The Writers' & Artists' Yearbook
Guide to
GETTING PUBLISHED

ALSO BY HARRY BINGHAM

fiction

THE MONEY MAKERS

SWEET TALKING MONEY

THE SONS OF ADAM

GLORY BOYS

THE LIEUTENANT'S LOVER

non-fiction

THIS LITTLE BRITAIN

STUFF MATTERS

The
Writers' & Artists' Yearbook
Guide to
GETTING PUBLISHED

THE ESSENTIAL GUIDE FOR AUTHORS

Harry Bingham

A &C BLACK • LONDON

A & C BLACK PUBLISHERS LTD

1 3 5 7 9 10 8 6 4 2

First published in 2010

A & C Black Publishers Limited
36 Soho Square
London W1D 3QY
www.acblack.com

A CIP catalogue record for this book is available
from the British Library

ISBN: 978 1 408 12895 4

Typeset by Country Setting, Kingsdown, Kent CT14 8ES

Printed and bound in Great Britain by Martins the Printers,
Berwick-upon-Tweed

To N

here is the deepest secret nobody knows
(here is the root of the root and the bud of the bud
and the sky of the sky of a tree called life; which grows
higher than the soul can hope or mind can hide)
and this is the wonder that's keeping the stars apart

i carry your heart (i carry it in my heart)

ACKNOWLEDGEMENTS

My thanks to all the team at A&C Black, who have been wonderfully
supportive throughout. Also to my agent Bill Hamilton for being,
as ever, the model professional. And also to Katie Fforde, Adèle Geras,
Helen Corner, Becky Swift, Emma Darwin, Jane Graham Maw
and Jennifer Christie, Fiona Inglis, Andrew Crofts, David Callaghan,
Veronica Henry, Peter Buckman, David Llewelyn, Tania Hershman,
Alan McKenzie, Penny Holroyde, Roger Ellory, Will Atkins, Mark Johnson,
Bob Miller, Sarah Broadhurst, Mark Le Fanu, Nick Marston, Sam Leith,
Alexandra Pringle, Jean Naggar, Annabel Wright, Paul Martin, Janine Cook,
Annabel Robinson, Bud McLintock, Alan Mahar, John Blake, Scott Pack,
Jeremy Thompson, Peter North, Stuart Profitt, Georgina Garett
and Caroline Dawnay for all their advice and help.

H.B.

CONTENTS

FOREWORD

I started writing because my mother gave me a writing kit for Christmas. I think she was fed up with me saying I wanted to be a writer but not doing it. She didn't think having three small children and a husband who was at sea half the time a good excuse, so she got together paper, pens, a dictionary, a thesaurus, Tippex, etc., and put it in a big box file. My resolution for that year was to start a novel. About eight years after that, I had a deal.

I was probably writing the wrong thing. I probably should have taken no for an answer from Mills and Boon a lot sooner, but I really wanted to be published. I have never wanted anything more, and I thought (oh so wrongly) that it must be easier to be published by a publisher who only wanted 50,000 words and who published over a dozen titles a month. When my last rejection letter said 'lacks sparkle', I accepted defeat. But I was a winner. I learned so much from the process when I came to write my so-called 'debut novel' I knew about forging on with the story, getting every page to count and to create characters. I didn't know much about plot but, thank goodness, you can put the plot in after you've written the book. It's on a par with having to jack up your house on acro props and putting in the foundations – definitely the wrong way round to do it, but it was possible. Just. Now I work really hard on having a plot before I start. Top tip!

So is writing the best job in the world? Well, it's a bit like being a parent. It's twenty-four seven, you feel guilty if you're not doing it, you constantly feel inadequate, you feel someone will find out that you have no idea what you're doing and will take your children into care or make you get a proper job, but I can't imagine another way to be. No experience is ever wasted, even the bad ones, and discovering one of your books has given people pleasure is the best reward there is. So it probably is the best job in the world.

Are you a writer? Will you ever be published – or stay published? Almost anyone you ever hear talk on the subject will tell you how tough the market is just now. They're right! It is tough! But it's always been tough and you have to ignore that gloomy fact. If you really want it enough, are prepared to carry on working, reading, editing, listening, you will do it. Every birthday cake I cut, every wishbone I pulled and the one four-leaf clover I once found had the same wish, that I would one day be published. And I was. But I suspect it was the sheer bloody-mindedness that kept me going on and on and not the four-leaf clover that did it.

I once met someone at a writing conference who reckoned if you tried to be a writer for ten years you would probably make it. At the time I thought it was fair enough – I was prepared to work at my craft for ten years. If you're prepared to put in the hours, making sure your work is as good as it can be, with no dull bits, no unhoned sentences, no one-dimensional characters, you can make it too. With this book at your side for support, for encouragement and for a persuasive kick, you're well on your way. Good luck, and happy writing!

KATIE FFORDE

INTRODUCTION

You've reached the last full stop. Your finger presses that final key, then withdraws astonished. You've reached the end! Your novel (or non-fiction book, or children's novel, or whatever) is complete.

It's hard to describe your emotions. In amongst them is the thrill of arrival. A Channel swimmer grazing his knees on the rocks outside Boulogne must feel something similar. It wasn't so long back that this project looked so dauntingly *huge*. So many miles to swim. So many words to write. The maths said that, if you just wrote so-and-so much every day, then you'd get there in the end, but as you gazed out over all the miles of empty space, the maths seemed impossible to believe; it simply ignored the multitude of ways in which this project could have spiralled off into uselessness or failure.

Another part of you feels pride. You did it! You say that little sentence over and again to yourself and it feels amazing every time. Putting aside your family and other loved ones, this is probably the biggest single achievement of your life. Sure, you've passed exams, secured jobs, won promotions – but so does everyone. Writing a book is a bigger, tougher, more serious challenge altogether. Maybe you know someone else who's written a book, but quite likely not. You certainly don't know many. You're special, and you know it.

And then, of course, there's another feeling bubbling up as well. Excitement. You'll send the book out to agents, you'll get taken on, you'll get a book deal in the UK, then in America too. And how about a movie deal? You aren't into counting chickens, but some of your scenes would be just amazing on screen and you've written a part that most actresses would die for.

Needless to say, when you tell people that you've finished your book, you keep most of these thoughts private. You tell people that there's still a long way to go, you know you need to revise a few things, that it can be tough to get an agent, that you aren't taking anything for granted. Yet, all the time your lips are saying exactly the right things and in exactly the right tone of voice, your thoughts are racing twenty miles ahead. The thrill of seeing your name on the *Sunday Times* best-seller lists. The pleasure of your first book review. Just how you'll introduce your book on BBC2's *Culture Show*. What you'll say to Martin Amis when you best him at the Booker Prize.

The joy of finishing a manuscript is to be relished. I've known it seven times myself, and hope to feel it again a good many times before I hang up my pen. It's a milestone of huge significance in a new writer's career. The only moments that compare with it are the pleasures of getting an agent, getting a book deal and – ultimately – actually seeing your very own book on the shelves of a real-life bookshop.

Yet completing a manuscript is the start, not the end, of a process. Revising a manuscript is tough. Getting an agent is tough. Getting a book deal is tough. Negotiating the whole publishing process so that you end up with a book you love and which is being marketed hard and well by people you enjoy working with – well, there may be times you wish you'd become a Channel swimmer instead.

Worse still, you'll often find yourself adrift in an industry that everyone but you seems to understand perfectly. Issues you didn't even know existed – the cost of getting into a three-for-two promotion; the near-impossibility of getting reviews for paperbacks – suddenly rear up to thwart what you had thought would be an ordinary part of the publication process. Such things afflict first-time writers particularly. By definition, first-timers have no experience to fall back on. On the other hand, many professional authors aren't vastly better off. An editor at a leading publisher might handle a couple of books every month. That means that, in six months, they'll have handled more books than a committed writer is likely to produce in a decade. And, of course, that editor is surrounded by other editors, has instant access to salespeople and marketers, and can call on any amount of expertise in design, PR and everything else. No wonder you feel like the novice in the room. That's just what you are.

This book is a guide for every writer who's completed a manuscript and doesn't know what to do next. It's a guide for writers who have found an agent but never got a book deal. It's a guide for those who have had the sheer delight of a book deal – and the sheer misery of a book that bombed with no clear reason why. In short, this is an instruction manual and a survival guide. It won't make the publishing process easy or certain. Nothing short of being an A-list celebrity will achieve that happy outcome and, even then, not always. But it will tilt the odds in your favour. It will forearm you with the information you need. It'll tell you about the pitfalls that lie ahead. It will draw a map of an industry that too often leaves its writers politely in the dark.

If you want to rattle straight on to the substance of the book, then please feel free to do just that. If you're the sort that likes to have 'i's dotted and 't's neatly crossed, then bear with me for a few other preliminaries.

First off, you should use this book just as you want. There's no need to read it cover to cover, if you don't want to. The book is broadly arranged to follow the publication process itself, so you can jump straight through to whatever part of it is currently baffling and enraging you. Do, however, keep the book at hand by your writing desk. Parts of the book which don't seem relevant now may become relevant in the fullness of time. You may want to refer back to it from time to time as well. As you start to get more experience, different sections of this book will echo differently.

Second, this book is designed to complement the *Writers' & Artists' Yearbook*. You'll find all the listings information you need in there. If your *Yearbook* is more than a couple of years or so out of date, then you may well want to replace it, as addresses do change and people do move around. The two books are designed to be used together.

Third and last, a word or two about me and about the experience and philosophy which underpin this work. For the first ten years of my career, I worked in the City as an investment banker. I enjoyed what I did, but didn't love it. As a child I'd always wanted to be a writer, but writing hardly seemed like a practical way of paying the heating bills.

Then my wife got ill. I needed to quit work to look after her. As I sat by her bedside (in a darkened room because her vision was problematic), I tapped away on a laptop, drafting the book that would one day become *The Money Makers*, my first novel.

In due course, I finished the book and got an agent. I was surprised how hard it was to get an agent, because I was pretty sure my book was OK, but eventually two agents offered repesentation at the same time. I chose one of the two; she sent my book out, an auction ensued, and a very nice book deal was the happy result.

That, perhaps, was the high point of my involvement with the industry. For sure, I went on getting some very attractive book deals. I sold five novels, all to HarperCollins, and have just completed a two-book non-fiction deal with Fourth Estate, an upmarket imprint of the same publisher. I fully expect to continue writing and selling books for a very long time to come. I've sold books in Japan and America, Germany and China, and in a broad scatter of smaller territories too. I've had book clubs making me their book of the month. I've clambered briefly on to best-seller lists. I've had some nice reviews and some stinkers. I've written for most of the national newspapers in the UK and articles about me have appeared in many of them as well. I've even, four times now, had film producers sniffing around my work and once got tremendously close to a movie deal.

All the same, my early cheerful belief that all I had to do was write good books and the rest would follow has long since evaporated. Publishing is *hard*. It's hard enough for publishers, but at least they can spread their risks over a whole host of titles. It's a lot harder for authors, whose risks are firmly pinned to a single frail manuscript.

What's more, a few years ago, I set up a new venture, The Writers' Workshop, a consultancy which aimed to help first-time writers. The business started out small and is now among the largest in its industry, using around eighty professional authors to offer help and advice to first-time writers. We cover pretty much every branch of writing from craft books and picture books through to fantasy sagas and highbrow literary fiction. Where work is strong enough to present to agents, we help with that part of things too. I doubt if there's anyone in the country who has pitched more books to more agents over the last few years than me.

Running the Writers' Workshop has hugely extended my knowledge of publishing. For one thing, it's opened my eyes to the problems that first-timers routinely face in navigating the industry. Agents who are dilatory. Agents who are useless. Agents who are outright scammers. These aren't *normal* problems, you understand: most agents do a good, thorough, professional job. At the same time, the problems aren't exceptional either. At the Writers' Workshop, we simply hear too many stories of woe to set them aside as once-in-a-century exceptions.

It's the same thing with publishing generally. As I've come to know the authors who work for us, I've learned again and again how challenging it can be for a writer to build a lasting career in this industry. I've gained some experience of what works and what doesn't. Equally, as I've deepened my connections with agents and publishers, I've learned ever more about the commercial logic which can be so perplexing to outsiders.

Through this book I've been able to prise my way further inside the publishing industry. I've spoken to dozens of industry insiders – editors, marketers, booksellers, books-page editors, and more – about their own roles and how they see the world. You'll find their insights scattered all the way through these pages. All that experience, theirs and mine, informs this book.

So much for my experience, but philosophy matters too. This book is written emphatically from an author's perspective. I know that you didn't come to writing to make money. Rather, I know that you came to writing from a sense of passion. A story you wanted to communicate. Characters you couldn't get out of your head. Information and insights you wanted to share with the broadest possible audience.

I have that perspective too. Writing for me is a passion from which I happen – miraculously – to make money. Yet that doesn't mean that the commercial side of things doesn't matter. On the contrary, I detest it when writers are treated badly, or sidelined, or pressured into agreeing to things which aren't in their (or often their publisher's) best interests. I hate it when writers are told half-truths because editors want to avoid the discomfort of conveying a few hard truths. I hate it when authors feel like they occupy the lowest rung of an industry that should really be setting them at the place of honour on the top. This book is certainly written from a place that honours the writer's artistic impulse, but it also passionately believes in the author's right to treatment that is fair and respectful to their commercial aims too.

This book offers no guarantees. Even forewarned and forearmed, writers are likely to find the publishing industry a tricky one to manage. Good writers often fail. Bad ones sometimes thrive. No industry handbook will ever put an end to those outcomes. All the same, you should use this book as your guide and compass. It will tell you what to expect, how to proceed, what choices to consider. If the outcome is less than positive – well then, at least you'll have made the best possible choices available to you. You'll have nothing to regret. If the outcome is fantastic, then so much the better. I'll be cheering you all the way to the *Sunday Times* No. 1 best-seller slot – and every fellow author will cheer you too.

HARRY BINGHAM
The Writers' Workshop

Part One

GETTING READY

MOTIVES AND EXPECTATIONS

Why do you write and what do you hope to accomplish by it?

The question seems so obvious that no one ever asks it. Writers write because they like it. Because they want others to read their work. Because they want to make some money. Different writers may weight those three things differently, but it would be a rare writer for whom one of those three motivations was altogether absent.

The question matters all the same, because the motivations are different and they need to inform how you proceed with your work and the expectations you set yourself. Some examples will illustrate the point.*

> EMMA, *literary novelist.* Emma started out as a short-story writer. She got some very positive feedback on her short stories and was encouraged to write a novel. She did so. She got an agent. The agent managed to secure a £3,000 deal for the book with a small, but highly esteemed literary publisher. The book got two or three nice book reviews. It did not earn any royalties over and above the initial advance. Emma continues to work full-time as a doctor, as she had always intended. She is currently searching for a publisher to take her second novel.

> RICHARD AND JENNY, *mental-health memoirists.* Richard and Jenny are a husband and wife team who collaborated on a memoir about Jenny's history of mental-health problems. The book was acquired by a publisher specialising in mental-health issues for no advance, but a share of royalties. The book has sold a few hundred copies only, but Richard and Jenny know that their readers are almost certain to be ones for whom the book came as inspiration and help. It hasn't reached many readers, but it's reached the right ones.

> JOHN, *commercial novelist.* John has a high-paying job as a management consultant. His first book – an adventure romp about a high-class thief – was bought for a good five-figure sum by a major publisher. The book went on to sell around 150,000 copies,

---

* The case histories in this book are all real ones. I've usually changed the individual's name and have simplified the exact sequence of events wherever appropriate, but have stuck closely to the core truth of what happened.

which meant there were decent royalties over and above that
initial advance. John's publishers have commissioned further
titles from him, and John continues to write them – without,
however, choosing to give up his existing job.

All these authors feel thoroughly pleased with what they've accomplished.
Emma wanted a commercial book deal, because of the quality standard it
represents, but the money itself was immaterial to her. She's probably never
earned so little money for so much work in her life. She doesn't have a huge
readership and is most unlikely ever to get one, but, then again, her work is
quiet, beautiful and unflashy. It's not the sort of thing to cause a splash, but
Emma wouldn't dream of adapting her tone to the market. She writes what
she wants to write and is happy to see that acknowledged by a good, well-
respected publisher, some nice reviews and some appreciative feedback from
her readers.

If, however, Emma had ever thought about building a career from her
work, then she'd made a colossal error right from the start. It's not that literary
fiction *can't* sell for decent amounts, just that it's only likely to earn significant money if it works hard to call attention to itself. Two of the most
dazzling debuts of recent years were Jonathan Safran Foer's *Everything Is
Illuminated* and Zadie Smith's *White Teeth*. Both books (one American, one
British) banged every drum there was to bang. They were funny. They were
raucous. They showed off a wide range of technique. Both books were jubil-
antly modern in their celebration of ethnic and cultural diversity. Just in case
there wasn't enough going on, Zadie Smith thumped an attempted suicide
right there on page one to grab and hold the reader's attention. Safran Foer
handed his opening credits over to one of the most hilarious and bizarre versions of English ever to hit the printed page.

Both Smith and Safran Foer are accomplished novelists. Nevertheless, it
wasn't quality alone that determined their success. They were novels that
deliberately created a din, that insisted on being given attention. Emma didn't
want to write like that. It's not her style. It's not the way her art chooses to
express itself. The outcome that she's enjoyed reflects the way the market
operates, and it's an outcome she's been entirely happy with.

For Richard and Jenny, the memoirists, a large audience might have been
positively unwelcome. Their work traipsed across sensitive territory. If they
had been asked to alter their work into a warts-and-all misery memoir, then
no matter how large the potential sales through mass-market outlets, I think
they'd still have said no. Other things mattered more. They've secured the
readership they wanted, with a publisher who understands their project.

As for John, he doesn't take his work too seriously, but he enjoys it. If he can combine writing and a career, he'll go on doing just that. If his book sales ramp up from where they are now, then just possibly he'll put the career on hold and pay more attention to his writing – but he's a smart cookie, and he knows how precarious the writing world can be. I suspect he'll hang on to the monthly pay cheques for some time yet. If I were him, I'd quite likely do the same.

FINANCIAL CONSIDERATIONS

The box below attempts to put some very crude figures to these thoughts. It's crucial to stress that in books, perhaps more than in any other industry, it's hard to set benchmarks for the price of a particular product (and your book will, of course, be considered as just that – a product). First of all, the market is always changing. The 2008-10 recession has, at the time of writing, buffeted advances. It would be nice to believe that, as the economy pulls out of recession, advances will come back to their previous levels, but personally I'd bet against it. The recession is more likely to have exacerbated and speeded up changes that had been in the pipeline anyway. More of all that later on.

Next, it's important to be clear that books are so wildly variable, that no table can offer more than the very crudest indication of possible outcomes. Although the table already includes some quite broad bands for the range of possible advances and likely sales, there will be plenty of books that fall outside those bands. In short, please don't hang your hat on these numbers! They're intended as the roughest of rough guides only. (And indeed, if and when you get an agent, they won't tell you what advance they're hoping to

Market segment	Typical advance	Typical hb sales	Typical pb sales
Poetry	£0–£100	–	50–500
Good self-published book	n.a.	–	10–500
Children's novel	£1–15,000	–	2,000–25,000
Niche literary fiction	£0–3,000	50-100	500–3,000
Niche commercial fiction	£0–3,000	–	500–5,000
Specialist non-fiction	£0–5,000	variable	variable
Mainstream non-fiction	£10–50,000	1,000–10,000	10,000–50,000
Mainstream literary fiction	£5–25,000	200–1,000	5,000–30,000
Mainstream comm fiction	£20–60,000	–	10,000–100,000

achieve for your book. That's not because they're mean and won't tell you. It's because they're experienced enough to know that their private guestimates may be way off the mark. And since we're tidily tucked away in parenthesis at the moment, let me also add that this section is likely to raise as many questions in your mind as it answers. Don't worry! We'll get to everything in due course.)

The first two items on the list – poetry and a decently successful self-published work – are included for the sake of comparison more than anything else. Poetry occupies at best a semi-commercial corner of the publishing industry. If you don't have a major reputation already (and preferably a Nobel Prize or a Laureateship to boot), then you are likely to be published only in a tiny print run by a specialist publisher who susbsists in part on government or charitable funding. There may be some money involved in the deal, but, if you choose to celebrate your success with a meal out at your local posh restaurant, more than likely you'll have eaten and drunk your way through your advance before you get to coffee and mints.

Self-publishing is still less commercial, in the sense that it's funded by the author him- or herself. The median number of copies sold by self-published authors is low: a few dozen, perhaps. There are, however, some more active self-publishing companies that (shock, horror!) actually try to sell the work they are so busy printing. A decent outcome with one of these better companies may see the author sell out a print run of 500 copies, and I've come across self-pub authors who have done still better than this.

When it comes to the wider market – novels and non-fiction, children's and adults – the range of outcomes splays out into a range so wide it's hard to find meaningful benchmarks. I've distinguished between 'niche' and 'mainstream' as a way to separate out large publishers from small, and 'big' books from 'little' ones. A big book can usefully be defined as any book that is expected to grab a real slice of retail promotional space. That is, space in one of the three-for-two promotions at the major specialist bookshops, or some similar promotion in the mass-market bookshops (which in the UK means WH Smith), and/or acceptance by one or more of the supermarkets. A little book is one that will be distributed to many or most bookshops, but which doesn't feature in any promotion. For many types of book – a 'How To' book on dog grooming, let's say – there's simply no chance of being included in a promotion, no matter how good the book might be.

As for publishers, there are essentially six major publishers in the UK. They are Hachette, Random House, Penguin, HarperCollins, Macmillan, Bloomsbury – the ranking is in terms of gross market share as it stands today. If you glance at the books on your bookshelf, you'll be taken aback by the brevity of this list. What about all those other names: John Murray, Orion, Little Brown, Pan, Picador, Transworld, Allen Lane, Fourth Estate, Ebury, BBC, Virgin, Piatkus and the rest? The answer is that each one of those names is an imprint – a brand name, effectively – of one of the big six. The big six companies are by far the best-funded publishers around and the only ones likely to pay out big advances.

After the big six, you get to a raft of independent publishers. Some of these are just excellent. Canongate, for example, has a huge and deserved reputation, as does the microscopic Tindal Street Press. Faber is – well, it's *Faber*, once the home of T. S. Eliot and publisher of no fewer than eleven Nobel prizewinners. Big doesn't always mean better. What's more, a number of quality independents have clubbed together to form the Independent Alliance, which gives them greater clout with booksellers.

In genre fiction too, there are some capable specialists such as Robert Hale, Allison & Busby, and of course Harlequin Mills & Boon. Nevertheless, good to excellent as some of these outfits may be, they don't have the financial resources of the bigger players. If it's the size of the advance that drives you, then you need to be seeking to shape a big book for a big publisher.

A further point to be borne in mind while looking at the chart is that a range of £20–60,000 (for mainstream commercial fiction, in this example) may suggest that the 'average' advance is therefore likely to be around £40,000. Not so, alas, since most advances will cluster towards the bottom end of these ranges. The big payouts do happen, but they're unusual and hard to achieve. You certainly shouldn't be counting on them.

CAREER DEVELOPMENT

The final point to be made is that the table refers to debut advances. As soon as you have some kind of sales record, your future advances will be determined largely by the number of books that you've sold in the past. More likely than not, that means your advance will be headed *down*, not up. That will strike almost every reader as bizarre and quite likely untrue. Surely (you'll be thinking), once you start to establish yourself, you'll begin to gather a readership, you'll get more reviews, you'll sell more books, and you'll start to prosper.

Impeccable as such logic seems to be, it's simply untrue. Publishers lose money on a significant proportion of all books they sell. Obviously enough, they don't knowingly publish loss-makers, but it's tremendously hard to tell in advance which book will sell and which won't. The result is that a large proportion of authors will see book sales that lag behind their advance by some considerable margin. These authors are likely to see a large drop in their advance when they come to negotiate a renewed book deal – if, that is, they're lucky enough to be offered a deal at all. Only where an author hits a sales nerve and achieves sales considerably in excess of expectations is their advance likely to climb significantly.

One recent case that came to my attention involved an author of classy historical fiction. She's had some very positive book reviews. She is represented by one of Britain's most able and best connected agents. Her first book sold well and her second book did even better. A major newspaper featured her novel in some kind of special offer and during that week she featured in the national top-fifty best-seller list, which is a terrific achievement for a literary novelist without much of a track record. At this point, she and her agent thought it would be a good idea to talk to her publisher about an advance for her third novel, then partially written. Because of the gloomy economic climate, both author and agent were expecting a reduction in the advance offered – perhaps a 30% cut. In actual fact, the publisher came back offering an advance that was a full 70% lower than before, an amount so derisory that in any other industry the offer would have represented an only semi-polite way to tell somebody that they weren't wanted.

Or take another recent example. A client came to us with a very well-written and unusual misery memoir. We helped him get it into shape, then took it to a very capable agent, who took him on and sold his book for an excellent £75,000 to one of the biggest publishers in the true-life-story area. The book sold so-so in hardback, but it wasn't really a hardback sort of book. In paper covers, the book leaped straight on to the non-fiction best-seller lists and stayed there for weeks on end.

Now, unusually, the author in question had a second volume of memoir as good as the first. (It's unusual, because it's rare that a non-celebrity has a life that lends itself to more than a single volume.) I've read both books and can genuinely say that there was nothing to choose between them. They were both excellent. Alas, the publisher decided that a few weeks on the best-seller list weren't enough to justify a further advance, so they didn't offer at all for that second book, which has remained unsold and unpublished. The author would have stood more chance of selling that second book if he'd never written or published the first one.

The publisher wasn't being foolish here. The market for these kinds of memoirs nosedived in between the first book and the second, and the publishers figured (probably correctly) that the author hadn't sold enough copies to have created brand value around his name. In short, although the author had done everything that could reasonably be asked of him, market circumstances were such as to turn him from a best-seller to unpublishable.

Facts like these will shock almost any industry outsider. They should shock you. Indeed, because these things are shocking, it's rare that agents or publishers discuss them fully with authors at an early stage of their development. As a consequence, it's commonplace for authors to import to their new career the assumptions and beliefs taken from their old one – assumptions that suggest talent will be rewarded, that seniority and experience will be appropriately valued. This approach, unfortunately, can very easily prove unhelpful to authors, since it makes navigating the various inevitable pitfalls of the industry so much more uncertain.

I speak from experience here. My first novel sold for a good, strong sum. It was energetically and successfully marketed by my publisher, Harper-Collins. The book was accepted into a number of major promotions and sold well. The second book sold less well – perhaps the cover design was not quite right? Perhaps the book itself was not quite as well judged as the first? Nevertheless, that second book was one of the summer books of the year in Britain's biggest high-street retailer. It was hardly a dud.

Fresh from experience in a more normal career, I assumed that I was doing well. My next book was better than either of my first two. I'd built a platform already. The next steps would be onwards and upwards, right? Full of confidence, I invested in a new house. I didn't move anywhere crazy, I just assumed that my income wasn't about to plummet. A bad move. In fact, the advance I was offered for my next couple of books was almost 40% lower than for the first pair. Looking back, and knowing what I know now, I'm astonished at how generous that offer was. The truth is, HarperCollins must really have liked my work and remained willing to pay over the odds to keep me. Nevertheless, that plummeting advance meant I was now in a house too expensive for my income and I was forced to sell it. (Fortunately for me, a crazy property market meant I made money on the deal anyway, but I couldn't have known that in advance.)

WRITERS' INCOMES

Another way to look at all this is by studying the median outcomes for different categories of writer. A 2005 survey conducted on behalf of the Authors' Licensing and Collecting Society studied the incomes of professional authors writing in a variety of genres. The results were as follows:

Novels	£13,000
Children's fiction	£15,500
Non-fiction	£8,000
Academic/educational	£10,000
Newspapers/magazines	£13,200
TV	£39,400

Do note that this table reflects the income of professional authors: that is, those who make more money from writing than from any other source. Needless to say, these authors are the most commercially successful authors around. If you take the income of all writers – professional and part-timers – then the median level is around £4,000, and has declined by more than a third over the past five years or so.

The survey also revealed that male professional authors earned more than women. This is most unlikely to be the consequence of sexism in the industry – many publishers are two-thirds or three-quarters run by women.* In my own career, I've had five editors, of whom only one was a man, and women at the most senior levels are commonplace. Rather, I suspect that, in households where the man is seen as the breadwinner, he feels the need to go out and earn some bread. That may well mean accepting contracts and assignments which wouldn't be enticing from a creative perspective alone.

Tellingly, it's also the case that, while 25–34-year-olds earn the lowest median income of any age group, 35–44-year-olds earn the highest median income (£18,000) and earnings decline from there on. There are probably a few factors involved in this earnings profile. One is that younger authors are (alas!) favoured by publishers. Another is the consequence of all those declining advances. If you haven't made it to the big time with your first novel or two, then you are quite likely to have to deal with lower advances or leave the industry altogether.

Finally, it's worth stressing that these figures relate to medians. Thus, to say that the median income from writing is £4,000 means that there are exactly 50% of writers who earn more than this figure and exactly 50% who earn less. Because there are a handful of super-well-paid authors around, the average (or mean) figure is significantly higher than these medians, just as the average income in any room would jump if Bill Gates happened to walk into it. The median is a better reflection of likely outcomes, however.

---

* That, incidentally, is why the pronoun 'she' is much commoner in this book than the pronoun 'he'. I've tried, very roughly, to reflect the actual gender balance of the industry.

THE IMPORTANCE OF PASSION

This section opened by asking about motives and expectations and has spent nearly all of its time discussing money. In a strange way, however, that takes us back to the heart of the question. There can be money in writing, but for most people, most of the time, there isn't very much. Authorial careers tend to be short and precarious. There's no sick pay. No health coverage. No unemployment benefit. No pension. Which, when you think about it, is liberating. You didn't start out writing your book to make money or pay the mortgage or buy that yacht you'd always dreamed of. You started it because of a passion to write, to communicate, to spin dreams and inform others.

Good. You need to hold on to those motivations, as they're the only ones which can reliably sustain you. That's not to say that you should give up thoughts of commercial success altogether. On the contrary, this book aims to give you a road map that will maximise your chances of selling books to the very limits of your potential. But selling books is as much about the desire to communicate, to connect with readers, to pass on your vision to others as it is about making money.

Because most authors will want to get as many readers as possible and (secondarily) to earn as much as possible from that readership, this book will concentrate on the centre ground of publishing: the territory of agents, of major publishers, of retail promotions, and all the rest of it. But not all authors will make it to that centre ground, nor should they necessarily want to. At the opening of this part, I mentioned three authorial trajectories: Emma, Richard and Jenny, and John. All four authors have done well, in terms of what they have got out of writing. The satisfaction is primarily artistic in Emma's case. For Richard and Jenny, their satisfaction came from having grappled some meaning out of their own personal battles, and from having been able to put that experience to use in the service of others. John, the only one to have clambered securely on to that centre ground, finds that he gets a kick from writing, he gets a kick from his fans, he likes the diversity that writing has brought to his life, and (even for a talented management consultant) the money is welcome. None of the four, however, has chosen to become a full-time professional. Most writers don't. The centre ground of writing isn't the only territory that matters, and this book will pay plenty of attention to the remoter corners of the landscape as well. Because commercial publishing won't be available to many, I'll talk about self-publishing as well.

It's important to remember these things as you read on. All authors need to find a meeting point between what they want to write and what the market will buy. You can't neglect the latter, because if you do you'll remain unpublished. But you mustn't even think of giving up on the former, because that will void your writing of the one purpose that you can entirely rely on: your own passion, the very thing that brought you to writing in the first place.

DON'T LOSE HEART

Things have changed tremendously since I published my first book in 1976. Back then, you wrote something, sent it to an editor who either took it or sent it back to you. Advances reflected what the publisher really thought your book might earn. I started out with Hamish Hamilton and I think the best-selling books of the day underwrote the rest of us who didn't do quite so well. Nowadays, every book has to have a healthy bottom line of its own and, if a writer doesn't cut the mustard financially, publishers are apt to let her go. When I started, a hardback novel for young adults would sell to libraries, but that's not the case now that library budgets are so small and paperbacks are what's most often bought. In children's fiction, at least for the moment, series seem to be more popular with publishers than standalone novels. Things do change, however, so I live in hope. Series are risky. If you sign a contract for three books and the first does very badly, contracts for the second and third can be cancelled. When I first started, the Net Book Agreement was still in place and EPOS (Electronic Point of Sale) was unknown. Now, every publisher can see just how badly your last book fared in the marketplace . . . a scary thought!

My first adult novel was auctioned for an amount of money I knew I would never earn back. With hindsight, this was probably not a sensible kind of advance to have, but it's easy to be wise after the event. My advice for new writers is: sign up for one book at a time and, whatever happens, don't lose heart. You have to write, as Chekhov said, 'without hope and without despair'.

ADÈLE GERAS
author of more than seventy books for children, young adults and adults

IS YOUR BOOK READY TO GO?

A typical literary agent will receive somewhere between 400 and 2,000 submissions a year. From that pile, he or (more likely) she will offer representation to one, maybe two, clients. Some agents will find themselves taking more than that, but others may go a year or more without taking anyone from the slushpile. It is presumably facts such as these which have given rise to a common misconception about the literary industry which depicts the whole shebang as some kind of Oxbridge conspiracy where people with posh voices throw commissions out to their friends while excluding everyone with the misfortune to have only one surname or to live in the North of England (or, worse still, the colonies).

If there is such a conspiracy, then I have yet to find it. The simple truth is that quality sells. There are some caveats that we'll come to in due course, but the caveats are much less important than the headline itself. Quality sells.

Naturally, what counts as excellent varies from market to market. A literary novel has to be impeccably written to achieve success. Commercial fiction needs to be competently written, but a galloping plot and a racy premise will speed a writer over many a shaky metaphor or leaden word choice. In the field of non-fiction, a writing style has to be perfectly capable of course, but such things as approach, tone, expertise and structure may all count for more. All the same, though the determinants of quality may vary, the need for it never does. When manuscripts don't sell, when they get rejected by agents, it's almost always because the darn things were never good enough in the first place, and that in turn means that writers are sending them out prematurely. The purpose of this section is to give you pause. Is your manuscript genuinely ready to send out as it is? Does it need more work? And, if so, are you capable of doing that work on your own or will you need outside assistance?

PAUSING FOR BREATH

Every now and then, we receive an enquiry which says roughly, 'I've completed the first three chapters of my novel. Do you think I should contact agents now or wait until I've written a little more?' The answer, emphatically, is that you need to wait. (With fiction, that is. The situation with non-fiction is a tad more complex – more of that in the next section.) You don't just need to wait until you have bustled your way to the final full stop. You need to wait until your novel is perfected. To properly professional writers, the first draft is just that: a working draft which may need to be completely rewritten. Indeed, I know one Costa prizewinning author whose working routine is: (1) write a complete first draft of her novel; (2) read it, then throw it away; (3) write a completely new draft; (4 – optional) repeat steps two and three; (5) work on the final draft to bring it all the way up to the required standard. Not every author is quite as committed to rewriting as that, but I don't know any quality author who isn't a serious rewriter of their own work.

One of the most important tips here is also the simplest: take your time. Once you've completed your manuscript, read it through once, then put it away in a bottom drawer. If you can, spend the next few weeks doing something entirely different. Go on holiday, take up sailing, run a marathon, have an affair. Come back to your project once enough time and life have elapsed to give you a sober view of it. Then reread your work from cover to cover. You can jot down thoughts as they occur to you, but try to avoid getting stuck into any real editorial work at this stage, because the editing will distract you from the big picture.

With luck, the rereading process will help shift your mindset. Any writer, as they're ploughing ahead with a first-draft manuscript, needs to keep themselves motivated. That can often mean living in a warm haze of self-deception, in which every sentence seems brilliant, every plot point inspired. Good. There's nothing wrong with that. I've been there myself and plenty of others are the same. When it comes to rewriting, however, you need to turn from Mr or Ms Indulgent to Mr or Ms Savage. You need to scour your work for its failures. You need to anguish about sentence construction and pick away at flaws in plot and character. If you aren't as ruthless as you were once kind, you simply aren't exposing your work to the kind of scrutiny it almost certainly needs.

What's more, you need to set no prior limits to how much rewriting may be required. I know one leading author who wrote four unpublished novels before selling her fifth. I myself deleted the opening 60,000 words of my first novel, because I realised that my writing had developed through the course of the book, and the opening material wasn't as good as the stuff later on. With my second novel, I realised that my first draft was rubbish, so I deleted the whole damn thing and started again from a blank screen. I'm not advising that you need to take action as radical as this, but I am saying that you mustn't rule it out in advance. What matters is quality and only quality. If you don't care enough about the excellence of your work, then your lack of care is certain to show. Agents and publishers have hundreds and thousands of other manuscripts to choose from. They are not going to take you on for your potential. They will only be interested in the merits of what you present on the page.

So take your time and get it right. As the roughest of rough guides for first-time writers, I'd suggest that reaching the final full stop represents an approximate halfway point. If you spend as much time on revising and per-fecting your work as you did on writing it in the first place, then you'll have got it about right. As you develop your skills, the time spent revising may drop – but only may do. In any case, you should forget about the time you spend. Effort doesn't matter; quality does. If what you produce is excellent, then the time you've taken to get there has already been rewarded.

GETTING HELP FOR FREE

Different writers work differently. In my own case, I wrote my first novel chapter by chapter. Because I had three (or three and a half) stories running in parallel, I didn't even write the book sequentially. I wrote it in three (or three and a half) separate strands, then assembled them all by spending two days in the living room on my hands and knees shuffling the chapters into an order that I was happy with and building a giant spreadsheet to keep track of it all. I then revised the novel intensively. I handed it out to family and friends and solicited comments. I was obsessive about detail. When one friend told me that I overused commas, I looked again at my manuscript, decided he was right and went through the whole thing – all 185,000 words of it – taking out the surplus (thereby inadvertently providing employment to the copy-editor who would in due course go through the entire script putting them all back in again).

I thought hard about getting external professional feedback on my work, but decided against it. I went straight out to agents. The first six said no. I didn't know it at the time, but my covering letter was disastrous and some of those first six would have rejected the manuscript without reading so much as a sentence. I thought again about getting professional feedback, but decided against. I went to six more agents and obtained two offers of representation. I was up and running.

I mention this experience, because I need to flag up a conflict of interest. I run a large editorial consultancy. We make our money from providing tough, expert editorial advice to first-time writers. There are some major virtues in going that route, which we'll talk about in this section, but I also need to be clear that the route is not right for everyone. It wasn't right for me. It's not, in fact, the route taken by most authors who end up in print. So, although it's worth thinking hard about taking external advice, you are by no means obliged to go down that route. Different writers need different things.

With that caveat in place, let's review what options are available for getting outside input. The first and most obvious source is family and friends. Most writers do solicit feedback from those around them, and they're probably right to do so. Friends and family are likely to come up with a few helpful observations. A plot issue here. An aspect of character there. These things matter and incorporating those insights will improve a book.

On the other hand, you need to be firmly realistic about how much to expect. There are only two sorts of people who have a genuinely expert grasp of editorial work and they are those with real editorial expertise inside a publishing house, and those who have written and sold work themselves. Unless your friends and family are all novelists and editors, you are unlikely to get anything approaching systematic and rigorous feedback. What's more, it's not enough that Uncle Fred has written an academic text on management theory. That will not equip him to comment on a novel. And though your dear Aunt Hephzibah has worked for ten years as an editor at the prestigious house of Sage & Parsley, you need to remember that she will only ever have worked on manuscripts that have already been accepted by agents and purchased by S & P. A publishing editor may not, in fact, ever have worked on an unsaleable manuscript or worked with an author who has yet to learn some important writing skills.

Since you quite likely do have some important skills yet to learn, you should certainly solicit comments from Uncle F and Auntie H, but don't assume that they represent the final word on anything. (Also, of course, editorial work is time-consuming to do properly, and often needs to be blunt to be useful. Busy lives and the importance of friendly relations may get in the way of the advice you're after.)

While on the subject of realism, let's just slay another myth. Agents do not give feedback to non-clients. If you send your material out to agents hoping to get feedback on your work, then you will be brutally disappointed. Agents receive 1,000 manuscripts for every one they take on. If they gave editorial advice to the 999 rejectees, they wouldn't have time to wash or eat, let alone do their job. Every now and then an agent may reject a manuscript with a handwritten note that adds a few words of editorial explanation, but this is rare and writers need to be cautious about placing too much reliance on those comments. If an agent is rejecting a manuscript, they may not have thought long and hard about that handwritten comment. If you do use these comments, then use them with caution. (For further thoughts on decoding agents' rejection letters, please refer to the section in Part Two on 'Communications from Planet Agent'.)

SEEKING EXPERT PROFESSIONAL HELP

In 1996, the first serious editorial consultancy in the UK came into being. Called the Literary Consultancy, it gave first-time writers the opportunity to pay for tough, expert editorial advice. The venture's two founders, Becky Swift and Hannah Griffiths, had understandable doubts about whether there would be a market for such a service. Would writers really, when it came to the point, value honesty over flattery?

Time, however, has erased those doubts. The Literary Consultancy flourished. Competitors sprang up alongside it. The heart of all these services is tough, expert editorial advice. Don't expect to use one of these services and be told that your book is great. That may happen, if your book genuinely is fantastic, but if your book is one of the 99.9% that will be turned down by an agent, then you are looking for the brutal truth about what's not yet working and how to fix it.

You'll certainly get a written editorial report. In the case of my own consultancy, the minimum length of these reports (assuming we're dealing with a full-length manuscript) is 3,000 words, but they often go well over that. Other leading agencies have different ways to ensure that their advice is genuinely comprehensive, but you can rely on them delivering a properly in-depth service. In addition, you may be offered a follow-up phone consultation, discounts on any further help, a mentoring service and more. Where manuscripts are of marketable quality, some agencies will do what they can to help the writer towards securing an agent.

There are now three major consultancies operating and a whole slew of smaller ones, many of them one-woman or one-man bands. The three large ones are:

Cornerstones	www.cornerstones.co.uk
The Literary Consultancy	www.literaryconsultancy.co.uk
The Writers' Workshop	www.writersworkshop.co.uk

Because I want to be even-handed in talking about my competitors, I've asked Helen Corner and Becky Swift to introduce their own agencies themselves. You'll see their comments in the box overleaf. There's no question, however, that all these three larger agencies are excellent at what they do. They're well respected by agents and publishers, and set a seriously high standard of editorial competence and integrity. The same is often, but not always, true of the smaller outfits too. (You can find their names by searching around online. Try a variety of different search terms as smaller operators are often restricted in how widely they can afford to advertise. The advertising section in the *Writers' & Artists' Yearbook* is also a good place to look.)

The business in the US works a little differently. In Europe, freelance editors are there to offer advice; it's down to the writer to use it wisely. In the US, you'll find that editors prefer to take on a much more hands-on role, actually reworking a manuscript themselves, sometimes doing all the work from tightening sentences and correcting spellings through to trimming plot or sharpening characterisations. Such a service is naturally very expensive. A decent editor will charge anywhere from \$0.03 per word to as much as \$0.10 per word. Measuring prices in cents gives a nice cheap feel to things, but, if your manuscript is 100,000 words long, those pricings mean you'll be paying out anywhere from \$3,000 to \$10,000 for help.

There are multiple risks in this approach. You may end up investing heavily in a project which is unsaleable. You may not be able to rely on the impartiality of the advice you're given. You may fail to learn the skills which you need to acquire if you are to build a lasting career. And so on. Nevertheless, there is certainly a place for such services, and, if you feel they're right for you, by all means investigate them. The longest-established quality editorial company in the US is The Editorial Department (www.editorial department.com). I've never heard anything but praise for its services.

There are also a host of freelancers available, whom you can make contact with either via the web or through personal contact at a writers' conference. Before signing up with anyone at all, do make sure that their qualifications are appropriate. A sub-editor on a regional newspaper should be good at editing journalism. He or she will quite likely not know what to do if presented with a novel. Equally, a PhD in History is a great thing if you want to write academic history books, but it is not an obvious qualification for offering editorial help with a children's novel.

Perhaps it's also worth saying that you'll find some critique services which offer to comment on a complete novel for as little as \$99. I have no idea who is crazy enough to use such services. No competent freelance editor I know would even read a novel for that amount of money, let alone offer detailed comments on it. Bad editorial advice is probably worse than useless because it'll set you off in the wrong direction altogether. This is a job worth doing right or not at all.

CORNERSTONES LITERARY CONSULTANCY

Helen Corner founded Cornerstones Literary Consultancy in 1998, and four years later the specialist children's division Kids' Corner. They provide editorial feedback on manuscripts of all genres, run self-editing workshops and scout for agents. To date, they've helped launch over fifty writers.

Helen worked at Penguin and part of her job was to process 'unsols' – manuscripts sent in by authors, not via an agent; and due to an automatic turn-down policy she wasn't able to provide feedback. A desire to help aspiring, talented writers increase their chances of being noticed by an agent or publisher led her to set up one of the founding literary consultancies. Their ethos is, if they can impart advice in five minutes that it might take an author a year to find out then that's a good thing, hence the free advisory line. You can contact Helen with any query or for feedback on opening material at helen@cornerstones.co.uk or look up www.cornerstones.co.uk

HELEN CORNER
founder of Cornerstones Literary Consultancy

THE LITERARY CONSULTANCY

The Literary Consultancy was co-founded in 1996 by Rebecca Swift and Hannah Griffiths. TLC was established to act as a bridge between the world of the writer and the publishing industry – and to help demystify the workings of the publishing world. TLC believes that, by engaging honestly with writers, they can progress with more clarity and realism. TLC sets out to help inform people writing at any level in the English language, and has also helped many clients find publication in various formats, and with both commercial and online presses.

In recognition of their original contribution to literature, the Arts Council provides core funding to TLC and pays for a quota of free manuscript assessments for high-quality, low-income writers. TLC also runs an original online mentoring service, co-founded with novelist Sara Maitland, literary events and creative writing holidays.

In 2009, TLC moved to the Free Word Centre in London which is a national and international centre for the promotion of literature with a public space.

BECKY SWIFT
co-founder of The Literary Consultancy

Finally, do be clear that, if you work with an editorial agency, you are doing so in order to improve the quality of your writing, *not* to impress agents. All agents will make their own independent assessment of a manuscript. All they care about is quality and saleability; the fact that the name of some editorial consultant is attached to a project won't make any difference to the final decision.

PICKING THE RIGHT CONSULTANT

I hope I've said enough to indicate that there are good editorial services and bad ones, and that many writers will get on perfectly happily without paying for help. Nevertheless, if you do choose to go ahead, it's critical to pick the right consultant for the job. Questions for you to think about include:

➢ *What experience does my editorial consultant bring to bear?*
There are four groups of people who can claim to have real editorial expertise. They are (1) professional authors; (2) current or former editors at good-quality publishing houses; (3) any present or former agent; and possibly (4) any professional creative writing tutor. My own emphatic preference is for authors. If you were building a chest of drawers, you might go to an antiques dealer for a verdict on its beauty, but you'd surely go to a carpenter for advice on its construction. Particularly now, when publishers tend to be more marketing than editorially led, someone whose editorial know-how comes only from publishing may not have what it takes to help you demolish and rebuild major aspects of your manuscript. It's also true that the closer your manuscript comes to being marketable, the more the skills of a publishing editor come into play.

With agents, there are certainly some who possess real editorial flair, but they are in a minority and I'd advise you to look before you leap. As for professional creative writing tutors, my personal advice is to look hard at their publication record. If they've sold full-length manuscripts to major publishers, then fine. If they've published some short stories, had some lit crit published in a literary magazine or two, pounded the stage as a performance poet, and are now working on a literary novel for the exciting new publisher HereTodayGoneTomorrow Ltd – well, don't be surprised if you feel let down by what they have to offer. There are a lot of creative writing courses in the world and not all of them are good.

➤ *What am I buying?*
If you're approaching a British or Australian consultancy, you'll almost certainly be offered an editorial report. That's the core of any editorial service and, if you get a really insightful report, then perhaps that's all that matters. On the other hand, there'll be plenty of times when you'll want to discuss aspects of an editorial report with the person who's written it. Some services offer such access as an automatic part of the package. Some do, but restrict it to an email exchange only. Others don't offer feedback beyond that intial report. Again, my own view (but I'm biased, remember!) is that you need direct access to your editor for two reasons. First, it's perfectly normal to have questions about what you've been told. You need to be able to address those questions in a flexible and open-ended way. Secondly, if an editor knows that there'll be no follow-up from the client, they may be tempted to skip too fast over issues that they know need to be addressed more fully. If they know they're going to be talking directly to the writer a few days after completing the assessment, they've got a strong incentive to take that extra bit of care. Other things to think about are whether your consultant can offer mentoring, copy-editing, hands-on editorial work, and so forth. This may be highly relevant to you or not relevant at all. Again, it's down to you to determine your priorities.

➤ *Does my editor understand and appreciate my own particular brand of manuscript?*
On the whole, good writing is good writing. A literary novelist with a taste for crime fiction may be an excellent editor of such fiction. Nevertheless, expertise matters. A non-fiction author should not be asked to comment on novels. (The other way round can often work fine, however, as non-fiction manuscripts are generally less complicated than novels.) Likewise, a literary novelist with no interest in crime fiction will probably make a bad reviewer of it. A horror novelist is not an obvious choice to work with children's fiction, and so on. The larger agencies have dozens of editors on their books and are usually well able to match writer to editor. Smaller agencies may have access to precisely the right expertise, but this is something to check out before you send your work in for review, not after.

➤ *What access will I get to agents?*
No honest editorial agency will guarantee to get your work taken on by agents. Life just isn't that simple. Nevertheless, the larger agencies all have excellent access to leading agents, as may some of the smaller operators, but you also need to be clear how precisely a given agency operates. For example,

an agency may commit *either* to tell you why your book is not yet marketable, or to do what it can to help you with the next step (which is usually, but not always, securing an agent). Other agencies are more selective. They'll help you if they think your book has the X-factor, but not otherwise. Or they'll help in return for a chunk of any advance. Or something else. If it's not clear from the company's website, then *ask*! Remember, though, all an editorial consultancy can do is make connections. If your manuscript is strong enough, then it'll find an agent without outside help. If it isn't, it won't find one, no matter what.

➤ *What about philosophy and outlook?*

Different editorial consultants have different ways of approaching their work. Some aim to help writers get the most enjoyment and fulfilment from their writing. Others are sternly focused on the path to market. Some use editors mostly from an industry background. Others use only professional authors. In fact, it's probably fair to say that there are as many different approaches as there are companies and no one size fits all. You need to work out what you want and are comfortable with, then choose the consultancy which best seems to fit your needs.

➤ *How much will it cost?*

Needless to say, there's a range of price and quality on the market. My own view is that bad editorial advice is worse than no advice at all, but I certainly don't mean to imply that cheaper services are always worse. If you find a solo operator with a credible track record and a sympathetic manner, who's willing to work hard with you in a way that you like and at a reasonable price, then you should certainly go for it. The larger operators are likely to be rather more expensive: detailed feedback on a typical manuscript is likely to cost in the region of £400–£500. Long manuscripts may cost a good bit more.

Working with a good editorial agency will significantly increase your odds of success, but it won't work miracles. At the time of writing, the Writers' Workshop has almost never received a manuscript which would have succeeded in finding an agent under its own steam. (The one possible exception was a manuscript with an awful first chapter but an excellent everything else. An agent might have read further than the opening few pages, but only might.) From that pool of manuscripts, we expect to help about thirty to forty clients in every thousand to go on to get an agent or publisher. In most industries, a success rate of 3–4% would suggest that the company involved was worse than useless. Given the one-in-a-thousand success rate of people applying independently to agents, however, that 3–4% success rate can also be seen as remarkably good. I can't say how successful other agencies are, but I would expect the better-known ones to have track records that are broadly comparable with our own.

It's also true that to focus on the *average* stats somewhat misses the point. If your manuscript is already strong, working with a good editorial agency may be an excellent way to haul yourself to the finishing tape. If your writing skills are not yet that developed, then you'll learn a tremendous amount from working with an editorial agency, but your manuscript is most unlikely to get from Mediocre to Dazzling in a single leap.

OTHER SOURCES OF HELP

Getting one-to-one feedback on your manuscript is the only way to get commentary that is entirely focused around you and your work as it stands now. Nevertheless, there are a whole host of other support services, some of which may be very helpful to you, either as a standalone exercise or in conjunction with something more focused.

➤ *Workshops*

There are a host of workshops available almost everywhere these days. The exact focus of each workshop will vary, as will the expertise of the tutor, the duration, the average experience level of the students, and so forth. Although most workshops will seek to address each writer's work in class, there's an obvious limit to how much time can be spent on any one individual's work. Nevertheless, a workshop can be a wonderfully systematic introduction to some of the big concepts in successful writing – and learning from the mistakes of others can be just as fruitful as learning from your own.

If you feel that a workshop would help you, then it most likely would: your own gut instinct on these things is normally reliable. The Arvon Foundation (www.arvonfoundation.org) is the UK's biggest provider of residential workshops, which are generally outstanding, but there are plenty of other companies providing residential and one-day workshops. (All the big editorial agencies, for example, offer such things.) You need to work out what exactly you want, then browse the net to find it.

Do make sure that your tutor is properly experienced – that is, that they have written and sold books to major publishers themselves. Do also check out what the student: tutor ratio is likely to be. Prices vary considerably, so keep an eye on costs.

➤ *Distance learning*

More likely to be useful for complete beginners. Once you've written a complete manuscript, or are a good way into a particular project, then distance learning courses are likely to be frustratingly non-responsive to your needs. Again, though, if you fancy getting structured help, then it may well be a good investment of time and money. The Open University has an excellent reputation and I know some of its tutors to be excellent. You can also try the London School of Journalism, which offers more than just courses in journalism, and Gotham Writers' Workshop, which is New York-based, but offers a variety of short, cheap and popular distance learning courses. Other options are available too: just browse around. The Open University course in 2009 cost £630 and ran over a 32-week period.

➤ *Mentoring*

Most people who think they want mentoring really want detailed editorial advice. Once they have that advice, they are likely to feel confident that they know what do and how to do it. Again, however, that's a general rule, and every rule has its exceptions. If you do think that mentoring would suit you, I'd suggest that you work with an editorial consultant as a first step, and just check that your working relationship can morph into a mentoring relationship if need be.

➤ *Creative Writing MA/MFA courses*

Most people reading this book are likely to have gone beyond the point of considering a university-level creative writing course, but the option exists and has become too popular to ignore. One obvious benefit of such courses is that you get to go back to college to explore your creative side. If your tutors and fellow students are inspiring and delightful, then you'll have a good time, you'll become a better writer, and you will certainly end up with a more thorough appreciation of good literature. For all these reasons, the course may be eminently worthwhile.

On the other hand, most of these courses believe that it's their job, first and foremost, to encourage students in their creative endeavours. That culture of encouragement has obvious merits but it can seriously mislead students as to the standards demanded by the publishing industry. Such courses can also leave students shockingly ignorant about even elementary matters to do with the business. On the day of writing this, for example, I got an email from an MA graduate of a well-known creative writing school asking me whether I thought that self-publishing or approaching agents was a better

CREATIVE WRITING COURSES

The only thing you need to write a publishable book is paper, a pen and a big library. But the right course, at the right moment, can make you a better writer, faster, than you ever could on your own.

On a good course you'll learn many things: to read as a writer; to find and imagine material and use it well; to sharpen and extend your technical toolkit; to make the most of feedback; to read your work as others do. It should also be a safe space to experiment and dig deep, to meet other writers, and share support and information. A beginners' course will help you to find your writing self, and an advanced course will arm you for the ups and downs of the professional writing life: the better you understand your writing and the sharper your technical toolkit, the more able you'll be to turn your hand to new projects.

But is it the right moment? It's best to wait to do a course till you've got as far as you can on your own. That way, you'll know something about your writing and your writerly self, and can decide what to accept, what to adapt, and what to ignore. Then look hard at the course: is it the right shape, level, focus? Is the teacher published? Experienced? A workshop which is vicious in the name of rigour can destroy your confidence; one which is anodyne in the name of supportiveness is little more use. If it feels really wrong then walk away, because you must protect your writing self. On the other hand, you must be willing to be challenged, because a good teacher will help you to go just beyond what you think you can do, and that's where the really exciting writing comes from.

EMMA DARWIN is a novelist and short-story writer. She is Associate Lecturer in Creative Writing with the Open University, and a senior editor and workshop leader for the Writers' Workshop. She has a PhD in Creative Writing from the University of London

first line of attack. If such questions haven't been properly answered in the course of the MA, then what on earth have the students been doing with their time? It's also rare to find a creative writing course which is as serious about genre fiction as it is about literary fiction. In short, by all means do explore this option, but, if your principal goal is to bring your work to publishable standard, then there may be options which are cheaper, less time-consuming and more likely to achieve success.

➤ *Writers' conferences*

These are very common in the US, less so elsewhere, but they provide an excellent way for first-time writers to meet professional authors, agents and editors. Most such conferences offer a good mix of keynote speeches, workshops and informal opportunities to make contacts. Most will also offer participants a chance to pitch their work direct to agents. Again, these conferences will certainly add something to your understanding of the industry and you should have a good time while you're at it. Don't, however, expect them to act like magic. If your work isn't strong enough to secure representation, then no matter how entertaining, witty, personable and polished you are when you meet an agent, you will not be taken on. As ever, it's the manuscript that matters first and foremost.

READING INTELLIGENTLY FOR THE MARKET

One of the commonest observations we agents make while reading through our slushpile, or when discussing with writers at creative writing seminars, is that so many novels are fluent and coherent but just aren't edgy or purposeful enough. The central idea, or character, or situation, hasn't been pushed far enough, or the story is just not conforming to the requirements of the genre where it naturally fits. The usual response from the writers to this is usually that writing isn't about pigeonholing in categories, it's about self-expression, and that writing can escape the shackles of genres, or the expectations of publishing, and often does very successfully. There's often a crime element in a historical novel, or a fantasy element in a contemporary one, or a historical element in a romance etc, and readers can fall in love with unexpected books.

But this is missing the basic point. Publishing is a competitive business, and publishers are shrinking their lists in a difficult retail climate. There's limited shelf space in the shops, and lots of books are vying to get it. Most readers set out to buy something familiar, or something they have heard on the grapevine is exceptional and different, and become pretty expert at what they like, even if they don't necessarily articulate it to themselves in the way that we in publishing do. Genres subdivide into different kinds, whether thrillers, sagas or historicals, according to the specific reading pleasure they offer, and new entrants into the market have to offer something distinctive or different within these sub-genres to attract the attention of agents, editors and readers.

If you are interested in attending a conference, then Poets & Writers (www.pw.org) offers the best guide to events in the US. In Britain, the Winchester Writers' Conference is well established, and there are others too, such as the Writers' Workshop's own annual conference. If you are interested in a particular genre, then the relevant authors' association may well run a conference that offers something for you – the most notable examples being the Romantic Novelists' Association and the Crime Writers' Association.

THINGS YOU PROBABLY DON'T NEED

Having just discovered the huge and wonderful variety of ways in which you can spend money on your writing, you may be relieved to know that there are some things you almost certainly don't need to do.

> *Books that rely on psychological suspense really have to pull that off: they're competing with television and film for excitement. Chick-lit, Aga sagas, romances etc. are genres that change their spots very regularly in response to readers' moods. It's a fast-moving as well as a competitive market. Publishers follow or try to predict these trends. Of course, once a book opens up a new vein of writing, publishers will exploit that as best they can. You do see lookalikes, but they have to be strong and quick off the mark or have genuine originality in their own right. Literary novels, the hardest category to define, have to provide exceptional writing, unusual sensibility, striking voices, and have a gripping narrative of their own.*
>
> *The point is that there must be one overriding purpose to any novel if it is to find readers: a voice, a character, a new twist on an established genre, the playing out of a drama. It is easy for readers to become expert in what's really good, what they like, and why. But too often I have found that writers set out to write without having read intensively enough in their chosen area, to know who they're writing for, what the standard is that they are trying to beat, or what the basic building blocks are. It is impossible to have read too much as a writer, but it is easy to have read too little. Much basic technique is picked up subliminally from reading: it can save years of frustration, and careful reading can reveal all the tricks of the trade and help you analyse the shortcomings of writers you don't think are up to scratch. There's a lot to learn and a whole industry's output to learn from if you're canny enough. Self-expression is for the self-published. Writing is for professionals.*
>
> BILL HAMILTON, Managing Director, A. M. Heath

Top of that list is copy-editing. Copy-editing is the process of working through a manuscript line by line to check for typos and spelling, punctuation glitches and awkward repetitions. A really thorough copy-edit may also clarify or adjust awkward sentences and tidy away any clumsy turns of phrase. Needless to say, no matter how thorough your own review of your manuscript may be, such things will always wriggle through the net, if only because at a certain point you start knowing your manuscript so well that you're not seeing it fresh.

So the manuscript that you're about to send off to agents will certainly have errors in it, some of them plain stupid ones. That doesn't matter. An agent will know that your manuscript hasn't been copy-edited and will also know that smart and capable writers are as prey to brainstorms as anyone else. So, although you should certainly aim to have a professional, clean and tidy manuscript (more about that shortly), you don't need to aim at perfection. What's more, copy-editing is, for most people, both an expensive service and a pointless one. It's expensive, because of the sheer amount of time required to do the job properly. (You should allow, say, £500-£600 to have a manuscript of normal length copy-edited in full.) It's also pointless, because agents are looking for strong stories, strong characters and strong writing. Fiddling around with commas and word repetitions is like trying to paint a room before you've even plastered it. Get the structural stuff right and let a professional copy-editor handle the minor stuff in due course – much further on down the road and at someone else's expense.

You also probably don't needs hands-on editing. As I've said above, in discussing the US approach to editorial work, you can find yourself spending a lot of money for such work. If the manuscript was close to publishable already, you could probably have done that work yourself given appropriate guidance. If it wasn't, it may well be that even $10,000 of professional assistance won't create a publishable manuscript. So take care before reaching for that wallet!

Inevitably, however, there can exceptions to both rules. If you are heading towards self-publication, then you do need to pay for copy-editing help, because no one else is going to pick up the tab for you. If you are writing a memoir about some shocking event that happened to you, perhaps it doesn't matter so much who writes the book as long as it's wonderfully well written. In such a case, then thinking about hands-on editorial help and/or ghostwriting can make sense. Do, however, check very carefully whether your ghostwriter thinks the resulting manuscript is likely to be commercially viable, and also what their track record on such assignments has been in the past. Even with good writing, some tales just aren't likely to be saleable. You may want to go ahead and work on it anyway, but just be clear what the range of outcomes is likely to be. If in doubt, just say no. It's easy to spend money and easier still to end up with very little to show for it.

CONCLUSION

If you've written your manuscript, paused for breath, then revised and edited as hard as you possibly can, you should now be ready for the next step: going out to the market. We'll turn our attention to that in a moment, but first we'll quickly review what's needed for a good non-fiction book proposal. If you've already completed your book, or if you're writing a novel (in which case, you just need to finish it), you can skip the next section and move on to the one after. If you're writing non-fiction, however, what follows is crucial – and is written especially for you.

HOW TO ASSEMBLE A PROPOSAL

If you are writing a novel, you need to complete it before you think of going out to agents or publishers with it. That's not complete as in 'type the final full stop, read it through once, then chuck it in an envelope to send off'. Complete, in this context, means make perfect. You need to edit, revise, polish, get feedback, re-edit, and so on until your novel is properly finished, and only then should you start to think about approaching the industry.

If you are writing non-fiction, however, things are more shaded, and it may not be necessary to write your book in full – or even a single word of it – before writing to agents or publishers. This section is about the non-fiction book proposal, and how to judge what you need to put it together. If you've already written a complete non-fiction book, this section may come a little late in your writing life, but you will probably still want to review it, however briefly.

NARRATIVE-LED NON-FICTION

Some non-fiction nestles close-up against the novel in terms of structure and impulse. A memoir, for example, needs rich characters, a strong sense of movement and story, and vibrantly described settings to succeed. That's pretty much a tick-list for writing a decent novel, except of course that the memoir needs to be true. The same goes for most travel writing and for many biographies. With all such works, you probably need to have written the entire book to convince an agent or publisher to take you on.

This rule isn't absolute, however, and there are certainly exceptions. If, for example, you are a journalist and you have a stunning story to tell – let's say, you were taken captive by the Taliban in Kandahar, made friends with them, then spent eighteen months living amongst them before returning to the West – then you can unquestionably sell your book on the basis of two or three opening chapters and a quick outline of what will follow. The same is true if you have a plausible writing background (which doesn't include business or academic writing) and you are writing the biography of some obviously interesting person. For example, if you're a TV writer and are collaborating with a famous mountaineer about a story of triumph and disaster in the mountains, again you can probably sell the book off three chapters and an outline of what follows.

On the whole, though, the rule is the rule. I know one writer who ghosted a memoir of the first woman to serve in the French Foreign Legion. That book sold for an enormous advance, but did so off a 'book proposal' that was almost one hundred pages long. In other words, the writer (who was very experienced both as a ghost and a journalist) was at pains to make sure that her proposal left nothing out in terms of story. There were gaps as regards characterisations, settings and a host of incidental details – but the agents and publishers were able to read the story at length, and knew that the author's prior track record guaranteed an excellent execution of the complete book. In such a case, a debut author would have been very well advised to write the whole damn thing before seeking to sell it. The same goes for any type of non-fiction which is largely story-led.

POPULAR SUBJECT–LED NON–FICTION

There's a further category of non-fiction, which is subject-led, but where tone and treatment is every bit as crucial. My own *This Little Britain*, for example, was a book which looked at all the ways in which British history diverged from that of its neighbours; my subjects ranged from the early adoption of the rule of law to why English spelling is quite so bananas. That's pretty clearly a book which would be interesting to publishers *in principle*, but the project's success relied entirely on my ability to deal with a broad range of subjects in an engaging way. The result was that I assembled a book proposal which comprised:

AN INTRODUCTION. The introduction was, in effect, both an outline of what the book would look at and a justification for why such a survey was important and worthwhile – a kind of manifesto for the book, if you like. The introduction was not only written with agents and publishers in mind but also the ordinary reader. In fact, the introduction that went into the book proposal was almost precisely the one that wound up in the book.

A HANDFUL OF SHORT CHAPTERS, collectively amounting to some 12-15,000 words. In the case of *This Little Britain*, the chapters were picked more or less at random. In a more structured work, it might be necessary to include the first three chapters. The crucial thing, however, is that you include enough material to allow publishers to form an opinion of whether you'll be able to convey complex material in an entertaining manner.

A 2–3 PAGE OUTLINE of the chapters that would follow. If the introduction and the sample material is strong enough, the outline may not actually matter very much. In the case of *This Little Britain*, the book's range of subject matter was so broad that I simply hadn't bothered to research it all at the book-proposal stage – I only wanted to commit to further work once I had a contract in my hand. As a result, many of my indvidual chapter outlines were cryptic in the extreme. They were essentially just a fudge, to indicate the territory that lay ahead, but without saying very much at all about the lie of the land in those areas. This technique wasn't simply acceptable: I don't honestly think that the publishers who bid for the book either noticed or cared that I was fudging. Why would they? I'd delivered half-a-dozen chapters that were funny, authoritative and thought-provoking. I'd indicated a host of further subjects that I wanted to tackle. That was enough. If you can outline the rest of your material without fudging, so much the better.

If you are writing a book in any popular subject-led non-fiction area, then a book proposal on broadly the above lines will serve you just fine. If you're not sure whether yours is a 'popular' title or not, then have a think about whether you could plausibly see it in the three-for-two section of a major store chain. If you can (and be honest with yourself: most people aren't as interested in your subject as you are), then it's popular non-fiction. If you can't – perhaps you've written a diet book, for example – then it may still be 'popular', in the sense that your style needs to attract people who aren't technically specialist.

If the work does aim at a popular audience, then you must write in a popular way. It doesn't matter that the subject is very important. It doesn't matter that your views could change the world for the better. It doesn't matter that you are supremely well qualified to pronounce on these things. You must write in a popular way. No shortcuts, no excuses. I emphasise this point, because by far the commonest error by writers of subject-led non-fiction is to concentrate too much on the subject and too little on the reader.

THE GRAHAM MAW CHRISTIE LITERARY AGENCY'S TOP TIPS FOR A PERFECT PITCH

A proposal is your sales pitch, firstly from you to a prospective agent and then, probably after quite a bit more work, from the agent to their 'hit list' of editors. But it doesn't stop there.

If the editor is interested, she will show it to editorial colleagues. If it clears this hurdle, the editor will take it to an Acquisitions Meeting – where it will have to pass muster with executives from Sales, Marketing, PR and Production. Therefore, your proposal needs to make a strong case for investing in your book – it also has to present you as authoritative and dynamic, someone capable of supporting its promotion when published. Expect to work on it for several weeks with your agent to perfect it. Then, once your book is signed up by a publisher, your proposal document will be adapted for the cover blurb, press release, sales conference and other in-house uses. So take the opportunity to put your ideas across in the clearest way possible.

A proposal should cover the basics: concept, market, competition, your qualifications, promotional ideas, the estimated number of words, the number of months it will take you to write it and a chapter outline. We find that 6–8 pages is about right, not counting any sample text.

☐ *Make it concise and skimmable for the time-starved, overloaded editor: this is not an opportunity to showcase your finely honed prose: save that for the sample chapters.*

☐ *Be clear, ditch the jargon and explain any terms – even if the editor is familiar with your subject area, others may not be.*

☐ Make a business case for a product that will build and improve on any similar products available to prospective buyers in a digital world. Ask your agent to check Bookscan for the sales of similar books. Read the competing titles.

☐ Reassure the publisher you are an authority on your topic by listing relevant credentials (not your life story) and sales of any previous books including overseas rights deals and serial deals.

☐ Define your market: what typifies your potential core purchaser, how many of these do you estimate there are (include statistics if possible), where do they live, what other books do they read, what other media do they consume and via which gadgets, and when are they most likely to buy? Suggest any secondary markets too.

☐ Explain why your book is particularly timely.

☐ Explain how you will front your title and proactively promote it, particularly online, at launch and beyond, using who and what you know about the subject and your market. Having your own blog or website is really important. If you can sell it yourself at conferences, talks and events, estimate the number of copies.

☐ Memoirs require a different kind of proposal. You will need to convey the narrative arc of the story (actions and events rather than ponderings) and explain how it will inspire readers. Your agent may team you up with a ghostwriter to draft some sample text or a full chapter outline.

YOU COULD ALSO SUGGEST

☐ Ways in which the concept could translate into other media.
☐ Alternative title/subtitles.
☐ Suitable experts/authors/public figures who might endorse the book. If you know any personally, then perhaps ask them to have a look at your sample text.

We really enjoy working on each proposal with our authors, and it needn't be a daunting task if you approach it systematically with these hints in mind. Think of it as good practice for editing your book after it is enthusiastically signed up by a publisher!

JANE GRAHAM MAW and JENNIFER CHRISTIE
Graham Maw Christie Literary Agency
www.grahammawchristie.com

If you don't entertain the reader, the book will fail. If you have to choose between entertaining the reader a tad more and informing her a tad less, go for entertainment every time.

TECHNICAL SUBJECT–LED NON–FICTION

Where a book proposal concerns a fairly narrow and technical subject, it can be fairly brief. A decent proposal might do no more than:

- ☐ *Outline the market.*
- ☐ *Identify the main existing texts.*
- ☐ *Explain why your proposed book brings something new and important.*
- ☐ *Outline your qualifications to write it.*
- ☐ *Summarise in a few pages the proposed outline of your work.*

If a gap in the market exists, and if you are amply qualified to fill it, you may not actually need to supply a single specimen chapter of the intended book. This book, for example, was commissioned by Jenny Ridout at A & C Black on the basis of a proposal that contained no sample material at all. She agreed with me that there was a gap in the market. My qualifications to write the book were very strong. The outline proposal seemed to have covered everything that was needed. And that was all she needed to know. Now, it's true that I came to this book with a proven track record (and indeed, I made sure Jenny had seen copies of my fiction and my non-fiction), but that only mattered because of my proposed subject. If my book had concerned fly-fishing, or computational techniques in statistics, or the history of croquet, no one would have expected me to come brandishing a publication track record.

Although you should certainly check out competing titles by going to several local bookshops (several, because if a given title is sold out in one store, then you may overlook something you need to know about), you can also learn a lot from Amazon. Although Amazon sales rankings don't equate to total sales through all retailers, you can get a good rough guide of which titles are selling strongly and which are also-rans. This can be an excellent method of identifying those titles which are likely to be your principal competitors. It's fine to use that information directly in a book proposal – I did just that when it came to identifying the direct competitors to this book.

Do also bear in mind who your target reader is. If your work is on com-putational techniques in statistics, your reader will almost certainly be obliged to read your book, or something else like it. They're either a professional, seeking to bring their skills up to date, or they're a student, getting ready to sit some exams. In these cases, competence and clarity is all you really need to achieve. If, on the other hand, your book is aimed at lay readers, you need to work harder to hold on to them. If you're writing a primer on parenting, however, although your potential reader has a real interest in work like yours, they're not obliged to sit through anything that bores them – so make your book fun! That means use anecdotes, use jokes, use snippets of personal experience. Think about text boxes, quotations, jokes, cartoons, bulleted lists, trivia facts, and the like. The more fun your book looks to a casual buyer, the more likely they are to carry it over to the till.

Finally, although getting the book proposal absolutely right matters a lot, once you've got a contract you should feel free to depart from the precise terms of the proposal, if you feel that would help the book. This book, for example, has already departed significantly from the outline I gave to A & C Black – apart from anything else, this section didn't even exist. That doesn't matter. If you're worried that a certain alteration is likely to worry your editor, talk it over. If you're confident that the changes you're making are both necessary and consistent with the spirit of the proposal, just go ahead and make the changes. Chances are that no one will notice. If you do it right, they certainly won't care.

THE IMPORTANCE OF ANGLE

The issue of angle is extremely important in any area of non-fiction where competing titles already exist. Since there are a zillion books already written, most subject areas will have obvious existing competitors. My book on British history, for example, was exciting because it found a new way to look at the past. If I had simply been reprising facts familiar from countless existing histories, I wouldn't have got anywhere.

There are, of course, certain books with no obvious predecessors: Dava Sobell's *Longitude* was one such book; so was Simon Singh's *Fermat's Last Theorem*; so was Kate Summerscale's *Suspicions of Mr Whicher*. These, however, are exceptions. Most titles have obvious competitors, and hence the importance of distinguishing your work from the pack.

Every now and then, someone comes to us with a manuscript that addresses some popular 'how to' area: diet, perhaps, or leadership/motivation. The writing may be perfectly good. The writer may be somewhat authoritative: perhaps they practise as a dietician or as a motivational trainer. The subject is clearly important enough to merit a book, since shedloads of books

JENNY RIDOUT'S TIPS
FOR YOUR SPECIALIST NON-FICTION PROPOSAL

Like any other product, your content has to satisfy a market need. So your non-fiction proposal should begin by addressing this, as it is the first thing your editor will look for. Explain what is driving the demand for this type of information and how your content meets the need. It could be changing exam requirements, new technology or the need for professionals to re-skill, for example. Knowing clearly who your target market is and their information needs will help you understand how to shape your content. What specific approach do you have that will make someone buy your book? Your editor will base her own in-house pitch (to get your book approved) very much on your initial proposal, so it is worth spending time on. Don't forget your editor will be pitching to a group of publishing professionals in-house, not experts on the chosen subject area, so do explain any technical terms or acronyms.

The competitive angle comes next. It is good to consider the strengths and the weaknesses of competing titles. The strengths will tell you a lot about what works. The weaknesses will point to where to differentiate. Remember, the competition may not be in book form – so consider what you are actually competing with. Just because there isn't a similar title on Amazon doesn't mean that there is no competition – it could be in the form of a course, or a free internet resource.

Having worked out in your mind what the market wants and your angle on the competition, now you can think about the structure of the content. In addition to chapter headings, describe the topics you will cover in each chapter and what your particular approach will be. This will help your editor get a real feel for the book. Also think in terms of special features (case studies, interviews, tables, graphs) and the benefits of those features to the reader. What will the reader be able to do as a result of having read your book? What special features of your content help them to do that? Again in the sales copy, these things will translate into what the industry calls USPs (unique selling points).

Remember that a good table of contents will also form the basis of your writing plan. It is the skeletal backbone, if you like, on to which you will hang your genius! Map it out, with topics listed under chapter headings, find regular slots for writing time, tick off completed sections as you go along, and in due course you will see your content build and feel a sense of accomplishment. Your editor will also have a very good sense of how you're getting along if you send regular status reports. Halfway through your deadline, for example, they will expect you to have half the manuscript complete. Your editor may like to look through your early chapters and provide comments or peer reviews at this stage.

Other things to consider: try to give an indication of the level of illustration. Is there any material that you would like to include that is not your copyright and for which permission will need to be sought and paid? What about video or web resources? Not sure how much material to write? You'll need to provide a 'guestimate' (grab a similar title off the shelf, count the rough number of words per page and you'll get a feel for how word count translates into actual pages). Your editor will put together an initial cost for the book based on this information and their estimated first print run, so this detail is necessary upfront and your eventual contract will also state the rough number of words you are aiming for. If you have answered all these questions in your proposal it saves the editor having to come back and ask, the project will move along more swiftly at the publishing end, and you will look more professional.

Can you help with marketing? Can you suggest organisations or websites that would be interested in featuring this type of book? Do you have contacts and leads that will help your publicist? Put these ideas in, as a clear route to market is as important as good content, so try to include this information.

Include a good biography – a few paragraphs will suffice. List previous relevant publications if you have them but most of all your biog should support why you are the best person to deliver this necessary content for the intended readership.

Most specialist non-fiction proposals will be peer-reviewed: your editor will seek one or two industry experts to comment on your outline and provide feedback. This is usually done anonymously and most authors welcome this constructive early input. It can be an early indicator as to how your book would be received in the marketplace and so it is worth taking seriously. You don't have to agree with everything (your editor will often have filtered out all but the most sensible comments), and the process usually results in some helpful ideas to make your book more relevant to the marketplace and sell more widely.

Finally, think hard about how long it will realistically take you to put your book together. Most people underestimate how long it takes to write a book, and most people have to do it alongside a day job and family etc. If this is your first book and you are not sure what to suggest with regard to a deadline to work to, ask your editor for advice. Remember that publication dates are based on manuscript delivery dates, so, if you slip your deadline, the pub date will slip, and this causes all sorts of disruption for the sales team, not to mention bad relations with booksellers and disappointed customers placing orders ahead of publication. So try to make it realistic, but not so far out that you put the project to one side.

Good luck – enjoy!

JENNY RIDOUT, Publisher,
Methuen Drama, Media and Reference, A & C Black (Bloomsbury)

are sold in these areas each year. Very often, however, the angle is completely missing. We are then obliged to tell the author that their book isn't distinguishing itself from countless other titles in the genre, many of which may have celebrity endorsement, or be familiar from TV, or already have bestseller status in the much larger US market.

The writer is often incredulous. 'But what I'm saying is *true*,' they tell us. 'My stuff *helps* people.' They're probably right. I have no reason to doubt them. But being right is not an angle. When a potential reader is browsing the dozens of available diet books, they're not going to know whether your arguments are true or not. They're going to look at the title, then the front cover, then maybe the back cover, then maybe flip casually at the contents themselves. That's it. That's how long you have to convince the reader that your strategy is the right one for them. That means you need to think about your book the way a brand-strategist thinks about canned beans, the way a copywriter thinks about a TV commercial. What's more, if you don't think about angle, an agent will. If your book doesn't have one – and a good one at that – it'll be turned down flat.

WHICH AGENT? WHICH PUBLISHER?

Most authors, well before they even finish their work, will get hold of a copy of the *Writers' & Artists' Yearbook*, flip through to the pages that list literary agents and pore over the runic text, trying to sense which of these sacred names are going to be The One. Depending on taste, you may also start to highlight names, compile matrices, compare websites, make phone calls or (who knows?) fashion an array of voodoo dolls out of candle wax and matchsticks.

I'm entirely in favour of all these activities and was as prey to them as anyone else at one stage in my career. On the other hand, I'd gently suggest that there are a number of more elementary steps that may be useful supports to the voodoo-doll and sacred-name procedure. The very first step to be taken is a simple one: do you even need an agent?

WHO NEEDS AN AGENT?

Not everyone needs an agent, and there are a fair few people in search of agents who'll never get one, simply because their book isn't agentable material. Equally, there are others who emphatically do need agents, who persist in sending their work to publishers and who will be doomed to failure until they shift their focus. There's also – inevitably – a middle ground where there's room for doubt. You might be better off with an agent, or you might not. There's no certain way to know.

YOU DO NEED AN AGENT, IF . . . If you are writing any kind of mainstream book, you need an agent. A mainstream book is anything that you might see in a prominent position in a major bookstore or supermarket. If you've written a novel (for adults or kids), you need an agent. If you've written a work of popular non-fiction, you need an agent. Travel books, memoirs, popular science, biographies, popular history and some 'how-to' titles all need agents. The reason why you need an agent for work of this sort is that the major publishers of books like these don't even look at unagented work. Without an agent, therefore, you are cutting yourself off from the most important possible market for your work.

YOU DON'T NEED AN AGENT, IF . . . If your book is highly specialist, you don't need an agent. An agent will take a commission, usually of 15%, on any money they make on your behalf. If your book is a specialist one – *The ABC of Snowmobile Maintenance, Avant-Garde Knitting for the Experienced Knitter, A Primer on Early Medieval Manuscripts* – it's not going to sell for very much money. 15% of not very much money isn't going to keep an agent in champagne and Marc Jacobs for more than a few seconds, so they simply won't have any interest in representing you. There are, however, publishers who do specialise in books just such as these. Motor publishers who want books on snowmobiles. Craft publishers who want books on knitting. Academic publishers who go all pink and giggly when a primer on early medieval manuscripts plops through their letterboxes. In all such cases, you need to cut out the agent and head straight to the relevant publisher.

YOU MIGHT WANT AN AGENT, IF . . . Needless to say, there's a middle ground where it's unclear whether an agent should or should not handle your work. Snowmobile maintenance texts fairly clearly only appeal to a small audience, but what about a *Field Guide to the Flowers of Britain*? As it happens, a client of ours wrote such a book and got a publication deal without an agent by going direct to a specialist publisher. On the other hand, I could imagine an agent receiving a proposal like that and thinking, 'Not my usual area this, but actually there must be a fair few flower-lovers out there, and maybe I could sell this guide for £3,000 and pick up a stream of royalty earnings over the years as well.' If that agent happened to be in need of a new pair of Marc Jacobs at the time, then that might just have been enough to clinch the deal.

Children's picture books are another major area of unclarity. There are some good agents who specialise in such texts. Equally, publishers are happy to look at unagented work. Do you need an agent or not? Well, no, you don't *need* one, but you may nevertheless *want* one. It's up to you. If in doubt, my advice would be to get an agent. If you fail, the worst that happens is that you've wasted a bit of time. If you succeed, you will probably get a better contract and a more professional start in the market than you would otherwise have done. Once you've established a decent name in the field and started to learn the ropes yourself, you may well feel better off managing your career by yourself. I know a very successful author of children's picture books and novels who took exactly that route.

One last word before leaving this subject. If you're unsure about whether you want an agent or a publisher, never make the mistake of approaching agents and publishers simultaneously. If an agent is interested in taking you on, they'll be extremely disconcerted that you've made prior approaches to publishers. If those publishers have already said no (perhaps because you approached the wrong editor in the wrong way at the wrong time), you'll have impaired the agent's chances of securing a deal and the agent will therefore be more likely to reject you too.

If by chance you approach a major publisher with a mainstream novel and get it accepted (a rare but not impossible occurrence), then you have the opposite problem – and a nice one to have. Although you'll be delirious about the acceptance, you'll also suddenly realise that you have no idea what you're doing and that you really, really need an agent. At that point, however, it's easy. All you need to do is contact a handful of agents, tell them you have a signficant offer from a major publisher and is it possible they'd like to represent you? Although agents will certainly want to read your work and make sure that they like it too, the commercial proposition is an easy one, as they know there's money to be made. It's a bit like asking a banker whether he fancies a bonus: the answer is always likely to be yes.

Though this sequence is rare, it's not unknown, and I know of at least one very high-profile author who took this route. The publisher who waded through the slushpile and found her work loved it and made an excellent offer. The author thought, 'By 'eck, I'd better get me an agent.' So she did just that. Her agent did what any competent salesman would do and auctioned the book off to the highest bidder. The initial publisher still loved the book and raised their offer to crazy new heights, but were still outbid by other publishers who raised their bid to heights yet crazier still. The moral of that story from the first publisher's point of view is never, ever bother with the slushpile, because, even if you do find jewels in it, they'll be snatched from you anyway.

TARGETING AGENTS: THE RULES

One of the questions we're asked most frequently is some variant of this one: 'I've written a novel which I'd classify as a ———. Please can you suggest which agents are interested in works of this kind?' Sometimes the blank is filled in with something fairly generic: 'a historical romance' or 'a political thriller'. Sometimes, however, those blanks are filled in with an astonishingly specific array of descriptors. 'A religio-political drama set in the court of Ferdinand of Aragon and incorporating certain philosophical arguments connected with the ethics of the later Reconquista.' Sometimes we honestly get the impression that, if we were to come back saying that we knew of an agent specialising in religio-political dramas in the court of Ferdinand of Aragon, but one with no prior expertise in Reconquistian ethics, the author concerned would stomp off in a huff, looking for someone who *really* understood his market.

All such queries are essentially misconceived. The simple truth is this: agents aren't very specialist. My own agent will happily handle commercial fiction and literary fiction and non-fiction. He'd handle thrillers and women's fiction; serious non-fiction and popular best-sellers. He needs to *like* the book in question. He also needs to believe that he can find a publisher to take it. But that's it. My previous agent operated in exactly the same way. So do a large majority of all other agents out there. The simple truth is that, if agents tried to specialise too far, their supply of saleable manuscripts would dry up very rapidly indeed, leaving them cold, poor, ragged and hungry.

Having said that, it's worth taking any obvious and easy steps to direct your work to those most likely to take it. Most agents who specialise in thrillers are men, for example. It probably makes slightly more sense for women's fiction authors to be represented by women. Some agencies will have informative websites that disclose what different agents are interested in. In such cases, it's worth visiting the site and directing your work to the appropriate person. In other cases, it's normally fine to ring up and ask if there's a particular agent who relishes your particular genre. That kind of simple, easy spadework is well worthwhile.

Agents often advise that writers research the agent and agency in detail before making an approach. This sounds like good advice, and perhaps quite likely is. It can, however, be harder to implement than it sounds. Let's say you're thumbing through the *Yearbook* and come across an agency which advertises itself as welcoming 'commercial and literary fiction and non-fiction'. That presumably includes your MS since it includes every possible manuscript. You then click through to the relevant website and find that the agency is enthusiastic about 'established and exciting emerging talent', that Agent X is very keen on 'literary and well-written commercial fiction'. What precisely have you learned from this research? I think the answer is that you've learned nothing at all. Of course, you can then always click through to an agent's list of clients, read half-a-dozen authors on that list, if you are not yet familiar with them, then seek to divine what precisely connects those six authors . . . which may, in fact, be very little, because everyone's tastes are to some extent personal and unpredictable.

An alternative method, often recommended, is to locate the agents who represent authors you admire in your particular genre, then approach them. Once again, however, I think this can be hard to achieve and of dubious value. First of all, it can be quite hard to find out who represents a particular author. Second, the whole thing can come to be quite mechanical. Many agents will have two or three star names on their lists and, if every covering letter that comes in to them mentions one of those three names, I imagine they'd soon stop taking any notice. Thirdly, the suggestion can actually be quite counterproductive. More than once, I've recommended a client to an agent, thinking that, since X already represents Y, she'll certainly be interested in my very Y-ish client Z – only to be told that X doesn't think she can represent both authors as they come across as too similar.

The general rule, therefore, is simple. Do the simplest research fast and effectively. Don't send adult fiction to someone who only deals in non-fiction. Don't send literary fiction to a house that only deals in commercial work. Thereafter, it's more a numbers game than anything. For most books, you can just send your manuscript fairly broadly with a decent hope that, if your work is strong enough, it'll be taken on. If you are writing for children or young adults, then use the *Children's Writers' & Artists' Yearbook* as your guide. By all means take some easy, sensible steps to refine your list of submissons somewhat – checking websites, making calls – but there's no need to go crazy. In the end, this is a numbers game.

You should aim to come up with a list of ten to twelve names, and send your work to them. Some of those people will reject your manuscript for essentially random reasons: the book you've written just doesn't happen to be their sort of thing. But not all dozen. If you send your work to ten to twelve agents and they all reject it, then your work isn't good enough. It's that simple. (Or almost – we'll talk about some complications in a moment.) If you notch up a dozen rejections, then rather than trying to scour the *Yearbook* for a host of new names to contact, you almost certainly need to look hard again at your manuscript. Since, by definition, your own scrutiny wasn't sufficient the first time round, you'd be very well advised to call on expert external advice, both in order to analyse the problem and to develop next steps. The alternative to not doing this may well be to give up on the project altogether.

It's also, perhaps, worth saying that, if you send your manuscript to literally every agent in the *Yearbook*, as some writers I know have done, then you are wasting their time and your own. If a dozen agents turn down your novel, then a dozen professional assessors of manuscripts have, in effect, ruled your manuscript unsaleable. If that's the case, you simply need to fix the manuscript. Even if you did find an agent to take you on, publishers are more likely to agree with the first dozen agents than they are with the solo contrarian voice.

BIGGER OR SMALLER? OLDER OR NEWER?

There are, depending a little on how you count, two or three large agencies in operation: Curtis Brown, PFD and United Agents. The latter two outfits have been through some turbulent times just recently, United Agents having been set up following a mass walk-out of agents from the old PFD. At one point, the PFD office was almost empty; United Agents were still sorting out permanent offices; and the two sides were growling at each other in court. All this made for good soap opera for a while, but no longer. Both agencies are capably managed independent agencies, and there's no reason to fight shy of either company because of a storm that's now long past.

As well as the three larger outfits, there are a whole slew of middling agencies. A typical middling agency might have four agents with a slightly larger number of people in support. Down at the lower end of the spectrum there are a number of one-man and one-woman bands, where the agent will also be opening envelopes, answering phones and sweeping the floors. The oldest established agency has been going for more than ninety years, while new ones are springing up all the time. (They're also disappearing all the time, of course. Because of the general pressure on the industry, which tends to concentrate more and more money in the hands of fewer and fewer best-sellers, the pressure on literary agents has been fairly acute at times too. It's not size, however, but quality that confers immunity to such pressure.)

On the whole, it's true that the more established agencies will have a longer list of clients, easier access to celebrity and established authors, and perhaps less of an appetite for new clients. On the other hand, even established agencies will have newer agents working for them and those agents will be working hard to build their client lists and make some sales. Equally, there'll be plenty of smaller agencies who are kept pretty busy by their existing clients and who will need to be dazzled by a manuscript to take on a new author. If a particular agent hasn't been in business long, she will certainly be looking to take on new clients, but then again she'll also be keenly aware that she needs to build her reputation with publishers, so she'll want to go out to them first with submissions that are very strong rather than marginal.

In short, although it's probably true that younger/smaller agencies are a little greedier for new clients than older/bigger ones, it's by no means a reliable rule. It's also not true that the letterhead of a big agency on a submission to a publisher will create shock and awe amongst those who receive it. A young, fairly inexperienced agent at a large agency won't have a lot of shock and awe at his disposal. An agent who's in business on her own will, if she has a strong reputation, command much more respect.

In the end, though, it's not about respect; it's about the quality of the manuscript submitted. If a newbie agent sends a MS out to six to eight properly selected editors, and that MS is fantastic, then the publishers will respond the way any market normally would: it'll push the price for that manuscript rapidly upwards. Likewise, if a highly well-known agent sends out a manuscript that isn't quite strong enough, no one will bid for it. Ten years ago or more, it would have been common to find capable agents boasting that they'd never failed to sell a manuscript. I don't think I know any long-serving agent of whom that is still true today. Publishers have cut their lists. They've become more conservative about their selections. It's not even that uncommon for a manuscript to be rejected by a publisher, with a note from the editor containing only praise for the writer and the writing, with a plaintive addendum to the effect that the folks from marketing weren't quite convinced. Those folks from marketing just don't care who an agent is, where they work, or what their reputation and track record may be.

I generally advise mixing your submissions up somewhat: approach some larger agencies and some smaller ones, some older ones and some newer ones. There's no overwhelming logic in operation here. If you want to do it some other way, then feel free. The only real purpose in mixing things up is that, if you do get more than one offer of representation, you may be in a position to compare and contrast the feeling of being one client amongst many hundreds in a larger agency, or one rather more significant client in a smaller one.

WHAT PERCENTAGE?

Not too long back, most agents charged 10% or 12.5% on commissions earned on home sales, and 20% on commissions earned on overseas sales – that 20% in effect representing 10% for the London-based agent and 10% for their overseas counterpart.

As median advances declined, agents noticed that their pockets were jingling with rather less change than had once been the case. So agents started to push their commissions upwards, and a majority of agents now charge 15% of home sales; the overseas percentage hasn't altered. This has, of course, been adverse for authors taken as a bloc. It does, after all, seem a little harsh to be paying 50% more commission, when median advances have declined by 33%. That's not exactly rewarding success.

On the other hand, it almost never makes sense to fight the market. Every now and then, I've come across first-time writers selecting agents according to how little they charge. That's a crazy procedure. A really good agent is the most important ally a writer will ever have. Really good agents may charge 10% or 12.5% if they are looking to attract clients to an expanding business, but most good agents charge 15% - and should be able to deliver far more value than that to their prospective clients. If you get more than one agent offering to represent you, then you can certainly ask – gently – about commissions, and it's quite likely that you'll be able to negotiate a little give in that 15%. But don't obsess about it. It's not worth it. Go with the best agent, not the cheapest one. After all, there aren't many things where the cheapest is always the best – and selecting your agent is a very, very big decision.

LONDON, NEW YORK, DUBLIN, SYDNEY?

For most people, it'll be obvious which publishing centre is right for them. If you're a Briton living in the UK or Europe, you need a British agent who, most likely, will live or work either in London itself or very close by. (There are a couple of decent agencies in Edinburgh, a couple in Oxford and a small handful of other good agents operating well outside the M25, but not all that many.) If you are based in Lincolnshire, you should not be looking for an agent based in Lincolnshire, because you don't want your agent to live close to you, but close to publishers. Since the main Hachette companies, Random House, Penguin, HarperCollins, Macmillan, Bloomsbury and most of the larger independent publishers are based in London, that's where most of the agents congregate too. That's not snobbery or metropolitian cliquism; it's common sense.

Likewise, if you are American or Canadian, and living in North America, your agent will, for similar reasons, almost certainly be based in New York. The *Writers' Market* is your best guide to the available agents.

If you aren't a Briton resident in Europe or a North American resident in North America, the issue of where to send your material becomes a little more complex. The following rules will be correct in most instances, but you need to be guided by common sense and some understanding of the market, not simply by the rules. But the rules first:

➤ *If you are Irish writing Irish-interest material*
Approach Dublin-based agents or publishers.

➤ *If you are Irish, but writing general interest material*
You are definitely better off going to a London-based agent, which sounds a little colonial, but, since the multinational publishers are based there, you need to head for London nevertheless. Do note that your material may be set in Ireland but still of general interest. Maeve Binchy is as Irish as a leprechaun dancing on a shamrock, but her novels are of universal interest, with multinational publishers to match.

➤ *If you are a South African, Australian, New Zealander or, indeed, hail from anywhere in the Commonwealth apart from Canada*
You have a decision to make, which could run one of three ways.

(1) If you reckon there is a healthy local market for your work, you can approach local publishers or literary agents. Selling to a local publisher doesn't have to mean giving up on your global ambitions. If you sell world

THE VIEW FROM DOWN UNDER

In my opinion it's rarely wise for Australian writers to approach publishers or agents in the UK or US direct. They will often use the geographical excuse to give an immediate rejection and then the door is closed, often for ever. If an Australian agent – who generally has good contacts in these places – gets an overseas agent on board, then you have two people fighting in your corner and the result will usually be much better for you.

I always caution writers against writing specifically for an international market. My heart sinks when I hear someone on the phone saying, 'This novel is sure to do really well in the US.' It's generally much easier to get an overseas sale once you have an established reputation in your home territory – and perhaps some best-seller listings and glowing reviews to show off.

Remember too that it's sometimes in your interests for your Australian agent to sell world rights to an Australian publisher – if they are offering reasonable terms and have a very good track record of on-selling overseas rights.

Most publishers are not accepting unsolicited manuscripts at all these days (possibly a result of the explosion of creative writing courses, and consequently of creative writers) and so an agent is the best first port of call. There is now an Australian Literary Agents' Association and all members must abide by certain rules and codes of conduct (such as not charging reading fees). They are listed at austlitagentsassoc.com.au. Always check websites on individual agents' submission guidelines before submitting material.

FIONA INGLIS
MD, Curtis Brown (Australia) Pty Ltd
www.curtisbrown.com.au

rights and are confident that your local publisher will make a real effort to sell those rights to publishers elsewhere, then you are effectively getting an agent and a publisher all in one go. You've got a decent hope of there being a local market for your work if it is clearly of a type handled by local houses. If you can offer some specific local interest into the bargain, then so much the better.

(2) If you reckon that the local market for your work is a little skinny, but your work has the quality and breadth of appeal to work elsewhere, then you can try a London agent. Strong work will be taken on by a London agent who won't have a particular problem that you might live half a world

away. However, because authors who live half a world away are less available for PR and are going to be considered somewhat less newsworthy by the British press, the hard truth is that you are probably at something of a disadvantage compared with British or Irish authors. Not a huge disadvantage, but a real one nevertheless.

(3) If you reckon that the local market is going to be too skinny for you, then you can alternatively approach agents in New York. There tends to be a slight expectation that Commonwealth authors will look to London first, and it's probably true that UK agents will be rather more accustomed to an international outlook than American ones, but these are minor factors in the scheme of things. Certainly if you have strong US connections via family or work, they should trump anything else. And in certain areas – say, fantasy/sci-fi – the North American market is livelier than the British equivalent, so that would also be a strong reason to snub the Queen and salute the President.

➤ *If you are British or Irish and living in North America, or if you are a North American living in Europe*
The world is your oyster. You could go either way. You are probably better off dealing with an agent located in the same continent as you, but if there are reasons for doing otherwise, then do otherwise. If you want to send your material to agents in both locations, go right ahead.

➤ *If you are Canadian*
So far, I've treated North America as a unit with New York as its hub. That's too simple. Canada has its own excellent publishing industry, and looks almost as much to the Commonwealth market as it does to the American. Many Canadian authors will secure a Canadian agent or publisher as a first step, then proceed from there.

➤ *If you are Indian or African*
It's perhaps worth emphasising that the publishing industry today is somewhat discriminatory – that is, it discriminates *in favour of* authors who aren't middle-aged white Europeans or Americans. A dazzling first novel by a Nigerian author may well sell for more than the same novel written by, for example, me. Indeed, I have had agents explicitly tell me that they are looking for brown-skinned authors. That's a barmy state of affairs if you ask me – I'd like a world where authors are judged only on the merits of their work – but it's certainly better than the other way round. Indian and African authors will be very welcome in London, but they'll also be very welcome

in New York. Again, most Indian and African authors will probably feel that London is a better first port of call, but it's marginal. It's also, just to be clear, absolutely fine if your novel is written in something other than Standard British English or Standard American English, but it must be fluent. Unless you are entirely comfortable in English as a spoken language, you are unlikely to have the fluency needed to write a novel. If you have that fluency, however, then drawing on your local version of English may greatly enrich your work.

And if those rules don't deal exactly with your situation, then use your head. If your work is good enough and your approach is professional enough, it probably doesn't matter all that much which door you knock on first.

TARGETING AGENTS: FANTASY AND SCIENCE FICTION

Fantasy and science fiction is an altogether more problematic area. There's a ludicrous snobbery which pervades the industry about this kind of speculative fiction. No matter that the *Iliad* and *Odyssey* fall into this category, that *Beowulf* does, that the *Morte d'Arthur* does, that Dante's *Inferno* does. And Shakespeare's *The Tempest*. And *Gulliver's Travels*. No matter, in fact, that many of the greatest works of world literature have been solidly 'speculative' in nature, the snobbery has solidified into something so pervasive that it's virtually impossible to find a way over or through it. There are some genuinely interesting fantasy authors writing today (for example, Neil Gaiman and Guy Gavriel Kay). Russell Hoban's stunning 1980 novel, *Riddley Walker*, is dystopian science fiction – and a classic of post-war fiction. Though the wonderful Haruki Murakami is normally categorised as surrealist, at times he's only a fingernail's thickness from being an out-and-out fantasy writer.

I, therefore, don't share this snobbery about speculative fiction, but I do, in part, understand it. The manuscripts that we receive range from very good to very bad. We get good thrillers and bad thrillers, good literary novels and bad ones. We also receive a lot of fantasy/sci-fi, some of which is very good. We've handled fantasy manuscripts which have gone all the way to getting agented and published. Those weren't manuscripts which were merely good by fantasy standards, they were just plain good stories, well told, which deserved publication irrespective of genre. The trouble is that we also receive a quite disproportionate amount of bad fantasy/sci-fi.

I'm not quite sure what the reason is. Often the writers are younger and less mature. Often (and usually disastrously) the novel in question has been inspired by a computer game. Often the writer seems to believe that having a strong imagination is an effective substitute for writing decent English. Whatever the reason, however, many agents have effectively closed the doors to fantasy/sci-fi, simply because the administrative burden of sorting through all the bad manuscripts has overwhelmed the likely profit from the handful of good ones. It's also true that publishers currently feel that the fantasy market is weaker than it has been in the past – one agent told me recently that she thought, if Philip Pullman were a debut author, his *Dark Materials* trilogy might have proved unsaleable in today's market.

(Though, if you'll permit a brief digression here, I think there's a question of mindset as well as mere economics. The novel is essentially a post-Enlightenment art form, expressing post-Enlightenment values. Fantasy fiction hijacks the novel and uses it as a vehicle for exploring pre-Enlightenment beliefs and archetypes – that is to say, the beliefs and archetypes which pertained through nearly all of human history and through every jot and syllable of prehistory too. To my mind, that means that good fantasy fiction should be able to explore some extremely interesting territory and in an extremely interesting way. Alas, most agents don't seem to share that view.)

In any case, the main point to arise from all this is that selling good-quality fantasy/sci-fi is harder than it should be. One good trick is to look at your book and see if you can reclassify it. A light science-fiction novel might be reclassifiable as a techno-thriller or a near-future thriller. A novel set in a post-apocalyptic future might 'explore the same territory as Margaret Atwood's *Handmaid's Tale*'. Fantasy novels are often able to masquerade as 'young adult fiction'. Sad as it is to say, these dodges are normally advisable, so long as they're plausible. If your 'techno-thriller' involves space suits and warp drives, then no one will believe your reclassification.

If reclassifying your work isn't possible, then you simply need to make the rounds of agents in the normal way. You'll need to do more work than usual in establishing which agents are potentially fantasy/sci-fi friendly. You should avoid those agents who simply reject fantasy on principle. One agent's website has a road-sign icon depicting a dragon barred by a diagonal red line through its chest. Most agents are more subtle in their distaste, but that only makes your job harder. With fantasy/sci-fi, you may need to go to more than the usual ten to twelve agents in order to get a reliable read as to the market for your work. Fifteen to eighteen agents might be a more realistic number to target – but, again, I would urge you to make sure that your manuscript is up to scratch before you send it out. The ultimate reason why most fantasy manuscripts are rejected is not that agents are snobs, it's that most fantasy manuscripts don't pass muster. Many of them don't even remotely reach the kind of quality threshold required. So, before sending work out, go back to the previous section and ask yourself as honestly as you can whether your work is truly ready to send out.

Finally, if you have solid reason to believe in the quality of your work (perhaps because an expert outside assessor has given it the thumbs-up), you may need to think of non-conventional routes into the industry. HarperCollins, for example, has enjoyed a good track record at setting up niche imprints that combine the nimbleness of specialists with the muscle of a large publisher. One such imprint is an outfit (entertainingly called Angry Robot) which is open to any author with a recommendation from an authoritative source. A literary agent would be the most normal kind of authority, but an editorial agency would do just as well. So would a professional author in the field. So would a magazine publisher or a competition organiser. So, if you do get turned down by agents, and really, truly have reason to believe that your work is strong enough to sell, then get that imaginative energy to work in finding unconventional routes into the industry. They do exist and quality will always sell in the end. You may just need a little extra degree of persistence.

TARGETING AGENTS: NICHE AREAS

Having stressed early on that most agents are generalists, I should also acknowledge that there are some niches, where specialist agents do operate. Sports books, TV tie-ins, cookery books, illustrated work and other specialisms do exist. If you've written a book in an area that you feel might have a niche of its own, then there's no way to check whether there's a specialist agency operating other than by browsing the pages of the *Yearbook*. If such a specialist does exist for you, then by all means send them your work, but don't necessarily despair of finding a non-specialist to represent you. Equally, the existence of specialists may also mean that your book is the kind of thing where a direct approach to a publisher is something you could consider.

TARGETING PUBLISHERS

If you decide that your work would best be sold direct to publishers, then the task of identifying those publishers is a little more complex than it is with agents. There are two basic techniques to use, which are best used in conjunction.

First, you should scour the pages of the *Yearbook*'s publishers section for any likely names. Whereas agents tend to give relatively little away either in the *Yearbook* or on their websites, publishers are very frank about what they handle. If yours is a craft book – those knitting patterns, maybe – then you are looking for a publisher of craft, fashion or sewing books. Just go through the *Yearbook* and make a note of any likely names. You probably want to cross-check those names against the company websites, just to be on the safe side, and doing so will also give you some further useful information about that company's emphasis and approach.

Allied to this approach, you should also go to the relevant section of a bookshop. Spend time looking for books in a vaguely similar area. Don't be too pedantic about this. Your book may be specifically about knitting, but any craft- or sewing-related title is relevant to you. When you find related titles, take a look at how the book is packaged and marketed – that information may well suggest some useful revisions you could make to your own text – but also note down the publisher's name and address. (You'll find that information on the page of tedious-looking small print at the front of the book.) Do make sure that you take the address in full. If you only use the *Yearbook* for addresses, you may end up with the central corporate address of some large conglomerate, which is quite likely to lose or neglect your submission. A big part of the trick of approaching publishers directly is to make sure that your submission lands as near as possible to the desk of the person most likely to appreciate it.

What's more, when you do approach publishers, you need to think very hard about the work from their point of view. Let's say, for example, you've written a book on classic motor bikes, and you've discovered a publisher that has titles on *Classic Cars*, *Classic Planes*, *Classic Ships* – but nothing yet called *Classic Motor Bikes*. Clearly, you're in a potentially strong position. But do take the time to study those other titles. If they all have a certain format – a jaunty prose style, text boxes full of trivia facts, comparison charts and the like – then you need to make darn sure that your book fits that basic mould. If it doesn't, that publisher won't want it and it'll be your fault for not properly adapting your work to the market.

Don't expect publishers to have the imagination to leap from the text that you've submitted to the text that you could supply if you had a contract to make the necessary changes. I yield to no one in my love and admiration for all publishing kind, but I'd no more rely on their imagination in such a context than I would hand my wallet to a jewel thief. You get to do the work. Then they get to say yea or nay. That's not fair, but there it is. Better to do that bit more work and secure the contract than do that little bit less and achieve nothing.

THE X-FACTOR IN GETTING PUBLISHED

The publishing industry is exactly like The X-Factor. *You start with tens of thousands of hopefuls, all certain that they are talented and deserve to be made into stars/published. Their friends and family are equally convinced, or at least have to say they are out of loyalty or blind love.*

These thousands of people turn up to auditions/send in their manuscripts, and the gatekeepers of television/publishing have a limited amount of time to try to spot the ones that the public will like and want to get to know better. Sometimes it will be obvious that someone has enormous talent, or is exceptionally attractive, usually it is not that obvious.

The majority, through sheer weight of numbers, will then be sent home/ have their manuscripts ignored or rejected. Even those who get through to the show/publication will still be ignored by the public/voted out and will end up disappointed not to have had their dreams come true and angry with those who have succeeded where they have failed.

Someone, of course, has to win — just as with every lottery. On The X-Factor *it will be Alexandra Burke and in publishing it will be J. K. Rowling, and then there will be the people who simply gain public attention because they are different and make people smile — John and Edward in* The X-Factor, *Katie Price in publishing.*

It is all quite fair because everyone has the same chance to lay their goods out on display and there are only a limited number of hours that we can all watch television or read books, so most of us will inevitably be knocked back.

There has been a spate of complaints in the media recently from published authors about the state of the publishing industry and how hard it is for new writers to break in and how unfair it is that the bad stuff gets published and the good stuff gets overlooked. But wasn't it always so? Is it possible that millions are transfixed by The X-Factor *because it is a giant metaphor for life? Publishing is also exactly like life — everyone who goes into it has ambitions, most will be disappointed.*

What to do about it? How do you beat the odds?

Well maybe, like Alexandra Burke, the secret lies in (a) having enough talent to start with, (b) working ceaselessly at your craft and (c) coming back for another go every time you are knocked back (she only won on her second time of appearing on The X-Factor).

Young talent is often knocked back and discouraged, but in the long run persistence will always pay off — in publishing as in life.

ANDREW CROFTS
novelist and ghostwriter (extracted with permission from his blog)

AVOIDING BANDITS

You should always use the *Writers' & Artists' Yearbook* as your source of information, or at least one of the other reputable directories available. The *Yearbook* demands references for all of its listings and will boot companies out if they are seen to be less than ethical.

Because of the vast number of people seeking to be published, there are inevitably also fraudsters preying on them. In particular, you should avoid:

> *Agents who advertise aggressively on the internet.* Real agents don't need to advertise any further afield than the *Yearbook*. There's a cluster of phoney US-based 'literary agencies' which relies on aggressive online advertising to secure clients. All writers are accepted as clients. (I know this, because I sent them some pages from a dishwasher manual and they wrote back to me congratulating me on my 'excellent commercial potential'. When I then sent them the full text of *Pride & Prejudice*, they sent an identical email.) Those clients are then asked to pay a small sum – $90, typically – for a 'critique'. These critiques are computer generated and all positive. Often there are follow-up requests for further relatively small sums of money for minor tasks. Then there's often a suggestion that self-publishing (with a sister company, though they don't tell you that) is the right course of action for you. These outfits are scams, pure and simple. Avoid them.

> *Agents who ask for money upfront.* It's rare to come across this now, but, when one dodgy agent goes bankrupt or (as happened in a recent case) flees the country, another one will sooner or later pop up in their place. Real agents don't ask you for money ever. I have never, ever given a penny to any agent or any publisher that I've had dealings with except, in the case of my agents, the commission due on money they've rustled up on my behalf. If you're asked for cash upfront, then – it doesn't matter what they call the payment or say it's for – just say no.

> *Publishers who advertise on the internet.* Real publishers get their books from agents or direct submissions. I'm not aware of any real publisher who advertises on the internet, but, even if there are one or two, the vast majority are self-publishing companies – or, to call them by an older name, vanity publishers. Some of

BRITISH VS AMERICAN AGENTS:
ONE WRITER'S EXPERIENCE

When I finished my draft novel, I decided (as an Irishman) to send my work off to London agents in the first instance. I picked my top sixteen UK agents and queried them all as per their guidelines (most required a snail-mail submission with covering letter, synopsis, first three chapters and a SAE). As Ireland no longer sells International Reply Coupons (IRCs), this involved purchasing stamps online, printing all the hard copies needed, personalising the letters, posting them off and waiting with fingers crossed.

Three months later, I received seven (out of sixteen) replies, all form 'Dear Author' rejections and no requests for partials. Only one agent allowed e-queries. She replied within thirty minutes and requested a partial, which she read and then passed on it about a week later. No replies at all from the other eight. Out of the seven snail rejections, maybe three submissions were read (to judge from the pages I received back). Now I am not complaining. I understand how this business works and I understand how little time agents have, and that they may have found a cause to stop reading on the first page.

Last week, I decided to start querying agents in the US, and the whole experience (while still filled with rejections) has been a lot more pleasant. First of all, the majority of agents take e-queries (which is great because each UK submission was costing me ten euros in printing and postage costs). Secondly, I've generally received an automated response letting me know the estimated response time, which is a nice touch (and, if I haven't had that, it's usually clear on the website). Thirdly, most agents have a website with a clear list of what they are looking for, so you don't waste their time or yours. In the UK, I found only the larger agents had such useful guidance.

Finally, I don't know if they just like my stuff more, but the first few rejections I have received have been a lot nicer. Instead of a form rejection, I am hearing things like 'I don't have the right editorial contacts to sell this, but it's a strong project and you should definitely pursue other agents.' I've also had two requests for partials so far, which is great.

It doesn't make a huge amount of difference to me whether I get taken on by a US or a UK agent, but my experience, such as it was, would lead me to query further in the US before trying again in the UK.

DAVID CALLAGHAN (not his real name)
is currently seeking representation for his historical novel

these outfits are honest, reputable and do a good job. Others are only a Rizla paper away from being out-and-out bandits. If you're aiming at commercial publication (and, at this stage, most likely you should be), then avoid all these people. You can always come back to self-publishing as an option later on.

PROTECTING YOUR COPYRIGHT

This section is short, because the issue it deals with is a phantom one. Although it's something that bothers many new writers, it really needn't trouble you at all. If you're not worried about copyright theft, then just turn the pages and move on. If you are, read on . . .

➤ *How do I protect my ideas?*
You can't. There is no legal mechanism in Britain or America or anywhere else at all for doing this. And just as well, since there are said to be only seven plots in the world – and Shakespeare, for one, was a serial recycler of ideas.

➤ *How do I protect my manuscript itself?*
In all signatories to the Berne Convention – that is, the entire known universe aside from Beetlegeuse IV and North Korea – the copyright in artistic or literary works (which includes any novel or any book of non-fiction) belongs to the creator. You don't have to sign documents, register at the Post Office, chain yourself outside Parliament, or video yourself writing the book to claim copyright. The copyright is yours from the moment that the words tumble from your fingers on to the page. I myself, in common with almost every professional author under the sun, have only ever taken two steps to protect my copyright. Those steps are:

(1) *Write a book.* That's what gives me the copyright in the first place.

(2) *Sign the contract that is put in front of me.* We'll deal with publishing contracts in a later section, but any standard contract will secure a statement of copyright for you in every book that is published under the terms of that deal. You don't have to raise this subject with your agent. You don't need to make a fuss about it with a publisher. You don't need to unlock yourself from the railings outside Parliament for just long enough to consult an intellectual property lawyer. You just need to check that your contract contains reasonably standard copyright terms – which it will – and then sign it.

If you're an ordinarily trusting type, then those two steps are the only ones you'll ever need to take yourself.

> *What if I'm strangely suspicious?*

Let's suppose, just for the sake of argument, that you are the suspicious type. If so, perhaps you're reasoning along the following lines: 'Aha, I may in theory own the copyright, but if some Evil Agent, Sinister Publisher or Malevolent Copyright Thief comes across my manuscript, and finds it to be a work of genius, then what's to stop them publishing it under their own name? How would I be able to prove that the MS was mine?'

There are several possible answers to that question, of which one of the strongest is a little financial maths. There are about a thousand manuscripts submitted to agents for every one which is taken on. Of that one in a thousand, the average advance may be as little as £5,000. In order to wade through a thousand manuscripts to find the jewel that may be lurking there, you'd need to pay someone at least – let's say – £10,000 for the labour and the risk of being caught. So the putative Malevolent Copyright Thief would need to be at least as stupid as he was evil in order to believe the copyright-thieving game was likely to be a profitable one.

If that answer doesn't satisfy you, then consider this. There isn't, as far as I'm aware, any known case of an agent listed in the *Writers' & Artists' Yearbook* indulging in copyright theft. It just doesn't happen. Agents have integrity. If they lost their reputation for integrity, their business would disappear over-night. Copyright theft just doesn't happen.

If you are still not satisfied, for peace of mind you can print off your manuscript, pop it into an envelope, then take it down to the Post Office and post it back to yourself, recorded delivery, so that there is a date stamp on your receipt. When the package arrives, *don't* open it – an unbroken seal proves that the contents of the envelope were inserted no later than the date on the postal receipt. All you need to do now is pop the envelope and the receipt into a secret hiding place, and you're done. There's not, in truth, a lot of legal force gained via these manouevres, but, if they make you happy, then who am I to stop you?

> *Alas, I'm actually paranoiac*

There will, however, be people who are certain that the moon landings were faked, that the CIA arranged 9/11, and whose cellars are full of bottled water, tinned food, shotgun shells and gas masks. For such happy souls, a mere receipted envelope will never be enough and something a little more rigorous is called for. Fortunately, there are a number of online services which should satisfy you. Of these, the best established and best known is run by the Writers Guild of America, West – the Hollywood branch of the main US union for writers. Because copyright ownership is somewhat more of an issue in the film industry than in the books industry (not because film people are evil, but because of the larger amounts of money at stake and inevitable overlaps between different script concepts), the WGA West offers a script registry service. It's mainly for film scripts, but you can use it for novels or any other type of written material. There's a smallish fee (currently $20) and your work will be logged in a way that puts ownership of your work beyond legal dispute.

If you are writing a film script, you should certainly use this service. If not, you don't need to, but you can if it helps you stop worrying.

➤ *I'm not paranoiac, I'm American*
If you are US or Canadian, the rights of the Berne Convention apply to you in any case, but there are evidentiary benefits of registering copyright. Having registered your copyright provides you with prima facie evidence of legal ownership and entitles you to sue for damages should your copyright be infringed.

Knowing this, plenty of North American authors are careful to register their work before submitting it to agents. From a legal perspective, you can't really take issue with the logic. Except that agents never steal work. It doesn't happen. It doesn't happen in London. It doesn't happen in New York. It simply doesn't happen. If you are ordinarily trusting, then just forget about the whole copyright business and focus on getting your manuscript excellent, then seeking an agent. That's all you need to do. Your agent and publisher will take care of everything else, including copyright registration. If you're still genuinely worried, then you can approach the US Copyright Office (www.copyright.gov) and register there. But you really, truly don't need to.

COPYRIGHT PROTECTED NOTICES

Finally, please, don't go writing 'copyright protected' warning notices all over your script when you send it out to agents. Don't put that little © symbol on every page. You already own the copyright and telling everyone that you do doesn't make any difference, except that you come over as pointlessly suspicious and amateurish. Just write the book. Make it good. Then send it out.

HOW I GOT PUBLISHED

I spent five years as a script editor and then ten years as a script writer before turning to novel writing. I had become frustrated by the culture of 'too many cooks' in television, sometimes getting to fourth-draft stage with a script and having to go back to the drawing board. The deadlines were also draconian, as I often had to turn a script around in twenty-four hours. I longed to be in charge of my own material and have control over the stories and characters myself.

I mentioned my desire to write a novel to my agent, Valerie Hoskins, whose excellent advice was 'Well, get on with it, then!' So I sat down and began Honeycote — *a romantic family drama based around a Cotswold brewery — and very quickly learned that being in charge of your own material is daunting indeed. Writing scripts had given me a firm grasp of narrative and an innate feeling for when to get in and get out of a story, but having total freedom was actually rather terrifying, and I had no editorial team to fall back on. I could either eat my words — or face the fear. I took up the challenge, but it wasn't the leisurely, pleasurable task I had assumed it would be.*

When I had finished 50,000 words of Honeycote, *I had an introduction to Araminta Whitley, a literary agent who liked it very much. She showed it to several publishers, and happily I ended up with a book deal. My eighth novel,* The Beach Hut, *is being published this summer by Orion Books.*

I was lucky to come from a background which helped with the discipline of novel writing, and that also gave me contacts. But the best advice came from Valerie when she told me to get on with it. You'll never get published if you don't grasp the nettle.

VERONICA HENRY
author of *The Beach Hut*, and other novels

MANUSCRIPT PRESENTATION

Your manuscript should be tidy and well presented, which these days, of course, means that it's been printed from a decent home or office printer. Your name and contact information should be on the title page. Each page should be numbered and, ideally, have your name and title in the header or footer. You should never use single line-spacing. Use 1.5 line-spacing or double. The 'Paragraph Format' menu on your word processing package will tell you what that means, if you don't already know. You should avoid any horrific howlers in your opening pages. If you commit a grievous sin later than that, it'll probably be attributed to a moment of sloppiness, not something more serious. Send your manuscript unbound and single-sided.

In truth, that advice is all you really need. No manuscript that obeys those rules has ever been rejected because of a format or presentation issue. There was, it's true, a period when New York agencies typically wanted writers to present their work in a Courier font, and to come up with a word count based off a crazily artificial method of calculating words, but those days are long gone. If you see a website that tells you about the importance of Courier and the intricacies of word-count calculation, ignore it. It's years out of date and, if you're submitting work to UK-based agents, three thousand miles adrift into the bargain.

Because, however, I'm well aware that numerous writers aren't satisfied without a much longer list of dos and don'ts when it comes to manuscript presentation, here, for your delight and delectation, is just such a list.

FONT SELECTION. Don't be freaky. Use a standard font. Times New Roman is an excellent default option. Georgia or Garamond are frequent substitutes. Unless you're American and like things old-school, then don't use Courier – it's just weird. It's quite common to see Arial used, which is a sans-serif font (that is, there are none of those little strokes at the tops and tails of the letters). This may work for manuscripts that are assertively modern or brash, but on the whole you're recommended to use serif-based fonts: they're easier to read over an extended period. For that reason, sans-serif fonts are mostly used for headings (as in this book) or as attention grabbers in advertising.

FONT SIZE. Use a font size of 12. Not 10 or 11: they're too small and strain the eyes. Not 14 or larger: that makes you look like a child. 12 is just right.

LINE-SPACING. Use either 1.5 or double line-spacing. You should simply be able to select all the text in your document (Ctrl-A on a PC, Cmd-A on a Mac in most word-processing programs), go to the 'Paragraph Format' menu and select the appropriate option. If you don't know how to do this, then ask somebody who does. Agents don't want the text to be properly spaced because they're going to making a host of editorial changes in between the lines. They want the text spaced so their eyes don't burn out.

CHAPTER BREAKS. Doesn't matter too much, but a page break at the end of each chapter is standard. You can number chapters any way you like, start the text halfway down the page, and play around with other minor format issues if you like, but you really don't have to. My chapters begin with a number or heading at the top, centred, in bold and one or two font sizes larger than the main text. The text begins a few lines down. If you want to get fancier than that, then it's up to you. But nothing weird.

PAGE NUMBERING. Your pages must be numbered. Must be. If you don't know how to insert page numbers in your word processing program, then ask someone who does. They can go anywhere: top or bottom; left, right or middle. No one cares.

HEADERS/FOOTERS. Again, not a huge issue, and I don't think the manuscripts I've sent out have mostly had headers or footers with my name and the MS title on. It's a nice touch, though, so do it if you know how to. I'd suggest using a font size that doesn't compete with the main text. If you know how to put the header/footer text in dark grey rather than black, you may want to do that too. But don't get hung up about it. No one else will.

TITLE PAGE. It should have the title. Your name. Your contact information (address, phone number, email address). The presentation can be stylish, but, if you think that your presentation is definitely stylish but just possibly weird, then play it safe. There's nothing wrong with a title in a large font (go crazy – try out 36 or 48), your name a few lines below that (in a smaller font size, 12 or 14), and then your contact info in the bottom right- or left-hand corner. You can have the word count on your title page as well, if the fancy takes you.

PARAGRAPH BREAKS. Business letters and documents have a complete blank line to separate paragraphs, but paragraphs themselves are not indented. (That is, the first line of the paragraph begins on the left-hand margin like everything else.) You, however, are not writing a business letter or a business document. You are writing a book. That means that there is no blank line to separate paragraphs, but the first line of every paragraph should be indented. To achieve that indentation you can either use the tab key in your word processing program, or you can set the 'Paragraph Format' menu so that you choose 'First Line' in lieu of 'None' in the indentation dialogue box. In terms of how far to indent your first line – well, it just doesn't matter very much. Less than 0.2″ is too small to register. More than 1.0″ is heading off into Possibly Freaky territory. I'd suggest that anywhere between 0.3″ and 0.5″ looks nice.

MARGINS. Go with the default page margins, or at any rate don't try to squeeze too much text on a page. An inch at top and bottom, with an inch or 1.25″ at the sides looks nice.

INDICATIVE COVER DESIGNS. What a great idea it would be to offer the agent a sample cover design to help them imagine what your book would appear like in print. You're not saying that your chosen image would have to be the cover, you're just giving the imagination something to work off. If you have access to a colour printer and some semi-pornographic graphics involving purple skies and women with tight clothes and implausibly long legs, then so much the better . . . Needless to say, if you so much as catch yourself starting to think along these lines, then take a cold bath until you stop. Hit yourself repeatedly over the head with this book, if you need to, whilst repeating, 'I shall not be freaky when it comes to manuscript presentation.' If you've got a genuinely lovely and appropriate black-and-white line drawing that will reproduce well, then you can think about including it on your title page. But, if you are in any doubt at all, don't do it. The manuscript is what matters. Images are neither here nor there.

SINGLE-SIDED VS DOUBLE-SIDED PRINTING. There was a time in the industry when printing your manuscript double-sided was tantamount to suicide. In these more eco-conscious days, I'd say that suicide would be too strong a term: serious self-harm would be nearer the mark. If your green conscience can bear to do it, then print the manuscript out single-sided. It truly is easier for an agent or editor to manage. If your green conscience finds this unbearable, print it out single-sided anyway, then go outside and plant a tree.

LOOSE-LEAF VS BOUND. Don't bind your text. No plastic comb binders. No treasury tags. No sheafs of little plastic envelopes with a chapter or two in each one. No lever-arch files. None of those metal clip things with two stabby prongs that would probably be your murder weapon of choice, assuming that you were obliged to kill someone while locked inside a typical corporate stationery cupboard. If it pains you to see your manuscript completely unbound, then treat yourself to a rubber band. Or go nuts: use two. The simple fact is that the industry works completely happily with unbound wodges of paper. The advantage of a wodge is that a busy agent or editor can take a chunk to read on a train or bus, without having to lug the whole thing around. The very idea may be painful to an author who assumes that their precious manuscript will be revered by its recipient, but that ain't going to happen. Express your grief by twanging those rubber bands, then leave well alone.

ENVELOPE TECHNOLOGY. When you take your MS down to the Post Office to mail off to an agent, the postal clerk is quite likely to ask you if there's anything of value in the package. The question is innocent. It just means, does the package need insurance? – but, to a budding author, the answer virtually screams itself: '*Valuable? Valuable? There is nothing more valuable in the entire world than this package. It's my north, my south, my east, my west. At this moment, to be perfectly honest with you, I'd sooner that my entire family was swept away in a tsunami – or thrown to the tigers – or boiled up in a gigantic, if excessively bony stew, than that anything should happen to disturb the swift passage of this package.*' These feelings are quite natural – I've been there myself – but they're also foolish. In particular, they cause would-be authors to develop a strange suspicion of all normal forms of packaging. To send a manuscript, you need a padded envelope. You put the manuscript inside the envelope. You write the destination address on the front of the envelope, and your own address in smaller writing on the back. Then you unpeel the little cellophane strip that protects the sticky stuff on the flap, and fold the flap down. That's it. That's all you need. Astoundingly enough, the sticky stuff has been put on the flap because research has shown it does the job. You do not need to study the envelope long and hard before deciding to use three entire rolls of packing tape to swaddle the manuscript, like a postal version of the infant Jesus. You do not need to send your manuscript recorded delivery, or special delivery or anything else. Envelopes work, that's why they exist. The postal system also works.

That's why it does. If I seem a little wired on this point, it's because every single week we receive packages that we need a circular saw to prise open. You are not helping your cause by expressing your anxieties in brown parcel tape. If anything, you are hindering it.

AVOIDING HOWLERS. I've already said that it's a waste of money to get your manuscript copy-edited, and it is. But attention to matters of detail is a genuinely reliable indicator of manuscript quality. If a writer has taken sufficient care over word choice, sentence structure and the rest, then they are almost certain to have cared about such things as punctuation, consistency and spellings as well. That does therefore mean that while a few errors will creep into your manuscript – and it's just fine if they do – you need to avoid any hint of a more widespread inattention. Given the importance of first impressions, you should take particular care over the first few pages. That means don't write *its* when you mean *it's* or vice versa – either way round, it's a criminal offence to get this wrong. Don't write *whose* when you mean *who's*. Don't anywhere talk about your 'fiction novel'. (All novels are fiction. Just call it a novel.) Don't make any errors of the sort that would make any self-respecting pedant want to hurl hard objects at you. If your own spelling or punctuation is poor, then ask someone competent to do it for you. Better still, learn the rules, then apply them diligently. You are unlikely to succeed until you do. There are some good texts that will guide you through the commonest issues. Take your pick from Fowler's *Modern English Usage*, Strunk and White's (much shorter) *Elements of Style*, *The Good Word Guide* or *Who's Whose*.

'Have we covered everything?' Harry wondered aloud.

The image of his first editor hovered in front of him.

'Dialogue formatting,' she said. 'You must cover that.'

'What, all that tiresome stuff about inverted commas?' he replied. 'How double inverted commas were once standard in the UK, but have now given way to single inverted commas? How Americans still prefer the double sort?'

'Well, yes, now that you mention it. But really, I meant how all the commas and capital letters work. And what about that thing about quotations inside dialogue? Like if I wanted to quote your comment about, "How Americans still prefer the double sort?" I'd have to dress it inside double inverted commas . . . except funnily enough, if I were American, when I'd have to go for single inverted commas to distinguish them from my ordinary doubles.' She thought a bit, then added, 'Hold on. I am American.'

HOW TO ENSURE YOU DON'T GET BINNED

Like every other reader, agent and publisher, we're looking for good stories, distinctively told. And though we receive up to a hundred submissions a week, every week, we look forward to reading them with a tingle of eager anticipation.

But the tingle quickly turns to irritation if we can't open the blasted envelope because it's so securely sealed with sticky tape you can't even get the point of a paper knife into a corner. First point: please don't make it hard for us.

You'd think somebody intelligent enough to complete a piece of writing would also know how to put the correct postage on the envelope. You'd be surprised how many submissions we refuse to accept because the Post Office want to charge excess postage (which includes a fee of at least a pound). Just as you might be surprised at how many Americans seem to think American stamps are valid outside America . . .

Before you've even put your material in its envelope, have you made the essential checks? Is it in a readable font (minimum 11 point), with reasonable line-spacing (we recommend 1.5), and plenty of paragraph breaks? (Nothing makes the heart and eyes sink more quickly than a vast slab of unbroken prose.) Are the pages numbered? Has every page been properly printed? Have you included your name, address and either an email address or an envelope with return postage?

More important even than these, are you sure you're sending your work to the right person at the right agency? If you read agents' websites, you should know what they're looking for, what they do and don't handle, whether or not they accept emailed submissions, and which person to contact. Yet we still get loads of stuff that our website makes it plain we're not interested in, often addressed to 'To whom it may concern'. As it's so easy to press the 'Send' key on a computer, this is at best laziness, and at worst bad manners. It's like sending your covering letter full of spelling mistakes and bad grammar. If you can't be bothered, why should we?

PETER BUCKMAN
Peter set up The Ampersand Agency after a career
in publishing and as a full-time writer.
The first book he took on turned into *Slumdog Millionaire*

DIALOGUE FORMATTING. In deference to the ghost of my first editor, let me add that you should also get your dialogue formatting right. The little snippet above gives you most of what you need to know. Please notice (1) that every bit of dialogue starts a new, indented paragraph, as does any action paragraph, such as the second line of the text above; (2) that commas, question marks and so forth live inside the inverted commas, not outside; (3) that you do not need a capital 'H' in 'he said', even if the preceding bit of dialogue ended with a question mark or an exclamation mark; (4) you don't end a bit of dialogue with a full stop, if you are running straight into a 'he said' or 'she said' – you use a comma instead; but (5) you do end a bit of dialogue with a full stop (as in the last line or so of the final paragraph above) when the sentence that follows is not a 'he said', a 'she said' or an obvious equivalent. If you apply those rules consistently, you're probably doing fine.

All this, in a way, is to give too much attention to the subject of presentation. The takeaway message from this section is a simple one. Take care to present your manuscript in a smart professional way, then stop stressing about it. Your manuscript will not stand or fall on how pretty it looks. It will stand or fall on how well it's written. That's where you should concentrate your time, care and attention. The rest of it is just a question of ordinary, competent professionalism.

NOTES FROM THE GATEKEEPER

I am the Gatekeeper. I police the borders, I man the drawbridge and am pledged to repel intruders. However, those who do get past me stand on the threshold of fame and fortune, in the citadel that is Publishing. Effectively, as a freelance Reader for a leading London literary agency, this is my role. Scary, isn't it?

My role is to undertake the initial assessment of all general and non-fiction unsolicited manuscripts that arrive at the doors of Conville and Walsh. Once a month, a white van pulls up outside my secret retreat and deposits up to five Post Office bags, containing up to two hundred part manuscripts.

C&W is one of a dwindling number of agents that still accepts unsolicited manuscripts from potential authors. We request up to fifty consecutive pages of manuscript, a covering letter and synopsis, plus a self-addressed, stamped envelope (SASE) if the enclosures are to be returned to sender. Other agents and publishers may have differing requirements.

The idea in asking for fifty consecutive pages is to enable the Reader to make an initial assessment as to the quality of the writing, the flow of the narrative and the strength of the individual voice. I have had as few as two pages and as many as four hundred. Both extremes are unwarranted.

The synopsis is a summary of the plot (we suggest one to two pages). The synopsis is not the equivalent of a book's blurb and should contain no claims as to market placement, no hyperbole and no comparisons with any published literature. It should be a simple, clear and immediately understandable summary of the main plot and themes contained therein. Don't hold back vital information. Too many authors seem to distrust agents and end up providing a truncated summary, with the proverbial 'All will be revealed.' Such detail must be revealed to the Reader, especially if there is an unexpected twist or plot development.

The covering letter should be no more than a courtesy letter, containing a very short, two-line summary of the manuscript, reference to any other published or unpublished work and relevant personal details. 'Relevant personal details' is not meant to include the following: information on the author's writing history from childhood onwards; lists of favourite books and authors; what the neighbours, friends and children think of their work. Be concise and be professional. Leave the manuscript to talk for you.

Personally, after skimming through the covering letter, I start reading the text straight away. I only refer to the synopsis if the quality of the writing, strength of the voice or some other element of the submission catches my attention. I then look at the synopsis to get an overall impression of the work, and to establish where the manuscript is eventually leading.

How the author presents the above package of papers is also important. I suggest you follow these guidelines.

☐ Put your full name, address and contact details on your covering letter and at the head of the first page of your manuscript.

☐ Number your manuscript pages, and provide an approximate word count for the full manuscript, ideally on the title page.

☐ Print your work in a standard, recognisable font, such as Times Roman 12 pt.

☐ Double space and include adequate margins.

☐ Do not ask for a written assessment of your manuscript. If rejected, you will receive a standardised courtesy letter (but see below).

☐ *Always check out the submission requirements of each and every agent and publisher that you propose contacting.*

☐ *Do submit to more than one agent or publisher at a time. This is quite acceptable practice, though check individual agents' requirements. Keep a careful note of those to whom you have mailed your work.*

☐ *I am reluctant to provide any tips on how to achieve good-quality writing, as that is well beyond the scope of this short piece. However, as a Reader, I can only impress on you the importance of the first half-dozen pages. If you fail to catch the imagination or light some spark in those opening pages, you will be struggling to retain a Reader's interest. Sometimes I do see poor openings that are redeemed by subsequent pages, but don't test the Reader's patience. Browse through bookshops and libraries to study how successful authors manage to grab the attention from the first line, then put extra effort into those opening pages. First impressions do count, especially when a Reader is faced with two hundred manuscripts. Make yours stand out.*

Things not to do would include the following:

☐ *Never sign your letter with initials only – 'J. K. Rowling', for example. Just use your name, 'Ms Anna Zanetti', for instance.*

☐ *Never wrap your paper bundle in ribbon or try to staple together. Paper clips or clamps will do.*

☐ *Never handwrite your covering letter, and do use plain, not lined, paper.*

☐ *Never include a photograph of yourself. You are not entering a beauty contest.*

☐ *Don't ever apologise for your work or talk it down in your covering letter. Have confidence in your own work and be proud of it.*

☐ *Never compare or liken your manuscript to any published authors. The agents will make such assessments themselves.*

☐ *Don't start chasing up the progress of your manuscript for at least six weeks. Only very rarely (once in five years, in our case) has a manuscript gone missing.*

☐ *Never send the only copy of your manuscript. Always retain a hard or electronic copy for yourself, just in case.*

☐ *Don't bother with dedications or acknowledgements. They're not needed yet.*

I have the greatest respect for each and every author who submits to us, and I do read every submission. The process at Conville and Walsh is that, out of two hundred submissions each month, I recommend between six and ten for the agents to follow up. Of this shortlist, perhaps two authors will be asked to submit their full manuscripts to the agents. Those authors rejected by the agents, at this stage, will get a more personalised rejection letter, indicating what worked and what was felt to be deficient. Of the authors who are asked to forward us their full manuscripts, possibly three to four a year will get through to publication. The statistics are not very encouraging, I know, but there are new faces appearing every year. The industry is not a closed shop.

In the last twelve months we have been fortunate enough to have discovered a number of fresh, new authors out of the so-called 'slushpile' – or 'talent pool', as I prefer to call it. Four of our new authors this year have, between them, grossed over £1.5 million in advances, and, of course, have the great satisfaction of seeing their work in print.

I look forward to seeing your work in front of me in the not too distant future. Good luck.

DAVID G. LLEWELYN
Reader, Conville & Walsh

TITLES, OPENING LINES, OPENING CHAPTERS

It's said – on the basis of what research I have no idea – that the average housebuyer makes their purchase decision within a few seconds of seeing a property. It's certainly true that any wise property developer takes plenty of care in ensuring good 'kerb appeal' – that is, making sure that the property looks good from the most casual of external inspections.

It's the same with manuscripts. On the one hand, no manuscript will be taken on by an agent or a publisher unless the whole thing is in very good shape. In that sense, you have to be as worried about the plumbing in your bathroom as you do about any weeds in your front garden. On the other hand, your manuscript is, in the first instance, going to be rapidly assessed by somebody who will be expecting to reject every new submission in that morning's post bag. That means that you simply can't allow any imperfections to manifest early on. Your manuscript also needs to do as much as it possibly can to capture an agent's attention from the start.

TITLES

Titles are odd things. There's one perfectly sound argument which says that, at this stage, titles don't really matter at all. I've published seven books before this one. Only one of those seven went to print with the same title that it wore when I first sent it to my agent or publisher. In all the other cases, the titles were changed, often several times, prior to publication, and sometimes for the oddest of reasons. For example, the title I initially gave to my fifth novel was *The Russian Lieutenant*. My agent liked the title. So did my editor. So did the sales team. It looked as though I was about to notch up only my second ever title-success. Then we got an excellent offer from one of the book clubs (now, alas, largely defunct). They wanted to place a large order, but told us that they couldn't sell any book with the word 'Russia' or 'Russian' in the title. It wasn't a political thing; it was just their readers were put off by that word. So the *The Russian Lieutenant* became *The Lieutenant's Lover*. I didn't mind too much either way, but it's symptomatic of how fast and randomly titles can change.

Agents and editors know all this perfectly well. In that sense, they shouldn't care too much what title appears on the document you send. It also shouldn't matter to a potential home-buyer whether the front garden is littered with leaves in autumn, yet matter it does.

Strong titles help. I'm probably worse than average at titles, so I can't offer a magic formula for success, but good examples abound. D. B. C Pierre's *Vernon God Little* had a pleasingly intriguing feel to it. So did Susanna Clarke's blockbusting *Jonathan Strange and Mr Norrell*. For my money, Yann Martel's *Life of Pi* was a bad book with a good title. The best-selling therapist M. Scott Peck attributed the huge success of his *The Road Less Travelled* in good part to his excellent title (purloined, of course, from the poet, Robert Frost). *The Brief Wondrous Life of Oscar Wao* also fared well at the tills, because of its entertainingly teasing title. And so on. If you can find a strong title, use it. If you can't, use an old trick, which is to write the longest list of titles that you possibly can. Aim to get at least a hundred possibles on to your list. More if you can manage it. Don't delete or censor yourself as you go. If you think of a rubbish title, stick it down on the list anyway. It may not look so rubbish when you look at it a second time, or it may spark a thought that leads to something better.

Once you have your list, leave it on one side for a day or two, then come back to it and see what looks good. Remember, you're not looking for the title that most perfectly encapsulates your book. You're looking for the one that'll sell it. The two things are very different goals, and only one of them matters. You also, by the way, don't need to say anywhere that your chosen title is provisional, because all titles are provisional until they go to print.

If the title you've selected has already been taken by another book and another author, then use your common sense. There's no copyright in titles, so there's nothing illegal in duplicate titles. If you've called your book *The Copper Moon*, and you discover that a minor author in the 1960s had a book by the same title, then there's no problem at all. Just stick with what you've got. If on the other hand, there's any realistic scope for confusion between your book and something else currently on sale, then change your title.

OPENING LINES

It is – or has become – conventional writerly wisdom that first lines matter a lot. It would be traditional for me at this point to trot out some well-known first lines of fiction and encourage you to imitate their literary and commercial excellence. Obedient as I am to my reader's every expectation, I herewith submit a handful of such opening lines for your review:

'Lyra and her daemon moved through the darkening Hall, taking care to keep to one side, out of sight of the kitchen.'
Philip Pullman, *Northern Lights*

'It was a queer, sultry summer, the summer they electrocuted the Rosenbergs, and I didn't know what I was doing in New York.'
Sylvia Plath, *The Bell Jar*

'As Gregor Samsa awoke one morning from uneasy dreams he found himself transformed in his bed into a gigantic insect.'
Franz Kafka, *Metamorphosis*

'It was a bright cold day in April, and the clocks were striking thirteen.'
George Orwell, *1984*

'I am an invisible man.'
Ralph Ellison, *Invisible Man*

'Granted: I am an inmate of a mental hospital; my keeper is watching me, he never lets me out of his sight; there's a peephole in the door, and my keeper's eye is the shade of brown that can never see through a blue-eyed type like me.'
Günter Grass, *The Tin Drum*

'The human race, to which so many of my readers belong . . .'
G. K. Chesterton, *The Napoleon of Notting Hill*

You better not never tell nobody but God.'

Alice Walker, *The Color Purple*

These are all, self-evidently, strong opening lines, and, if you have a strong opener, then good for you. It'll help matters, if only just a little.

But don't go crazy. It can be an error to chase too hard after that golden opening line. Too hard a chase tends to end up with an opening sentence that smacks more of contrivance and effort than of real talent, and your first sentence needs to lead on to a first paragraph and a first page which cohere and sound good together. If your novel isn't the dazzling opening sentence kind of novel, then don't worry too much. Most novels aren't.

OPENING PAGES

My approach, however, is a lot more hard line when it comes to opening pages. Plenty of writers worry about submitting the first three chapters to agents because 'my story only really gets going later on'. That, let's be clear, is not acceptable. When I first read *War and Peace*, I remember thinking that the story took about a hundred pages to get going. In *The Good Soldier Svejk*, I'm not sure that the story ever actually gets going, though it's entertaining to watch it try.

These days, whether you are writing genre fiction or commercial fiction, you must grab the reader hard and early. If the reader doesn't have a strong sense of the story by the end of Chapter 1, you probably need to delete your first chapter and rewrite it – or perhaps, better still, just start with Chapter 2. Equally, if you are writing non-fiction, the purpose and importance and momentum of your book must be apparent early on. If you play fast and loose with this injunction, then your book will very likely not sell and, however good the rest of it may be, it probably doesn't deserve to. So get it right.

It is also important that you commit no mortal or venial sins against the Gods of Good Prose in those opening pages, as a reader is making up their mind whether to read further. Once they've made the decision to read on, then the odd embarrassing slippage will be forgiven. Early on, you can't afford to give anyone the excuse to stop. And if you don't know what a mortal or venial sin is, then don't worry. I'm about to tell you.

HOW TO GET A SHORT-STORY COLLECTION PUBLISHED

One of the joys of writing short stories — apart from constantly meeting new characters and situations — is the opportunity to publish single stories as you build a collection. Whether in magazines, short-story competitions, multi-author anthologies, short-story podcasts or radio broadcasts, this not only boosts confidence and is good publicity — and may even earn some money! — it adds to your writing CV. In a tough climate, having a good writing CV impresses potential agents or publishers: it says that not only are you publishable but you know how to sell yourself.

When you have a collection ready — which may be planned, perhaps with a theme linking the stories (although this is not necessary), or just something that happens when you realise you have enough stories for a book, a minimum of 130 pages or so, roughly 30,000 words — there are several ways to look for a book deal. The traditional route is through a literary agent. However, agents today commonly respond that it is very hard to sell a short-story collection without the promise of a novel. Sending your manuscript straight to one of the large publishing houses will probably elicit a similar response.

The main publishers of short-story collections today are the small, independent presses, often not-for-profit. You can submit to them directly, without an agent. They usually ask for three stories, and then the full manuscript if they are interested in your writing. There is no need to submit only to independent publishers in your own country, try further afield too.

Another avenue which is becoming more popular is to enter your collection for a contest in which the first prize is publication. A number of American university presses run such contests, and the concept is spreading. There are also 'chapbook' contests: a chapbook used to refer to slim, often hand-bound, poetry collections, but the term is also now used for short-story collections. The small presses that publish short-story chapbooks often invest a great deal in presentation, hand-stitching the covers and experimenting with different formats.

Being published by a small, independent press may not carry the prestige of a 'big name' publishing house, and authors will often have to do a great deal of the book promotion themselves and are unlikely to receive an advance on sales. However, these presses pride themselves on their investment and individual attention to every book and author they publish. Good luck!

TANIA HERSHMAN

A former science journalist, Tania is the author of *The White Road and Other Stories* (Salt Modern Fiction, 2008), which was commended by the judges of the 2009 Orange Award for New Writers. She is founder and editor of 'The Short Review' (www.theshortreview.com), a website dedicated to reviewing short-story collections

COVERING LETTERS

When I came to send my first novel out to agents, I thought I knew what I was doing. I was pretty certain that my novel was a strong, saleable proposition (as, indeed, it was). I had also spent ten years as a Mergers and Acquisitions banker at a top American investment bank, in the course of which I had learned to pitch my wares. Pitch hard, pitch pushy. So I wrote a covering letter that briefly introduced the novel and outlined the brand concept that would unite my future *ouevre*. I don't quite remember what else went into that letter – though I do remember that I made free use of bullet points and was more than willing to share my thoughts about the American market – but I do know that it would have been a leading contender for that year's World's Worst Covering Letter Award. The first six agents who received my package either sent standard form rejection letters or didn't bother to reply at all. Utterly mystified, I sent my package out to a further six agents and this time my fishing line came back with two little fishes wriggling on the hook.

The moral of this story is twofold. First, that covering letters matter. Second, that they don't matter all that much. The one absolutely central, critical, crucial and decisive point is that your manuscript is excellent. If your manuscript is strong enough, then even the World's Worst Covering Letter is unlikely to prevent you from getting an agent, though it may certainly delay your journey there. As for the covering letter itself – well, there's just no need to write a bad letter. This section will tell you how to write a good one. But all a covering letter really needs to do is not to be so awful that it stops anyone from looking half-seriously at the manuscript itself. The same is true of the synopsis. It's well worth avoiding some basic mistakes, but you don't need to get into a pickle over minutiae. If your covering material is decent, and your approach to agents is businesslike, then your success will be determined by your manuscript itself – which is just as it ought to be.

WHAT A COVERING LETTER NEEDS TO DO

A covering letter has one main role: not to be so bad that it puts anyone off looking at the manuscript itself. If an agent turns from the letter to the MS, then the letter has succeeded. That is a fairly low hurdle to clamber over.

If you care to set your sights a little higher, you may want to make the agent turn *with interest* from the letter to the MS. That's a bit more of a challenge, but still hardly insuperable. One very senior agent once told me that the best covering letter she'd ever received ran like this:

> Dear Sirs,
> I have written a book and am looking for a literary agent.
> Yours faithfully,

Personally, I'd say that was a little on the skimpy side but, as you can see, this bar is not set particularly high.

Assuming that you want to write a slightly longer letter, what should that letter seek to accomplish? There are no rules here, but I'd say that a good template for a covering letter might run like this:

☐ *Use the right name! Address your letter to a named agent, not to the agency (unless you are told to send it to the Submissions Department, or whatever). Do make sure that the agent actually exists. A. M. Heath is a fine and thriving agency, but the good Mr Heath has long since passed into the great library in the sky. Needless to say, if you try to use a mail-merge program to create your covering letters, you are likely to get yourself into a pickle.*

☐ *A one- or two-sentence introduction to the book: title, word count, genre.*

☐ *A somewhat longer paragraph introducing the book at greater length: the theme, the setting, the protagonist, the premise – but not a detailed plot exposition.*

☐ *A shortish paragraph introducing you.*

☐ *A sign-off.*

Thus, if I had not been attempting to win my World's Worst Covering Letter award, the letter I sent out for my first novel might have looked something like this:

> Dear Random Agent,
> I'm writing to introduce my first novel, *The Money Makers*, an adventure yarn of some 180,000 words.
> The novel opens with the death of the multi-millionaire Bernard Gradley. Angry at the indolence of his three sons, Gradley has written his will so as to force them into action – and competition. Each son is given three years to make a million pounds, starting from scratch. If one succeeds, he inherits everything. Should they all fail, Gradley's millions go to charity. The

book is a fable of modern-day treasure hunting, and one that becomes complicated by growing emotional and ethical dilemmas as the young men get closer to their goal.

I'm a former investment banker myself, 31 years old, and currently caring for my wife, who has been struck down (temporarily, we hope!) with a neurological illness.

I'd be delighted if you felt able to represent me. Please don't bother to return the manuscript, but I've enclosed a postage-paid envelope for your reply.

Yours,

Harry Bingham

That is, I hope you agree, a fairly simple letter. If you are capable of writing a saleable manuscript, then you are surely capable of writing a letter like the one above. It's not, however, entirely devoid of subtlety. Although the letter mostly presents the novel as a good old-fashioned adventure romp, the final sentence of the second paragraph strikes a slightly different note: hinting that the book, though fun, isn't without its more thoughtful side.

Likewise that dart into parenthesis – '(temporarily, we hope!)' – has a twofold job. First of all, it's a marker of social awareness. It's a big thing to tell a stranger about a major disease that's affected your wife, and the little lightening of mood is a way to signal, 'Don't worry, I'm not going to get all heavy on you.' Furthermore, the willingness to vary the tone of a fairly neutral business letter suggests a certain degree of authorial confidence. (Having said which, this author's confidence was dented when an agent told him that no exclamation marks should *ever* appear in a covering letter, which is probably good advice.)

Those are little things, no doubt, but I'd say that any agent who's halfway interested in a good old-fashioned yarn will have her interest piqued by such a letter. Instead of turning to the manuscript itself with a weary sense of duty, she'll most likely turn to it with a slight quickening of interest. That's hardly winning the war, but it's a tiny opening victory, which is all you can hope to achieve at this stage anyway.

Finally, you should also note that the letter says almost nothing about plot. It doesn't need to. A synopsis is there to do that. The letter doesn't even grapple with all the subtleties of the premise. (What if more than one son makes a milllion pounds? Is Gradley's money divided or does it go only to the son who has earned the most?) Indeed, the letter entirely neglects to mention that Gradley had a daughter, but excluded her from the competition altogether, for reasons of his own. These things don't matter – or, rather, they don't matter at this stage. You are writing a letter of introduction, not one of exposition. Keep it short, keep it simple, keep it clear.

WHAT A COVERING LETTER CAN HOPE TO DO

In smaller agencies, it'll quite likely be an agent who deals with the morning post. In larger agencies, it's more likely to be support staff. If you feel cast down by the idea of mere support staff opening your post, you shouldn't. Although many agencies pay atrociously, they do nevertheless secure a high calibre of recruit, often youngsters with the ambition of entering the profession properly in due course.

In addition, all agencies are well aware of the need to take on new clients. Although an agency can survive perfectly well off its existing clients if it doesn't take any new ones on for a year or so, writers are seldom immortal. Unless an agency refreshes its stock of clients, it will gradually wither and die. I know of only one (rather eccentric) London agency which is, and has remained, more or less closed to new clients over a period of years. Everyone else – well, they need clients and are constantly looking for them.

That's not always the impression those agencies give. It's a commonplace of rejection letters that 'the agency is not actively seeking new clients at this time'. That statement is, almost always, a lie. True enough, the agency is unlikely to have declared at its last board meeting, 'We must get new clients *now!*' An agency isn't going to put up ads in Leicester Square, start handing out fliers on the London Underground, or grabbing passers-by and interrogating them about any plot ideas they may have; so in a sense the agency can honestly say it isn't actively seeking new clients. But it's on the lookout for them, nevertheless. If an excellent writer happens to send through an excellent manuscript, then the agency will be on to that writer like a shot. Indeed, the weary old formula about not actively seeking new clients or not having slots available on its list (as though there are any such things as slots!) is simply a con. It's a way of fobbing an author off in a manner that is calculated not to rile them too much.

Alas, I think these circumlocutions are unintentionally confusing; unhelpful to writers who, in their ordinary lives, expect people to say what they mean. Sometimes what people mean may be disappointing or upsetting. Fine. So be it. I'd say that writers, as a group, are as robust and capable of dealing with disappointment as any other group on the planet, or perhaps more so, since we know to set our expectations low. On the whole, then,

I think that writers would welcome the same degree of plain speaking from the books world as we expect to encounter in every other part of our lives. If the news is disappointing, then we'll handle it.

In any case, the point here is a simple one: agents want clients. Their businesses depend on securing a small but steady stream of excellent new writers. That in turn means that, when support staff are entrusted with the task of looking at new submissions, they are trained and monitored carefully, so that no promising writer slips through the net. Covering letters can be very useful indicators of excellence, and staff will be trained accordingly.

This means that, although a straightforward letter, such as the sample one above, is a perfectly fine method of introduction, some writers may wish to set their sights a little higher. In particular, if you are a literary author, you may well want to make sure that you strut your stuff in the covering letter as much as you aim to do in the book. If you are a superbly well-qualified non-fiction author, then making that authority fully apparent in your letter is also highly advisable.

The reason for this is that very often a manuscript may have missed its target, but may nevertheless succeed in advertising your essential competence. For example, we once worked with a literary author whose work was stunning, but too complex, too long and with a story that took too long to get going. That manuscript, had it gone straight to agents as it was, would have been rejected for those reasons. All the same, a really intelligent covering letter plus a manuscript that showed obvious potential might well have intrigued an agent anyway. With a little luck, that author might have received a letter that said, in essence, 'We can't sell this manuscript, so can't offer you representation, but we think you're a class act and do come back to us if you have something more commercial to offer.' With a little more luck, the author might even have received a letter which briefly identified the major editorial issues and invited him to come back with a revised version in due course.

Likewise, if you are a highly qualified author of non-fiction, even if your existing manuscript or proposal has missed its target, a covering letter which hints at what you would be capable of, given the right kind of guidance, is a strong invitation to an agent to pick up the phone and get talking.

Indeed, it's worth being clear at this point that it's fairly commonplace for agents to say, 'We like *you*, but we don't think that this manuscript is yet right for the market, so we'd like to talk about some possible alterations.' When I wrote the proposal which would eventually turn into *This Little Britain*, a book of popular historical non-fiction, I got precisely that response. The agent I spoke to told me that he liked the concept and liked my prose style, but felt that I needed to make the book more easily digestible if it were to sell. Over a period of about six months, I reworked the proposal. My initial book, which was fairly serious and would have had chapters of some 10–15,000 words, morphed into something significantly lighter in tone and made up of a lot of bite-sized 2–3,000-word chapters. During this period, the agent I was working with was not formally my agent. We didn't have a contract and he was not representing me. Only when he actually had a proposal from me that he believed to be saleable did we sign on the dotted line with each other. Thanks to my concept and writing ability, and his nose for the market, we ended up with a proposal that sold in a keenly contested auction, very swiftly and for a lot of money.

The anecdote illustrates one of the single most important aspects of an agent's function: they know the market and are there to relay it to you. Because of my work as a literary consultant, I'm more keenly in touch with the market than nearly any other writer out there. All the same, I don't know as much as any properly competent agent. Their day job is selling books into that market. They are constantly in touch with editors and publishers, sensing what's in demand, what's not. An agent who likes your work enough to talk to you about revising it is someone who needs to be listened to very carefully indeed. You may not like the idea of the proposed revisions. I didn't like the idea of revising *This Little Britain* in the way that my agent first suggested. But writers need to compromise. You need to find an intersection between what you want to write and what the markets wants to buy. If that means shifting from your initial conception, then so be it. You don't get to make the rules. The market does.

If your covering letter is elegant, intelligent and intriguing, then you are maximising your chances of entering into productive dialogue with an agent, even if your manuscript itself has missed the target. You may still wish to follow the basic template given earlier, or you may wish to expand on it a trifle. If you are pitching to a US agent, then you can allow yourself a little more salesmanship than would be appropriate in the UK – but, if in doubt, less is more. No agent has ever taken on a client because that client is good at praising themselves.

Whatever else you do, you should keep your letter fairly brief. Most letters will fit comfortably on to a page. Some few will spill over to a second sheet. No decent letter will be any longer than that. And, of course, no letter that's halfway competent will commit any of the sins covered in the section that follows.

COVERING LETTERS: THE MORTAL SINS

You are a writer. Your covering letter is trying to pitch your skill with words. You are quite possibly hoping to make a living by putting words together in an entertaining and compelling fashion. That means that your letter must read well. You can no more afford sloppy sentences or clunky constructions in this letter than in the manuscript itself. Yet such errors are hideously commonplace. (I know this because we offer a free covering-letter review service, so we get to see an enormous number of such letters.) Although first-time writers often complain that an agent may not even have read their work before rejecting it, why on earth should an agent waste their time on a submission which displays a feeble command of English? If I were an agent, I'd move swiftly on too.

Some of the sins are glaring ones:

✗ 'Its my first novel' – *should be 'It's'*.

✗ 'This is my first fiction novel . . . ' – *it's not a fiction novel, it's a novel.*

✗ 'My main character, whose got the power to . . . ' – *should be 'who's' or 'who has'.*

✗ 'The protagonist Rachel has to go away . . . ' – *there should be commas around the word 'Rachel'.*

✗ 'The hero should of been killed, but . . . ' – *'should have' not 'should of'.*

And so on. If you don't feel confident about such things, then you aren't ready to send your work to agents. You *must* have an excellent command of written English. That isn't snobbery on the part of the industry; it's common sense. You wouldn't hope to be a dancer if you were too unfit to get out of bed; you wouldn't set out to be a cook if you were a total klutz in the kitchen. Likewise with your writing. It's all very well to have a story that you want to tell, but telling it means using words – and that means using them skilfully or, at the very least, competently.

More commonly, the sins we come across are less glaring than these. They're still sins, however, and will debar you from the paradise that is agency representation. For example:

✗ 'The protagonist, Richard, has to go to battle and he fights hard but gets wounded and has to crawl away and hide in a cave and stay there until nightfall.'

✗ 'The adventure drama is one of suspense and intrigue which culminates ultimately in a showdown that pits the forces of good and evil against each other but in a way that maybe puts more shades of grey in there than is common in these things.'

✗ 'Joanna is hopefully a really sympathetic heroine (at least I think so), but she does have faults too, so she isn't all good.'

✗ 'Enfolded in silken luxury and with maidservants and marble palaces, her every waking hour is a blissful annunciation of peace until the dread hour when Evil comes to stalk in on her.'

I hope I don't have to tell you why these sentences should make any self-respecting agent want to screech, but in among those shockers you'll find problems with punctuation, run-on sentences, poor use of abstractions, some horrible old clichés, sloppy use of colloquialisms, careless sentence construction, incorrect word choices and more. If I were an agent and encountered any of these sentences in a covering letter, I wouldn't bother to turn to the manuscript. I'd know for sure that any writer capable of inflicting those monstrosities on me has not written a book that I want to read. So do reread your covering letter carefully before sending it out. If you fear that your English may not yet be up to the right level of proficiency, you need to improve your skills with the written word before you even think of sending your work out to agents. If you need to get help, then get help.

COVERING LETTERS: THE VENIAL SINS

Finally, there are a host of lesser sins, which don't have to do with command of the language, but which should nevertheless be avoided. Those sins – many of which I managed to commit with my early entry for the WWCL Awards – include the following beauties.

✗ *Overselling your book.* You don't need to push your work. Simply sending it to an agent is enough. It's the manuscript's job to sell itself. Your covering letter just needs to introduce it.

✗ *Overselling yourself.* If you are very well qualified to write about a particular subject, then say so. Otherwise, no one is all that interested in who you are. A swift sentence or two about you is plenty. The manuscript is the star of the show, not you.

✗ *Talking about the US market.* You know nothing about the US market. An agent does. So shut up about it.

✗ *Talking about the movie potential.* See above. Only doubled.

✗ *Talking about merchandising opportunities.* See above. Only trebled.

✗ *Talking about why the world needs this book.* Neither agents nor publishers are interested in ending world poverty. They are interested in making money. If they think they will make money by buying your book, they will buy it. If not, they won't.

✗ *Talking about how good it's been for you to write the book.* Agents don't care. Publishers don't care. See above.

✗ *Comparing yourself to exceptionally successful authors.* It's usually fine to say that 'this manuscript occupies the kind of territory normally associated with Patricia Cornwell' (or whoever), because that's simply identifying the kind of novel you've written. But don't say, 'I see myself as the new Patricia Cornwell' or 'My prose style is reminiscent of John Updike.' In the first place, you're probably deluding yourself. In the second place, it's for an agent to make those kinds of judgements. So shut up.

✗ *Talking about the excellent feedback you've had from friends and family.* Your mother loves you. Good. Keep it to yourself.

✗ *Grossly overstating the market.* 'My book is about pilots and aeroplanes – and we've all been on aeroplanes, haven't we?' Yes, and everyone who has ever flown is certain to buy all books that make mention of aeroplanes. Your logic is impeccable. What an excellent marketing ploy.

✗ *Mentioning the website you've constructed.* If you run an online organisation that bears directly on the subject of your book, then mention it. For example, in pitching this book to A & C Black, I took care to mention my involvement with the Writers' Workshop and The Word Cloud, our online writers' community. Because these organisations give me direct access to the target audience for this book, these facts were highly relevant. But if your website is not directly connected with the book – or if your book is a novel, in which case no website is all that relevant – just don't mention them. Setting up a website specifically for your book won't impress anyone.

✗ *Wittering on.* It is no doubt a source of continuing delight and pleasure to you that you once won a story competition when at primary school. You should feel proud and happy to have got an A grade at A-level.

Your cute little story about running the parish magazine is certain to have the vicar chortling to himself in the vestry. But now is not the time and place for such disclosures. Keep your letter short and taut. The manuscript is what matters.

✗ *Feeble attempts at humour.* It's much harder to write humorously than it is to speak humorously. Something that sounds good in your head when you post a submission off on Friday evening may sound horribly limp and contrived to the mildly hungover person ripping open your envelope at 9.30 on a busy Monday morning. If you genuinely have a wit and lightness of touch that comes over well in print, go for it. If not, or if you're in any doubt, then leave well alone.

✗ *Excessive confidence.* 'I will call your office shortly to set up a meeting, where we can discuss this further.' Anything of this sort alienates the agent almost instantly.

✗ *Gimmicks.* Agents love gimmicks. Oh yes. Little novelty gifts. Letters that have the word 'SEX' in big capital letters, before that beloved phrase 'That got your attention, didn't it?' A covering letter that talks about 'you' as the protagonist. ('You are in a locked room. Water is seeping up through the floor. You estimate you have half an hour to live unless you can find a way out . . . ' Excellent stuff!) All these things are wonderful, of course, and bring a depthless measure of hilarity and warmth into an agent's lonesome life. But couldn't you do more than this? How about enclosing a plastic dustbin which you refer to as a filing cabinet? What about making reference to your impending suicide? Surely you can rack your brains and find a good comedic use for some tomato ketchup or a toy gun? Agents really, really love all that. They love it so much that your manuscript will go straight into that plastic dustbin and never, ever come out.

YOUNG, BEAUTIFUL AND EXOTIC

According to a report in the *Independent on Sunday*, when Zadie Smith sent *White Teeth* to the well-known agent Andrew Wylie, her covering letter ended, 'I'm six foot tall. I'm nineteen years old, and I don't exactly look like the back of a bus.' *White Teeth* was a stunning debut novel, but there's no question that Smith's age, beauty and exotic provenance substantially increased the advance that her agent (who was not, in the end, Andrew Wylie) was able to achieve. That's not because publishers go all wobbly-kneed in the

PITCHING GRAPHIC NOVELS

The key to success in graphic novels — as in any other type of storytelling — is to make sure you thoroughly understand what your target audience is looking for and give them what they want. Sounds easy enough, but this is a real minefield when it comes to comic strips.

The medium of graphic novels is unlike any other area of fiction. What is considered mainstream in graphic novels — superheroes in brightly coloured leotards — is very much niche in the more mainstream media like films and novels. Conversely, what is classed as mainstream in movies and books — war, romance, historical fiction — is very much niche in graphic novels. Go figure.

So there's a dilemma for an aspiring graphic-novel author. Play it safe and pitch a superhero story, or try to be original and edgy and offer up a western or a crime mystery?

There's risks in both strategies. With costumed heroes, there's a heap of competition; with less common genres, there's the publisher's natural wariness of commercially risky subject material.

While it's true that even established, big-name professionals like Dave Gibbons and Frank Miller can often encounter resistance when they offer esoteric subject matter to publishing houses, some of the biggest successes in graphic novels have come from way out of left field. Art Spiegelman's Maus *and Harvel Pekar's* American Splendor *spring to mind.*

So the best advice to offer the novice graphic-novel author comes down to the same as should be offered to any creator. Pick a subject that you feel passionate about and believe in with every ounce of your being. Because if you don't believe in your project, how can you expect anyone else to?

ALAN MCKENZIE
is a graphic novelist and author of *How to Draw and Sell Comic Strips*

presence of beauty, but because they calculate correctly that youth and loveliness make for some terrific PR opportunities. Sure enough, the newspapers couldn't get enough of their new literary star, and the book was launched with far more publicity than usually surrounds a debut novel. Though the book would have deserved to sell well, no matter who its author, its sales were certainly boosted by Smith's PR advantages.

These facts raise the question of how to deal with age and beauty in the covering letter. Let's start from the happy assumption that you are six foot one, eighteen years old, and have recently excelled in competitions both for lingerie modelling and for nuclear physics. On the one hand, it does help to mention these things. On the other hand, you can easily come across as a pushy oaf if you do it wrong. Some delicacy of touch is therefore called for.

If you have remarkable achievements to your name (those prizes for nuclear physics and lingerie modelling, for example), then you may want to attach a short biography that makes brief reference to them:

2009 – Nobel Prize for Physics (joint winner).
2008 – Miss Lingerie's 'Best Basque Wearer' Award (runner-up).

That would do fine. If the things you want to stress aren't quite as tangible as that, then I'd generally recommend that you hint at rather than shout about your assets. 'I am a highly personable eighteen-year-old,' for example, would be a good way to indicate that you are exceptionally stunning and cause most photographers to faint with longing. The truth is that, no matter how gorgeous and talented you may be, you will only get taken on by an agent if your manuscript is up to scratch. If it ain't good enough, it ain't good enough. An agent is almost certainly going to want to meet you before they agree to represent you, and once they've made your acquaintance they'll know all about your physical charms and will certainly let publishers know about them in full. In other words, you can let the agent boast on your behalf. At the opening stages of your approach to agents, you can afford to play it fairly cool.

Being young and beautiful is by no means the only PR asset a person can have. At the time of writing, I'm trying to find a home for a client of mine. The client isn't particularly young. He's white, British and middle class, like so many others. But he has had an exceptionally well-travelled life and, in the course of writing a book about kidnap, he was himself kidnapped while in the Niger Delta. That, to put it mildly, suggests a hook for a future PR campaign. Another client worked for years as a TV presenter, before she switched her attentions to writing. She too had an obvious PR asset that was well worth a mention. Your covering letter needs to allude to such things in a way that is clear, but not crass.

Let's now look at the much more common issue of writers who aren't young, aren't pretty and aren't exotic. The fact is that good writing tends to come with maturity. Many terrific writers have first picked up their pens in their fifties and sixties. Indeed, Mary Wesley's first adult novel was published when the author was seventy-one, from which point she went on to write a total of ten best-sellers, aggregating more than three million copies in sales (and, incidentally, launching the career of Catherine Zeta-Jones, who rose

WRITING FOR CHILDREN

Books for children are enjoying a cachet hitherto unknown. In the last decade and a half, Rowling and Meyer have contributed much to a climate that has put books written for 'children' at the top of the best-seller lists, and delivered a bottom line publishers wouldn't have dreamed emanating from the children's division.

It is a phenomenon that these two authors have created a public consciousness of children's books, not usual. Writing for children is a specialist area, as is agenting for children's books, and the not-yet-published author is best served by an agent with expertise and experience in this area.

The bar for getting published in the children's market is about as high as it's ever been but, judging from our submissions pile, people still think, because they're shorter and because a handful-size test market at the local primary school seemed to enjoy it, that getting a children's book published is easy. It's not: the market is smaller, the readers are capricious and it takes real skill to tap right into the psyche and emotions of the audience.

So my advice would be, before you think about submitting your children's proposal, really imagine yourself reading it to fans of the likes of Julia Donaldson, J K Rowling and Robert Muchamore. It is really good enough? Then revise it, read more books and revise it again.

Study the market too. The most common mistake I see in the submissions we receive is that from an author who has read just enough to know that the proposal might have a commercial application in the market, but not nearly enough to know that the proposal is derivative or the style old-fashioned. It might seem obvious, but the submissions that stand out are good ideas, well written. Also, do your research thoroughly. It should be an effort to submit a proposal, so make sure it gets into potentially favourable hands and always double-check the submissions policy. We moved offices 18 months ago. When submissions arrive from the old address, the forwarding label may as well say 'don't bother, because I haven't'.

PENNY HOLROYDE
is an agent at the Caroline Sheldon Agency

to stardom in the TV adaptation of Wesley's *Camomile Lawn*). Not bad for a retirement project.

As far as I know, neither Mary Wesley nor other late bloomers were still involved in the lingerie-modelling game when they picked up their pens, and, if they were, their best days were probably behind them. With such people, I tend to advise that the covering letter draws a graceful veil over the entire issue. If being sixty-two is something of a disadvantage – and that's all it is; it's not a killer blow – then say nothing about it. Let an agent fall in love with your manuscript, then deal with everything else later. There's simply no need to disclose anything negative about yourself in the letter. After all, and as I've said often enough in this section, it's the manuscript that matters. Nothing else really does.

THE SYNOPSIS

Nothing, but nothing, stresses a writer more than their synopsis – and there's no need. Synopses are easy, and arguably the least important part of the overall package. You won't sell a book because of a good synopsis, nor are you likely to fail to sell it on account of a bad one. But every element of the package contributes to the impression you make, so it's worth getting it right.

The synopsis is not a blurb. It is not there to pitch the book. You are not trying to advertise something, entice interest, get the pulse racing, or anything else. A synopsis is a simple outline of the book itself.

Because synopses aren't all that important, you will come across a variety of different recipes for the best way to cook them up. A good middle-of-the-road recipe would be as follows:

☐ *A synopsis should be 500–1,000 words long.*

☐ *It should provide a summary of the book's plot.*

☐ *It should introduce the main characters.*

☐ *It can, especially with a literary novel, introduce some of your thematic concerns.*

☐ *It does not have to give away the ending itself.*

☐ *It should be written in fairly neutral language . . . but that doesn't mean you can write badly or make basic errors of punctuation or language. You can't!*

☐ *If the book is non-chronological in structure, then your synopsis should be non-chronological too.*

☐ *The synopsis should tell the story, not talk about the book. So don't say, 'At this point the novel introduces Tara, who is . . . ' Say, 'Tara is . . . '*

☐ *The synopsis doesn't have to contain every plot element of significance. It can't and it won't.*

☐ *Most of the rules in the section on 'Manuscript Presentation' apply to the synopsis too, but, if you want to squeeze the text up more than double line-spacing permits, then feel free to do so.*

Occasionally, you'll see people advising you to produce detailed notes on each character and their development, detailed chapter outlines, and more. I can't see why on earth any agent would ever want that, and I also can't see why you should waste your time with such things. If those things are useful to you as a working tool, then use them by all means, but don't go sending them out to agents. An agent and a publisher care about the manuscript. Nothing else really matters. No publisher has ever asked me for a detailed character outline of my main characters, and I doubt they ever will. Who cares? It would be easy to draw up a wonderful outline of a character who's wooden on the page, or a dreadful outline of a glorious one. So save your puff and keep things simple. If you manage a synopsis which ticks all the boxes on the list above, you're doing fine. If you spend more than a day on the exercise, you've got too much time on your hands.

Last, and just as with covering letters, it's probably true that the North American market welcomes slightly more salesmanship than does the British one. Don't go to extremes, but, if you want to pitch a little, then feel free.

MAKING YOUR SYNOPSIS STAND OUT

If you want to make the synopsis stand out, you can attempt a little more. The thing that matters most about the story is sometimes *premise* and sometimes *shape*. A 950-word synopsis of a detective story, say, may be perfectly accurate but also quite complicated. It can be hard to read such a synopsis and get a sense of the overall arc of the story. So, before you launch into a synopsis proper, you could allow yourself a few lines which present the premise or shape of the book. You could set those lines in italics to distinguish them from the synopsis proper.

Thus, if you are introducing a thriller about diamonds, your intro might run something like this:

THE DIAMOND MERCHANT

Roy Harding loses $500,000 of diamonds in a hit-and-run raid in Amsterdam's de Clercqstraat. But why did the thief look like a senior Dutch politician? And why was the girl in the getaway car Harding's ex-wife?

That would be a good example of a quick outline of the premise. If you think that the shape of the book is more important, then your intro might run a little more like this:

THE SONS OF ADAM

Alan and Tom, raised as brothers, quarrel on the battlefields of WWI. Alan comes to believe Tom is dead and goes on to found one of the world's greatest oil companies in his honour. But Tom isn't dead, and he has good reason to hate Alan. In the oilfields of California and West Texas, a second great oil company is born . . . and a feud that lasts until D-Day itself.

(If you hate the sound of that second book, then please keep your thoughts to yourself. It's an outline of my third novel.)

Both introductions offer a snappy, memorable introduction to the most important aspect of the story. The detail which follows is there for anyone who wants to read on, but the introduction has already told anyone reading that you know what your story is and what's special about it. That means that your synopsis has already achieved most of what it needs to do.

But, as I say, most writers stress much too much about the synopsis. They don't need to. It's just not that important. Time, then, to think about approaching Planet Agent itself.

Part Two

PLANET AGENT

APPROACHING AGENTS AND PUBLISHERS

Good. You've got your manuscript in shape. You've got a covering letter. You've got a synopsis. You've done your research and picked the names of a dozen or so agents that you're intending to approach. You're ready to launch.

SINGLE SUBMISSIONS VS MULTIPLE SUBMISSIONS

Agents would really like it if you didn't go sending out your manuscript to all and sundry at the same time. They'd like it if you sent it to them on an exclusive basis. They'd like it if you allowed them to work at their own pace, making due allowance for the fact that they have very many other important things to do. They'd also like it if they didn't have to compete with other agents. These things would all make their complicated lives very much easier.

Plumbers would also like it if you never got two quotes for the same job. Insurance companies would prefer you not to visit price-comparison websites. Thieves would like you to leave your windows open, and Bill Gates would be mightily obliged if you would update your software three times a year and pour hot goo into any iMacs you happen to come across.

You are not, however, obliged to spend your time caring for the needs of plumbers, insurance companies, thieves, Bill Gates or agents. You should behave in a responsible, professional way, but that doesn't mean you should be duped into behaving in a way which is grossly against your interests.

For one thing, Planet Agent is an orb that revolves more slowly than most writers would like. A really good agency might aim to respond to 90% of submissions within two weeks. More typically, an agency may take more like six to eight weeks to respond. If holidays or the major book fairs (London, Bologna, Frankfurt) intervene, then that eight could easily stretch to ten or twelve. You need to remember that the primary task of agents is to take care of their existing clients. Putative new ones are never a priority.

So much for the time lags. Let's say that your book is good and saleable, but not so obviously strong that every agent in town will be biting your hand off for it. It may well be that you need to reach ten or twelve agents before finding the one who's right for you. Multiply ten agents by six weeks, and you have already spent more than a year on the search. Multiply a dozen agents by a dozen weeks, and you have spent almost three full years chasing round after representation. If you have the genes of Methusalah, are starting out young, and are taking plenty of chewable calcium, then perhaps you will manage to fit in a decent career before osteoporosis sets in. For the rest of us, however, I'd advise a more pressured approach.

For another thing, competition is good. Normally, when you spend a lot of money on something, you will consider your choices very carefully before making your selection. Yet, although you may well end up spending a great deal of money on your agent, the difficulty of getting an agent in the first place means that you may well get desperately little choice as to where that money goes. Almost always, you'll end up saying 'yes' to the first agent who says 'yes' to you.

On the other hand, if you approach several agents at the same time, and more than one agent comes back to you with an interest in representing you, then so much the better. Go and meet both agents. Talk to them. See who you like better. See which agency feels like a better fit for you. Feel free to ask awkward questions: is that 15% commission negotiable? How do they handle any possible film interest? How can they help your career development? What if you also want to write children's books/screenplays/non-fiction?

You may get a sense that the agent isn't utterly comfortable being grilled in this way – but so what? That 15% commission *is* open to negotiation. That doesn't mean that all agents will be happy to show some flexibility – many, perhaps most, will not – but there's no law of the universe which sets commissions at 15%. (Indeed, there *is* a law, not of the universe exactly, but of every country in the developed world, which prohibits price-fixing. That means that there's nothing to stop one agent undercutting another on price, should they wish to.)

There are other issues too, perhaps more significant ones. Different agencies handle film interest in different ways. Some agents are more thoughtful than others when it comes to career direction. And so on. Plumbers, remember, don't particularly like you getting rival quotes, but, if you don't go ahead and get them anyway, I bet you've got some very expensive plumbing. Quite apart from anything else, agents make their money by getting different publishers to compete for manuscripts, so it would be a bit rich for them to complain about having to compete for your custom.

When you do make your multiple submissions, I'd suggest dividing them into two waves of five or six submissions and leaving six weeks or so between waves. If you really want to motor, then a single wave of ten to twelve submissions should do just fine.

FIRST THREE CHAPTERS VS THREE SAMPLE CHAPTERS

The standard package to send to an agent is a covering letter, a synopsis and three chapters of your book. Some agents, however, take care to specify the *first* three chapters; others ask for 'three sample chapters'.

If you have written a novel, then, irrespective of what an agent asks for, you must send the first three chapters. If you cull some random chapters from elsewhere in the novel, then they're almost certain to feel bafflingly incomplete. Some writers will feel themselves wanting to protest at this point. You may, for example, feel that your early chapters are of an introductory nature, and your story doesn't get properly under way until Chapter 4 or Chapter 5. If that's the case, then you need to rewrite your book. This is the twenty-first century. Attention spans are short and competing media are everywhere. Your story can't start in Chapter 4, or Chapter 3, or even Chapter 2. It can't start anywhere except Chapter 1. If your book hasn't yet achieved that early lift-off, then it isn't ready to go out to agents. Pull the opening apart and rebuild it until you're completely satisfied.

If your work is narrative-led non-fiction, the same still applies, perhaps not quite as absolutely, but almost. If your work is subject-led non-fiction (such as this book, for example), it doesn't matter where those three chapters are culled from. Just pick whatever you think looks most powerful.

Incidentally, you can include a prologue without counting it as a chapter. If your chapters are unusually short or unusually long, then you should adjust the three-chapter rule accordingly. You're aiming to send out about 10–12,000 words in total, ending at a natural break.

'NO UNSOLICITED MSS'

Some agencies use their entries in the *Writers' & Artists' Yearbook* to state that they want no unsolicited MSS. ('MSS' is simply the plural of MS, which in turn simply means 'manuscript'.) The part of the formula that more often perplexes writers is the 'unsolicited' bit. What on earth does that mean? How is an agent going to solicit your manuscript from you, if they don't even know that you've got one? And how can an agent stay in business if they cut themselves off from the flow of good but unsolicited manuscripts that exist?

There are two answers to these conundrums. (Or perhaps three: the literary-industry-as-Oxbridge-conspiracy theory would provide one sort of answer, albeit a false one.) The first answer is that some agencies want you to send them a query letter before sending through your manuscript proper. The purpose of a query letter is effectively to say, 'I've got a great MS on the subject of ————. Would you like to see it?' If you get a positive response, your manuscript has been solicited, and you're welcome to send it. In a sense, there's no more to the 'no unsolicited MSS' message than that some agents don't want to have their offices flooded with paper.

On the other hand – and this is the less salubrious part of the answer – many agencies will feel that they are well enough connected already. They may have a good track record in poaching talent from other agencies. They may be good at persuading celebrities or high-profile academics to sign up with them. They may get plenty of good business from word of mouth. They may be good at identifying journalists who can be 'converted' into authors. They may have some good talent-spotters at creative writing schools. They may have strong links with an editorial agency. More likely, they'll be thriving because of a combination of many of these things. In such cases, then the 'no unsolicted MSS' message is really no more than an obscure way of saying, 'Please go away and stop bothering us.'

Personally, I don't much like this approach. The literary industry feels astonishingly closed to first-time writers and anything which increases that impression is hardly welcome. On the other hand, you're not under any obligation to work with agents who don't particularly invite you in, and there are plenty of other agencies who do. So either send in your query let-ter and hope for the best, or simply turn to other, more welcoming, outfits. There are plenty of them.

EMAIL VS PAPER

I have no idea why most agencies don't welcome submissions by email. It would save paper and it would save time. Since 90% of submissions are rejected after a fairly swift perusal anyway, that perusal could be done as easily and comfortably on screen as via hard copy. There are some significant players who operate exclusively via email and say that the whole thing works much more efficiently and at much less cost to the environment. In any case, and for whatever the reason, most agencies do demand hard-copy submissions, so you should go ahead and oblige them. If an agency explicitly says that email submissions are fine, then they truly are.

The real problem arises for those living overseas. The post from South Africa, for example, is notably unreliable. The post from Australia is reliable, but hardly the cheapest if you're sending a dozen substantial packages to London. What's more, most agents ask for a 'stamped self-addressed envelope' to handle replies. That's easy if you live in the UK, rather harder if you live overseas. There are, to be sure, something called International Reply Coupons, but they are so little used that many overseas post offices have no idea that they exist. On the whole, I recommend a blunt approach here. Just send in your MS hard copy (if that's what's demanded), and say in your covering letter, 'Because I live in Australia/NZ/South Africa/Timbuktoo/ the Sea of Tranquility, I'd be grateful if you could reply by email to me on ————.' If agents are halfway helpful, they'll reply as requested. If they're not, you didn't want them anyway. And in any case, of course, silence always implies rejection. If an agent loves your book, they're hardly going to refuse to get in touch because you've supplied an email address not an IRC.

APPROACHING PUBLISHERS

If you're writing to publishers instead – well, the same guidelines broadly apply, except that publishers can be more variable in what they say they want. Take a look at what they specify, then do your best to comply, at least roughly.

If publishers say that they won't look at submissions except via agents, it's usually best to take that statement at face value. Although, in fact, all the major publishers do look at unsolicited work every now and then – perhaps a friend of a friend is an editor there, or knows someone who is – it's often best to avoid these back channels anyway. First of all, if your work is strong enough to secure an offer from a major publishing house, then it's also strong enough to get you an agent. Secondly, if you are not represented by an agent, then it's all too common for editors to make some vague expression of interest, then just let the submission drift for months. I've known writers who have been in a state of limbo with major publishers for months and even years like this. The writer is puzzled by the inordinate delays, but worried about submitting the work elsewhere while it's still hanging in the balance. When push comes to shove, however, the work is nearly always turned down and without any useful reason being given. ('While we really admired your work, we just didn't love it enough to make an offer. But these things can be very subjective and we do wish you the very best of luck elsewhere.' Gee. Thanks.) No agent would put up with these delays, but you're in a weaker bargaining position and there's nothing you can do about it.

In short, if you're approaching the mainstream: do it right and get an agent. If your book is more of a niche product, then by all means go direct to publishers. A well-presented manuscript, a strong covering letter and a professional synopsis or outline are your tools of entry.

COMMUNICATIONS FROM PLANET AGENT

You've sent your manuscript out to agents (or perhaps to publishers. This section will mostly talk about agents, because that's where the majority of authors submit their work – correctly – in the first instance, but what follows is largely true no matter where you send your work.)

You know that Planet Agent rotates at one-fourth earth speed, so you know to adjust your time expectations accordingly. You have your fingers and toes crossed. You notice that you have substantially increased your intake of your drug of choice (builders' tea, coffee, red wine, cigarettes, dark chocolate, hash cookies, coca leaves, opium), but nothing you can't handle. You think you're keeping things vaguely under control – baby not dead; husband still speaking to you – but you have a creeping suspicion that you may be vibrating in public, you can't precisely remember the last time you used a bar of soap, and it has become somewhat disturbing that perfect strangers approach you in the street saying, 'Are you sure you're all right?'

And then on the doormat arrives a letter with a London postmark . . .

HOW AGENTS WORK

When it comes to decoding responses from agents, it helps to know first of all how they work – and that means understanding the concept of triage. The term is a French word, whose literal meaning is 'sorting' or 'sifting', but whose use in a medical context originated with the French doctors treating the wounded of the First World War. In the most basic form of triage, the battlefield wounded were sorted into three categories:

Those likely to die, irrespective of medical treatment.
Those likely to live, irrespective of medical treatment.
Those for whom immediate medical care can positively affect likely outcomes.

Brutal as the system sounds, it saved lives and was immediately copied by both Allied and German medical services.

In the agency business, things are slightly less life-and-death than this, but the sorting process is similar. The three groups of manuscripts are roughly:

OBVIOUSLY UNSUITABLE. *Don't bother to read more than a page or so.*

MARGINAL. *Read the entire submission package, before deciding to reject.*

INTRIGUING. *Read the entire submission package, before deciding to ask the author for the entire manuscript. When the manuscript arrives, it will be read in full and carefully thought about before being accepted or rejected.*

The triage will often be handled in the first instance by support staff, but these staff are recruited and trained to handle the job well and properly. Agency support staff often go on to become full-time agents, or publishers, or indeed authors. (I know at least three authors who started out in this way.) What's more, because agents know that the long-term success of their business depends on an effective triage, the operation will be carefully and responsibly supervised.

Do bear in mind that, if the average agent receives 1–2,000 manuscripts a year, that equates to somewhere between 20 and 40 submissions every week. There won't be any member of staff whose full-time job it is to handle such things, which means that handling submissions nearly always has to be fitted in around other things. That does mean that response times can be a little variable, to put it mildly. The Frankfurt Book Fair (in October) and the London Book Fair (in April) are periods when all agencies are crazily busy.

In terms of ratios, I'd say that different agencies work differently, but the 'obviously unsuitable' category perhaps amounts to around 80–90% of submissions. In these cases, the manuscript will be rejected because:

➢ *The premise of the novel or manuscript is unappealing.*

Many agents, for example, will be hostile to fantasy, no matter how strong the manuscript (another reminder of the value of doing your research properly beforehand). But there are plenty of other manuscripts likely to be swiftly rejected if it seems to the agent that their authors have misjudged the likely market. It's hard to give useful examples of such misjudgements, as they are so legion. But, for example, there's not much of a market now for the kind of novel that features weedy country vicars, braying aristocrats, fierce horsewomen and cricket clubs run by people called something like Colonel Blenkinsop. Likewise, there is not a lot of appetite for 'novels' that include large chunks of personal philosophising on life. Nor is there a big market for childhood memoirs, one third of which is made up of poetry. And so on.

➢ *The prose style is bad*

It remains astonishing to me how many writers (including many who are eminently capable in their outside lives) are careless about their prose. If you want to be a writer, you can no more be careless with your prose than a painter can be careless with his paints. Prose matters! You may think that no sane person can reject your manuscript without having read it in full, but, if your prose is weak then your manuscript is weak. Since a rapid assessment of your writing quality can be made by reading no more than a page or two, plenty of failures happen at this stage. The only way to avoid such failures is to get to grips with the minutiae of putting together decent sentences.

That's it. If the premise is potentially a marketable one and the prose style looks strong, then an agent or an agent's reader has to read further to make a decision.

The second category is assessed with much more care. If a reader makes their way to the end of the three chapters and they're still happy, they'll quite likely refer the package to an agent for joint discussion. If they find something to bother them, on the other hand, then a rejection is likely to follow. From your point of view, a rejection is a rejection and it doesn't make much difference whether the decision has been made relatively swiftly or relatively slowly. If, for example, your manuscript is nicely written but has profound plot problems, then it may certainly take two or three chapters (or more) to determine the extent of the plotting issues, but that doesn't mean that you've 'done better' than someone whose perfectly plotted book is facing instant rejection because of poor prose quality. In both cases, the manuscript may need to be torn apart and reassembled before the writer has a realistic chance of publication. In any case – and subject to some further comments below – you are unlikely to know why you've been rejected or whether your submission has even been read to the end.

If a reader and an agent both read a submission package and decide that they want to see more, they'll get in touch asking to see the full manuscript. If you haven't got the full manuscript – or you do have something, but only the first three chapters are in shape to go out – then you've created a problem for yourself. At this stage, an agent's interest is still only faint. If you send them work which isn't up to scratch, you'll be rejected. If you ask them to wait and come back to them in three months' time with a properly edited work, you may well have missed your window of oppotunity. The only sensible advice is to send nothing out until you're properly ready.

If you do send in the full manuscript, then you're in the last and final stage of the triage. You may still be rejected at this point. There are, after all, plenty of things that can go wrong from Chapter 4 onwards, but, whatever happens, you'll know that you've made it into the top few percentiles of all work submitted to that agency. Do be aware, too, that the entire manuscript has to be as strong as those first three chapters. It's no use hoping that agents will see the potential in your work and take you on in the hope of a glorious future. That ain't gonna happen. The manuscript you send in has to be dazzlingly good.

THE STANDARD REJECTION LETTER

Most agencies will use a standard form letter for the bulk of their rejections. That letter is likely to feel a little cold. It certainly won't invite any further interaction. It'll say something to the effect that this is a subjective business and will wish you luck elsewhere, but a no is a no is a no is a no. Even a manuscript so poor that a swift glance at the opening sentence would be enough to dismiss it will receive that standard form rejection letter, so don't try to read between the lines for something positive. There isn't anything. That doesn't mean that your novel is a total disaster. Remember that 80 or 90% of submissions (or more) will receive that standard letter, so you can't even tell whether you're at the top end of that range or plumbing its depths.

You should also be very careful about trying to intuit how good or bad your work is from the speed of an agency's response. A fast response could just imply that your package arrived in a quiet week that was a good one for dealing with new submissions. A slow response could mean that your work sat on a shelf somewhere for eight weeks, then was rejected out of hand.

In short, there aren't many clues you can get from a standard rejection letter. Just crumple it up, throw it away and move on. All writers have had them.

THE 'NICE' REJECTION LETTER

Sometimes, authors will experience the strangely mixed joy of a 'nice' rejection letter. Occasionally, that'll be a standard letter with a handwritten note on the bottom. Sometimes it'll actually be a personal note with not a whiff of standard letter anywhere near it. Such nice letters are commoner after the full manuscript has been requested – and, indeed, I'd say it was bad form to ask for the full manuscript and then not offer any comment at all if it's then rejected.

In such cases, you should assume that most of what an agent says is broadly true. So, if they say, 'We really liked this,' then they probably did. Perhaps they're being a bit more emphatic about their liking than was really the case, but they wouldn't go to the trouble of saying anything unless they really did have some positive feelings for it.

Likewise, if they say, 'We just felt we wouldn't know how to sell this,' then they are being nothing but truthful. After all, if they quite liked something and were sure they could sell it, they'd probably take it on.

There are other common comments, however, which you should treat with some scepticism. My personal bugbear is the comment, 'We didn't find your central character sufficiently sympathetic.' What is that supposed to mean? Does it mean that *American Psycho* is a rubbish book? That *Macbeth* is a rubbish play? That nobody could possibly build an appealing series of commercial novels around Hannibal Lecter? Indeed, James Bond – one of the most popular heroes of all commercial fiction – is a drug-taking, sadistic, sexually predatory snob.

I don't mean to suggest that the agent is trying to play mind games with you by saying something which can't possibly be relevant. Rather, the standards of editorial insight among agents and readers vary wildly. The 'unsympathetic central character' nonsense has come to be a convenient euphemism which translates as, 'We didn't quite like your book enough but aren't quite sure why.' I'd say that, in a large majority of such cases, a really good editorial assessor would be able to say precisely what isn't working with the book and what needs to be done to fix it. Making the central character someone who likes baking cakes and working with children is not the answer.

That's not to say that you can't or shouldn't make use of editorial comments from agents, but do use them with caution. We fairly often receive manuscripts from clients who have been told by an agent that X is the problem. I'd say that about a third of the time X really is the problem and the agent has (succinctly, but accurately) identified it. About a third of the time, there is a problem and X is indeed one of its manifestations, but the underlying problem is deeper and has more ramifications than the agent's swift summary understood. Then, in the last third of cases, X simply isn't the issue at all. There are issues, for sure, but concentrating on X just won't get the poor old writer any closer to the target at all. In fact, by concentrating their energies on the wrong thing, the writer will be moving further from the target, not closer.

A good rule of thumb to apply in these situations is to ask yourself whether a particular comment rings true with you. If you find yourself thinking, 'Dammit! I knew X was a problem but I hoped I'd hidden it well enough,' then the comment in question is almost certainly spot on. If you find yourself thinking, 'Well, I hadn't thought this was an issue, but Agent Badger here tells me that it is and who knows more about books, really, me or Agent Badger?' then you may well want to take the goodly Badger's advice with a small spadeful of salt.

In summary, 'nice' rejection letters are a genuinely positive sign. They indicate that you are in the top 5% or 10% of submissions. You may also glean some specific, helpful, relevant insights to your work. But don't start treating these bulletins from Planet Agent as infallible. They're nothing of the sort. If they chime with you, use them. If they don't, ignore them. If you're not sure, go and pay for proper editorial support from a properly qualified editor. Even then, you'll need to use your judgement about which of their comments you want to work with, but you'll be in a position to have a much more in-depth discussion before making any decision.

THE INVITATIONAL REJECTION LETTER

If an agent really likes something but is sure that he can't place it as it stands, he's in a slightly delicate position. He can't tell you that, if you change certain specific things, then he'd be happy to represent you, because he can't responsibly offer representation until he's got a complete, saleable manuscript in front of him. On the other hand, he doesn't just want to send you away with a 'nice' rejection letter, because he does see potential in your work and would like to work with it.

In such cases, you'll often get a response which invites further collaboration. Below, for example, I've included a real letter from an agent to an author. (I've changed one or two names, admittedly, and shortened it.) The letter is long. It's thoughtful. It's got a clear plan of action. All these things are clear signs that the agent is genuinely interested in collaborating.

> Dear Wilma
>
> Forgive the delay in getting back to you with my thoughts but it was the London Book Fair last week which seemed to take up all of my time.
>
> Anyway, I have now read *Romeo and Juliet* and enjoyed it a lot. It is great escapism, in the way Webster is, and there is an enthusiasm to the writing which one can't help to be swayed by. [...]
>
> In order to live up to this potential, I do think, though, that the book needs quite a bit of work, namely in terms of the architecture of the story ... At the moment, the storyline/s aren't tight enough so that the whole thing feels too baggy and at the centre there is no one strong narrative strand that gives the whole story narrative tension and momentum.

I would suggest that you need to rework and make more of the main rivalry to be found in your book – i.e. that between Tybalt and Romeo – because it seems to me that it is this which is/should be your main narrative focus. If you can set this up earlier, and then play this out as the story progresses, slowly cranking up the tension to a big climax, it will help give the whole book focus. [. . .]

The background is the rich and wealthy. Juliet is really the only character who isn't from this life. [. . .] Is is worth making her the centre of a love-triangle between Tybalt and Romeo? This might give the book a more obvious 'centre'. The other area you need to work on is Romeo's characterisation. [. . .]

If these comments strike a chord, then I would be delighted to see a revision of the manuscript along these lines. If you'd prefer to try your luck elsewhere, then let me wish you the best of luck with that. Whatever happens, I enjoyed reading this!

Yours
Steve

It's worth noting that the agent is talking about some pretty big changes here and offers no guarantee that he'll accept the finished work. That means that you, the writer, will need to decide what to do. In this instance, the writer decided that Steve was completely right about Juliet, largely right about Romeo, and mostly wrong about the Tybalt/Romeo rivalry. So she amended the book as she felt was right, not as the agent himself recommended in detail. She did, however, succeed in creating a tight central story and felt the resultant book was very much better.

Steve is currently reading the manuscript. It won't bother him that Wilma hasn't followed his exact recipe for improvement. As a matter of fact, he probably won't even look back at his original letter to refresh his memory about what his recommendations were. All that really matters to him is that, when he reads the manuscript through, it seems to sing. If Wilma's changes have got it to sing, Steve's just got himself a new client. If, for whatever reason, Steve ends up turning the book down, Wilma will go on to other agents, confident that she has a much stronger product to pitch.

If you get an invitational rejection letter, and its broad message makes more sense to you than not, you should proceed much as Wilma did. If the letter makes no sense to you, this probably isn't the right agent for you.

There's one last possibility to think about here as well. An agent may well get back to you not with editorial commentary exactly, but with detailed thoughts about the market for your intended work. Very often, the thrust of those comments is likely to be 'dumb down', 'make accessible', 'sharpen focus'. Many authors resist such suggestions, but need to be very cautious before doing so. When it comes to purely editorial matters, you are the author and you, ultimately, are the boss of your own work. Others can advise. Only you can pronounce. On matters to do with the market, on the other hand, agents know what they're talking about and you don't. Even if you hate the message, you would do well to ponder it hard – and, if necesary, go down to a bookshop and ponder it there.

And, as you're pondering, make sure that you focus on the right slice of the market: that is, debut books written in the last few years. That is your market. The fact that Virginia Woolf did X or William Faulkner did Y is of no relevance to you. Famous authors of more recent vintage are of no use to you either. It's all very well to say of your complex literary novel that it's no more demanding (say) than John Banville's Booker Prize-winning *The Sea*. Banville's novel succeeded because Banville already had a large reputation. If Banville had written that book as a debut novel, I suspect he would have been unable to sell it in today's market. That sounds grossly unfair, and it is, but if you want to get published you need to take the market as it is, not as you'd like it to be.

THE SOUND OF SILENCE

Agents and publishers are often poor when it comes to the common courtesies. I once worked with a client who wrote a capable, professional adventure yarn. It probably wasn't quite strong enough to attract the biggest commercial publishers, but was certainly strong enough to give some of the smaller publishers food for thought. He wrote a calm, professional query letter to around a dozen publishers who sold work of this kind, then sat back to wait . . . and wait . . . and wait.

In an email to me, he commented:

> I have still had no luck with the small publishers. Mostly, they don't
> bother with the common courtesy of replying to emails, which I
> find rather irritating and arrogant. I don't understand how people
> who make their livings from the work of writers seem to feel free to
> simply be rude to them. Yes, I know they are busy. We're all busy.

He's right. Publishers and agents do make their living from writers. Rudeness should be unacceptable, irrespective of whether the writer involved is a client or not. The trouble is that the industry has evolved a blunted sensitivity to these things, so that what would be rudeness in any other context has come to be seen as perfectly normal. That doesn't make it acceptable, however. It isn't. Just don't take it personally.

You may also find yourself encountering rejection letters which seem spiky, almost to the point of rudeness. (These are more likely to come from publishers, simply because agents are almost certain to use a standardised rejection letter, which won't be friendly but won't be outright hostile). For example, although my literary consultancy doesn't normally operate as an agent, we do occasionally present clients' work direct to publishers. We did so recently with a true-crime story, written by the villain himself, but with lots of hands-on editorial input from a very accomplished literary novelist. The resulting manuscript was superbly written and eye-popping in what it revealed about our client's particular line of work. We sent the work to various publishers, all of whom were active in the true-crime market. Our covering letter made it very clear what kind of manuscript we were dealing with.

One of those publishers responded promptly but acerbically, asking us with contempt whether we really thought that this publisher's readers would be interested in such a 'crude and unsympathetic' character as the one portrayed in the book. Their rejection was intended to sting, and it did. One would be tempted to say that their comments were fair enough. There's no question that our client, as he came across in the book, was unsympathetic. But – duh! – he was a criminal! And this was a publisher who specialised in books about criminals! What on earth did this publisher believe the criminal fraternity to be like? A true-crime imprint that restricted itself to books about gentleman thieves and art-collecting contract killers might, you'd think, end up with rather few titles to its name. It was a daft rejection letter, and intentionally, pointlessly rude. (This particular story ended well. Another true-crime publisher snapped up the book and was delighted to do so.)

The point to bear in mind, however, is that you may well encounter slowness, rudeness, prickliness and a degree of non-responsiveness that you can only hope to encounter in the outside world if you try to get customer services help from your telecoms provider. I'm afraid to say, that's life – or, rather, that's life as a writer. Just shrug it off and move on. It's not you, it's them.

HOW NOT TO GET PUBLISHED

If ever you wished to consult an author about how not to get published, then I would be your man. Notwithstanding the fact that the first book I published was the twenty-third I wrote, it was actually fifteen years from the moment I put pen to paper until the moment I received that phone call offering a publishing contract. Why? Very simply, because I approached publishers directly, and never really secured the services of a stubborn and dedicated literary agent.

Even my first book was contracted directly to the publisher, and it was my editor who said I had to get an agent. There was no question in his mind about the vital necessity of an agent, and now, several years and several books forward, there is no doubt in my mind either. An agent believes in you. He believes in your work. He takes a percentage of what he has helped you make. He doesn't charge you for services before the fact. You are paying an agent for his experience, guidance, judgement, contacts, his ability to get you a better deal. If you make nothing, then neither does he. An agent – over the years – has built a network of contacts and acquaintances in the publishing industry. He will know that a sci-fi novel should go to so-and-so, whereas a romance should go to someone else. This takes the 'luck' option out of it. He uses what he knows, more importantly who he knows, to get your script on an editor's desk. And that editor is going to take your script seriously because of your agent's recommendation.

I have no idea how many unsolicited manuscripts are submitted to the UK publishing collective in any given month. Thousands? Tens of thousands? The percentage of those that make it into print is infinitesimal. Yes, the work has to be good. Yes, the work has to stand out. But it has often been said that some of the best books you will never read are in people's desk drawers. Why? Because they didn't know what to do with them. They didn't know who to send them to. Back at the end of 2006 I wrote an article called 'How Do You Get Published?'. I posted it on my blog. It's still there. That was based on fifteen years' experience of doing it wrong. It gets read more than any other article I have ever posted. It's the article I get more emails about than any other. I wish this book had been around then, but, if you want my advice in three words, get an agent.

R. J. ELLORY
best-selling and prizewinning author of *A Quiet Vendetta*
and other works (www.rjellory.com)

AREN'T WE MISSING SOMETHING?

As you tick off the subject headings in this section – the standard rejection, the nice rejection, the invitational rejection, the sound of silence – you may start to feel that perhaps we've missed something. And we have. Every now and then, it does truly, genuinely happen that an agent (or publisher) asks to see your full manuscript – and they like it! They want to take you on!

You start to uncross your fingers and toes. You get out the hoover for the first time in – how long? – and are slightly alarmed at what you find on the floor. (A few chocolate wrappers, fine. But what are all those chewed up leaves? And why do those biscuit crumbs smell so funny?) Life returns to normal. Your baby has grown rather alarmingly, but is still alive and healthy. Your husband is still speaking to you and perfect strangers no longer have that worried look on their faces.

Most of the time, agents will break the good news via email or phone, though there may still be some who use letters. It's fairly rare for an agent to use that first communication to say outright that they'd like to represent you. Mostly, they'll say that they loved your book and would be eager to meet up. If you come over as hopelessly rude and arrogant at that meeting, you might be able to convert an acceptance into a rejection, but nearly always an agent is asking to meet you because they want and expect to represent you. So you can go to that meeting in good heart and cheerful confidence.

Oh yes, and, if you reacquaint yourself with a bar of soap before you go, so much the better for us all.

AN INTRODUCTION TO PLANET AGENT

Meeting an agent is a thrilling moment. It's your first proper entry into the literary community, the first time you're there by invitation. Enjoy it.

If you're youngish and scrub up nicely, then scrub up nicely. That's not because agents are swayed by such things for their own sake, but because they know that publishers know that the print and broadcast media prefer people who look good in photos. If you're not young or if you look like something made of dough and old mattresses, it's not a big deal. People are after your skill with words; the rest of it is secondary.

Aside from that, be prompt and pleasant. You are potentially about to enter a business relationship that will endure for many years. Agents just don't want the pain of working with someone arrogant, rude, abrasive or anything else. So be nice and be businesslike, but again don't worry too much. The manuscript is the main thing and the agent already likes it. That's why you're here.

Curiously enough, although you are likely to be nervous at this first meeting, it's the agent who has more reason to be. For sure, you'll be giddy with excitement, but the agent knows that your manuscript is marketable and that you may well have sent it to other agents. That means that there's a whiff of competition around, whether or not anyone makes that fact explicit. Although you need to present yourself well at the meeting, the agent is also pitching to you. It's their turn to sell themselves.

You should expect a meeting of about an hour. There'll be some chit-chat, some flattery, perhaps a cup of tea and a biscuit. Once the biscuit is nibbled and the tea has cooled, however, the agent will lean forward and say, 'So. What do *you* want to ask *me*?' This is not a good moment for your mind to go blank. Nor is it a good moment to start gabbling the first questions that come into your head. ('Do you ever get confused about how to pronounce the "r"s in "literary"?' 'What did you think of Keira Knightley in *Atonement*?' 'Have you ever actually read *War and Peace*?' 'Erm . . . erm . . . the capital of Colombia?')

As a matter of fact, it might be around now that you realise you don't actually know what agents *do*. Just as well, therefore, that this section is here to tell you.

WHAT AGENTS DO

> *Agents are there to sell*

Agents are salespeople. That's the heart of their job. Like any good salesman, they are paid on commission. Like any good saleswoman, they know how to pitch and who to pitch to.

A large part of their sales skills is understanding the market – in this context, understanding which of the various publishing houses are going to see the most value in your work, because it's those houses who will bid the most for it. Agents also, however, need to know individuals. A certain sort of manuscript might be obviously right for (let's say) Ebury, a large publisher of general non-fiction. But Ebury is a big outfit. Who is the right person for this book? An agent will want to choose somebody who'll be really passionate about the manuscript, but also someone authoritative enough to command widespread support in the organisation. One editor might be perfect for a book about a troop of commandos in Iraq. Another editor might be right for an affectionate memoir of farming life. Your agent needs to know the various different editors well enough to pick the right one for your book.

He also needs to pick the right sales strategy. Because books are more varied products than used cars or double glazing, there's no one way to sell a book. With a really commercial offering, an agent will almost certainly pick a small group of publishers – typically six to eight – and get the MS out to them all at the same time. Where a manuscript has an obvious preferred publisher, an agent may sometimes give that publisher a two-week 'exclusive', in the hope that a good deal can be tied up quickly. With manuscripts that are going to be a little more tricky to place, a publisher may try a more select group of three or four editors in the first instance, or perhaps approach just one.

> *Agents are there to negotiate*
In the most ideal of all ideal worlds, you'll have multiple publishers bidding for your book, in which case the main components of any deal more or less negotiate themselves. In other cases, the negotiations will be more one-on-one. If the agent pushes too hard, he risks the publisher walking away. If the publisher offers too little, she risks the agent taking the manuscript else-where. Either way, your agent needs to be an effective negotiator: dogged on your behalf, but wise enough to close the deal when the moment is right.

> *Agents are there to sell your work overseas*
Some work will sell well overseas. Most manuscripts, alas, are likely to pick up only pocket-money abroad. Nevertheless, your agent needs to secure whatever can be secured.

In a majority of cases, that'll be done through a network of 'sub-agents'. Thus, the XYZ Agency in London might use the ABC Agency in New York to sell its work there, the Agence DEF to sell work in Paris, and so on. Don't be confused by the term 'sub-agent'. A sub-agent is simply an agent: the ABC Agency in New York has plenty of its own clients, and more than likely uses XYZ to handle its own activities in London.

A good agency will make sure that it has excellent sub-agents in the major territories and will sell actively to the minor territories when the annual book fairs come round. A really good agency may also be selective. It might think, for example, that the ABC Agency in New York would be the perfect outfit to handle your slim literary novel, but that the JKL Agency would be better if your next book was a rip-snorting bodice-ripper.

Most of these issues, however, should barely trouble you. An agent is there to handle such things. You're there to pick up the cheques.

➤ Agents are there to supervise

Every now and then publishers mess up. You don't have much experience, so you may not notice if they do. An agent does, and it's their job to pick up any problems early and address them responsibly.

➤ Agents are there as mediators

If you get into a disagreement with your publisher, the agent is there to mediate. That doesn't necessarily mean taking your side. Sometimes it'll mean telling you that you're being an idiot. Some of the time, your agent may deal with a problem directly with your editor. Other times, a really good agent will see the need to go racing up the chain of command at the publishing house and secure proper attention for the issue in question. When that happens, it's very good agenting – particularly if everybody ends up as friends afterwards.

➤ Agents are there to manage your career

If selling is the heart of an agent's job, then career development is perhaps its soul – but you need to have a realistic idea of what's involved.

An agent isn't about to whip up movie deals for you. They won't get you a column in *The Times*. They won't come to you with a slew of interesting book commissions. They won't get you gigs on radio, place features in the Sunday press, or introduce you to Jeremy Paxman. It's not their job to do any of those things; it's not something they're expert at. What they can and should do, however, is ensure that any book ideas you have are properly considered and right for the market.

For example, once upon a time an author came to an agent with a number of ideas for a possible book. The author outlined the first idea – his best one, as he saw it. The agent said hmm. He tried out his next idea. She said hmm. And so on down the list, until they had considered and disposed of the first five. The author then, rather gloomily, started to outline his final idea. He had long been a football fan and wanted to write about what that felt like . . . .

That book became a many-million-copy best-seller. It sold as well as it did mostly because the author was and is an extremely capable writer, able to articulate and dissect the anxieties and contradictions of modern urban man. Yet it also sold because it was a book in tune with its time and its public. It sold because the market was ready for just such a book.

It's that kind of guidance that an agent can offer. You are the creative. It's up to you to originate and develop ideas. But your agent knows the market. He will know much better than you what editors are looking for, what retailers will be willing to promote, and what markets are flourishing. Between the two of you, you need to find the sweet spot where the stuff you want to write intersects with what the market wants to buy. That's where success lies.

AGENTS AS EDITORS

It is also part of an agent's role to help you shape your work for the market, but explaining the way agents work editorially needs some delicacy. On the one hand, agents aren't looking for potential. If you send your manuscript to agents knowing that it's rough around the edges, it'll be rejected and quite right too. Your work needs to be dazzling, nothing less.

It's also true that a significant proportion of agents aren't editorially centred by nature. The most obvious alternative line of work for an agent is as an editor in a major publishing house. The fact that they've chosen to be an agent not an editor is normally a telling one. There are exceptions to this rule, of course. As we'll see a little later, publishers themselves are much less editorially centred than once they were, so occasionally you'll get editors who come to agenting so that they can work with authors in the way that they always really wanted to.

In general, however, agents do not tend to be editorially focused – not in the old-fashioned sense of this term, at least. In today's literary economy, very few agency business models allow time to work through countless new drafts of a manuscript. Such an investment of time may prove wholly uneconomic, and agents may not have the skills or inclination for it anyway. You should not assume that you and your agent will be going on long country walks, smoking pipes or discussing sentence structure in post-war American literature. That is not going to happen.

Having said all this, agents know that they can't send work to editors until it's glittering and perfect. If they go out to the market at all prematurely, they'll either fail to get a deal or they'll fail to get a deal as good as they ought to. (The reason being that a modern publisher can no longer take an imperfect manuscript to an acquisition committee. No amount of fine talk about an author's potential will convince the sales team to take a risk on something that's not yet ready for market.) Agents will also, as I've said previously, have a nose for the market that you can't have. It's not enough for a book to work in purely literary/artistic/intellectual terms. It must satisfy the needs of the market, no matter that the market can sometimes be crass or even downright barmy in its requirements.

What's more, agents will sometimes see that a particular manuscript has an X-factor, something so strong and uncommon that it merits extra input. For these two reasons – shaping something for the market and to bring something to its maximum degree of editorial potential – an agent may want you to make changes to your script.

Sometimes, those suggested changes will be very broad brush indeed. 'This is a great story, but the cast list needs to be cut down and I really need to feel more emotion from the protagonist. I'd love to see the script again if you rework it that way.' I've witnessed editorial interchanges between agent and writer which could be summarised almost as briefly as that. These suggestions aren't really editorial ones, in the sense that the entire task of developing and implementing a plan of action is left to the writer. If you're an excellent writer, then you may not need more than this kind of nudge. If you're not, you may need to get outside help.

Other times, you'll get a more detailed plan of action – such as the plan outlined in the 'invitational rejection' letter quoted in the previous section. On still other occasions, you'll be told something about the market for the book, and asked to reshape your book accordingly. In such cases, you're unlikely to be given any detailed set of editorial comments. The assumption will be that you're a competent writer and that, if you know where your work needs to end up, you'll figure a way to get it there.

Whichever of these possibilities applies to you, the chances are that your early encounters with an agent will include some kind of editorial commentary or intervention. It's hard to offer general advice as to how best to respond, but the best rules of thumb would be:

EDITORIAL CHANGES. Make changes if you think they would improve your book, and not otherwise. You're the boss.

ADAPTING THE BOOK TO THE MARKET. If the agent tells you that your manuscript needs to be rejigged for the market, then you need to listen very carefully indeed. Here, the agent is the boss.

Do note that, if you don't produce a manuscript that the agent loves, he or she won't represent you. If, therefore, you reject their editorial commentary, you run the risk that you lose the agent. In the end, though, this will be a hypothetical concern for most authors. If an agent has an editorial concern, they are probably right that a problem exists, though they may incorrectly understand the exact nature of the problem and their proposed solution may well not be right. If you respond vigorously and effectively to the underlying concern, then you're most unlikely to lose the agent's support.

AGENTS AND PAID EDITORIAL ADVICE

There are a couple of last complexities to deal with, before leaving the topic of agents and editing for good.

First, some agents may occasionally say, 'Look, I love this book, but it's not yet in shape to sell. Since I'm not particularly patient or gifted at editorial work myself, I'd suggest you use a professional editor to help you.' Usually the agent in question will recommend a particular option, which may be an individual freelancer, or might be one of the larger literary consultancies. If you do hear this, you can almost certainly take the agent at face value. They probably do love your book. They probably aren't the right person to work on it. They certainly won't be getting any kind of kickback from the editor in question. If you feel yourself that there may be aspects of your manuscript that need work, then it's probably a good idea to take the agent's advice as enthusiastically as you can.

Secondly, there are now one or two literary agents who also offer editorial advice. Those two services are kept quite distinct. Becoming a client on the literary agency side doesn't require you to pay for editorial advice, or vice versa. This (fairly natural) combination of services is in fact prohibited under the articles of the agents' trade association, the Association of Authors' Agents – the reason being that the AAA is dead set against any literary agent charging an upfront 'reading fee'.

The AAA's opposition needn't necessarily trouble you, however. First of all, these agents *aren't* charging a reading fee. As agents, they work in the regular way, operating on a commission-only basis. As editors, they work in the normal way of things for editors, charging by the assignment. They say, and they mean, that the two services are kept entirely distinct.

Secondly, although all members of the AAA are trustworthy operators, that doesn't mean that non-members are automatically untrustworthy. Indeed, I know a past President of the AAA who believes that combining editorial and agency services is likely to become ever more common in the future, and wasn't very troubled by the prospect.

Having said all this, it's still fairly rare for agents to work outside the AAA rules, so these are not issues that are likely to confront you. (And just for the sake of clarity, I *am* saying that it's OK to work with an agent who happens to offer paid-for editorial services, but who makes no linkage between those services and and his commission-only services as a literary agent. I am *not*, however, saying that it's OK to pay a reading fee to an agent, or any upfront fee no matter what name it's given. It's not OK! Those upfront fees are always a sign of literary agents to be avoided.)

THE AUTHOR AS PRODUCT

The final thing to say about agents is perhaps the most important. I was once chairing a workshop at the Hay Literary Festival, where we had a very capable editor and a senior agent on the panel. Talking about their different outlooks, the agent commented, 'The thing is, to an editor, a successful product is a book that sells well. To an agent, the successful product is an author whose career flourishes.' The editor nodded and agreed.

At the time, that shocked me – not least, because the editor in question was my own editor from Fourth Estate. Back then, I still assumed that publishers still had some ambitions to create authorial careers, however hedged in those ambitions might be by other realities. The truth, however, is that publishers now focus almost all their efforts on the book, not the career. That means that the only professional you'll have to nudge and guide your career will be your agent. For sure, publishers will play a massive part if your career does take off, because such breakthroughs can only come about from vigorous and imaginative publishing. Yet the focus of publishers will always be on the book deal that is actually signed up. Only you and your agent will have a longer horizon. For that reason, it's very common for an author and agent to stick together for years and decades. You are most unlikely to have a relationship with your editor that endures nearly as long.

For this reason, chemistry matters above all. An agent may tick all the boxes on competence, but, if you simply don't feel comfortable with him, it's not certain that you've got the right agent. Because it's so tough to get an agent in the first place, you may be more or less forced into signing up with him to start with, but you don't need to feel locked in. If the time comes to change, then change. In the end, the only person responsible for your career is you.

THE COOLING CUP OF TEA

Knowing all this, when an agent asks you if you have any questions, you are now in good shape to put down your cup of tea and say, 'Yes, I do have some questions. Perhaps we could quickly run through them . . .'

The next section suggests a possible list.

THINGS TO ASK AN AGENT

If you have only one agent interested in your manuscript, then the frank truth is that you're likely to accept an offer of representation, no matter what the agent says in response to the questions that follow. On the other hand, it can still make sense to ask them for three reasons. One, because the agent's answers will let you know what you expect from the future. Two, because those answers give you something to refer back to if you don't get the service that was initially promised. And three, because, once you've gobbled up your biscuit and agreed with the agent's lavishly flattering assessment of your work, you still have some minutes to fill in before it would be polite to go cartwheeling down the street kissing random passers-by.

Not everyone will want to ask all the questions that follow, but, if you adapt the list below to your own sweet ends, you'll be doing fine. Needless to say, if you have questions about any editorial comments made by the agents, then you'll need to deal with those too.

➢ *How many agents work here and what's the set up?*
If you were half-awake when you looked at the *Yearbook* or the agents' website, you already know the answer to the first part of this question, but it's well worth just exploring in a little more detail exactly how an agency operates. An agency with just two agents will typically operate with a fair degree of consensus and overlap. If your agent is away on holiday when some urgent issue comes up, then the other agent is quite likely to have enough background to give you a sensible response. That may be harder with a larger agency (though it's also true that issues in publishing are seldom that urgent). On the other hand, a larger agency may have a level of specialisation that you think is helpful. For example, a slightly larger agency may have a 'Mr Thriller' or 'Ms Children's Fiction' on their team. That degree of specialisation won't run all that far – almost certainly, the agent who mostly handles thrillers will also handle material in other genres, and there'll be other agents in the agency with thriller writers on their books. Nevertheless, knowing the approximate set up is a good place to start.

➢ *What is your own background?*
Some agents will have spent their entire career in literary agencies. Others will be émigrés from publishing, in which case you want to check that they

have worked as commissioning editors at major houses. There may be other career paths that lead to a solid base in agenting (for example, a good book publicist might be able to make the switch), but feel free to probe away. The core skill of an agent is knowing the publishing world very well. An individual can get that by being an agent, but not necessarily by being a member of an agent's support staff. They can also get it by being an editor, as long as their position was sufficiently mainstream. So, for example, someone who spent most of their professional working life commissioning textbooks for an academic publisher is not likely to know the industry well enough to represent general fiction. If an agent tells you that they worked for fifteen years at a publishing company you've never heard of, make a note of the name and use the *Yearbook* and/or the internet to check the company out. There are plenty of large publishers whose names aren't well known to the ordinary reader, so you don't need to worry if a name doesn't click with you in the first instance.

➢ *How many clients do you have?*
Most writers are shocked when they learn how many clients a well-established agent is likely to have – often somewhere in the region of 120. Few of those clients will write a book every single year. Many will, in fact, never write a book again: agents often handle the estates of dead authors whose backlists are still selling. Smaller agencies often tend to have fewer clients per agent; larger ones to have more. But there are no firm rules.

➢ *How will you sell the book?*
Via a mass auction involving eight or so publishers? Or a more selective auction? Or a more selective approach still? You should ask the agent to explain their thinking.

➢ *Will you accompany me to any meetings at the publisher?*
Any agent will tell you that they expect to keep an eye on the publication process, but some mean it more than others. Asking them if they'd expect to accompany you to meetings is a good way to find out just what they're intending.

➢ *Are you happy getting tough with publishers?*
A crucial question, although you won't really learn the answer to it until you reach some pivotal moment in your career. Nevertheless, you may be able to learn something from the agent's answer. Are they able, for example, to cite a recent dispute with a publisher where they hung tough and got

results? Naturally, most disputes need to be resolved amicably, but there will be times when an agent needs to be willing to show teeth. If you get the impression that an agent is likely to fight shy of confrontation, then you may well have someone who's going to back down when you most need them to fight your corner.

➢ *How closely do you work with authors when it comes to developing new projects?*
Obviously any creative ideas will come from you, but a good agent will want to winnow away bad ideas as early as possible and supply encouragement and direction for the good ones. When you ask this question, be alert to the kind of reply you get. All agents know what the right answer is and will do their best to give it. But the best agents will be talking about something that they do regularly and encourage; less capable agents may drop clues that this isn't something they do as a routine part of their business.

➢ *Are you taking on me or my book?*
Let's say things go badly and the agent fails to sell your work. Are they still going to offer all their help and support as you develop your next project? You need them to say yes – and to mean it.

➢ *Do you ever 'terminate' clients and, if so, how does that process work?*
A slightly strange question perhaps, but the issue is this. It happens far too often that an agent takes on a client, fails to sell the work, then wishes they'd never taken the client on in the first place. The businesslike approach would be to contact the client, tell them that the business relationship isn't working, and – politely and respectfully – to end it. Alas, far, far too many agents prefer death-by-neglect. What happens is that the client stops gettings quick answers to any emails, then the replies get testy, then there's a weird emotional outburst of some sort which the client has done nothing knowingly to provoke. The relationship is then terminated with tears and recriminations. This should be totally unacceptable behaviour on the part of the agent, yet it's common enough that I hear of such things at least once or twice every month. Asking questions about this upfront may not help much, but you never know – perhaps it might.

➢ *How do you handle foreign sales?*
One of the clearest ways in which larger agencies have an edge over smaller ones is that it's easier for larger outfits to have specialist staff for overseas sales. Nevertheless, plenty of smaller agencies are well equipped themselves. Perhaps they've trained a member of the support staff to handle such things,

or perhaps they have an arrangement with a specialist foreign rights agency. It's easy to overestimate the amount of cash which will come to you from abroad; nevertheless, you want the chance to grab as much of it as you can.

> ➤ *Who is your US sub-agent?*

You want to know that the US sub-agent is a good, well-respected agency in its own right. A really strong UK agency may work with several different sub-agents, choosing which one to work with on a project-by-project basis according to their strengths. The follow-up question that you're burning to ask – and may as well ask, if it puts a stop to the burning – is:

> ➤ *Do you think you'll be able to sell my book into the US?*

Any halfway competent agent will want to evade the question. The appetites of the US market are strangely unpredictable to those based outside it. Some books which would seem to have obvious American appeal get nowhere. Others, which seem to be narrowly British in flavour, are enthusiastically accepted. Certainly, you'd be unwise to assume that getting a British deal means that you'll get an American one. It doesn't work like that.

> ➤ *How do you handle film interest?*

The biggest agencies have their own film and TV departments, so effectively you'd be getting all-in-one representation on both the books and the film and TV side. Smaller agencies tend to wait until they are contacted by some branch of the film/TV industry about a particular property and then pass that enquiry on to a specialist film agency. If any money emerges from the process, then you'll be paying your literary agent 10% for making that connection. Either way, large agency or small, the process is going to be largely a reactive one. Perhaps some of the best agents at the best-connected agencies may propose a project to a producer or director and toss your books into the mix, but this is a rare event. Mostly, what happens is that a production company will happen across your book (and they do keep an eye on publishers' forthcoming catalogues) and make an enquiry. The truth is, given how little money ever actually lands in authors' pockets from the movie business, you shouldn't be too exercised about the whole question.

> ➤ *Are you a member of the Association of Authors' Agents?*

Nearly all agents are members of the AAA. Those that aren't are still probably eminently reputable beings – as long as they're listed in the *Writers' & Artists' Yearbook*. If they're not in the *Yearbook* and they're not members of the AAA, then they still may be absolutely fine (perhaps, for example, they are very newly established), but it's worth asking them exactly why they're not.

There's one last issue, not a question exactly, which is worth bearing closely in mind as you chat. It's this: does your agent 'get' your book. Does he love what you love in it? Is your understanding of the market the same? Do you both have a similar sense of how your career might develop? These are things to be felt out rather than interrogated directly, perhaps, but they're critical all the same. If your first book is literary fiction with a crime twist, and your agent wants to pitch you as a crime writer of class, then that could be confining into the future. On the other hand, the agent may have a sharper sense than you do of how the market will wish to pigeonhole your book. Worth investigating anyway.

WHAT IF TWO AGENTS OFFER REPRESENTATION?

If you make multiple submissions (as you should), then it is possible that two agents will offer you representation at much the same time. This, in fact, happened to me when I was looking for agents with my first novel. (As a matter of fact, to be precise, I was offered representation by three agents, the last of whom, however, seemed weirdly slippery and didn't appear actually to have read my book. He belonged to a well-known agency, but acted un-professionally from the first and I never got close to signing up with him.)

If you do get two offers of representation, then good for you. That's just as it ought to be. You now need to go and meet both agents and ask them a slew of questions, broadly along the lines of the ones above – and never forgetting to talk about any editorial issues which they may have raised.

There is no hard and fast rule as to who you should pick. Or rather: the hard and fast rule is to trust your gut instinct. The two non-crazy agents who offered to represent me were (1) the MD of a large and famous London agency, and (2) one half of a two-woman agency that hadn't been in existence all that long. I met both people, and was very impressed by them both, but thought that I would feel happier with the dedicated attention of a smaller agency, so I ended up rejecting one of the best-known agents in London. I never once felt that was the wrong decision. On the contrary: for me, it was the right one. Somebody else might have made the opposite deci-sion and felt it was absolutely the right course of action for them. Personal chemistry matters a lot. Remember that you'll potentially be working with this person for years to come.

You should also feel free to negotiate a bit. That 15% commission may be negotiable. You don't need to come over all aggressive about it. Just say in your sweetest voice, 'Gosh, I wonder if that 15% is negotiable at all. It's just that I suspect the other agent may be willing to offer me a discount.' If they say no, so be it. No one will be offended that you asked.

At the same time, don't go nuts. Don't try to start a bidding war or anything like that. It's far, far better to secure the services of an excellent agent at 15% than a mediocre one at 10%. A good agent will earn you way more than that 15% in the long run. If an agent refuses point-blank to consider any reduction in their take, then don't be offended or surprised. Agents have businesses to run and they do need to be properly incentivised to work hard on your behalf. If you have a slim literary novel for sale, and no realistic hope of a huge readership for it, then any move you make to reduce that agent's incentivisation is probably directly contrary to your own best commercial interests.

Another tip: if you do get two offers of representation, consider splitting your representation. For example, if you write for both adults and kids, having a different specialist for each could make good sense. Likewise, if a large agency offers to represent you directly for film and TV work, you should jump at the opportunity, even if you use a smaller agency to handle your fiction. But be careful with these things. If your core agent is confident that they can handle your children's writing, let's say, then you will probably want to work with them and would be wise to do so. Having a deep relationship of trust and co-operation is worth a vast amount, in this industry most of all.

SIGNING UP WITH AN AGENT

You've written your book. You've found an agent who loves it. You met her and got on well with her. You've handled any editorial changes that were needed. As far as the agent is concerned, your book is now ready to sell – which means that you and your agent need to sign a proper contract. Remember that, until your agent offers you a contract, you aren't being represented – and the reason will almost certainly be that you haven't yet delivered a manuscript which the agent believes to be saleable. So get that editorial stuff right, get your manuscript over to 'your' agent and have her give it the final thumbs-up. As ever, don't rush that job. The manuscript matters more than anything. It's better to get it precisely right slowly than roughly right fast.

A TYPICAL CONTRACT

The contract you sign with an agent is likely to be simple and self-explanatory. The occasional agent may go in for a four- or five-page contract that's full of gobbledegook, but a more standard approach is a simple two-page contract letter. That letter is likely to look rather like this:

Dear Persephone,

This letter confirms our agreement whereby you appoint us as your agents to act exclusively on your behalf for the sale of your work throughout the world, including but not limited to book publishing, motion picture, TV, radio and electronic publishing rights.

This sentence appoints Parminter & Pickle as your literary agency – your contractual relationship is with the firm, not the person. It's thrilling to see that phrase 'motion picture' in a contract, no?

We undertake to represent your interests to the best of our ability and will conduct negotiations on your behalf, subject to your reasonable approval in all cases.

This simply requires P&P to act with appropriate professionalism. It doesn't mean much though.

We shall promptly remit to you any money due to you and which we receive on your behalf. Our commissions, which shall be deducted from those disbursements, shall be as follows:

Agents are generally very prompt in handing over any money they get from publishers – but the dosh always lands in their bank account first, not yours. When you do get payment from an agent, they'll have knocked off their commission from the total.

On home sales – 15%
On US sales – 20%
On translation rights – 20%
On film & TV rights – 20%
[On one-off journalism – 15%]

These are now standard commission rates. 'UK sales' actually means 'UK and Commonwealth sales', where 'Commonwealth' has a meaning unknown to geopolitics, because it includes Ireland and excludes Canada, presumably annoying both. I've put the journalism commission in square brackets because not all agents will even involve themselves in this area. It's not their core skill-set and the money is small. If you arrange journalism with a newspaper directly, you won't owe your agent anything.

We have the right to reimburse ourselves from any money received on your behalf for expenses incurred for you relating to (i) the photocopying and mailing of manuscripts and other associated material, (ii) the purchase of books for submission to overseas publishers, and (iii) any other expenses that may, exceptionally, be incurred on your behalf and only ever with your agreement.

This is also standard. When material is submitted to publishers, you'll end up picking up a photocopying bill if the MS is subsequently bought by a publisher. Likewise, if you get published in the UK, then agents will have to buy a number of copies off your publisher for submission overseas. In my ten years of writing, I have never paid a penny in 'exceptional' other costs, so it's not something to worry about. Do also note that, if your manuscript doesn't sell, you wouldn't pay an agent for the photocopying and mailing.

This agreement may be terminated by either side, sixty days after written notice has been given.

That means just what it says.

After termination, we shall no longer undertake any new negotiation or representation on your behalf, but . . .

Ditto.

. . . we shall have the irrevocable right to continue to receive the full commission above on all money due under all contracts which we have negotiated on your behalf, or which derive from them, or which are renewals or extensions of them.

This needs a tad more clarification. If you ditch your agent just after they've sold your sensational manuscript – The Life and Loves of Prince Philip *– to MegaBucks Publishing Ltd, then your agent, quite rightly, thinks themselves entitled to all commission on that contract both now and in the future. This clause secures that right for the agent.*

Our right to receive money from these publishers and to deduct the commissions due may only be varied or revoked with our agreement in writing.

This is belt-and-braces stuff – just rehashing and emphasising the previous point.

We agree to continue to represent your interests with respect to such contracts unless you instruct us otherwise and our commissions shall remain due on any improved terms under such contracts, whether or not we negotiate such improved terms ourselves.

More belts. More braces. Agents really, really don't like the idea of those tasty little commissions slipping away. It's all fair enough though. Don't worry about it.

You agree to hold us harmless for any breach of contract in respect of any agreements with publishers or co-authors signed by you.

If there are legal fisticuffs arising from any contract you sign, then agents are taking care to keep their heads down. Fair enough.

This agreement shall be governed by the laws of England and Wales.

Obviously.

Please signify your agreement to the terms of this letter by signing and returning both copies of this document.

Sign it. Post it back. You're done!

Yours sincerely,

Peter Parminter,
Senior Agent, Parminter & Pickle
Literary Agency

If you do receive a letter that's much more complex than this, then feel free to ask for a full explanation of any clauses you don't understand. Agents don't need to have contract letters that are long or complex, so they should feel happy to explain themselves in as much detail as you need.

If you are a member of the Society of Authors, then you can certainly ask them to cast an eye over any weird-looking clause. If you aren't a member of the SoA, but are entitled to become a member, it may be worth signing up for that free legal advice alone.

On the whole, though, the contract with your agent is not something to fret about. It's a simple and uncontroversial document. It's most unlikely to cause you a bother either now or in the future. On quickly then to more interesting things . . .

LIFT-OFF

You've now written and polished your manuscript. You've secured an agent who loves your work. It's now down to that agent to send it out to publishers.

Sometimes, an agent will tell you exactly which editors at which publishing companies your MS is going to; sometimes they won't. Almost never will an agent *discuss* that decision with you. That's partly because they are the experts here, but also because the entire agenting industry has evolved an attitude towards writers that's reminiscent of the way doctors of the 1950s treated their patients: with proper professionalism, of course, but preferring an air of professional mystery to one of open frankness. If you want to know who your book is going to and why it's going to those people rather than others, then ask. It's not a secret and you have every right to be told. If you don't care too much, then that's fine too. Your agent has every incentive to get this critical part of the job exactly right.

But as your manuscript noses off into the void, like some NASA probe voyaging out into the asteroid belt, you might suddenly notice that you know about as much about the books trade as you do about the asteroid belt – and have seen far fewer movies about it. Before you head off to your local video store to see if they can remedy the deficiency, you might prefer to use this book instead. After a brief interlude that deals with various alternatives to agents, we will turn to the book trade itself: understanding it and working with it.

ALTERNATIVES TO AGENTS

For mainstream non-fiction and for all fiction, you need an agent. For niche publications, a direct approach to publishers is perfectly appropriate. But the publishing world is a complex ecosystem, and inevitably there are various other alternatives that you may need to consider.

MACMILLAN NEW WRITING

Because agents don't want to take on anything which stands a real chance of not selling at all, or not selling for very much money, they have become increasingly risk-averse. At the same time, publishers often pay out significant advances for work that never makes a profit. As a result, a few years back Pan Macmillan, a large publisher, decided to launch an imprint called Macmillan New Writing.

The idea of the imprint was simple. It would take on fiction that (in most cases) hadn't succeeded in finding an agent. It would offer no advance, but instead offer authors a non-negotiable standard-form contract. That contract would pay writers a 20% share of the publisher's net receipts, a 50% share of all rights revenues, and otherwise be more or less in line with standard industry practice. The calculation based on net receipts differs from the usual royalty-based one, but is slowly becoming more normal and is already standard in some parts of the industry. (What it means is that publishers are gearing royalty payments not to the recommended retail price of a book – which has much less meaning now than it used to – but to the amount of money that a publisher actually receives from retailers. Since the second amount of money is a lot less than the first – £3.20 for a mass-market paperback, let's say, instead of the £6.99 cover price, the proportion due to the author is correspondingly higher.)

A 20% net receipts payout isn't wonderful, but is reasonably generous nonetheless. It's possible for an author who does well to make more money under this arrangement than they would under a more conventional contract. What's more, authors whose work flourishes under the MNW umbrella will then be offered further contracts under one of Macmillan's regular imprints.

Initial reaction was mixed. Agents worried that getting rid of advances was just one more way for publishers to exploit authors, but MNW settled down and started publishing. Their books made a little money. Not much, but enough to justify the venture. Their authors were thoroughly happy to be published by a major-league publisher and were never made to feel like second-class citizens within it. In its own small way, the experiment has been a success. Indeed, as advances plunge towards ever lower levels and net-receipts-based contracts become ever more common in the industry, you could perfectly well argue that MNW was simply a prescient forerunner of the way the industry at large was going.

On the other hand, while I think that MNW was an intelligent and worthwhile innovation, it's a second-best solution for most novelists. If you don't have an advance, your rewards may be meagre and your publisher has

FRESH WORK FROM DEDICATED AUTHORS

We set up Macmillan New Writing as a way of finding the best new novelists writing in all genres – authors who would go on to have a long-term relationship with Pan Macmillan. We decided not only to accept 'unsolicited' submissions of debut fiction direct from authors, but to welcome them. It's true that we don't pay anything upfront, but otherwise MNW titles are published in the same way as other Pan Macmillan novels, and by the same team.

Because our authors are part of a major publishing house, we're able to offer them more clout in terms of rights, sales and publicity than most independents. Ryan David Jahn's debut, Acts of Violence, *for instance, has just been reviewed in every broadsheet paper in the country (plus the* Mail*) – a rare occurrence for a debut novel, from any house. And Texan author Ann Weisgarber's* The Personal History of Rachel DuPree *was shortlisted for the Orange New Writers Award and longlisted for the Orange Prize – and we recently sold rights to Viking US. What Macmillan can do, which many other, smaller houses can't (with or without an advance), is to make things happen.*

Truly superb, lasting writers are very rare. What I'm always looking for is fresh work from dedicated authors – something surprising, loveable and gripping. In other words, precisely the same things that readers are looking for.

WILL ATKINS
Editorial Director, Pan Macmillan

less at stake in your book's success. If you don't have an agent (and most MNW authors don't), you're going to be less well protected in the event that things start to go wrong in the publishing process. What's more, MNW hardly represents an easy option. Submissions pour in at the rate of around 500 a month, of which perhaps just one will be accepted for publication. That's a better acceptance rate than agents offer, but not much.

If you've tried sending your work out to literary agents without success, then in almost every case you are better advised to take a long hard look at your manuscript than to try to creep in to the industry by what is and will remain a back-door route. If you really make your manuscript as strong as you can possibly make it and still have no luck, then by all means try MNW. Its authors speak highly of it and it has some fine successes to its name. Even the back door can lead to the penthouse.

AUTHONOMY

Another recent and interesting innovation has been Authonomy, a HarperCollins website which encourages writers to submit their work and review the work of others. Each month, the five manuscripts most highly rated by their peers are passed to the appropriate HarperCollins editor for review. Thus far, a number of Authonomy manuscripts have been accepted for publication. Several of these weren't 'true' Authonomy manuscripts, in the sense that the writers already had an agent and a separate process was under way in any event, but there have been some proper successes as well: instances where manuscripts were taken on that might never otherwise have come to HarperCollins' notice. With non-fiction in particular, the site has achieved a considerable degree of success.

Inevitably, the system has its flaws. Peer review doesn't always lift cream to the surface. In particular, if your manuscript is worthy and affecting, it's likely to do better under such a system than it might do if more professionally and dispassionately assessed. It's also true that such sites tend to encourage frenzied networking as a way of boosting your position in the rankings. That introduces a set of factors which have nothing to do with either literary quality or market appeal. It also means that, if your work doesn't shoot up those rankings, then you shouldn't lose too much sleep over your failure.

These points, however, are rather picky ones. Any system in the world has its problems and there's much to be said for variety. I know one author whose manuscript floated straight to the desk of the senior HarperCollins editor responsible for that particular genre, and the MS was properly assessed and came tremendously close to being taken on. That would not have happened without Authonomy. Although that author's manuscript was, in the end, rejected, it was a close call and she felt delighted to have made it even that far. On another occasion, she might have made it all the way.

Overall, Authonomy is never likely to be a first-line solution for most authors, but it doesn't set out to be. It offers one more way into the industry for writers, and the more entrances that are made available the better. It's a terrific innovation and it'll be interesting to watch it develop.

PAYING TO ADVERTISE

There are also a number of independent websites which promise, for a fee, to display your work, so that agents and editors can talent-spot you on their pages. Some simply ask for an outright fee. Some encourage you to become a member of an online community, where this is one of the benefits offered.

Others will introduce some kind of peer-review system of their own. Or whatever.

The main thing to know about any such site is that the premise is a con. No agent in history has ever walked into her office and thought, 'Gee whizz, now where in hootin' heck am I going to find me some unsolicited manuscripts? If only there was a website where I could find stuff like that!' Much more likely, the agent's office will be awash with unpublished manucripts.

THE AUTHONOMY COMMUNITY

authonomy.com *is a unique talent-spotting writing community conceived by editors at HarperCollins. Concerned that the traditional slushpile system was failing to discover the best books, we wanted to find a better way of connecting talented authors with keen editors – using the Web was the obvious solution.*

authonomy *works very simply. Writers post several chapters of their work (minimum 10,000 words) for visitors to read online. Members of the site discuss and recommend the best writing that they find, and all these recommendations are combined to create a league table of the most popular manuscripts. Each month the top five manuscripts are considered for publication by appropriate editors within HarperCollins.*

authonomy *has proved quite effective at spotting talented writers. In our first year of operation, HarperCollins signed deals with four new authors discovered on the site, two writing fiction and two non-fiction. Many writers have found agents, and several have been approached by publishers other than HarperCollins – the manuscripts on* authonomy *are available for anyone to read and discover.*

But beyond this success, we're really pleased that the authonomy *community itself has become a very helpful resource for writers of all types. Its busy message boards echo with lively debate and thoughtful advice on all aspects of writing and publishing; many writers find much motivation and support from making contact with a network of like-minded people outside their immediate friends and family. And* authonomy *authors often learn as much about their own writing from critiquing other's work as they do from receiving feedback themselves!*

MARK JOHNSON
Head of Digital Communities, HarperCollins

The problem isn't finding them; it's filtering, assessing and responding to them. I dare say that since the arrival of the internet there have been examples of agents picking material up from these sources, but I'd guess that the success rate is maybe only one tenth the (already miserable) success rate achieved by authors who seek to do things the regular way, with stamps and envelopes.

I'm not saying therefore that you should never become a member of online writing communities – indeed, I run one myself and participate actively. It's just worth being aware from the outset that such communities are not good places to sell your wares. If that's how a particular community or website is pitching itself, then it's being less than honest with you.

Part Three

HOW THE
BOOK TRADE WORKS

THE MARKET

The article quoted above is not fiction. It appeared just as I was completing the first draft of this text. When I spoke to Benedicte Page to get permission to quote this article, she told me, in effect, to watch this space. There would be more articles, more doom-laden still, appearing in the coming weeks.

Now it is just about possible, I suppose, that, by the time this book gets to a final draft, by the time it gets copy-edited, typeset, bound and sold, the position will be reversed. Perhaps author advances will rebound. Perhaps they'll be even higher than they were before (not that that is, or ever has been, saying much). Perhaps by the time you're reading these words, authors will have a gleam in their eye, a spring in their step.

But nobody thinks so. No agent. No publisher. No bookseller. No industry observer. I haven't spoken to a single industry participant who thinks that the position is about to get better for authors. Most think it is likely to go on deteriorating. As it does so, the very fabric of publishing as we know it is likely to come under strain. The loyalty that binds agents to authors, for example, may be threatened if authors are now worth anything up to 70% less to the agent than they had been previously. Many authors will need to think hard about whether they can afford to stay in a 'profession' that no longer pays most of its participants a living wage.

These are frightening but real questions, and, before we move any further ahead in understanding the publishing process, you need to understand the market that publishers are selling into. It's that market which will shape your future.

THE MARKET

Bookselling is a strange game. On the one hand, it's an industry which has been astonishingly static over the centuries. In around 1439, Johannes Gutenberg invented a printing press that used a corkscrew press, oil-based inks and movable type to simplify and cheapen the business of reproducing the written word. William Caxton learned these techniques from Continental printers, and returned to England in 1476 in order to set up a press in Westminster, where he printed Chaucer, Malory and other titles calculated to set fifteenth-century hearts a-racing. These books posed an unanswerable challenge to the old monk'n'quill technology, and books started to come down in price.

Their price would continue to tumble relative to incomes until, at the start of the eighteenth century, books became cheap enough that something like a mass-market product became possible. A new art form was invented – the novel – and for the first time the daughters of dukes, the wives of cloth merchants and the housemaids of both began to tremble, gasp and weep over the adventures of people who didn't really exist.

In the nineteenth century, steam-cylinder printing arrived – an event that's celebrated by no one today except a few Industrial Revolution technology buffs. For all history's neglect, the invention was arguably the most important advance in communications technology since Gutenberg himself. The invention took Gutenberg's basic insight and mechanised it. Printing became still cheaper. Mass-market newspapers flourished. So did mass-market novelists, to such an extent that it's guestimated that one in ten Victorian Britons had read Charles Dickens, the most commercially successful novelist of his era.

The mass-market revolution, however, was not yet over. In 1934, the great Penguin publisher, Allen Lane, searched a station bookstall for something he could read on the way home. (He apparently hadn't thought to borrow something from his host that weekend, a certain Agatha Christie.) He found nothing to his taste and decided that it was time for a whole new invention: the paperback. The new books appeared in 1935. They were priced cheaply, but contained the same quality content as you'd have expected to find from any quality hardback publisher of the era. Within just twelve months, Penguin had sold 3,000,000 paperbacks. George Orwell was disgusted, writing, 'In my capacity as reader I applaud the Penguin books; in my capacity as writer I pronounce them anathema . . . If other publishers follow suit, the result may be a flood of cheap reprints which will cripple the lending libraries and check the output of new novels.'

It had now been five centuries since Gutenberg first slapped ink on paper, yet the essential product remained stunningly similar. Gutenberg would have been amazed at how cheap Allen Lane's paperbacks were. Allen Lane would have been astonished at how beautiful Gutenberg's printed volumes were. But the essential product simply hadn't altered in any of its essentials. Indeed, it's perhaps the least altered technological product ever invented. Digital technology may be about to change that – probably *is* about to change it – but at the time of writing we remain on the cusp of that revolution, not inside it. The chief executive of a major publishing house recently chided her authors for not coming up with more interesting multimedia content for the digital era,. On the other hand, very few fiction authors are actually asked by their publishers to produce such content.

These things will change and change rapidly, but at the time of writing (January 2010) we remain solidly within the era of the book. How those books are bought and sold shapes the economics which will, if you sell your book, shape your finances too. And whereas the core product has remained largely unaltered, the way books are sold has been changing rapidly of late.

THE SELLERS

In the good old days, when men smoked pipes and women wore tweed, books were sold in bookshops, on station bookstands and the like. In the heady era of innovation around the time of the first quality mass-market paperbacks, Penguin tried out a machine called the 'Penguincubator' where you could drop some coins in a slot and come away with a paperback, but (alas!) the deliciously named invention joined the rusting pile of history's failures. Books were books, and you bought them in bookshops. Things were clear and simple, even if pipe smoking was bad for the health and tweed got scratchy in summer.

These days, the picture is more complex. Nielsen Bookscan data suggests that the books market divides up roughly as follows.

Market shares (2008)	By value	By volume
Chain bookshops	36%	34%
Independent bookshops	10%	9%
Supermarkets	10%	14%
Online retailers	16%	13%
Discount bookshops	3%	7%
Other shops	9%	12%
Direct mail	13%	11%

Note that the first column above divides the market by value – that is, the number of pound coins jingling in the tills at the end of the sales day. The second column considers the number of books actually sold. Because the supermarkets, in particular, are heavy discounters, they account for a significantly higher percentage of the market when measured by volume than when measured by value. Indeed (and using a slightly different dataset), in 2009, the *Bookseller* reported that one in every five books in Britain is purchased at a supermarket, with Tesco's comfortably in the lead.

Among chain bookstores, by far the most important are Waterstone's and WH Smith, who between them account for the lion's share of the chain bookshops' slice of the action. (In 2007, those two chains accounted for approximately 20% and 13% of the books market, respectively. Tesco, the most successful supermarket retailer of books, accounted for about 5%.) Borders, prominent though its bookstores were in some town centres, has been bankrupted by the combination of poor strategic decision-making and unrelenting market pressure. (At the time of its collapse, Borders in the UK was no longer connected with the US store chain of the same name, which was, however, facing financial challenges of its own.) Independent bookshops have been declining for years, but there is some reason to hope that (at the very least) a bottom has been reached, as unprofitable stores are eliminated and the remaining ones do better than they used to at providing modern shop layouts, places to sit, coffee bars and the like. What's more, as the high-street chains struggle, today's independents are in a fine position to profit from their traditional strengths: knowing their customers, and being able to communicate passion for the books they're selling.

Amazon has a mighty presence in the popular imagination and it'll be a surprise to many readers to see that the entire online sector is less important to book retail than supermarkets, and that the independent bookstores are collectively almost equally important. For all that, Amazon has had a huge influence because it has achieved growth by across the board discounting, including very high discounts on key titles. It's also interesting to notice what a huge number of books are being sold in places that aren't bookshops at all – garden books selling in garden centres, genre fiction in post offices, gift books in tourist attractions, and so on.

The picture in other markets is broadly the same. The supermarket book-selling revolution has probably gone further in Britain than most other places, but it's happening everywhere. The assault of the online discounters is like-wise ubiquitous. In the end, although the exact numbers may vary from place to place, the overall picture is remarkably consistent.

DISCOUNTING AND NARROWING

What's more, the retail picture is united by two broad forces, which together have proved toxic to all but a handful of authors. The first of those forces is discounting. Back in the good old days, you couldn't sell a book at a discount even if you wanted to: the Net Book Agreement was there to prohibit it. Similar restrictions were in place in many other jurisdictions.

Since the demise of the NBA, discounting has become legal. And since the rise of the supermarkets and Amazon, discounting has reached levels that had never been seen before: half-price offers, three-for-two promotions, supermarkets selling a newly issued paperback for £2.99. These forces have conspired to push down the average selling price of a book from about £7.50 in 2005 to more like £6.70 today. If you want to guess whether (1) publishers are earning less money, (2) retailers are earning less money, or (3) authors are earning less money as a result of all this, then I'm afraid you won't be winning any prizes for a correct answer.

The second force is an even more dangerous one. Supermarkets are fine places, but they're not bookshops. Where a decent independent bookshop might try to stock 10,000 titles, a typical large supermarket might stock a total of just 40. Of those, the majority will be either celebrity-led or written by authors who are already best-sellers, leaving precious few slots available for authors who do not already have huge sales chalked up against their name. Given the huge market share of the supermarkets, that means that new authors are likely to find themselves excluded from 20% of the market before they've even started.

The narrowing of the book trade, however, goes well beyond the supermarkets. Much has been made of Amazon's 'long tail', its ability to sell a range of titles that even the largest bookstore would struggle to load on to its shelves. Many of us – myself very much included – have hugely benefited from that choice as consumers. Yet that long tail contains a nasty sting. If you're selling a non-fiction title, then Amazon will help you out. For example, if you have written a book on bee-keeping and you call it something sensible, such as *A Manual of Bee-keeping*, then anyone who types the obvious search term into Amazon will come across your book. Jolly good. For new authors of fiction, however, Amazon is a deeply hostile place.

Amazon is good at selling best-sellers, or celebrity-led titles, or non-fiction, but it has no good way of leading people towards interesting new novels by authors that its customers have never heard of. In a bookshop, that's a simple matter: you put titles on the shelves and let people browse. Amazon, however, has no easy mechanism that allows browsing for such titles. On the contrary, if you look up a title written by a debut novelist, you'll find a section on the page which says, 'Customers Who Bought This Item Also Bought' – followed by a selection of titles from famous authors. Needless to say, if you search for the books of those famous authors you won't then be led to the work of interesting debut novelists. In other words, Amazon is always pushing best-selling fiction at its customers. If you already know a novel that you want to buy, Amazon is a fine place to buy it. If you don't and just want to browse, it's unlikely that you'll come away with the work of a less than well-known author. Thus, if you're a first-time novelist, you can probably chalk up the online market as another place where you're not likely to sell your work in any volume.

So thank goodness for the bookshops, eh? Doughty defenders of literary variety, there to stick up for the full range of literary expression. Three cheers for the bookshops . . . except that perhaps two cheers might be sufficient. On the one hand, bookshops are indeed the new novelist's best outlet by a country mile, so hooray for that. On the other hand, they too play their part in constricting and narrowing the market. Those three-for-two tables at the front of the shop are great for consumers, but they hardly encourage browsing in the shelves beyond. In 2005, according to the Competition Commission, the top 5,000 titles accounted for around half of all book sales, despite the fact that 180,000 new titles were published in that year and 2,000,000 titles were in print. Thus, for all the huge floor space boasted by many modern bookshops, they are working hard to keep their customers focused on a small group of best-selling (and heavily discounted) titles at the front of the shop. The result is, once again, that debut authors have far fewer opportunities to grab the reader's attention than you might guess from the outside.

Because these developments are all too well known in the trade, a mainstream publisher today is highly unlikely to offer for a book unless the editor believes that the book will (1) get decent uptake from the supermarkets, (2) get a major promotional slot at WH Smith, or (3) get a major promotional slot at Waterstone's – and, ideally, will achieve two or three of those feats at once. Since those slots are few and far between, one consequence is that publishers have been cutting their lists – that is, publishing fewer titles. Since they're hardly going to turn away books by best-selling authors and their ilk, they've turned their hatchets to 'established' authors who have yet to cause a sensation at the tills, and they've reduced the number of debut novels purchased.

CONSEQUENCES

It would be nice to believe that, if fewer titles are being purchased, the average standard of those titles must therefore increase. Perhaps to some limited extent, there's truth in that, though I've seen no evidence for it myself. Rather, what's happened is that the market has become ever more conservative in its choices. Editors have come to believe that bravery doesn't pay, that safety matters.

My own career, thank goodness, has yet to be adversely affected by this timidity, yet, in my role as literary consultant, I've been able to watch with horror just how conservative the market has become. For example:

> ➤ *The thriller*
A client of ours wrote a book which mashed together the two genres of mystery novel (where every clue is cunningly concealed for the reader to tease out, if they can) and shoot-'em-up thriller. The protagonist was a PR-troubleshooter, parachuted into a failing American football club. We found the author an agent with some ease. That agent sent the book out to editors, and got numerous favourable responses . . . only to find that the sales and

marketing types at those publishers vetoed the acquisition, on the grounds that because the book was a thriller it needed a protagonist with a background in the Special Forces. That, in today's market, is apparently what thrillers need.

➤ *The literary novel*
Another client of ours wrote what seemed a dazzlingly good MS, beautifully, wittily, economically written, and in a tone and style that was entirely its own. The book was written in the first person and concerned a man who was certainly nuts, and might or might not be dangerous to boot. The book nudged the reader first one way and then the other as it laid clues, increased suspense and planted red herrings. (The book ended with a gloriously bloody murder, thereby settling the matter once and for all.) It was a terrific read, but it wasn't conventionally plotted. A conventional plot would have seen mounting external pressures conspiring to crush a fragile sense of sanity. This author did something far more interesting: he left external pressures out of the equation almost completely. His protagonist was as nuts and as dangerous at the start of the book as he was at the end; all that changed was the reader's is-he-isn't-he perception. It's been one of the best novels, published or unpublished, that I've read in the last few years – and yet this author couldn't even find an agent to take him on. His crime: he had dared to be different.

➤ *The historical drama*
Another book we handled was a terrifically well-written historical drama set in Victorian England, exploring a fascinating but little-known side of that era. There's no question at all that the writer wrote beautifully, characterised well – and, indeed, made our editor cry both times she read the manuscript. Yet we had difficulties with that one too, with one agent suggesting that the manuscript was too quiet. As the writer himself commented to me, 'I'm totally bewildered by these comments. I just can't understand how a book containing necrophilia, child abuse, murder, pornography, illegitimacy, poverty, insanity, dementia, prostitution, syphilis, drug-taking, flagellation, unrequited love, class conflict, suicide, cricket action, boxing, race relations and lashings of violence and sex . . . can possibly also be described as quiet. Please, please, please enlighten me.' There wasn't much enlightenment to offer, except that the book wasn't *showy*. It was subtly wonderful, not braggartly so. These days books have to display more self-advertisement.

I could, unfortunately, extend this list of examples much further, only it would be too dispiriting to do so. I can say, however, that every single one of those books deserved publication. The thriller was substantially more interesting than many of its published competitors. The historical drama did all that could possibly have been asked of it. And the literary novel was quite simply exceptional: better than two of the last three Booker Prize-winning books I happen to have read recently.

Just as bad, perhaps, even if you do play by the rules and avoid doing anything too unconventional, you still aren't guaranteed success. If you write a very good book and don't breach any of the unspoken conventions too drastically (a *little* bending is a good thing, now and again), then you will almost certainly be able to find yourself an agent – but that agent may not be able to place your work. One crime writer we handled got herself an agent without too much fuss, and he then circulated her book to all the normal suspects. It was rejected by every single editor, but not one of them disliked the book. Not one. On the contrary, every rejection email was full of compliments for the book and its author. Where reasons for rejection were given, they were often contradictory: one editor, for example, blamed the book's South African setting, while another editor singled the setting out for particular praise. The book ended up selling for good money to a German publisher, but in the UK it ended up selling to a third-tier publisher for a purely notional sum. There was nothing wrong with the book – as the German deal proved – but in an age when mainstream publishing has narrowed its gates too far, then deserving books will find themselves beating vainly at the walls.

(I do want to be clear, however, that these are not typical outcomes. If your manuscript is being rejected by agents, then there's almost certainly something wrong with it. That's true at least 99% of the time, and probably closer to 99.9% of the time. If you get taken on by an agent who loves your work but fails to sell it, then you are allowed to blame the market – but, even then, your work might usefully do with a third opinion on its merits.)

A CARTON OF YOGURT

Since I'm busy depressing you, I may as well add a little further to your pile of woes, while you have that nice bottle of Prozac so conveniently to hand.

Most writers, if asked to gauge the shelf life of their product, are confused by the question. If that Prozac is making you feel a little giddy, you might even find yourself winding up into a spot of oratory: 'Shelf life? Shelf life?

Does Milton have a shelf life? Does Chaucer? Does Homer? The work of the pen is beyond compare, greater than kings, stronger than armies, broader than oceans, beyond time itself. Was it not the Bard himself who wrote, "So long as men can breathe or eyes can see, / So long lives this, and this gives life to thee"? Put that in your pedantic little shopkeeper's pipe and smoke it!'

Shakespeare, however, lived before the advent of the three-for-two promotion. Those three-for-two tables and their equivalents won't stock your book for ever. As a matter of fact, retailers *sell* these slots to publishers. In the commercial-fiction market, for example, the single most important promotional slot is probably the 'WH Smith Book of the Week'. Although sales of any such book will be very much higher in the week of its elevation than they would be otherwise, the cost of that slot to the publisher is quite likely to wipe out all profit on those book sales. Publishers nevertheless go ahead and pay up, because they are effectively buying themselves a prominent chart position in the weeks that follow. (I should also say that specialist non-fiction is unlikely ever to secure in-store promotional slots of the kind we're talking about here, which is both good news and bad news for the authors of such books. More about that in a moment.)

Because publishers won't want to go on paying out large sums on your book for ever, and because every month brings new titles out to compete with yours, and because the first flush of PR hype and author interviews will quickly fade, it won't be long before your book leaves those promo slots for ever.

I don't want to alarm you unduly. Your novel will last longer than a pint of milk. It may even, just about, last as long as one of those pre-pack soft cheeses that need a month or so to ripen. But to be on the safe side, if you want to guestimate the shelf life of your book, then buy a carton of yogurt on publication day. When that carton has reached its best-before date, your book has probably also reached its. Your book will then slide from the three-for-two tables (or similar) to the shelves around the side of the store. Your sales will slump by the regulation 5,000%. If your book was in a supermarket, it'll disappear altogether. Your book's life has, pretty much, come to an end.

Once your book's sales have tailed off enough that the bookstore decides to make room for a new slew of titles, your book will disappear completely. It's still the case that bookshops take books on a 'sale or return' basis, so your publisher will find themselves taking receipt of a load of unsold stock, some of which may be kept in the warehouse to meet a trickle of future sales, and the rest of which will probably be pulped and recycled.

There'll be nothing you can do about any of this. The narrowing of the market has seen to that.

Finally, it's worth re-emphasising that these considerations apply to many books but not all. They apply to any novel and all children's fiction. They apply to broad-spectrum non-fiction of all kinds: Steven Levitt's *Freakonomics*, Bill Bryson's *Shakespeare* or any of his travel books, Richard Dawkins' *The God Delusion*, Kate Summerscale's *The Suspicions of Mr Whicher*, Dava Sobel's *Latitude*, and so on. But they don't apply to any specialist works of non-fiction.

Consider this book for instance. No sane retailer will want to pop it at the front of their bookstores and promote it heavily. By its nature, it will only appeal to a small proportion of the store's potential customers – namely, the proportion wise and diligent enough to have written a manuscript of potentially publishable quality. Indeed, the retailer knows that these customers will be motivated enough to go and seek out specialist work, no matter where in the store it might be shelved. If you bought this book in a bookshop, then you almost certainly went to the back of the shop to find it, into a basement or up some stairs. What's more, you probably went specifically to seek it out, or at least to see what selection of similar books the shop might have. If, on the other hand, you bought any of the more general non-fiction titles listed above, then you were most likely very close to the front of the shop when you first came across the book.

For books like this one – that is, specialist, subject-led non-fiction – retail promotions simply don't matter much. They will, in publisher's jargon, 'backlist' successfully – that is, sell on well after publication date. They will probably never have had a significant sales boost from retail promotions, nor do they require such promotions to establish themselves in the first place. The downside of this specialism is that you never get the huge sales kick of a nationwide promotional campaign. The not insignificant upside is that they will quite likely be earning their authors and their publishers money year after year.

WORD OF MOUTH

I'm aware I'm entering dangerous territory here (Prozac is a wonderfully safe drug, but an overdose is still something to be avoided), but I've not yet come to the end of my bad news.

Many newbie authors have a happy faith in 'word of mouth'. After all, J. K. Rowling's first book was turned down by one and all, no? And her publisher had hardly written 'world domination' into their budget projections. But kids started reading the books, and talking about them, and the books were firmly supported by librarians, and mums and dads started to get hooked as well, and they started talking about them too, and more and more kids in more and more countries were bitten by the bug, until the film industry took hold and made sure that everyone knew all about the heroic exploits of a certain bespectacled boy wizard.

All this is (more or less) true. It's also so rare that it's exceptionally hard to find examples of word of mouth lifting a book from obscurity to best-sellerdom. J. K. Rowling is a dazzling example, but I honestly can't think of any others. That's not to say that word of mouth isn't important – it really, truly is – but for that magical force to kick into action you almost certainly need (1) a strong position in all those store promotions and supermarket slots, (2) a strong PR campaign behind you, and (3) press attention that gains a momentum all of its own. Without those things, word-of-mouth simply can't get traction. When you hear the phrase 'word of mouth best-seller' used about newly released titles, that best-seller will almost certainly have enjoyed heavy promotion and as much media campaigning as it was possible to secure *before* any word-of-mouth sales started to kick in.

The difficulty of modern authors in building reputation, sales and readership is compounded by the terrible swiftness with which publishers will desert their authors. Turning to literary fiction, let's suppose that your career follows that of the young Graham Greene, the author of such twentieth-century classics as *Brighton Rock*, *The Third Man* and *The Power and The Glory*. Greene's first book was critically successful, though it achieved no great sales. His next two books did poorly on both fronts. A modern novelist in that position would effectively be at the end of their career. Indeed, a modern novelist would quite likely not even have been able to get beyond the second book; their career would have been over. A publisher wouldn't have offered a new contract. Even if a smaller house had offered a book deal, the lack of promotional space and PR heft would have meant obscurity almost for sure. The same is probably true for plenty of others.

To any new author, these ruminations will be deeply disturbing, yet it's worth stressing that the situation is a fairly natural outcome of ordinary competitive markets. If we put aside purely literary concerns – and the career concerns of first-time writers and mid-list authors – then on a purely economic basis it's easy to argue that the books market is doing precisely what it ought to do. There's no diminution in the number of books being bought and sold. Consumer prices have fallen. The producers of unsuccessful products are rapidly eliminated from the market. Retailers focus their attention on the products that consumers are keenest to buy. All this mirrors what happens in any other consumer marketplace.

The same relentless logic applies equally to authorial advances. Suppliers of the most successful products have their advances bid upwards, thanks to competition among publishers. Suppliers of the least successful products have their advances reduced. Since agents still have to battle an unending supply of unpublished manuscripts, it's not clear that any of these commercial pressures have impaired the supply of literary product.

THE TWENTY-FIRST-CENTURY READER

There's a further consequence of all this: namely, a shift in the reader's expectations of a bookshop. I remember as a teenager going to Mandarin Books, an independent bookshop in Notting Hill Gate. It wasn't a huge shop by any means. It had no books out on tables at all. Mostly books were shelved spine out; every now and then books would be shelved with covers facing out. I used to browse in that bookshop seldom expecting to *recognise* a book. I didn't expect to find books about which I could say, 'Oh, that's Nigella-Jamie-Gordon-Delia's latest book,' or 'Yes, I heard about that on the radio,' or 'Oh, he's that bloke off the telly' – let alone (mercy be!) 'Oh, yes, she's that bird who's always getting her kit off in the tabloids, so she must surely be an exquisitely talented author too.' The delight of going to a bookshop was to discover the unknown. I relied to some extent on the extraordinary knowledge of the people who ran that lovely shop, but mostly I was just there to truffle up something new.

Contemporary marketing techniques have changed that expectation. Readers now enter a bookshop expecting something familiar. Names they've heard of, books they've heard mentioned. In Borders the other day, I saw a rack of shelves with a slogan that said something like 'Try Something New Today'. I cheered inwardly, because I thought that here was a chain bookseller doing its damnedest to bring wonderful but little-known works to a broader audience. I was so happy I was ready to kiss someone.

Then I got up close and saw that the shelves were dedicated to the works of one man: Michael Chabon. Now I like Michael Chabon. He's a gifted, entertaining author of style and subtlety. But something *new*? The man leaped to literary celebrity with his very first book. He's camped out on the *New York Times* best-seller lists. He's won a Pulitzer Prize, a Hugo Prize, a Nebula Prize and more. His books receive countless positive reviews on both sides of the Atlantic. The idea that his work is unknown is simply ludicrous.

Bookshops, even relatively upmarket ones, have lost the confidence that they can introduce genuinely new work to their customers and expect them to buy it. Perhaps they're right. They, after all, have access to their own sales data, and they're certainly shrewd enough to test carefully what works and what doesn't. They aren't the real culprits here. We are.

THE NEWSPAPERS

Newspapers too have seen their roles changed over recent years. It was never the case that newspapers reviewed all books. Papers have tended to ignore genre fiction, especially in paperback, no matter that it's the stuff that most people actually read, preferring instead to review hardback non-fiction of the sort that generates a decent book review. Many of those book reviews were never really intended to advise readers whether or not to buy a particular book. Most people, for example, would much sooner read a review of (let's say) a Home Secretary's memoirs than read the book itself. Even in the past many books were widely reviewed and achieved meagre sales. Nevertheless, for professional writers, those reviews mattered. They gave some authority to the paperback edition; they supplied quotes for the next hardback to appear by the same author ('Praise for Jo Brown . . . '). They also, even if in a limited way, gave authors a route to build from critical to commercial success.

These days, review pages are ever fewer. Some mid-market national newspapers have eliminated their books pages altogether. Even the grander newspapers have less review coverage than ever before. What's more, most of the review space is effectively allocated in advance. If your book comes out at the same time as that of a Big Name author, it will be the Big Name that has priority every time. The same thing with non-fiction. In essence, newspapers have come to reflect the industry at large: narrowing the range of what gets attention, shining the light of attention on to ever fewer titles.

It's also very important to understand that quality alone achieves nothing. If your book has a bad cover and the PR effort flops, then it won't sell, no matter how fantastic the content. It won't matter, because no one will know. Newspapers will ignore it. The booksellers won't promote it. Readers won't buy it, because they won't even be able to find it in the bookshop or know to search for it on Amazon. Any nascent word-of-mouth campaign will die in its infancy.

BUILDING A NEW MODEL

HarperStudio was launched in April 2008 as an imprint of HarperCollins dedicated to experimenting with alternative approaches to trade publishing. There is a lot right with our business, certainly; we still have millions of readers, and thousands of talented authors who want to reach them. But over the past decade several ominous trends have threatened our ability to publish profitably in a way that is sustainable for the future.

The first of these is escalating author advances. As the biggest best-sellers have achieved higher and higher sales, publishers have become willing to bet larger and larger advances for books that might be the next mega-hit. The result is that unearned advances are the biggest drain on publishing profits. In an attempt to bring down the level of unearned advances, HarperStudio offers authors maximum advances of $100,000 per book, while paying each author 50% of the profits. While most authors still prefer the largest possible advance, we've signed up more than sixty authors now, many of whom could have been paid a higher advance against a royalty elsewhere.

The second issue we're trying to address is returns. The current industry data shows new adult hardcover titles averaging 40% in returns. A business that has to take back four units out of every ten it produces is not a healthy business, of course. So HarperStudio offers booksellers a choice between traditional discounts for returnable purchases and a higher discount for non-returnable purchases. The very largest and very smallest accounts still prefer returnability, but we do have many accounts between those extremes working with us on a non-returnable basis, with good results so far.

And finally, since traditional marketing such as paid advertising is too expensive for trade publishing budgets, especially given how ineffective it usually is, we are dedicated to experimenting with less expensive/more effective marketing and publicity online. There are new tools for book promotion online every day, with very little risk in experimentation.

BOB MILLER
CEO, HarperStudio

Such things aren't rare events; they're commonplace. They're much commoner, in fact, than their opposite: a good book getting the recognition it deserves. Getting published is hard enough. Staying published is getting harder every year.

THE GOOD NEWS

This section has been unremittingly pessimistic in its tone so far, although I honestly don't think that most authors, publishers or booksellers would dispute its basic message.

But it's not all bad news. Book sales continue to be high. The English-speaking world is still full of avid book buyers. Even in recession, the tills keep ringing away. So the first piece of good news is simply this: the market for books isn't vanishing any time soon.

It's also true that writers still dominate the writing game. For sure, if your book is hardback non-fiction and it's being published at Christmas time, then it's quite likely to fall victim to the celebrity steamroller. It's also hardly inspiring when the Galaxy British Book Awards invites former Spice Girl Geri Halliwell to trill gushingly over her career as a 'children's writer' before handing out the Children's Author of the Year Award – a prize for which Jordan, a model, was shortlisted. Nevertheless, it's still the case that most best-selling books are written by writers: not chefs, not TV personalities, not pop stars, not actors. Agents and publishers know this, and the demand for dazzling new authors remains strong.

What's more, success is possible. New authors do sometimes manage to clamber over all the obstacles facing them and achieve success – and, when that success comes, it's likely to be on a larger scale than ever before. One agent, for example, was talking to me about one of his superstar clients. He said that, if her debut novel had been published fifteen or twenty years ago, and if absolutely everything had gone right for it, it might have sold 100,000 or even 150,000 copies. Any such achievement would have been hailed as a triumph, the best possible outcome. In fact, her debut novel was published just a few years back and has recently notched up its one millionth sale. The narrowing of the market is responsible for successes like this, as it drives ever more sales towards ever fewer titles. That may be bad news for all those authors who have seen their sales gobbled up by the million-selling block-buster, but it's presumably rather nice for the blockbusting author herself.

Last of all – and this last point simply reiterates the single most important message of this book – the joy of creation remains the same as it always has done. If you write mostly for pleasure, and only partly for money, then a dif-ficult publishing market can only ever have a limited effect on you. As long as your work is strong enough to find some kind of publisher, then you'll still have a readership, no matter that it may be smaller than your work deserves.

And you'll win not only joy, but honour too. In my dark past as an invest-ment banker, I worked on some huge, landscape-altering deals. I worked hard, did well, was respected. And no one ever thanked me. No one ever wrote me a personal note saying that my work had moved them, or touched them or meant a great deal to them. I did my work. I got paid. And that, pretty much, was that. When it came to the launch of my first novel, however, people became effusive. Everyone *congratulated* me, as though I'd simultaneously passed an exam, got married and had my firstborn child. When people started to read my books, I became used to a little trickle of communications – emails, letters, online reviews, word-of-mouth comments from friends of friends of friends. Some of these communications were pedantic or silly, but most weren't. Most were heartfelt expressions of thanks from people whom I'd never met. I could have spent a lifetime as an invest-ment banker and never enjoyed any such gratitude from either clients or colleagues. This is still a good industry to be in – it's just getting ever harder to crack.

Part Four

GETTING YOUR BOOK DEAL

A PUBLISHER'S OFFER

Your agent will have decided how to sell your work. For highly commercial work, that'll often be via an auction involving six or eight major houses. Other times, work will be carefully introduced to a more select shortlist. Still other times, an agent might choose to go direct to a single publisher to see if an appropriate deal can be struck without any kind of auction. The agent's rationale for choosing a particular sales process may well be opaque to you, but you don't need to worry. If you have any questions about the approach being deployed, then ask away, but remember that your agent knows the industry and that their commercial interest is aligned directly with yours. Some books just aren't suited to the mass-auction approach and an agent won't get more money for them (let alone the right publisher for them) by trying to shove them down that road nevertheless. So trust your agent and let them do what they do.

HOW PUBLISHERS WILL APPROACH YOUR MS

A couple of decades back, your manuscript had to delight and dazzle your putative editor. If the editor was entranced, then he or (less commonly at the time) she generally had the authority to acquire it whatever anyone else in the company may have thought. This editorial independence certainly allowed editors to follow their instincts. It also allowed them to take on manuscripts that were brimful of potential but which needed a significant degree of reworking to get them right. It also, however, marginalised the people in sales and marketing whose job it would be to sell the resultant book. It wasn't, in the end, the right way to do things.

These days, after a long period in which corporate managements have professionalised every aspect of publishing, the acquisition process is thoroughly collaborative, just as it ought to be. Sales people bring their intimate knowledge of retailers' likes and dislikes to bear. Marketing people comment on how easy the book will be to market. The editor remains the fulcrum of this whole process. It'll be her job, if she believes in your manuscript, to whip up support for your book. She'll ensure that people across the firm are reading it (or, to be precise, reading some of it. The people who are less directly involved with your book may well read just 50 to 100 pages to get a decent flavour of it. It is still impressive, however, quite how much reading publishers do.) She'll do what she can to ensure that the acquisition committee meeting gives your book a thumbs-up. The more strongly she believes in your book, the more of her own authority she'll be willing to put on the line in support of it.

If and when your book is taken on, it'll be taken on with the support of the firm, not just the support of a given individual. When the book is a biggish acquisition and when an auction is a hotly contested one, it's perfectly common for the firm's chief executive to get involved in reading the manuscript and offering their verdict.

All this is good news and bad. It's good news in the sense that a 'yes' from a publisher these days brings with it genuine consensus and the commitment of the firm. It's bad news in the sense that your manuscript can't simply make an idiosyncratic connection with a single editor who happens to like what you do. It has to appeal across the board. You need to get editors loving your prose style and the salespeople convinced of your marketability. In order to win the all-round support of the firm, a contemporary manuscript has to have something to offer on every front.

IF THE NEWS IS BAD . . .

Ten or fifteen years ago, senior agents would often boast that they had never once failed to sell a book. These days, such a record would be exceptionally rare. Even well-known agents working at major agencies will have the occasional failure.

As with many things in publishing, the harsh news may take a long time to become apparent. An editor may be interested – will need to talk to the sales and marketing team – may make positive comments – then end up saying no. A first batch of submissions may be rejected, but the feedback from the second batch may seem stronger. If that second batch ends up getting nowhere, then surely Desperation Press of Banjo Creek, Arkansas (motto: 'we print anything') will end up making an offer, however modest. As each successive round of submissions will last weeks and months, it can easily take a year to establish that, alas, despite your scintillating prose and your agent's high expectations, there is no market for your book.

In such cases, you need to learn as much from the process as you can. Often enough, an editor will reject the manuscript by email to your agent. Those emails may just be bland – 'I'm sorry to say we just weren't confident that we could find a sufficient market for this book' – but they may often contain more substance. In any event, an agent and editor will often chat, no matter how briefly, about your manuscript, and those chats will often contain vital clues about why your work is being rejected.

You will not, in all likelihood, have direct access to those exchanges, which are, after all, addressed to the agent, not to you, and written on the assumption of confidentiality. Nevertheless, even if these comments come filtered by your agent, they're well worth having. Very occasionally, the comments will effectively amount to nothing much more than, 'We liked this book and wish the author well, but it didn't quite blow us away.' In such cases, you simply need to write another book but write it better. Other times, there'll be something more substantial to work with. A children's author might be told that they need to ensure that their work has series potential (i.e. that the protagonist is in a position to star in a number of further adventures). A thriller author might be told that he needs to bring more geopolitics into the action alongside shoot-'em-up set pieces. A literary author might be told that her style is too quiet for the market. Such things are almost always frustrating for the author concerned. 'But famous author X did it like me!' or 'Best-selling title Y was even worse in that respect than mine.' Complaints like this are universal and often at least partly justified. Nevertheless, you are selling your manuscript to publishers not directly to readers, and it's a foolish author who refuses to learn from the feedback that they're given.

In most cases, I'd say that a wise author will normally jettison the rejected manuscript, rather than try to make it fit to sail. If a particular editor has requested to review the manuscript again after certain changes have been made, then that's a different matter, but in most cases a rejection is a rejection. Forget it and move on. You should certainly do all you can to incorporate any lessons learned from the effort to sell your first project as you start work on your second.

In an ideal world, that second project will enjoy your agent's careful supervision. I don't mean that your agent will be reading each chapter as it tumbles from your printer. Far from it. But a good agent should want to know what your next project involves and to give you feedback once you have an outline and/or some sample material. Listen as carefully as you can to what your agent tells you. It's easy for authors to pick selectively from what they're being told – indeed, it can be hard not to do that – but you'll get the best results by listening hard and responding seriously.

Do also note that agents – like their kith and kin in publishing houses – can often be weirdly averse to putting things in writing. Anyone who has an ordinarily successful background in other industries will expect some

kind of written follow-up to major business meetings. I don't mean that anyone these days would feel the need to keep minutes or write a formal business
letter, but it would be normal to exchange an email which confirmed the
salient points of any action plan. If such things aren't recorded, they can be
forgotten. Given that you are new to this industry and will simply be ignorant
of many of the market-related issues which a commercial publisher has to
grapple with, you'd have thought that agents would be particularly concerned
to ensure that their killer points were being accurately retained by their
clients. In actual fact, such written communications are surprisingly rare.

You'd do well, therefore, to take on that task yourself. Write to your
agent, saying something along the lines of: 'Dear Jon, many thanks for our
very useful discussion yesterday. I believe that the major points we discussed
were as follows . . . If I've missed anything or got the emphasis wrong, do
let me know – otherwise I look forward to getting stuck in. All the best,
Jen.' If you have missed anything, your agent should pick it up and let you
know. If not, you are setting forth with reasonable confidence that your
course is a good one.

If you are trying to gear up for that second project and find that your
agent has become increasingly unresponsive, then it may well be that the
agent wants to ditch you as a client. In a more businesslike profession, that
ditching would be done properly. The agent would contact you to say that
they were proud to have represented you, consider that they may have
misjudged the market, and feel that they may not be the right person to represent you in the future. The communication – by email or phone – would
be courteous, prompt and unjudgemental. Alas, such communications are all
too rare. From my observation of the industry, it's almost more common for
agents to allow a relationship to die of neglect than to end it properly. Such
behaviour is unprofessional and irresponsible, but it happens all too
frequently.

If you think that you are being left to die of neglect, then you may as well
take the matter into your own hands. Write a polite and businesslike email,
saying that you've appreciated all the agent has done for you, but you want
to be sure that this is the right ongoing relationship for you both. Say that
you'd be pleased and proud if the agent wanted to continue to represent
you, but, if they felt it was right to terminate your relationship, you'd understand perfectly – you'd just like to know. The point of the email is not to tip
the agent over into declining you as a client, but to make it easy for them
to separate themselves if that's what they want to do anyway. You haven't lost
anything by become unagented again. It's much better to have no agent than

to pretend to yourself that you have representation when, in all truth, you don't.

It's also worth saying that there is a small group of agents who would never opt for the 'die of neglect' strategy when the 'major emotional tantrum' one is so much more satisfying. The typical pattern with such agents is that a certain project is taken on with much enthusiasm. The news from the first and second round of submissions is less than positive. Email communications become slower and slower. Phone calls are not returned. The poor old client – who, in their regular life, is a normal human being with normal human expectations of ordinary business behaviour – nudges for a response on a particular point, only to be greeted with a sudden and wholly disproportionate outburst on some issue which the author had never even known was an issue at all. In such cases, just terminate the relationship and be pleased it's over.

GETTING AN OFFER

The foregoing paragraphs are important ones to have at the back of your mind, of course. An author needs to be prepared for all contingencies. Yet you know, and I know, that your book is something pretty special. No sane publisher will be turning it down any time soon. Even now editors will be emerging excited from meetings with marketers and publicists, wide-eyed at the broad horizons of possibility opening on every side. It is, in short, about time that one of them will be making an offer.

When they make an offer, they will make it direct to your agent, almost certainly by email. That email may or (more likely) may not be forwarded on to you, but it quite likely looks something like the one below, which is an edited and abridged version of a real publisher's email, suitably altered to protect identities.

> Dear Agent,
>
> I'm thrilled to say that I'm now able to make an offer for Persephone's wonderful memoir. As you know, I've been really keen from day one and happily my colleagues throughout the company have also fallen in love with this incredible story. We are all really keen to publish it, and believe we are best placed to make it a tremendous success.
>
> I thought it might be nice for Persephone to see some of the fabulous feedback I've had, so let me present a small selection of quotes . . .

'Really special . . . just brilliant'

'Great voice, a very likeable character'

'Touching and affecting'

'I love it!'

'Let's hope that's a portent of what's to come!'

As you may know, we've had great success with similar titles here at XYZ Publishing Corp such as the classic *My Life in Cross-Stitch* by Hermione Melville and the recent best-seller (24,000 copies since April) *Crochet Hooks and Button Holes* by Charlotte Dickens. We would aim to position Persephone's memoir very squarely in this market, and believe we have the track record to make it a real success.

What we'd like to do is ensure that, through the title and cover, the focus is on Persephone and her remarkable story. One of the fantastic things about her writing is its lovely evocation of time and place – she conjures up the atmosphere of the age so brilliantly – and yet, for all its occasional darkness, somehow the story retains a charm and innocence that is incredibly touching. I'm sure you'll agree that this is what makes Persephone's story unique. We feel that the book will be most successful if we can present and edit it in a way that reflects this.

Our feeling is that we have an opportunity to shape the book a little more, and also come up with a title that really positions the book squarely within the best-selling tradition of recent sewing-related titles. We suggest *It's Just Sew Me*, but this is something we'd be happy to discuss further with you in the context of a deal. We have some further, relatively minor, editorial issues which we'd like to discuss in due course.

I have attached a formal letter containing all the details of our offer, but I'll quickly summarise the basics here . . .

Yours,

A. N. Editor

Several things are of interest about this communication. The first, and most important, is that the editor has read the work and genuinely loves it. The quotes from others in the publishing company will be genuine too. Publishing is an industry that does work on enthusiasm. If the editor in question weren't enthusiastic, she wouldn't be offering for it.

The second point is how focused the editor is on the market. The author of this particular memoir (which, of course, had nothing to do with sewing) had no idea that she was writing for a certain segment of the memoir market. It wouldn't have occured to her that her book would be judged against the commercial success of various other titles, none of which dealt with the same subject as hers. Yet the editor would certainly have checked out the market with some care. She'd have worked out how retailers would bracket this title. She'd have checked recent sales figures for some of the leading titles in the genre. She'd have gauged as carefully as she could how this particular memoir was likely to fare, given the market context, and made her offer on that basis. Her comments about changing the title would have been made with a view to cementing this particular memoir's place in a certain commercial niche. If the agent or author involved had been foolish enough to resist altering the title, then the offer might well have been withdrawn altogether. The editor's market focus isn't foolish or narrow-minded. It's part and parcel of her job, which is to sell as many copies of a particular book as she ever possibly can. That means thinking as hard about the market as any decent author will about her prose style.

As for the outline terms of the offer itself, an editor will not, at this stage, seek to detail every last term of the contract. Publishing contracts are pretty standard things. Of course, from time to time, there will be special circumstances which demand careful contractual elaboration, but for the most part one contract will look much the same as another – and, indeed, any established agency will have agreed a standard form or 'boilerplate' contract on behalf of their authors, which will form the basis of every agreement between those two firms. At this stage, therefore, an offer letter will confine itself to an outline of a few crucial terms – notably the size of the advance and the level of a few key royalties.

I'll discuss those royalties in much more detail when we come to look at the contract itself, but for now let me just reiterate that an agent negotiates this kind of thing for a living. His interests are exactly aligned with yours, so you don't need to worry too much about whether he's getting the best possible terms for you. He'll most certainly be doing his damndest to do so. It's not just his duty calling him – it's his income.

THE AUCTION

In the best of all possible worlds, a flurry of opening bids will give way to one or two, or just possibly three, publishers duking it out for your book.

I've been in that happy position twice in my career, and it's a curious place to be. Mostly, of course, it's delicious. Every day, another offer. You're richer today than you were yesterday; richer yesterday than the day before.

At the same time, it's a rather peculiar sensation. These publishers aren't fighting over *you* – they haven't met you. They're fighting over your work. What's more, their competition doesn't take the form you rather think it ought to. The various editors aren't vying with each other to demonstrate their understanding of your intellectual or literary project. They aren't anxious to discuss your next project, or how you see your career developing. Instead, they're just hurling bundles of cash at you and talking to your agent. Don't get me wrong. Anyone who would like to hurl cash at me should feel free to do so; they may do it all day long for all I care. I don't mind the sensation, but it is an odd one, for all that. I hope that one day you feel it too.

Because publishers are all looking at the same market, and because their methodologies for calculating advances are all essentially identical, it's surprisingly common for an auction to end with two publishers offering the exact same, or almost the exact same, amount. Again, I've been in this position twice, both at the start of my fiction career and the start of my non-fiction one. On both occasions, major publishers of impeccable reputation were offering identical amounts to publish my work. At this dizzy point in your life, you are in the wonderful position of being able to choose your publisher. Even better, you get to *reject* someone: an author finally able to reject the rejecters. Life gets no sweeter than this – and a new section is called for, all the better to relish the moment.

CHOOSING YOUR PUBLISHER

Your agent has sent your book out and been overwhelmed with offers. You are delighted with your agent, but are happier still to have your own estimation of your talent so emphatically confirmed. The auction frenzy subsides and you have two publishers offering the same, or very similar, amounts for your book. You need to choose one to accept, knowing that your career may rest on the rightness of your decision.

The first point to make is that both publishers are probably fine. Publishing is not the kind of industry where to be first is everything, to be second nothing. Although publishing markets vary from country to country, within any one country one large publisher looks very much like another. If any publisher tries something distinctive and successful, that innovation will quite likely be rapidly copied by everyone else. If a particular publisher happens to do well at attracting editorial or marketing talent to its four walls, the chances are that other companies will swoop in to lure it away. In my own seven-book career (this book is the eighth), two of my editors and two of my publishers have been headhunted by other firms. One other editor left as the person whom she replaced during a maternity leave returned to work. I've worked with more publicists than I can quite remember. In short, much as you may love the particular bunch of people who sign up you and your book, it's relatively unlikely that the same bunch will still be present as the second book in your (probable) two-book deal slithers its way towards the paperback shelves.

Nevertheless, you are presented with a choice and you may as well make it as best you can – and that means choosing between what is put in front of you, not trying to guess what it might look like in the future. It's also worth saying that you should, if at all possible, *meet* the rival publishers. If you've already got a fair bit of industry know-how, perhaps it'd be OK just to talk to the competing editors by phone, but really, if you can, go and talk to them. It's a big decision.

Your agent will certainly accompany you and will talk things through with you beforehand, but many agents will be fairly passive when it comes to setting the agenda for the meeting. Your potential publishers may be less passive, but their overwhelming concern is to come across as such wonderfully delightful people that you'll just tumble into their embrace. It's certainly not in their interest to bring up any potentially awkward topic of conversation that may nevertheless have a crucial bearing on how your book is published. In short, you need to take control yourself. Use this section to set the agenda, adjusting it as necessary to meet the demands of your particular book. You don't, by any means, need to come with a publishing strategy of your own. You aren't in a position to develop one, let alone execute it. But you should ask enough questions to ensure that you come away from the meeting knowing as much as you need to about how your publishers intend to publish your work, and what they are like as people to work with.

There's no set format for these meetings. I myself was once ushered into a boardroom and offered – rather oddly – a huge platter of cheese and celery sticks. More typically, you'll be shown into a functional-looking conference room and offered coffee and biscuits. You'll most certainly meet your putative editor. You will probably also meet that editor's boss (who probably calls herself a publisher). You will quite likely also meet a publicist. You may meet someone from the paperback side, if the publisher is the sort to separate out hardback and paperback publishing. You may just possibly meet others from management, sales and marketing. The whole meeting will probably last around an hour.

WHAT TO LOOK FOR

Crude as it sounds, the number of people who come to greet you means something. So too does the seniority of those pumping your hand and (in my case) offering me lumps of mature Stilton. If a company really wants your book, then it'll push the boat out. If a Chief Executive pops by to say how much they love your work, you can discount some of what they're saying: it's most unlikely that they'll have read more than a few dozen pages of it. Nevertheless Great Personages don't make the trip down from the management suite for any old person, and it means something that they've come down for you.

Just as important, you should take stock of those little flattering comments that fall so sweetly on your ears. Your editor will certainly be saying nice things about your book. She couldn't possibly not. But what about the others – the PR person, the paperback person, the scrawny chap from marketing? If they nod and look sage as your editor is speaking, it's likely enough that they've read a hundred pages or so of your book – enough to thoroughly familiarise themselves with your genre, tone and style – but haven't gone much further. If, on the other hand, they weigh in with stories about how they were kept up late reading your book, how they cried at your ending, or anything else along those lines, then you can take those comments at more or less face value.

Enthusiasm matters hugely. One author recently made a high-profile move away from the publisher who had brought out her previous seven books to a smaller outfit which wasn't offering any more money or better terms. What made the difference was enthusiasm. This author felt her publisher was now handling her in a professional but unenthused way. She calculated – correctly in my view – that her interests would be better served by publishers who would bring both professionalism and passion to the game. Even if the financial outcomes ended up identical (and they may well not), you'll have more fun and a better feeling about the enthusiasts.

YOUR EDITOR'S COMMENTS ABOUT YOUR WORK

Similarly, you should listen carefully to anything the editor says about her personal response to your work. Things may be said in passing that strike you as somehow missing a critical aspect of your writing, or as pigeonholing you in a way that you don't want to be pigeonholed. These remarks aren't casual and you shouldn't dismiss them. That's not to say that interpreting them is easy. Your editor is your interface between your manuscript and the market. You don't want her to present your work too crudely, yet you can't afford to have her be too timid in her approach to the market either.

Much of the rest of this book will deal, in one way or another, with the knotty problem of approaching the market, so I won't expand on that subject much more here. Just be alert to the issue. You want your editor to understand your book. You also want her to have a sales strategy that is decisive, clear and forceful. If either needs to win, then it needs to be the latter every time, but in an ideal world both things will happily co-exist – and you will certainly be happier with an editor who never loses sight of the more subtle aspects of your manuscript. So note any comments: those you like, those you don't, those you aren't sure of. You can reflect on them at greater length in due course.

You should also, of course, ask about any editorial changes that the editor has in mind. At this point, you'll only get the broadest of broad-brush comments. They'll also be offered very tentatively, because the editor will worry that you're going to go off in some authorly huff if anyone suggests that your work is capable of further improvement. You, of course, aren't anything like that – and, as it happens, I think damn few authors are. Nevertheless, don't be fooled by that tentative approach. However gently your editor introduces something at this stage, as soon as the ink dries on the contract that gentleness will harden into iron. If you think your editor's comments are simply wrong, then say so now. Get as far into the issue as is necessary to resolve it. If you think the comments are broadly right and helpful, then so much the better. That's an excellent sign that you'll see eye to eye when it comes to the nitty-gritty.

HARDBACK VS PAPERBACK

Often enough, the publishers who are bidding for your book will have essentially the same publishing strategy in mind. That should hardly be surprising, given that they're selling the same kind of products into the same market. Yet it's remarkable how often strategies do vary, in particular when it comes to the big question of how to launch.

Traditionally, books were sold in hardback first. Hardback buyers got the pleasure of big awkward books that looked nice on a bookshelf, and they were (for some strange reason) happy to pay about twice the cost of a paperback for the privilege. (Libraries used to like hardbacks for the more logical reason that they needed books robust enough to withstand plenty of handling, but libraries are not the major buyers that they once were.) Because the simultaneous availability of a cheap paperback version would wreck the saleability of the hardback, paperbacks traditionally launched nine months to a year after the hardback. For a typical book, paperback sales would be perhaps five times greater than hardback sales but, because hardbacks retailed at double the price of paperbacks and had a higher unit margin into the bargain, hardback publishing remained a crucial part of any large publisher's strategy. What's more, hardback publishing continued to be more prestigious, the pulp aura of the mass market having never quite left the paperback side of things. That, then, was how the world worked. It was daft in some ways, but everyone understood it.

Gradually, an alternative model began to evolve. For certain books – notably genre fiction of any kind – the vast bulk of potential sales lay in paperback. That wasn't just a question of price. It was also that paperbacks are for readers who really want to read: on the subway, on a beach, on a train, in a lunch hour – wherever and whenever the mood struck and the hour offered. Paperbacks weren't just for the unwashed mob any more. They were for people like you and people like me, with brains and with money.

Now the trouble with the old model of publishing for books whose sales potential lay in paperback was that all the launch costs and effort went into supporting the hardback. You couldn't launch a hardback without spending money on it, but that ate some of the paperback's marketing budget. More to the point, any PR effort would have to be concentrated on the launch of the hardback. (That's because newspapers are only interested in 'new' news and, by the time a paperback followed the hardback on to the bookshelves, its existence would have nothing newsworthy about it.) The old hardback/paperback model was therefore forcing some publishers into the paradoxical position of heavily promoting a product which *wasn't* expected to sell and cannibalising the sales effort behind the product which *was* expected to sell.

A new model therefore emerged. Quite simply, for some books, the hardback stage was eliminated. Books (particularly books by debut authors) were launched straight into paperback, with all the sales and marketing budget and all the PR effort focused hard on that single product. This change is bizarrely recent. My first novel was published in February 2000. When discussing that launch with the team at HarperCollins (who at that stage were still bidding against another large company for my novel), I found them oddly timid about their paperback-only strategy. It was as if they were worried that I might be insulted if my novel were sent out into the world without the dignity of hard covers. The team at the other publisher, as it happened, were still attached to the hardback-first model, and therefore offered a completely different launch strategy.

(Just to confuse things still further, another very recent innovation has been to launch hardbacks and paperbacks simultaneously. The notion is that some people prefer hard covers, so it makes sense to make a high-value, high-margin product available to them, while making the regular product available to everyone else. By launching at the same time, all PR and marketing costs can be concentrated on one launch, not two. This paragraph, however, sits in parenthesis, because the model is new, has not been widely adopted and is not, if you want my frank opinion, likely to endure.)

Finally, even if both your possible publishers are going to follow a traditional hardback-then-paperback route, they may well have different internal structures. Some publishers place one person in charge of a particular title, for both its hardback and paperback versions. Others separate out the two functions, so that the person who oversees your hardback edition will be different from the one who oversees your paperback edition. The standard justification for such a divison of roles is that it brings a fresh set of eyes to the paperback-publishing process. If there are things that have been handled poorly in the hardback, they can be picked up and corrected with the paperback.

That's the theory. There's also the risk that the person who handles the paperback wasn't responsible for the initial purchase decision, has little investment in the title and is simply concerned to bash out a paperback from the material developed for the hardback. I've seen it done both ways, either with my work or with other people's. There's no certainty as to which route is better, though, if the decision were mine, I'd prefer to have one editor with whom I got on well overseeing everything. If that's not available, I'd want to meet my putative paperback editor at the same time as I met the hardback team. And if that's not possible – and I was expecting to sell many more copies in soft covers than in hard ones – I'd leave the meeting knowing that one of the people most important to my publishing future wasn't even present.

I've talked at length about this issue because, if you are talking to two different publishers with two different publishing strategies, then you should probe their rationales carefully. Why is your publisher taking the approach they're planning to take? What are the pros and cons? What makes most sense to you? As a broad rule of thumb, the more 'commercial' your title is, the more it makes sense to launch it straight into paperback. The more literary or highbrow your title, the more a hardback-first approach is called for. (And newspapers remain much less likely to review paperback-only titles than ones that come out first in hardback.) But there's still a broad middle ground where approaches vary. If you are presented with different approaches, then you need to make your best assessment of where the greatest advantage is likely to lie. It is, of course, tempting to be seduced by the glamour or prestige of a hardback, but you should resist the seduction. Sales matter. Nothing else does. You'll have all the prestige and glamour you could possibly want if your book is a sales hit. More to the point, it's sales and only sales which will ensure you have an enduring, profitable career. (Although for literary fiction, literary prizes and a strong critical reputation will do a lot to repair the damage done by mediocre sales.)

PRICES AND FORMATS

Although the hardback/paperback issue is probably the single biggest decision to be made when it comes to launching a book, it's by no means the only one. Standard mass-market paperbacks come in two different sizes, though (for debut authors) only one more-or-less universal price point. Trade paperbacks are soft-covered, but hardback-sized, and come often with a hardback-sized price tag. Hardbacks also come in pocket-sized 'demy' editions, which have paperback-style compactness alongside hardback-sized prices, as well as larger, more luxurious and more expensive full-size editions. The table on the opposite page shows the approximate norms which prevail at the time of writing, but variants abound, in relation to both price and production.

You don't need to get too involved in the intricacies of all this. You should, however, understand exactly how your publisher is proposing to sell you and why. If they're launching you in hardback, are they thinking of a compact demi edition? Or a full-size, high-price one? And why are they making the choice they're making?

You're not, of course, a publishing expert, and there's a temptation simply to shrug and accept that your potential publishers know what they're doing. Yet, if you are meeting two publishers with notably different strategies, then,

Format	UK Price	US Price	Size
		MASS–MARKET PAPERBACK	
A-format	£6.99	$7.99	110 × 178 mm
B-format	£6.99	$7.99	130 × 198 mm
		TRADE PAPERBACK	
C-format	Variable: up to £16.99 / $16.99		135 × 216 mm
		HARDBACK	
Demy	Variable: typically £12.99 / $14.99		130 × 198 mm
Full	Variable: typically £16.99 / $24.99		Variable

like it or not, you have to choose between them. If you choose the one with the strategy that you're most comfortable with, if things do go pear-shaped in due course, you will at least have the comfort of knowing that you made your decisions as wisely as possible.

LAUNCH DATES

Another huge decision to be made concerns the timing of any launch. The two major sales seasons in publishing are Christmas and the summer holiday reading season. The 'Christmas' season starts in about September. Indeed, if there's a huge title being launched in September (as there was, for example, with Dan Brown's *The Lost Symbol* in 2009), then the Christmas selling season may even edge into August (and, yes, I share your distaste at that particular thought). The Christmas season is the traditional period for launching hardback books by big names, both popular and serious. It's also the major season for gift books, for cookery books and for celebrity-led titles. From the debut author's point of view, Christmas is both tempting and dangerous. It's tempting, because a Christmas best-seller may well sell more copies than a best-seller at any other time of year. It's dangerous, because perfectly good books can tumble beneath the celebrity and big-name steam-roller and be splatted from sight.

Summer, on the other hand, is the season of paperbacks, of beach reads, of popular fiction. Because sales are strong in summer, that's also the period when big-name authors are most likely to release their paperbacks, thereby potentially crowding out lesser names.

It's common, therefore, for debut authors to be launched at a time when competition is thinnest, anywhere from January to April, for example. Again, however, different publishers will have different approaches. That may partly be down to different sales strategies. It may also be because of varying access to retail space. If, for example, a particular publisher is confident that they can get you on to the shelves of a major supermarket in August, that would be a strong incentive for them to launch you then. A different publisher with a different publishing schedule and a different set of retail relationships may want to launch at some other point.

Again, the more you understand about what your publisher is doing and why they're doing it, the more you'll be in a position to assess which of two rival strategies makes more sense to you. Yours is never going to be an expert verdict, but it will be *your* verdict and therefore one that you'll be able to live with more comfortably, come what may.

Do also note that lead-times in publishing can be weirdly long. A publisher will want at least six months in which to sell the book into the trade. So, if you strike a deal today, then the absolute earliest you'll see a book on the shelves is in six months' time. If your book is red-hot topical – let's say, it's a biography of a major celebrity who has just (and, I hope, coincidentally) died – then perhaps a publisher will rush it out sooner. But red-hot topical does mean just that. If Iran happens to be in the news at the moment, and your book is a memoir of your Iranian childhood, then that is not red-hot topical, nor even close. For nearly all books, that six-month lead-time will be sacrosanct.

What's more, six months is the shortest time that it takes to launch a book. I sold my first novel one October. The publisher wanted an early spring launch, in order to ensure maximum paperback sales potential. Since we'd already missed the catalogue for the spring coming, we had to wait another full year – that is, a full seventeen months from striking an agreement. That's on the longer end of things, but it's not extreme. It's as well to know these things in advance, as it'll allow you to assess the publisher's commentary about launch strategy with something like calmness and intelligence.

TITLE AND DESIGNS

I've talked a little about titles in an earlier section, in particular drawing attention to the way that they're liable to change rapidly. Nevertheless, it's well worth ensuring that you know what your potential publisher's thoughts on titles are. If they like your title, all well and good. You'll presumably be happy with that. If they want to change it, then what they want to change it to may tell you a lot about how they're thinking of packaging and selling your book.

For example, I once worked with a client whose excellent memoir told the story of his life as a teenager in a British reform school of the late 1950s. Reform schools were for criminal youths. They were tough, aggressive places, and my client (who had, in fact, done nothing criminal to start with) was forced to become tough and aggressive himself in order to survive. The book was hard, masculine and full of fighting and foul language. Its original title was *Dead Before Christmas*, the phrase deriving from a threat made to the author when he first arrived at the school. There's no question that the title suited and accurately summarised the book's content.

However, the publisher who bought his work decided that they would sell his work as a misery memoir. Since such memoirs have an almost universal cover design – soft pastel images of sweet children with large, appealing eyes – the publisher decided against doing anything radical with this one. Since *Dead Before Christmas* sounded too tough for the kind of cover they intended to use, the publisher altered the title to the pleading *Please Don't Make Me Go*. The cover image showed a small boy – much younger than the author was in the period covered by the memoir – staring out with the compulsory large, appealing eyes. The new title and cover design made an absolute nonsense of the book's content.

Now I don't tell this story as a warning. The fact is that the book leapt onto the non-fiction best-seller charts and stayed there for weeks. But I do say that knowing the kind of titles your publisher is thinking about will tell you a huge amount about how they are thinking of marketing your book. If you're talking to two different publishers and they have different approaches to the title, then be very alert to those differences. They won't be casual; they'll be highly significant as to the entire marketing posture with regard to your book. You may well have views on which stance best captures what you have to say. You may well have views on which position will generate the higher sales. In almost every case, if there's a conflict between the two, you'd be well advised to go with the higher sales.

The issues are rather similar when it comes to cover design. At this stage, there won't be a cover design developed for your book, so it doesn't make sense to ask to see one. But you can and probably should ask to see any comparable titles that the publisher has produced. The books that they pull out to show you will almost certainly tell you a lot about how they see your own title. What's more, even if they can't show you a precise cover image, they probably will be able to say something about the kind of design they have in mind. Although those ideas will always be presented as the very sketchiest of all sketchy thoughts, the truth is that those sketchy initial ideas have a habit of turning into fact, so again, if you don't like what you hear, then now's the time to find out.

MARKETING AND PR

You may also want to raise the subject of marketing and PR, but, if you do, then do so with low expectations. As we'll see further in a later section, marketing budgets have largely been eaten by retailers, who in turn have largely given away their extra revenues in the form of discounts to their customers. The result is that publishers these days have almost no cash left with which to market a book. If your potential publishers do sketch out any significant marketing plans, take careful note of them. If they say nothing, then feel free to ask, but do so gently. Most likely you'll just be told (truthfully enough) that somebody just ate their wallet.

On the PR front, things are a little different. A good publicity campaign can achieve widespread coverage of your book at relatively low cost to the publisher. Column inches of editorial matter are also worth two or three times the same number of column inches of advertisement, so publicity is quite likely more efficacious too. On the other hand, although you should certainly feel free to talk about PR (and you will probably be introduced to your future publicist at this initial meeting), there won't yet be much to say. The publisher will have a firm commitment to rustle as much publicity for you as they ever possibly can. At the same time, they are months away from launching that campaign and will have little or nothing to say in detail about it now. So feel free to ask. By all means, try to get some feel for your publicist, and whether you could work with them. But don't expect anyone to have a detailed plan of action. It's way too early for that.

CHEMISTRY

So far, this section has been all coldly rational about things. That's all well and good, but rationality alone misses the crucial element of chemistry.

Do you get on with your editor? Do you like your publicist? Do you feel they liked your work and understood it and genuinely meshed with some of its deeper themes?

If you meet two different groups of publishers and you come away entranced by one bunch and feeling solidly businesslike but un-elated about the second, then you will almost certainly go with the first. Both with my

A TOUGH WORLD OUT THERE

I don't want to be a killjoy, but it's a tough world out there and I believe the easiest part of a book (if you have the talent!) is writing it. The most difficult part is selling it, first to your agent/publisher and then to your public. You could go internet only but most authors will want to see their books in the shops, so you do need a middle-man. These middle-men are independents, supermarkets, Waterstone's, WH Smith and Amazon, and they are all hungry for profit. These middle-men are tough people, but if they don't buy it what chance is there of your public ever seeing it? A glorious review is nothing if the book is invisible.

The independents score on knowing their stock, giving service, having attention to detail and putting their customer first. They acquire a large amount of their stock through wholesalers, a 'middle' middle-man, and they need to know, or at least feel, that your book is good. These independent booksellers are your friends, but there are only some 1300-odd of them, so you'll need to reach well beyond them in order to succeed.

The rest of these middle-men I will lump together under the heading of 'central buyers'. These retailers want to know that your book is good, but their main concern is profit. Let the publisher invest in your future and nurture an author they believe in. All these retailers believe in is their bottom line and, if the book doesn't work, they can return their unsold stock.

Consider, for a moment, the supermarkets and WH Smith. Their buyers are retailers. Last year your book buyer may have been buying stationery or toys. To climb the management ladder, they may soon be chief buyer of DVDs or cards, so they need to screw the best deal they can. Is your book any better than the next? Does it matter? No. They have a display that needs a certain number of new titles, yet many more titles than that are being produced. What to choose and why? Discounts, deals, marketing spend, cover artwork, topicality, media exposure and the price of the display area, that's what makes their decision. They may believe they like to support authors but they actually rely on past records. What did that author do last year?

Much the same philosophy occurs in Waterstone's and Amazon too. (New authors score on this front, by the way: no track record can be a positive.) It's all down to your publisher's enthusiasm and spend. Your book may be better than X's, but is your deal better? Getting it published is one hurdle, getting it sold (the publisher's responsibility) is a much larger hurdle. Be satisfied, if necessary, with a slow sales climb and trust your publisher. In a tough marketplace they know how to do it.

SARAH BROADHURST
has long written the 'Paperback Preview' column for the *Bookseller*
and also selects fiction for lovereading.co.uk, a site for booklovers.

own work, and when acting as agent for a number of my clients, I've observed that chemistry trumps rationality every time. Or, perhaps more accurately, I've noticed that chemistry just gets to the right answer quicker than rationality can.

It is worth ploughing through all the previous headings in this section – if only because you need to have something to talk about at your meeting and you may as well be talking about stuff that matters. Also, if you get on well while talking seriously about the publication of your book, then that's a much more significant omen of success than it would be if you were just chatting and wondering how much Stilton you're expected to eat.

DECISIONS

Once you've met your two possible publishers, sit down with your agent, talk it over and make a decision. You don't absolutely have to make a decision that same day or the next one, but the truth is that you've probably made up your mind already. Take a deep breath and say yes to the publisher you liked the best. It's now time to sort out money and sort out a contract. It's to those happy topics we now turn.

ADVANCES, RIGHTS AND ROYALTIES

There is a good argument to suggest that you don't really need to worry yourself too much about advances, rights and royalties. If you have an agent, then your agent will negotiate these things on your behalf. They know what they're doing. Their interest is in line with yours. Just let them go to it. Quite apart from anything else, if you've achieved some kind of auction process, the auction will have flushed out the best price the market is willing to pay for your work. If no auction was achieved, you are not in the strongest possible negotiating position, so you'll just need to take the best you or your agent can manage to achieve.

If your book is a smaller title and you therefore don't have an agent to represent you, then the sums of money involved are likely to be small enough that you don't need to bother very much either. Perhaps sometimes you might be offered an advance of £1,000 when you might, if you were pushy, be able to force that to £1,500 – in which case, negotiate as hard as you feel you want to. For the huge majority of authors at this end of the market, the issue isn't the money, but getting your work into print. If that's the case, then don't get too hung up on commercial details. Remember that what matters most is working effectively with your publisher to maximise sales. And, for smaller titles and with smaller publishers, you may not be offered an advance at all. A book deal struck on the basis of a zero advance and an acceptable level of royalties may well represent a fair balance between your commercial interests and your publishers.

(Just to be clear, however, a zero advance is very different from a negative advance. If you are asked for money upfront – by way of 'author contribution', 'subsidy publishing', to defray 'production costs' or anything else – then you are not being offered a commercial deal. What you have in front of you is just one more variant of vanity publishing. That may, in fact, be the right way forward for your work, but, if so, it's something you should only do with your eyes open. A later section deals with the whole set of issues involved in self-publishing.)

Overall, therefore, few authors will really need to stress about the matters in either this section or the next. Big book deals should be handled via agents, who will effectively look after your interests. In smaller book deals, the sums of money are generally so small that you just don't need to worry too much. If you think you may have a large book deal in front of you and you *don't* yet have an agent for any reason, then get one now. If you have an offer from a mainstream publisher, then getting an agent will be simple, since agents will be confident that you are a money-making prospect for them.

Having said all that, however, this section will guide you through the main financial elements that make up a book deal. That way, when your agent starts talking about serial rights, you won't be tempted to say, 'er . . . Kelloggs?'

THE ADVANCE

Authors' advances are the bit of a book deal that get the most media coverage. It's the only element which is guaranteed, and for that reason is the most important. I've made a good living as an author, because I've always achieved high advances for my books. The subsequent sales of those books have often been disappointing, sometimes because of sloppy publishing, sometimes because of outrageous bad luck – and once or twice, perhaps, because my books weren't as good as they should have been. Nevertheless, if I'd been forced to subsist on royalties only, I'd have had some fat and happy years, but other years when I'd have been reduced to eating the bark off trees. If you want to avoid a year or two of grazing bark (and if, of course, your book is the sort of thing that could plausibly attract a significant advance), then you need to do all you can to achieve a good offer. That's your agent's job, not yours, but it's worth knowing a little about what he is up to and what any outcome means.

First, you need to understand what an advance is. Crucially, it's yours. It's not refundable. It's your money to keep even if the book sinks like a stone. (Assuming that you've delivered the manuscript, of course. If you are commissioned to write a book and then never deliver it, you will be asked to refund any advance you've received, and quite right too.)

On the other hand, you don't get the advance *as well as* royalties; you get it by way of an advance *against* royalties. We'll deal with this subject in plenty of detail in just a moment, but for now think of them as a payment made for each book sold. Let's say, for example, you get 50p per paperback copy sold. Let's also say that your advance amounts to a pleasantly healthy £10,000. In order to receive one single penny in royalties over and above that advance, you have to sell enough books to completely cover the £10,000. In this example, you'd need to sell 20,000 copies of your paperback, earning 50p on each one, and thereby clearing your advance of £10,000. If you go on to sell even more copies of that selfsame book, then and only then do you receive a single penny of royalties. In this situation, you are said to have 'earned out' your advance, and you are quite likely to have a very happy publisher.

On the other hand, earning out isn't everything. Back in the good old days of publishing, when lunches were long and very liquid, authors didn't expect much by way of advance. They expected to receive payment largely by way of royalty. As literary agents started to come on the scene, however, they drove advances up and up, to the point now where it is perfectly common for a decently successful author never to see a royalty cheque at all. Indeed, one agent told me that, if ever a royalty cheque crossed her desk, she regarded it almost as a sign of failure: an indication that she hadn't forced the bidding high enough in the first place. That may, perhaps, have been rhetorical overstatement, but the point remains sound. When you agree a contract with a publisher, your advance is a known amount. That's the least you will get paid. It's also, in all likelihood, the most. So don't go crazy imagining a future of fat advances followed by plentiful royalties. That's not likely to happen. Usually, it's one or the other, seldom both.

It's also worth knowing that you don't get the advance all at once. It's normally sliced into chunks and fed to you piece by piece. The normal pattern for mainstream fiction and non-fiction is as follows:

25% payable on signature of the contract;
25% payable on delivery and acceptance of the manuscript;
25% payable on 'first' publication (normally the hardback version);
25% payable on 'second' publication (normally the paperback).

Some of the time, of course, these events coincide. If you are selling a novel, for example, you won't get an agent or a book deal until your manuscript is complete and polished. The signature of the contract will therefore take place simultaneously with the acceptance of the manuscript, so you'll get both chunks of money at the same time (or the contract will dole out the money in equal thirds, instead). Equally, if you are being launched straight into paperback, the first and second publication will take place at the same time, so the last two payments will also come simultaneously. The exact payment pattern will vary, so do check your particular contract for the schedule of payments.

Do also note that occasionally publication schedules will slip wildly for reasons that have nothing to do with you. If that does happen to you, and you find yourself short of cash that you had legitimately expected to receive, talk to your agent or your editor. Your publisher may well be happy to make the payment earlier than strictly required by the contract. Certainly, rather than get into financial distress, you should feel free to ask about these things. If people can help, they probably will.

It's also worth noting that the above delivery schedule will apply to most novels and to most non-fiction aimed at a broad audience. If you are writing a much narrower type of non-fiction – like this book, for example – you are quite likely to receive your money in just two chunks, the first on signature of the contract, the second on delivery of the manuscript. This rather simpler arrangement has the happy effect that, once you have done your work, you get paid for it. Because of the delays between delivery and hardback/paperback publication, it's not uncommon for authors of more popular work to wait two years or more to receive their advance in full.

ROYALTIES – THE DUMMIES' VERSION

The whole business of royalties can get very complex very quickly, so we'll start with a simple version that nevertheless tells you at least 90% of what you need to know. Royalties are either paid as a percentage of the published price, or a percentage of the price received by the publishers, termed 'net receipts'. Net receipts are the revenues received by the publisher after sales at discount to booksellers and distributors, so they take into account the wide variety of discounts and make no assumptions about price in a post-Net Book Agreement age where booksellers are at liberty to offer discounted pricing to the consumer. For certain areas of publishing, such as specialist non-fiction and academic publishing, net receipts are the norm.

In this simplified explanation, there are only a handful of royalty rates that matter: those for hardbacks and those for paperbacks. In both cases, the royalty rate itself may step up the more books you sell. As an example, fairly typical of the rates offered by mainstream publishers today (depending on the publisher and the type of book published), royalties could be as follows:

Hardback royalties
10% of published price for first 5,000 copies sold
12.5% of published price for next 5,000 copies sold
15% of published price for all copies after the first 10,000

Paperback royalties
7.5% of published price for first 30,000 copies sold
10% of published price thereafter

The more your book sells for by way of advance, the more an agent is likely to be able to push successfully for better royalties. Even then, however, it's more likely that you'll see a stepping down in the thresholds than an increase in the percentage rates offered. Thus, for example, an agent might be able to get that 10% paperback royalty rate to kick in from 15,000 copies rather than 30,000, if the manuscript involved was very strong.

If you are selling a niche manuscript to a niche publisher, then you shouldn't necessarily expect to see those higher royalty rates featured in your contract at all. That's not because the small publisher is making a fortune by ripping you off, it's more likely because nobody involved is going to make any real money on the deal and book sales are highly likely to be modest in any case. What's more, if your book (for example) is heavily illustrated, your royalties are likely to be lower and without any escalator element (that is, no additional percentages once certain thresholds have been met). Again, that's not because you're being ripped off, it's because the costings of these books are inevitably rather different.

It's useful for authors to understand how royalty rates translate into real money. So let's start with some assumptions. (Highly simplified ones, inevitably. We get to some of the complications in the next section.) Let's say your agent has won you a £30,000 advance. You have a royalty schedule like the one above. Your hardback sells at £15. Your paperback sells at £7. Let's say your book does tremendously well. You sell 8,000 hardbacks and 50,000 paperbacks. The royalty maths look like this:

First 5,000 hardbacks sold	5,000 @ £15 × 10%	£7,500
Next 3,000 hardbacks sold	3,000 @ £15 × 12.5%	5,625
First 30,000 paperbacks sold	30,000 @ £7 × 7.5%	15,750
Next 20,000 paperbacks sold	20,000 @ £7 × 10%	14,000
Grand total of royalties earned		42,875
Less: advance against royalties		(30,000)
Balance due to you		£12,875

You won't at any stage need to perform these calculations for yourself. They'll be made by your publisher, who will send you twice-yearly statements. Your agent, in principle, will check these things, though independent checks have shown publishers nearly always get them right anyway. In short, if you don't want to do the maths, then you won't need to. It's just good to have an approximate understanding of what the maths might look like. It's also perhaps worth noting that, for reasons known only to them, publishers have evolved a form of royalty statements almost wholly inscrutable to outsiders – a class which most certainly includes their authors. So, if you receive a royalty statement and are mostly baffled by it, you are not going to be alone in your puzzlement. If you want to ask your agent or editor about it, then do.

E-BOOK ROYALTIES

The first huge qualification to make regarding the above calculations has to do with e-books. In the past, authors made money from hardbacks and paperbacks. The level of those royalties has been determined by decades of negotiation and competitive pressure, and there's relatively little variation in the way they are determined. Clearly, however, the world is changing. In the future, it is widely expected that publishers will be making a significant proportion of their sales as e-books. Equally clearly, that emerging market has very different economics (because, for one thing, production costs are minimal) and will be sustained by a very different retail landscape (because the role of bricks-and-mortar sellers is likely to be more limited).

On the other hand, it's utterly unclear (at the time of writing, in January 2010) what this new market is likely to look like. In 2009, the Society of Authors called for e-book royalties to rise as high as 75% of the publishers' net receipts (in cases where the book has a well-established following). While the SoA was making this call, the prevailing level in the market was somewhere closer to 20–25%. Some publishers were seeking to push that rate down to 15%. I'm aware of at least one publisher whose standard terms offered just 10%.

And that's simply to focus on the relatively narrow question of how an author will get paid. Broader and more important questions also remain unanswered. The music industry suffered a major (and apparently permanent) revenue contraction following digitalisation, and well-known problems involving piracy. On the other hand, Hollywood appears to have benefited from digitalisation, as DVDs have proved to be a more attractive and commercially successful product than videotapes ever were. Will publishing be more like the music industry or more like the film industry? Nobody knows. My own guess – and it's no more than a guess – is that piracy will not prove to be as destructive to the books world as it was to the music world. We'll see.

For now, authors simply have to trust their agents to position them as strongly as they possibly can. If you don't have an agent, then take advice from the Society of Authors. As long as you're as well positioned as you can be, given the state of play in the market at the time you're signing your contract, you've done all you can be expected to do.

ROYALTIES FOR ROCKET SCIENTISTS

If you don't want to know any more about royalties – well, you probably don't need to. Many authors never see a royalty cheque anyway (because, in more mainstream consumer markets, advances are often not earned out) and calculating these things is never going to be your task. Nevertheless, some people just like to know about these things, and, if so, this section is for you.

➢ *Export sales*
All the calculations above assume that your sales are 'home' sales: that is, sales made in the publisher's home market (typically English-language sales anywhere in the EU). Your publisher will, however, also be selling your book abroad, in which case your royalty will be payable not on the published price of your book, but on the price received or 'net receipts' by your publisher.

That might sound sensible, if MegaCorp (UK) Ltd is selling to the independent Kiwis'R'Us Publishing (NZ) Ltd; but the larger publishers are highly international concerns, so mostly you'll find that MegaCorp (UK)

Ltd has just sold your book to MegaCorp (NZ) Ltd. Although it may seem unfair to see in some cases a 50% reduction in your royalty just because your book is being sold by a different arm of the same organisation, the truth is that there are additional costs for any publisher in selling books into a new market, so some royalty reduction certainly makes sense, whatever. In any case, this is not an area where you will be able to effect much change, or one that is likely to make much difference to you either.

➤ *Deep discounts*

The good news about supermarkets and 'pile-'em-high' booksellers is that they sell a lot of books. The bad news is that they drive a hard bargain with publishers, and you will find yourself being squeezed as a result.

The system operates via a set of 'deep discount' royalty reductions. Thus, if your publisher sells a £7 book to an independent family-run bookshop, they might be selling that book at a price of £3.50. The bookshop makes a profit of £3.50 when they sell the book. The publisher has made their money. Everyone's happy. But a supermarket, for example, might want to sell the selfsame book at a price of just £5.00. The supermarket can't make money if they're paying £3.50 for the book, so they'll insist on paying no more than (say) £2.80 for it. Where the independent shop bought the book at a 50% discount to the published price, the supermarket is buying it at a 60% discount. A fairly standard set of 'deep discount' royalty reductions might be as follows:

Type of book	Discount	Royalty payable reduction
Hardbacks	at a discount of 52½ to 57½%	⅘ of prevailing rate;
	at a discount of 57½ to 62½%	⅗ of prevailing rate;
	at a discount of more than 62½%	10% of price received
C-format pb	at a discount of 52½ to 57½%	⅘ of prevailing rate;
	at a discount of 57½ to 62½%	⅗ of prevailing rate;
	at a discount of more than 62½%	10% of price received
Mass-market pb	at a discount of 55 to 60%	⅘ of prevailing rate;
	at a discount of 60 to 65%	⅗ of prevailing rate;
	at a discount of more than 65%	10% of price received

These reductions can eat a long way into your royalty payment. A regular 7.5% published price royalty payable on a £6.99 paperback gives you slightly more than 50p per book sold. That same book sold through a supermarket at a discount (to the supermarket) of 65% on the cover price will yield you just over 31p. Nevertheless, as your agent and publisher will certainly tell you, supermarkets can do so much to expand your readership that it's a foolish author who worries about the decline in per-book royalties. On the contrary, you should be absolutely delighted at the sales and the exposure that comes from access to such a huge volume of potential readers.

➤ *Other royalties*

The royalties we've discussed so far apply to books printed and sold in the regular way, but not all books are sold in this way. Book clubs, though much reduced now compared with their days of glory, still buy significant volumes of books to be sold on, at low prices, to their members. Because book clubs don't pay much to the publisher for each book purchased, you will get 10% of the price per book received by the publisher. So if the books are sold at a discount of 70% to the bookclub, you would get just 10% of the publisher's 30% of the cover price – or about 20p per copy. Although even quite large book-club deals won't bring you much revenue, they bring in some and they get your book into the hands of more readers than could otherwise be the case.

The same kind of logic applies to other non-standard forms of book-selling. You'll get about 20% of the price received by a publisher on the sale of e-books, to be read via Amazon's Kindle, the Sony Reader, Apple iPad or whatever other devices that are currently en route to market. Because the technology and the market is moving rapidly here, there's no fixed consensus on what the appropriate payment to the author should be. Agents are trying to hold the line at 20–25%. As with most things royalty related, just trust your agent to know the current state of play and to get the best deal possible for you.

With audio books, sold in the form of cassette or CD, you should expect to get around 10% of the price received by the publisher. For audio books sold through digital downloads, you can expect to get about 15%.

RIGHTS

We've dealt thus far with advances and royalties. There is one third ingredient of your income as a writer which deserves mention, namely sales of rights. Though technically in a different category, rights sales operate rather similarly to royalties, so this section will be brief. As before, the main point to remember is that any 'income' you achieve by rights sales will be set against your advance. Since most advances are never earned out, what follows is more likely than not to be somewhat theoretical.

The rights that are most commonly sold are 'serial' rights. Typically, for example, a newspaper might pay £2,000 or £3,000 for the exclusive right to print a chunk of an upcoming non-fiction work, normally around two or three weeks in advance of publication. An author would typically expect to earn 90% of the proceeds of that 'first serial rights' sale. If a second serialisation deal happens (which is much less common), the author's share typically falls to more like 75%.

If a publisher has bought world rights to your MS, you would also expect the lion's share of any proceeds derived from its sale overseas – typically 80% of USA rights and 80% of translation rights.

For most other rights sales – radio reading and other audio, anthology and quotation, large-print, educational and a whole host of other curios – you should expect to divide proceeds about 50/50 with your publisher. You may well prefer not to sell your publisher rights to sell your MS to the film and TV industries, preferring to retain these rights for yourself, but, if you do grant these rights to the publisher, you would normally expect about 75% of any net proceeds. More of film rights in another section.

IF YOU DON'T HAVE AN AGENT

If you don't have an agent, then the advice given at the start of this section – don't worry about any of this; your agent will handle it for you – may strike you as somewhat less than satisfactory. As a broad rule of thumb, however, if you are offered terms broadly in line with the terms outlined in this section, then your publisher is offering you a perfectly fair deal. If you can squeeze things higher, by all means do so. If you can't, at least you tried. Some small publishers operate on budgets so minuscule, and are driven so much more by passion than by money, it would hardly be reasonable to mind if they do end up offering terms worse than those set out in this section.

VARIANTS

Do note that this section approximately conveys the state of play in the market at the time of writing for a typical deal with a mainstream consumer publisher for a mainstream fiction or non-fiction work. Every book deal, however, is different. The market changes rapidly. Different publishers have to respond to different pressures. As the retail climate alters, the prevailing level of royalties will change too. If you are being offered terms worse than those laid out in this section, you should certainly feel free to talk to your agent or publisher about those terms. But don't do so aggressively or with any conviction that you are being treated in bad faith. You probably aren't.

THE SOCIETY OF AUTHORS

Finally, if in any doubt about anything in this section or the next, most particularly if you don't have an agent, you should become a signed-up member of the Society of Authors, something you can only do when you have been offered a commercial book deal. The annual membership fee is £90, with a reduced fee (for the poor and youthful) of £64. The Society will give you free, expert and supportive advice on any publishing contract. They are also a trade union representing and standing up for authors. It's a force for good, so it's an outfit well worth supporting no matter whether or not you have an immediate need for their services. If you do get into any difficulties with your publisher, and your agent is either uninterested or useless, then the Society of Authors is your best and surest protection. If you weren't a member when the problem arose, then you won't be covered by their umbrella. So sign up.

YOUR PUBLISHING CONTRACT

When I first received a publishing contract, I read it through and asked my agent about anything I didn't understand. She was surprised, telling me that as far as she knew no authors ever bothered to read a word of the document before signing it. You could, I suppose, argue that authors are perfectly right to be this little bothered by what they sign. After all, their agents will have negotiated the best possible terms they can and the contract itself mostly represents a record of good sense and standard industry practice.

I don't personally advocate quite such a laid-back attitude. You are entering into a major commitment and a long-term contractual relationship. The contract may look about as appealing to read as an insurance document cross-bred with a tax return, but it's only a few pages of fairly ordinary English sentences and you are a writer, after all. You're allowed to be terrified of numbers, but this is only words. Furthermore, by entering into a contract with a publisher, you aren't just agreeing to sell your manuscript, you are also making a number of further undertakings that you will need to abide by. It's easier to do that if you know what they are.

UPS AND DOWNS OF SURVIVING AS AN AUTHOR

In this excellent book, Harry Bingham draws on his wide experience as a professional writer to give a vivid insight into the ups and downs of surviving as an author. There are many rewards, but a gushing flow of royalties is seldom one of them. With the book market in a fragile state, it is tempting to grumble; getting published is not easy and staying published can be even more problematic, as many mid-list authors are finding. Even the most patient authors at times find their dealings with publishers exasperating. Yet for most authors their writing remains a compulsive and pleasurable addiction.

Even in tough times publishers need new books. As Doris Lessing wrote in our journal, The Author, *'It does no harm to repeat, as often as you can "Without me the literary industry would not exist: the publishers, the agents, the accountants, the libel lawyers, the departments of literature, the books of criticism, the reviewers, the book pages – all this vast and proliferating edifice because of this small, patronised, put-down and underpaid person".'*

You will gather that the Society is pleased to help members by giving detailed advice on contracts: with publishers, agents, broadcasters, film companies and theatres. Conscious that writers spend much of their time alone and that a few nagging worries can sometimes become all-consuming, we aim to be able to answer queries on almost any business aspect of the profession quickly and sympathetically. One of the pleasures of working at the Society of Authors is we can never anticipate who is going to be in touch or the nature of the enquiry. The general areas that we cover include, for example, contractual issues with publishers (occasionally with agents), fees for talks, avoiding copyright infringement, minimising libel risks, saving tax and clarifying royalty figures.

The Society lobbies the government and the book trade on behalf of the profession (e.g. over the funding of Public Lending Right or royalties on e-books). We also administer many prizes and grants for writers. But the heart of our work remains giving individual advice to members on any business or legal query. You can find out more at www.societyofauthors.org.

MARK LE FANU
General Secretary of the Society of Authors

ANATOMY OF A CONTRACT

Fortunately, it's not that hard to predict what your contract will look like. It'll look rather like the one set out in the rest of this section. That's partly because each contract deals with broadly the same set of rights, obligations and contingencies, partly because publishers have, over the decades, come to adopt a largely common approach to dealing with them. If you have an agent, then it's likely that your agent will have negotiated a template or 'boiler-plate' contract with your publisher to cover all relationships between the two firms. That template will then simply be modified to reflect the particular terms and needs of your deal. The potential list of variations is too long to go into here. The contract below relates to a deal for a single book without illustrations, without quotations of other people's work or other potential complexities. For highly illustrated work, the terms offered are likely to be less generous than in the example below, simply because the writer's role is relatively smaller and the costs of production are significantly higher.

THE TWO-BOOK DEAL

Of these other possible complexities, the only one likely to affect most readers of this book will be the two-book deal. If you are selling a novel, or a certain type of mainstream non-fiction, publishers nearly always make an offer for two books rather than one. In a standard two-book deal, you'll sell (let's say) the novel that you've already written and you'll agree to write a further manuscript under the same terms and conditions. You'll have plenty of time to write that second manuscript, though the days of infinitely elastic deadlines are probably drawing to their close. Do check to see what dead-line your publisher is proposing for delivery of the second manuscript and be sure that you're comfortable meeting it. If you think you may need more time, then ask. On the whole, publishers are more than happy to grant plenty of time; it's just that they're apt to get snappish when agreed deadlines are blithely ignored.

(It can work the other way, mind you. I once met a novelist who had no idea that she should expect to get a two-book deal. When her agent secured just that, she was terrified. She was due to meet her publisher in two weeks' time and she had written just the one novel. She felt like a naughty schoolchild, who'd failed to do her homework. Nothing fazed, she took a fortnight off work and wrote fourteen hours a day, so that, when she met her publishers, she was able to deliver not one manuscript but two. The agent and publisher were astonished – as was I, when I heard the tale.)

While still on the two-book theme, do also note that your second manuscript needs to be something like the first. If you sell a wonderful, upbeat chick-litty romance to a publisher, then don't come to them with some literary novella about suicidal Frenchmen by way of your second offering. What they will want is another wonderful, upbeat chick-litty romance. For now you are only an author. Your publisher is trying to turn you into a brand. Don't make that task any harder than it already is. If you want to write gloomy existential fiction as well, then feel free to write away. Just use a pen name and sign a different deal with a different publisher.

TWO FINAL COMMENTS . . .

Two final comments before we get to the contract itself.

The first is that, despite the essential sameness of nearly all publishing contracts, it can take an uncannily long time to produce them. It's not uncommon for it to take three months from agreeing a deal to signing the contract for it. Given that the principal terms of the deal have already been agreed, and given that standard form ('boilerplate') contracts already exist between all major agencies and the major publishers, it's not quite clear to me why these things take as long as they do.

Nevertheless, they do take time and you need to adjust your expectations accordingly. What's more, protracted contract negotiations are only very seldom a sign that there's something radically amiss. I've never heard of a publisher offering a deal and then withdrawing it, unless there were some genuinely exceptional circumstances involved. In other words, if you're offered a deal, you can rely on it, even without proper documentation. And the reason why publishers take their time is partly that they have other things to do and sorting out your contract isn't their top priority. If you really want to accelerate things, then by all means seek to chivvy things along by talking to your agent and editor – though you should keep your expectations about the likely impact of the chivvying set fairly low.

Finally, before we consider the contract detail itself, let me repeat the advice with which I closed the last section. If you want a career as a professional author, then I would strongly advise you to become a member of the Society of Authors. Your agent is your first line of defence, but agents can die, move, retire, go mad, get drunk, fall ill, lose their wits, find God, go gaga, have visions – or, in short, be afflicted with any or all of the disorders which routinely affect agent-kind. Your only certain refuge in this vale of tears is the Society of Authors. It costs you £90 a year and you feel all authorly every quarter when you get their magazine. They also offer free, intelligent advice on any publishing contract you ever sign.

A SAMPLE CONTRACT

While every contract is different, they do have a lot of similarities. This one is for a sale of world rights. The contract text is in roman lettering below. My comments are italicised and follow each paragraph. I've avoided one or two possible minor complexities in what follows, so don't be surprised if the contract placed in front of you has one or two wrinkles over and above what follows.

Also, just to be clear, this contract is an amalagmation of various different contracts, sourced from various different publishers. It is *not* the standard contract offered by the publisher of this work (A & C Black), nor by the group (Bloomsbury) which owns A & C Black – nor, indeed, is it the standard contract of anyone else at all. It's a representative mixture, that's all. The contract that is placed in front of you for your signature is therefore likely to differ from the one below in a variety of material respects, and the only way you can determine what those respects are is to read carefully the document in front of you.

MEMORANDUM OF AGREEMENT

made this — day of —— 20— between William Shakespeare, c/o A Literary Agency, London (hereinafter called the 'Author' which expression shall where the context admits include the Author's executors administration and assigns) and Megacorp Publishing PLC of Megacorp Square, London (hereinafter called the 'Publishers' which expression shall where the context admits include the Publishers' successors in business and assigns and any imprint of Megacorp Publishing PLC whether under its present or future style) whereby it is mutually agreed as follows respecting a work by the Author at present entitled *Romeo and Juliet* (hereinafter called 'the said work')

> *The preamble identifies the two contractual counterparties, namely you and the publisher. Although you will (assuming you have an agent) always be 'care of' your agency, your agent is not a party to this transaction. The date of the contract will only appear once it's been signed by all parties. The bit about executors and assigns (in the clause that relates to you) means that your heirs will continue to benefit from the contract, even if you are knocked over by a bus.*

The bit about successors in business and assigns means that, if your publisher is bought up by someone else, or changes their legal structure in some other way, the resultant entity will still be bound by the contract.

1. The Author hereby grants to the Publishers during the legal term of copyright the sole and exclusive licence to publish the said work in volume form in all languages throughout the World subject to the conditions following.

This is it! You are selling your book. This is the clause that hands over the rights in your manuscript to the Publisher. Copyright protection in the UK lasts for the duration of the author's life plus the first seventy years thereafter. The rules in the US are somewhat more complex, but share the same broad principles.

2. The Author hereby warrants to the Publishers:

i. that he has full power to make this Agreement,

ii. that he is the sole author of the said work and is the owner of the rights herein granted,

iii. that the said work is original to him and has not previously been published in volume form in the exclusive territories covered by this Agreement,

iv. that the said work is in no way whatever a violation or infringement of any copyright or licence,

v. that all necessary permissions for the use in volume or serial form of all copyright material quoted in the said work have been granted and any fees payable to copyright owners have been or will be paid by the Author,

vi. that the said work contains nothing obscene, blasphemous, unlawful, defamatory or libellous,

vii. that the said work contains nothing which has been obtained in violation of the Regulation of Investigatory Powers Act 2000, the Data Protection Act 1998, or the Official Secrets Act 1989,

viii. that all statements contained therein as purported facts are true,

ix. that any recipe, formulae or instructions in the work, if followed accurately, will not injure the user or any other person, and

x. that the work does not breach any right of privacy nor any duty of confidence.

Your excitement at para 1 is likely to dissipate rapidly on encountering para 2 (which often appears much later in the contract). Sections i to v above are saying that you are the author of the book (you haven't nicked it from anyone else and have secured whatever permissions are required). You also need to confirm Sections vi to x above that the material is lawful in various other respects. Most authors will find it easy to make the warranties listed above. Some will need to pause for rather deeper consideration – and may need to peruse the section on libel in this book with some care. You do need to read the above paragraph, and, if you have any hesitations about any part of it, then ask. You may get into hot water if you don't.

Do also note that (in books that make extensive use of quotations from copyright material) most authors will not *have solicited all the permissions required before signing this contract. Indeed, it's hard to obtain a permission without a book deal in your pocket, because those whose job it is to hand out permissions always ask about publishers, publication dates, print runs and the like. Nevertheless, as long as you obtain all permissions in good time, it doesn't really matter to anyone whether you have them at this point or not. If your work is an illustrated one, it may be that the publisher will pick up the costs for clearing permissions. A publisher also often picks up the costs of indexing the work, should this be required.*

Likewise, the requirement in the contract that 'all statements contained [in the book] as purported facts are true' *needn't bother you too much either. It is, in fact, extremely difficult to produce a book-length work of non-fiction and to make no factual errors whatsoever. But, if you get the big things right – and especially the things that may verge on the defamatory – then you should be OK. The publishers are highly unlikely to suffer any financial loss from a few minor errors of fact, which means that any liability you have to them will remain only theoretical.*

The Author hereby agrees to indemnify the Publishers against all actions, proceedings, claims, demands, losses, damages and costs (including any legal costs or expenses (and VAT attributable thereto)) properly incurred and any compensation, cost disbursements, and VAT paid by the Publishers on the advice of their legal advisers to comprise or settle any claim (provided that the Author has been consulted by the Publishers) in consequence of any breach (or alleged breach) of this warranty or of any negligence on the part of the Author in the preparation of the said work. The Publishers reserve the right to insist that the Author alter the text of the said work in such a way as shall appear to the Publishers appropriate for the purpose of removing anything which on the advice of the Publishers' legal advisers is considered objectionable or likely to be actionable at law but any such alterations or removal shall not affect the Author's liability under this warranty and indemnity herein contained.

Should the said work become the subject of a complaint alleging libel, the decision of the Publishers as to whether or not to repudiate liability to contest an action if proceedings ensue or to settle the claim upon such terms as they may be advised shall be final and the Author shall have no grounds for action against the Publishers in respect of its implementation provided that the Author has been consulted.

The warranties and indemnities stated above shall survive the termination of this Agreement.

> *This is the scariest clause in the contract. You – little old you – get to idemnify Megacorp plc against any costs that it may incur as a result of libel action, or any other actual or putative breach of your undertakings in the first chunk of this paragraph. It doesn't matter whether the claim for libel (or anything else) is upheld in a court or not. Indeed, your publisher may choose to settle any claim, whether or not you want them to. The publisher's only obligation is to consult with you before they take action – they certainly don't have to take any notice of anything you may say during that consultation. And your publisher can then require you to pick up every single one of the costs, legal and other, that they've incurred in the process.*
>
> *Needless to say, under these conditions bankruptcy could very rapidly ensue, even if you are blameless, and it's hard to argue that this clause is genuinely fair to both parties. Nevertheless, the risks will be rather theoretical for most authors. You need not to have stolen your material from anyone else. You need to avoid libelling anyone. You need to avoid doing anything else that's stupid or wrong. And if you manage to do those things all right, you should be just fine.*

3. The Author has delivered the said work to the Publishers and the Publishers have accepted it.

> *This will be true for almost all first-time novelists and for many authors of non-fiction. If, however, you are obtaining a book deal on the back of a proposal, there will be language here requiring you to deliver a complete manuscript by a particular date – and you should get on and do just that. If you don't produce the material by the required date, or if the work you produce is of poor quality and the publisher rejects the work, then you risk having the work turned down*

for non-delivery or non-acceptance. So do your work properly and well, and do it on time. If you are having problems, then talk to your publisher. They would always rather know about problems well in advance.

4. The Publishers shall publish the said work within eighteen (18) months of the date of this Agreement unless prevented by circumstances over which they have no control or unless mutually agreed, and subject always to Clause 2.

Publishers can't not publish your book. The contract doesn't simply require that they pay you the agreed sums, but they do in fact get your work into print. It would be normal to see a deadline in the contract that allows for some slippage. So, if, for example, everyone is intending to see you published within 12 months, then the contract might use an 18-month deadline. It would be highly unusual for this deadline to be breached.

5. The Publishers shall pay to the Author

That is a beautiful word, is it not? The fourth one, I mean. Simple, precise and so sweet on the ear.

(a) The following royalties:

(i) on a hardcover edition published under the Publishers' own imprint:

HOME SALES: Ten per cent (10%) of the published price on the first three thousand (3,000) copies sold; twelve and a half per cent (12.5%) of the published price on the next three thousand (3,000) copies sold and fifteen per cent (15%) of the published price on all copies sold thereafter.

The section on royalties will explain this lot in more detail. Note that the level of royalties tends to ratchet up once a certain level of sales has been achieved. Hardbacks earn higher royalties for the author, both as absolute amounts and as a proportion of sales.

HIGH DISCOUNT SALES: On home sales where the discount is fifty-two and a half per cent (52.5%) or more, the royalty payable shall be four-fifths (⅘) of the prevailing royalty. On all hardcover home sales at a discount of sixty per cent (60%) or more, the above royalties shall be paid at a rate of three-fifths (⅗) of the prevailing royalty.

Again, see the section on royalties for more on this. When publishers have to reduce the wholesale price of books to lure retailers on board, authors have to share the pain of these discounts. Supermarkets typically drive a very hard bargain, so your royalty rates from supermarket sales will be lower – but your sales stats will be a darn sight better.

EXPORT SALES: Ten per cent (10%) of the price received by the Publishers on the first three thousand (3,000) copies sold; twelve and a half per cent (12.5%) of the price received by the Publishers on the next three thousand (3,000) copies sold and fifteen per cent (15%) of the price received by the Publishers on all copies sold thereafter.

You need to read the text carefully to make out what's going on here. When it comes to sales in your home market, you receive a royalty based on the recommended retail price (RRP) of your book. When it comes to export sales, you receive a royalty based on the publishers own net receipts – which may be half or less of that RRP. For this reason, it's a lot more profitable for you to sell a thousand copies of your book in your home market than it is for you to sell the same number overseas.

(ii) On mass-market paperback editions published under the Publishers' own imprint:

HOME SALES: Seven and a half per cent (7.5%) of the published price on the first twenty thousand (20,000) copies sold and ten per cent (10%) of the published price on all copies sold thereafter.

HIGH DISCOUNT SALES: At a discount of fifty-two and a half per cent (52.5%) or more, the royalty shall be four-fifths ($\frac{4}{5}$) of the prevailing royalty. On all paperback home sales at a discount of sixty per cent (60%) or more the above royalties shall be paid at a rate of three-fifths ($\frac{3}{5}$) of the prevailing royalty.

EXPORT SALES: Twelve and a half per cent (12.5%) of the price received on all copies sold.

See the comments under hardback royalties.

(iii) On trade paperback editions published under the Publishers' own imprint:

HOME SALES: If the Publishers' first edition, ten per cent (10%) of the published price on all copies sold. If not the Publishers' first edition, seven and a half per cent (7.5%) of the published price to ten thousand (10,000) copies sold, ten per cent (10%) of the published price thereafter.

HIGH DISCOUNT SALES: At a discount of fifty-two and a half per cent (52.5%) or more, the royalty shall be four-fifths ($\frac{4}{5}$) of the prevailing royalty. On all trade paperback home sales at a discount of sixty per cent (60%) or more, the above royalties shall be paid at a rate of three-fifths ($\frac{3}{5}$) of the prevailing royalty.

EXPORT SALES: Ten per cent (10%) of the price received to ten thousand (10,000) copies, twelve and a half per cent (12.5%) of the price received thereafter.

> *See the comments under hardback royalties. 'Trade paperbacks' is the slightly baffling term given to paperback books that are larger and more handsomely produced than ordinary mass-market works.*

(iv) On remainder sales: ten per cent (10%) of the sum received from the sale of any copies sold as a remainder, i.e. at less than two-fifths ($\frac{2}{5}$) of the published price and above cost. The Publishers shall give the Author an opportunity of purchasing some or all of the remainder copies at the remainder price such option to be exercised if at all within twenty-eight (28) days of notice being given to the Author of the Publishers' intention to remainder the said work. It is agreed that no remainder sales shall be made within twelve (12) months of first British publication. No royalty shall be paid on copies remaindered at or below cost.

> *But your books won't be remaindered, will they? If it comes to it, you'll be given the right to buy them up before they are.*

(v) On Publishers' e-book – the royalty to be mutually agreed.

An e-book will be the text of and any illustrations in the work in whole or in part in digitally accessible and/or electronic form for the purposes of reading/viewing. No enrichments shall be added without Author's consent. All terms to be reviewed two (2) years from first publication of the work.

> *A very hot topic in publishing right now, and that phrase 'royalty to be mutually agreed' is simply a sign that no one today knows what is a fair and sustainable royalty going forward. If you do see a number here, anything in the range of 20–25% is consistent with industry practice at the time of writing (January 2010), and anything lower than that is worth questioning. But these things are susceptible to rapid change – an unusual situation in an industry not known for rapid change. A wise agent will require that any e-book royalty*

arrangement is reviewed every two years or so, in order that you don't find yourself disadvantaged by rapid and unpredictable developments. 'Enrichments' is a nice phrase and it means all those add-ons that digital formats can provide – music, video, interviews, illustrations, interactive gaming, and who knows what else. Again, no one knows what a digital book might look like in three years' time, so the language is designed to provide plenty of flexibility. Many contracts, however, will simplify all these issues by simply agreeing an e-book royalty and fixing it into perpetuity. So long as that royalty is at a fair market rate at the time the contract is agreed, you don't have too much to worry about.

(vi) On Publishers' own Audio exploitation: use by the Publishers of the work in abridged audio form, physical version, a royalty of seven and a half per cent (7.5%) net receipts to 7,500 copies and ten per cent (10%) thereafter. On Audio Download, a royalty of 15% net receipts.

Audio books are a well-established format, so the royalty schedules here are better established. The ones here would be typical.

(vii) On the Publishers' large-print editions: ten per cent (10%) of the price received.

(viii) On the Publishers' educational editions: ten per cent (10%) of the price received.

(ix) On all sales of unbound sheets: ten per cent (10%) of the price received.

(x) On Sales Outside Normal Sales Channels: ten per cent (10%) of the price received.

Ditto, though the sums here are likely to be minor. 'Sales Outside Normal Sales Channels' includes such things as door-to-door sales, mail order, etc.

(b) An advance on account of all payments due to the Author under the terms of this Agreement of:

[£10,000] TO BE PAID AS FOLLOWS:

[£2,500] on signature of this Agreement by both parties

[£2,500] on delivery and acceptance of the said work

[£2,500] on first publication of the said work

[£2,500] on second publication of the said work

This is your advance — £10,000 in this example. Note that you don't get the advance plus royalties. You get the advance as an advance against royalties. So, if your book never accumulates enough sales to pay off your advance — and very many books never do — then you won't ever see a royalty cheque. The section on royalties explains more.

The schedule of payments here is typical of most novels and mainstream works of non-fiction that come out in hardback first. For more specialist non-fiction, you'd normally see a chunk of your money on signature and the balance on delivery. First publication generally means hardback publication; second publication — you guessed it — refers to the paperback edition.

6. In the event that the Publishers publish the work under the Megacorp imprint in the United States of America, they shall pay to the Author on sales of such American market edition(s):

(a) on hardback editions: ten per cent (10%) of the US catalogue price on the first 5,000 (five thousand) copies sold and twelve and a half per cent (12.5%) of the US catalogue price on all copies sold beyond the first ten thousand (10,000), and fifteen per cent (15%) thereafter;

(b) on paperback editions: seven and a half per cent (7.5%) of the US catalogue price on all copies sold;

(c) on copies sold outside the United States of America or outside normal trade channels or at a discount of fifty per cent (50%) or more or to book clubs at a price inclusive of royalty: ten per cent (10%) of the net amount actually received by the Publishers;

(d) on electronic books: twenty-five per cent (25%) net receipts.

You won't always see this clause — it's only here because this contract represents a sale of world rights, and this clause is here to ensure that Megacorp (UK) plc can't agree to publish the book via Megacorp (US) Inc except under agreed rates. Most authors will probably sell UK and Commonwealth rights to their book separately from the North American rights, in which case this clause becomes redundant.

7. The Publishers shall render statements showing royalties and all other monies due to 30th June and 31st December in each year after British publication within three (3) months of such dates and shall then pay all monies due to the Author, except that if the sum is less than fifty pounds (£50.00) they may hold it over until the following royalty period.

I'd love to know how long this clause has been standard in the industry. With modern technology, it would be simplicity itself for publishers to calculate royalty payments quarterly and make payments within 30 days of each quarter's end. But back in the good old days of high desks, coal fires and quill pens, these things took time and it's that Dickensian timetable which still operates today. So, royalties are calculated every six months, then paid within a further three months, meaning that it may take you as long as nine months to get your hands on your money.

The books of account of the Publishers so far as they relate to any matter arising out of this Agreement shall be open to inspection by the Author or the Author's duly authorised representatives by appointment at any reasonable time, and at the Author's expense. In the event that errors are found in excess of fifty pounds (£50.00) in the Publishers' favour, the cost of that investigation will be borne by the Publishers.

You have the right to audit your publisher's royalty accounting, though you are highly unlikely to want to do so. The Society of Authors makes regular random checks of publishers' accounting systems and finds that errors are in fact very rare. When errors do arise, however, they are more often than not in favour of the publisher, which suggests that there's room for a little improvement yet.

The Publishers shall have the right to set aside as a reserve against returns twenty per cent (20%) of any royalties earned on the Publishers' hardback edition of the said work and twenty-five per cent (25%) on a paperback edition and audio edition of the said work, and a reasonable reserve against returns for the US edition, as shown on the first royalty statement after publication or reissue and to withhold this sum up to the third royalty account thereafter, following which all monies due shall be credited to the Author's account at the time of the next royalty statement.

Publishers sell books to retailers on a sale or return basis. (Or rather, nearly all of them do. There are moves afoot to try to change that, but the system is so far resisting change.) As a result, selling books to a retailer doesn't necessarily mean that you've made a sale. It's perfectly possible for your publisher to get out (say) 10,000 books to retailers, then find that 5,000 of them come back again in due course. To handle this problem, publishers can make an allowance for possible returns against any royalty payments that would otherwise be due. That won't reduce the total amount of money that you receive, but it does alter the timing of when you get it.

8. The Publishers may with the consent of the Author grant licences in the said work and divide the gross sums received from the sub-licence as follows:

Book club:

(A) where the Publishers manufacture: ten per cent (10%) on a hardback edition and seven and a half per cent (7.5%) on a paperback edition of the Publishers' receipts to the Author.

	Author %	Publisher %
(B) Where the Book Club manufactures:	50%	50%
Condensation in volume form:	50	50
Large print:	50	50
Hardback reprint:	To be mutually agreed	
Paperback reprint:	To be mutually agreed	
Anthology and quotation:	50	50
One-shot periodical or newspaper rights:	50	50
Digest:	60	40
Straight Reading Rights:	75	25
Electronic/digital:	To be mutually agreed [*or often 50/50*]	
Braille and non-commercial recording:	50	50
First local serial rights:	90	10
Second local serial rights:	75	25
Translation:	80	20
Audio:	50	50

All monies received in respect of such sales and due to the Author (providing the advance due under 5(b) has been earned) shall be paid to the Author within thirty (30) days of receipt of such monies by the Publishers, except for sums of under one hundred pounds (£100.00), which would then be included in the next royalty account.

This clause deals with how proceeds from various other sources are divvied up between author and publisher. The proportions above are roughly representative of the market today (though, remember, every book and every deal will be different). Large-print rights relate to books printed in large text for the visually impaired. Braille rights are often given away gratis, so the shares here are often purely theoretical. First serial rights relate to any excerpts from your work published in a newspaper or periodical prior to publication of your book. Second serial rights relate to excerpts published after your book has appeared in print. Of all the rights in the paragraph above, the most commercially significant one is likely to be translation rights, where some quite large deals may be achievable. Remember that this contract makes a sale of world rights to a given publisher. Most deals won't sell everything in a single bundle, so it would be more common for you and your agent to retain translation rights at this stage, so that your agent can seek to sell them subsequently to different territories.

9. [The Publishers shall receive no shares of any monies received from the performance on sound radio or television of a play based on the said work either for a single performance or in instalments and it is further agreed that in the event of a motion picture or television film sale being made of the said work and on notification of such to the Publishers interest in any broadcasting or television rights in the said work shall automatically cease.]

You wouldn't normally sell film and TV rights to a publisher in the first instance, and this clause is just making that clear. The clause is in square brackets, however, as it's not really needed and often doesn't appear. It's not needed because the contract makes clear what rights are being sold. If you haven't sold a particular right – such as the TV and film rights – then the contract doesn't strictly speaking need to say anything further, though it's common to see words to the effect that 'rights not explicitly granted under this contract are reserved for the author'.

10. The Author shall receive on publication five (5) copies of the Publishers' hardback edition of the said work and ten (10) copies of any paperback edition published by the Publishers and shall be entitled to purchase further copies for personal use (but not for resale) at thirty-five per cent (35%) trade discount, such copies to be paid for on presentation of the Publishers' invoice. The Publishers shall send to the Author at least two (2) copies of any other edition of the work published by or under licence from the Publishers. The Publishers shall supply the Agent with two (2) presentation copies of the Publishers' hardback edition and five (5) copies of any paperback edition published by the publisher and two (2) presentation copies of any other edition of the work published by or under licence from the Publishers. The Author's copies shall be sent direct to his agent at: A Literary Agency, London.

You get some free copies of your book when it comes out. You can also buy further copies at a discount — 35% in this instance, but commonly as much as 50%.

11. The Publishers shall consult the Author and obtain his approval over jacket copy and design, such approval not to be unreasonably withheld or delayed. The Author shall be shown proofs of the jacket and consulted thereon, but the final decision shall be the Publishers'. No changes in the title or text of the said work shall be made without the Author's consent, such consent not to be unreasonably withheld or delayed. The Publishers shall inform the Author of the number of copies in the first and subsequent printings, if so requested.

OK, first the good news. 'No changes in the title or text' of your work can be made without your consent. In other words, when it comes to content, the Publishers can't so much as change a comma unless you're happy for them to do so. This is the one area of the whole publishing process where you truly are king. Enjoy it.

The less good news is that your rights are much more restricted when it comes to other aspects of your work. The language in the first sentence above actually yields the author more power than is awarded by some contracts — that is, it gives you a veto right over jacket copy and design, so long as your veto is not 'unreasonably withheld or delayed'. Other times, you'll see language which gives you the right to be consulted, but does not oblige the publisher to take the tiniest bit of notice of your opinions. As a practical matter, publishers will want you to like their jacket design and neither you nor your editor will want to get all legalistic about the matter. But it's worth remembering that this is an area where your rights are typically more restricted, which means that you can't behave like a diva and expect to get away with it.

Finally, do note that the clause above does oblige your publishers to tell you how many copies they're printing, if you ask them. As it happens, there is a lot more information that they could and really should give you. These days, after all, print runs tend to be fairly short and rapid, so you can't necessarily estimate sales expectations from the initial print run alone. Much more to the point are questions like, 'What chain bookstores are entering my book into their promotions?', 'What is the uptake like from the supermarkets?', 'How is my book going to be positioned in the travel [train stations and airports] sector?', 'Are there [a few weeks after publication] any indications about the level of returns?' If you know to ask these questions of your editor, she'll do her best to tell you, but publishers seldom volunteer this crucial information of their own accord, and what they do tell you is not always to be relied upon. The sad truth is that you will most likely be left mostly in the dark until you get your royalty statement – which, remember, could arrive as long as nine months from publication date. If you ask me, publishers should communicate much better than this. To them, your book is only one amongst very many. To you, it's everything.

In ample time prior to Publication, the Author shall be sent a questionnaire inviting him to supply personal information relevant to publicity and marketing and to suggest who should receive review/free copies and to say whether he wishes the typescript of the work to be returned.

Self-explanatory, but not something found in every contract.

12. If any alterations from the copy as delivered to the Publishers be made in the proofs by the Author the expenses incurred by the Publishers in making such alterations over and above the sum of ten per cent (10%) of the cost of setting the said copy shall be borne by the Author. The Author shall be notified if his corrections are likely to exceed ten per cent (10%) of the setting costs. The Publishers may deduct these costs from any monies payable to the Author under the terms of this Agreement or may present the Author with an invoice for payment, which the Author will settle within sixty (60) days of receipt.

This clause dates from the time when books were set by men in brown coats bending over trays of metal type. If an author made changes to the text after it was set, then the author was creating cost and expense for the publisher, for which the author, quite rightly, would be liable. What I'd love to know, if anyone has figured out how this clause would actually operate now that the whole process is electronic. In any case, it doesn't really matter. Don't make extensive changes after the page proofs have been delivered. If you do, you may end up paying for it – and, more to the point, you will be messing a lot of people around.

13. If at any time the Publishers allow the said work to go out of print or off the market in all UK trade editions and shall not have reprinted and placed on the market a new edition or impression within six (6) months of receiving written notice from the Author then all rights in the said work shall revert to the Author forthwith, except for any existing licence agreement or contract entered into by the Publishers prior to the date of such reversion.

For the avoidance of doubt, the said work shall be considered to be out of print if there are fewer than one hundred (100) copies of the hardcover edition and/or fewer than one hundred and fifty (150) copies of the paperback edition in stock or if sales of the work total less than one hundred (100) copies in two (2) consecutive accounting periods.

Another one of those clauses that has become a hot topic recently. In the good old days, a book was out of print when there was tumbleweed blowing through the relevant bit of the publisher's warehouse. 'Out of print' meant that the last box of books had been shipped and the publisher was not ordering a reprint due to declining sales. Old-fashioned contracts saw to it that authors could ask for a reversion of rights (i.e. they would take back all the rights in the book) if the book (i) fell out of print, and (ii) the publisher had no plans to get it back in print, within some set period following the author's request. These clauses allowed authors to reclaim their rights, with a view (for example) to selling them on to another, more active, publisher; with a view to revising the text for a new edition with someone else; or indeed, just to have the pleasure of repossessing rights to the work.

These days, however, print-on-demand technology has made it easy for publishers to order a print run of as little as one single book. So someone turning up at a bookshop in the year 2025 could theoretically ask for a title by Ms Forgotten Author, published to universal derision in 2010, and order themselves a copy — a fact which publishers can use to argue that their books never go out of print, so that they would never have to see their rights revert to the author.

The argument is, in a sense, pointless. Publishers shouldn't really care about allowing rights to revert on books that were no longer selling. These things do tend to matter to authors (whose interests go well beyond the solely commercial) and should not matter to publishers (who should care only about the pounds and pence). The evolving compromise is now to be found in clauses like the one above, which essentially says that, once sales have dwindled to below a certain point, the book will be deemed to be out of print, no matter what the technological situation. If your reversion clause contains the first paragraph above but not the second (that is, not the one defining what 'out of print' actually means), it may well be that the clause is in effect meaningless.

Two final comments on what won't, for most authors, be an issue of very great concern. First, depending on the type of book, many publishers will successfully keep a book in print with fewer than 100/150 hardbacks or paperbacks respectively. Those figures are about right for more mass-market titles. They'd be too high for smaller, more specialist works. Secondly, many authors won't even want to insist on a rights reversion, even if they're theoretically entitled to ask for it. After all, a publisher who isn't selling very many copies of your work may still be selling some, and those few may be better than none at all. But this isn't a huge issue, so not another word on the subject.

14. If the Publishers fail to fulfil or comply with any of the provisions of this Agreement and shall not within one (1) month after written notification from the Author rectify such failure or if they go into liquidation otherwise than for the purpose of reconstruction or when a receiver is appointed this Agreement shall thereupon terminate and all rights in the said work forthwith revert to the Author who shall be free to license any other person to publish the said work notwithstanding anything to the contrary contained or implied in any part of this Agreement and without prejudice to any claim which the Author may have either for monies due and/or damages and/or otherwise.

If the publisher goes bust – most likely as a consequence of their failure to turn you into the global best-seller that you surely ought to be (!) – then the rights in your work revert to you. If your publisher breaches this contract and doesn't remedy that breach within a month, again the rights revert to you. Many contracts won't contain a clause quite as beefy as this one – very often, for example, a publisher would need to default on their payment obligations to you before you can demand a reversion of rights. Disputes over relatively minor matters (e.g. has anyone sent you your free copies or not?) are obviously unlikely to trigger this clause, no matter what the contract says.

15. This Agreement expresses the entire understanding of the parties to this Agreement and no rights, licences or other interests are granted to the Publishers other than those specifically set out in this Agreement.

Belt-and-braces stuff, perhaps, but in a period of rapid technological change it's worth being clear about who's selling what to whom. This clause simply makes it clear that, if you aren't explicitly selling a particular right in your work, the publisher is not entitled to exploit it.

16. The Publishers undertake that the name of the Author shall appear in its customary form with due prominence on the title page, binding and jacket of every copy of the work issued by the Publishers and shall include in all copies of the work a complete and correct copyright notice as follows:

© William Shakespeare 20— (20— being the year of first publication)

Mostly self-explanatory. 'Customary form' means that your name appears the way you normally write it. Thus, my name appears as 'Harry Bingham' on my books, no matter that my full legal name is Thomas Henry Bingham. If you happen to be called, let's say, Daniel Brown but always call yourself Dan, then you will simply have to discuss with your publishers how to present your name so that you are properly identified but in a way that doesn't confuse or mislead readers who might be looking for the next book about shenanigans in the Vatican. On the whole, publishers prefer to avoid making use of pseudonyms – because it is hard to achieve maximum impact from publicity activities, if you and your book go by different names – but the preference is not very marked. I was once asked to change my name to a woman's name (for a German edition of one of my novels) and I know a woman who became a man for the purposes of publication.

17. The Author hereby asserts his moral right to be identified as the author of the said work, and the Publishers undertake:

to print with due prominence on every edition of the said work published by themselves the words 'The right of William Shakespeare to be identified as author of this work has been asserted by him in accordance with the Copyright, Designs and Patents Act 1988';

to make a condition of contract with any Licensee concerning any edition of the said work to be published in the United Kingdom that a notice of assertion in the same terms as above shall be printed with due prominence in every edition published by or further licensed by such Licensee.

All this simply requires your publishers and any parties who buy the right to sub-license your work (e.g. for those large-print books for the visually impaired), to assert your moral rights to be identified as author of that work. If you don't know what moral rights are all about, you probably don't need to know. The assertion of authorship which matters most is your name in big letters across the front of your book. That's the one that's going to make your mum happy, anyway.

18. If any difference shall arise between the Author and the Publishers touching the meaning of this Agreement or the rights and liabilities of the parties hereto the same shall in the first instance be referred to the Informal Disputes Settlement Scheme of the Publishers' Association and, failing agreed submission to such scheme by both parties, shall be referred to the arbitration of two persons (one to be named by each party) or their mutually agreed umpire, in accordance with the provisions of the

Arbitration Act 1996 or any amending or substituted statute for the time being in force.

A good and sensible clause, which tries to keep you and your publisher out of court in the event of a dispute. You should always, in any event, try to settle any dispute amicably and sensibly via your editor and agent before you take any further steps whatsoever. If your contract does not contain such a clause, you might want to think about suggesting it.

19. This Agreement shall in all respects be governed by and interpreted in accordance with the laws of England.

   Self-explanatory, except that they are the laws of England and Wales, are they not?

20. If at any time the Publishers consider that the copyright in the said work has been infringed and the Author after receiving written notice of such infringement from the Publishers refuses or neglects to take proceedings in respect of the infringement, the Publishers shall be entitled to take proceedings in the joint names of the Publishers and the Author upon giving the Author a sufficient and reasonable security to indemnify the Author against any liability for costs; and in this event any sum received by way of damages shall belong to the Publishers. If the Author is willing to take proceedings and the Publishers desire to be joined with the Author thereto and agree to share the costs, then any sum received by way of damages shall be applied in payment to the costs incurred and the balance shall be divided equally between the Author and the Publishers. The provisions of the clause are intended to apply only in the case of an infringement of the copyright in the said work affecting the interest in the same granted to the Publishers under this Agreement.

   Not a clause that's likely to trouble you much. If someone infringes your copyright, and your publisher wants to take legal action, then you can (i) agree to share the costs of the lawsuit and divvy up any proceeds 50–50, or (ii) choose not to incur any costs of the lawsuit but also give up any right to any proceeds that may arise. Either way, however, you agree that the publisher can sue in their name and yours, so long as (if you have chosen not to incur any costs) they give you a legally binding indemnity against any such costs.

21. The Author shall not during the currency of the Agreement without the consent of the Publishers prepare or cause to allow to be published

other than by the Publishers any written material which shall be an expansion or abridgement of the said work or of a nature likely to prevent the sales of either copies or of rights in the said work.

If you sell your work, you sell it. You can't sell The Complete Encyclopedia of Trilobite Fossils in the Lower Thames Valley *to publisher A, and then seek to sell* An Expanded Encyclopedia of Trilobite Fossils in the Lower Thames Valley *to publisher B. Nor* An Abridged Encyclopedia *to publisher C. Nor any other obviously competing work.*

22. The Author agrees that before publication he will undertake not to publish or broadcast the said work or cause to be broadcast or published any material about the said work in the exclusive territory without prior consultation with the Publishers.

You can't engage in PR activities relating to the book without talking to your publisher in advance. You shouldn't even want to, either.

23. Advertisements may not be inserted or printed in any edition of the said work, whether issued by the Publishers or their licensee, without the Author's written consent, except for listings of the Publishers' or their licensee's own works of a similar nature where there would otherwise be blank pages at the end of a paperback edition of the said work.

You won't suddenly find yourself endorsing products without your consent, the one exception being that publishers can advertise comparable books on their list in those pages at the back of the book.

24. This Agreement and the rights and licence hereby granted may not be assigned or transmitted by the Publishers without the prior written consent of the Author, such consent not to be unreasonably withheld save as herein expressly provided.

In the mortgage industry pre-2008, you never really knew who owned your mortgage, because everyone was flogging their rights to everyone else. It's not like that in publishing, where publishers aren't allowed simply to sell their rights in a work to some other party. If they want to do that – and they're most unlikely to – they need your permission first.

25. All statements of accounts and all monies shown thereon to be due under this agreement shall be paid to the Author's agents, A Literary Agency, London, who are hereby irrevocably authorised to collect and

receive such monies and to charge the Author their agreed commission on all sums payable by the Publishers to the Author during the validity of this contract and any extensions and renewals of it and the Author declares that the receipt of the said A Literary Agency shall be a good and valid discharge in respect thereof and the said A Literary Agency are hereby authorised to negotiate as agents for the Author in all matters arising out of this agreement.

All the money coming your way as a result of this agreement will go to your agent in the first instance. Your agent will help themselves to your commission, to VAT on that commission, and may also charge a few minor fees relating to photocopying and the like. You are also agreeing that your agent is authorised to negotiate matters arising from this agreement on your behalf.

26. (a) The Publishers may use or permit others to use the Author's name and likeness, the title of the said work and selections from the said work in advertising, catalogues, promotion and publicity related to the publication and/or licensing of the said work including (but not limited to) broadcast (without charge) by radio, television or cable or distribution via any form of electronic transmission including online or satellite-based data transmission.

You agree to let the publisher use your name and mugshot, plus chunks from the book itself, in publicising your work.

(b) The Author will make himself available to promote and publicise the said work as the Publishers shall reasonably require particularly during the two (2) weeks at the time of publication, the Author's agreed costs in such promotion to be borne by the Publishers.

Self-explanatory – and of course it's very much in your interest to be as co-operative here as you possibly can be. To be prudent, I wouldn't go on any long holiday in the four to six weeks around publication. It's rare that all PR activity takes place within a single fortnight.

27. It is hereby agreed that the Publishers shall have first refusal of (including the first opportunity to read and consider for publication on fair and reasonable terms) the next work of adult fiction by the Author suitable for publication in volume form, such work shall be the subject of a new agreement between the Author and Publishers on terms to be agreed between the parties hereto, such terms to be fair and reasonable.

The Publishers shall give their decision on the said option work within
one (1) month of their receipt of synopsis, outline or complete typescript
copy of the option work.

> *This clause — or versions of it — will appear in most contracts that are placed
> in front of you. This is a delicate area and one well worth understanding. The
> issues are these.*
>
> *On the one hand, your publisher is making an investment not simply in this
> book, but in you and your future career. That means they thoroughly deserve
> first dibs on your next work . . . if, for example, it's a work of fiction, or the
> kind of mainstream non-fiction work which aims to appeal to a broad audience.
> (If the work is a narrowly subject-led manuscript, you probably shouldn't offer
> and your publisher probably shouldn't ask for first refusal rights on any further
> work. If you are contemplating a series of further works on the same or closely
> related subject areas, that probably merits its own careful discussion.)*
>
> *On the other hand, don't think that those rights of first refusal don't cost you
> anything, because they do. If publisher B would, in principle, be interested in
> acquiring rights to your next novel, but they know that publisher A already has
> first refusal rights, publisher B is much less likely to go to all the effort of
> bidding assertively for the book, because they (rightly) fear that the effort may
> be wasted. The competitive playing field is not, in this instance, an even one.*
>
> *For novels and broad-spectrum non-fiction, the above clause represents a
> normal way to resolve this tension. And, of course, when it comes to selling
> your next MS, your agent will be able to guide you through all the thickets
> that will arise at the time.*

Publishers   . . . .

Author   . . . .

> *You'll normally receive two or three copies of the contract and will be asked to
> sign and return them all, without dating any of them. As soon as you do that,
> the publisher will sign and date each copy. You'll get one, your agent will
> (probably) get one, and your publisher will have one. Needless to say, this is
> a document that's worth filing somewhere safe.*

LIBEL AND OTHER ROUTES TO BANKRUPTCY

Everything in your contract matters and you will, naturally, read it attentively from cover to cover before signing it, but there is, for most authors, only one area with the potential to render you bankrupt, destroy your marriage and leave you begging for coppers outside Chancery Lane tube station.

That area, of course, is libel – an issue for only a small minority of authors, but if you are in that minority you *must* be sure of handling it correctly, as you may well pay very dearly for your errors if you don't. Authors who need to worry about these things certainly include the authors of 'misery memoirs', where the wrongdoers are still alive. They may also include the authors of current affairs or investigative-type books that make serious allegations about individuals or corporations. It is, however, rare for a novelist to have to worry, and most non-fiction simply doesn't go into the sort of areas from which libel claims are likely to arise. My career, for example, has never got close to brushing up against any libel issue, and I'd be surprised if it ever did. Most authors will be in the same position.

Nevertheless, you need to be safe, not sorry, and if you're in any doubt then read attentively on.

LIBEL

In law, you have defamed a person if you make statements in any publication which (i) expose him to hatred or ridicule, (ii) cause him to be shunned, (iii) lower him in the estimation of 'right-thinking' members of the public, and/or (iv) disparage his work. If you make such a statement about someone, that person can go to court to seek compensation for the harm you have done to their reputation. The object of the law is to balance the rights of free speech against protection for the reputation of individuals. For historical reasons, and in comparison with other modern democracies, British libel law is rather more favourable to the libelled and rather less favourable to the author than is true elsewhere, which means that any author publishing in the UK needs to be even more careful about these issues.

There are, however, some important restrictions to the scope of the law and some valid defences. In terms of the scope of the law, it can be helpful to know that you can't defame the dead, so (as far as libel goes, at least) you can say whatever you like about them. It can also be helpful to know that you can only defame individuals; you cannot defame an entire class. So, if, let's say, you want to attack a particular psychiatrist, you may well get into trouble if you do so (though we'll come to some possible defences in a minute). If, however, you wish to say nasty things about *all* psychiatrists, then you are safe from the libel courts. Do note that, if you are determined to say something defamatory about a particular individual, changing their name or altering their identity in other relatively modest ways will not help you. If the individual's identity would be clear to those who knew them sufficiently well, you may still be libelling that person and you need to take very great care in what you say about them.

You should also be clear that *any* published statement can give rise to libel. It doesn't matter if you have chosen to self-publish your book rather than seek publication in the normal way. If you distribute a significant number of copies of your book, you are spreading allegations about someone and the question of libel does therefore arise. It's true that the level of any damages is likely to be lower (because damage to reputation will be less, the fewer the people who are aware of the allegations), but that may not be a great comfort to you when the libel writ pops through your letterbox.

The same comments also apply to comments made online. Although the law here remains murky and under development, all you really need to know for now is that statements made online can give rise to a libel claim. Beware.

There are, however, defences against such a claim. The first and best is that what you say is true, but (in Britain) *you must be able to prove its truth*. It's not enough for you to show that what you say is probably or quite likely true. You must be able to provide a courtroom quality of proof for your allegations. That can be a big ask and in many cases what it really boils down to for an author is that your particular allegation has already been tested in court and upheld.

Specifically, first-time writers most often encounter concerns about libel when they are writing about difficult or unhappy periods in their life. Let's say, for example, that you are writing a memoir in which you state that your stepfather used to physically abuse you. Clearly, that allegation is a defamatory one, as any 'right-thinking' individual will think worse of a child-beater. You can't protect yourself by changing the individual's name, as you probably have only one stepfather, in which case it is obvious – to anyone who knows your family – which individual you are talking about. You can't simply change a few facts and call the memoir a 'novel', unless you change things so extensively that you are no longer writing a memoir at all.

For most authors in this position, the only way to be sure that you're safe from libel is if your stepfather's abuse was ever exposed in court and resulted in his criminal conviction. If he has been convicted, then you are safe to expose the full detail of what he was convicted for. Naturally, you will make many statements in your book that you can't prove individually, but you probably don't have to. If the thrust of your book is to describe your step-father's abusive habits and your father has already been convicted of the physical abuse of children, then you are very likely in the clear . . . though do read on to the end of this section for some important further comments.

Other valid defences to a libel claim are that your statements are fair comment – a test which requires that your statements are statements of opinion, that they are based on true facts, that you genuinely believe what you say, and that you are not inspired by malice. This defence lacks the crystal clarity of the previous one and, if you believe that you are covered by it, you will certainly want to take proper legal advice before proceeding. A further defence is that your comments are protected by privilege – for example, it is generally fine to report on anything that has already been said in parliament or the courts. More recently, a further defence against libel has arisen, namely that your comments have been made in the public interest (subject to meeting certain criteria as to how the material was researched and published, and whether the subject of the allegations was given the opportunity to respond). Again, if that's the defence you have your eye on, you will certainly want to take advice before proceeding.

Three final comments before moving on.

First, you don't ever want to get anywhere near a libel court. It doesn't matter whether you win or lose. It doesn't matter whether (if you lose) the damages awarded are large or small. The costs of the court case – financial and emotional – are likely to rip your life apart for longer than you care to contemplate. If in doubt, play it safe.

Secondly, plaintiffs in a libel case generally name both the publisher and the author. Your publisher is unlikely to know all the facts connected with the putative libel, so the author–publisher contract generally places quite a heavy burden on the author. As a rule, your contract will almost certainly make you extensively liable for bearing the costs of any libel claim, whether or not that claim is upheld.

Furthermore, your publisher will have the right to decide how to defend the case and whether a settlement is appropriate. You may not agree with the publisher's decisions here, but you won't be able to take issue with them. In effect, the publisher gets to make the decisions and you get to pay for them. Once again, therefore, any sane author will do whatever they can to stay away from the libel court.

But thirdly, you don't want to paralyse yourself either. None of these issues arises until you get into print. If you are writing a memoir about a troubled childhood, then just let rip. Say what you want to say. Express yourself with freedom. Don't worry about what a libel lawyer might think, because if you do that you will find yourself barely able to construct a single sentence. When you have completed your memoir, and made any revisions that you want to make, you should start taking the libel issue seriously.

If you are heading for commercial publication, then your publisher will have a depth of experience in these issues that you can't have. For all that your publication contract is very onerous on the libel front, publishers are well aware that a successful libel claim against them is likely to end up costing them a serious amount of money (if only because you may already have been pushed into bankruptcy). So talk openly to your publishers. Be honest. Raise any concerns you may have. You should do as much as you can at this stage to ensure that the book which heads for the printing press is as safe as possible from attack. If you skimp on effort or openness at this stage, you may come to regret it very much down the road. If the issues are plainly serious ones, then you may even want to take your own independent advice, which will cost you a penny or two, no doubt, but your own interests are not identical with those of your publisher and securing your own advice may well be a sensible step.

PRIVACY LAW

Article 8 of the European Convention on Human Rights promises a 'right to respect for privacy and family life' and the 1998 Human Rights Act incorporated that convention, and that promise, directly into UK law for the first time. Alas, the new law has not brought clarity – or, at least, it has not brought clarity *yet*. A spatter of landmark cases is helping to define how the law might work, but a settled case law has yet to be achieved. This lack of clarity, however, is unlikely to affect you, as few authors are likely to be affected by privacy law concerns, unless, that is, you happen to be moonlighting for a tabloid newspaper or gossip magazine at the time.

If, however, you are writing a book that does expose somebody's private life in a way that they might find objectionable, you simply must take proper legal advice before proceeding. Again, you probably don't need to be excessively concerned during the writing process itself. Fear about your legal position will make it hard to write fluently, and your publisher will possess the right resources and experience to help settle any delicate issues that may arise from your manuscript. So write the book, find a publisher, then take advice – and that does mean *take* it, not simply listen to it.

PLAGIARISM

If you want to ruin your life, then on the whole I'd recommend libelling someone – preferably someone famous, litigious and rich – as your optimal authorial strategy, but other options do exist and the prudent self-destructive author will want to review them all. (Syphilis was, of course, once de rigueur for such authors, to be replaced more recently by alcoholism. But fashions change. Syphilis is now curable, and alcoholism is less saleable than it used to be. Even hard drugs are *so* last year. My review of options is therefore, rather boringly, going to confine itself to legal matters.)

Plagiarism occurs when you use or closely imitate the language or thoughts of another author and pass them off as your own. Thus, if you were to take the above section on libel and paste that into your own work, representing it as your own wise thoughts on the subject, then you would certainly be guilty of plagiarism. Such acts are, however, relatively rare. It's also hard to believe that they ever happen by accident, which means that it's relatively simple to avoid plagiarism. just don't nick other people's work and pretend that it's your own.

There is, of course, a rather more subtle point lurking here. What precisely constitutes the close imitation of another person's thoughts? Shakespeare took material for *Macbeth* from Holinshed's *Chronicles*. Was he guilty of close imitation? My own novel *The Lieutenant's Lover* was certainly influenced by Pasternak's mighty and wonderful *Dr Zhivago*. (I've never seen the film, but read the book two or three times as I was researching my novel. Pasternak's writing was so wonderful that it sank in further than I'd have liked. My book would have been better if it had had more imaginative distance from that great work.) Was I guilty of close imitation?

Because all literature exists in constant imaginative reverberation with itself, courts – quite rightly – tend to construe the 'close imitation of thought' test very narrowly. It's fine to be influenced by something, even over-influenced. What you can't do is cleave to someone else's storyline and characters in a way that takes their work, changes the language and then represents it on the page as your own. If in doubt, you would do well to make full and generous acknowledgement of those sources that have most inspired you. If in serious doubt, you would do well to have someone proficient to read both texts and advise you on whether there is a case to be made against you. (To the extent that plagiarism involves word-for-word textual copying, you may be liable for copyright infringement.) As I say, though, it's hard to believe that real plagiarism ever happens by accident, so the simple rule is just don't plagiarise others, and you almost certainly won't get into trouble.

COPYRIGHT INFRINGEMENT

Copyright infringement occurs when you reproduce a substantial part of other people's work by copying their words, whether you acknowledge it or otherwise, but you don't seek permission in the appropriate way. (Except under certain quite limited circumstances, for example for the purposes of criticism and review, an acknowledgement will by and large be irrelevant when it comes to determining whether copyright has been infringed.) And do remember, of course, that permissions may have to be paid for.

There is no hard and fast rule for what qualifies as substantial, so, depending on the material, even a sentence or two might be considered substantial copying. Again, it's simple to get these things right. If you are quoting copyright work, then you need to seek permission. Most often that permission will be granted for free. Sometimes you will need to pay something for the pleasure. But just be diligent, make your requests, and you won't get into any trouble.

NIGHTSHADE WINE AND YEWBERRY COMPOTE

The last excitingly novel way of ruining your life is to incorporate a recipe or instructions in your manuscript liable to cause death or injury to anyone attempting to follow them. Thus, if a famous TV chef happened to include in their cookbook a recipe for wine made out of deadly nightshade, or a fruit compote made out of lethally poisonous yewberries, then they'd quite likely be facing a spate of claims for damages. Again, relatively few authors will find themselves in this position, but, if you are contemplating a book of toxic recipes or home experiments that may, if they go a tad wrong, blow readers' houses sky high, you may wish to adjust course before it's too late.

IF IN DOUBT . . .

Finally, while these guidelines will be sufficient for the great majority of authors – few of whom will ever need to give these matters deep consideration – they will not be sufficient for everyone. The final and most important rule is this: *if you are in any doubt at all about your legal position in relation to libel or anything else, then take professional advice prior to publication.* If you don't, you may regret it. And on that sombre note, we can leap forward to things altogether more appealing. It's time to talk about book covers.

TOWARDS WORLD DOMINATION

Chronologically speaking, your agent is unlikely to start selling your work overseas until you've got a settled manuscript. That means waiting till you've worked through any editorial issues with your home publisher. It may even mean waiting for bound proofs or actual hardback copies of the book itself. Nevertheless, since this part of the book has dealt with rights and contracts, it makes sense to complete that discussion here, before moving forward to talk about the process of publication itself.

ENGLISH-LANGUAGE SALES: WHO SELLS WHAT TO WHOM?

For most writers, the largest slice of their income will come from home sales to their home publishers. There's something counter-intuitive in this. No matter where your home market is, there are a lot more book buyers and book sales outside it than within it. I've sold books to China, Japan, the US and Germany, plus a fair few other territories as well. In total, that has given me exposure to a vastly larger number of buyers than I've had via my home market alone.

Taken together, those territories have substantially supplemented my total income from writing – but that's it. It's a supplement, a side order of fries, not the main course itself. The reason is that publishing markets are still more domestic than international. It remains a lot easier for an author to make a big splash in their home market than overseas, so – for most authors, most of the time – it's in the home market that you should expect to make the most money. Furthermore, when it comes to selling books into non-English-language territories, publishers are having to adjust their sums to take account of translation costs. Since those costs are effectively coming out of your advance, the value to you of unit sales overseas is likely to be less than it is at home. There are exceptions to these rules – the handful of genuinely global mega-authors who sell as well in Tokyo and Berlin as they do in New York and London. But this book isn't really aimed at giving advice to the mega-authors. They don't need it.

For the rest of us, the following rules are likely to apply:

➢ *If you are British*

Your agent is likely to sell 'home' rights in a bundle that includes Britain, Ireland, continental Europe, Australia, New Zealand, South Africa and a slew of other territories besides. Note that the right to 'continental Europe' gives your home publisher only the right to sell English-language work in those territories. So, if you are published by GodSaveTheQueen Ltd in London, and by Schwarz-Rot-Gold GmbH in Germany, then the former gets to sell English-language books in Germany. The latter possesses the rather more valuable right to sell German-language books in Germany. In both cases, those rights extend across the entire EU because of rules connected with the single European market.

While there can often be weirdly fierce disputes between British and American publishers over who gets to sell in marginal territories (Hong Kong being a notable example), and, though there was a very long-running (and entirely lunatic) dogfight between British and American publishers over who got to sell books in continental Europe, none of these issues is likely to make a significant financial difference to you. The one real question mark concerns Canada. Your agent will probably want to sell Canadian rights to your British publisher if he thinks that a US deal is unlikely. If he wants to shoot for a US deal, then the Canadian rights will be kept back from the UK publisher's package, because the US rights will be easier to sell as part of a package that includes the whole of North America.

➢ *If you are Irish*

You'll be treated as though you're British, so the above paragraphs will probably hold true for you too.

➢ *If you are American*

Your home publisher is likely to acquire English-language rights to US, Canada and the Phillippines, plus a range of other territories too. The pattern of these rights blocs all feels a bit post-colonial, but then again it *is* a bit post-colonial. But it's how the publishing world continues to work.

➢ *If you are Canadian*

A Canada-based publisher selling Canadian authors to the Canadian market is likely to acquire rights only for Canada. You will, therefore, be looking to find a US publisher (to cover the US, the Philippines and other ancillary territories) plus a UK publisher to handle Britain, Europe and Commonwealth territories aside from Canada. If, on the other hand, your MS has been purchased by a US publisher in the first instance, you would count yourself as an American for the purposes of working out the division of foreign rights. If your MS was bought by a UK publisher, you count as a Brit.

> ➤ *If you are Australian, South African, a New Zealander or other Commonwealth citizen*

If you have a home publisher, then that publisher may have bought world rights (in which case, they'll be looking to sell them on at the big international book fairs) or UK and Commonwealth rights (in which case, they'll seek to have your book published by partners in London and elsewhere), or rights to the local market alone – in which case, you or your agent will be seeking to sell the book more widely.

If all this seems pointlessly confusing – well, yes, perhaps it is, and there's no doubt that my summary above vastly simplifies a number of quite contentious issues. On the other hand, you shouldn't be left to navigate these perils on your own. If you have an agent, they will simply steer you calmly through these things and let you know what's been done when it's been done. If you don't have an agent, you should certainly discuss international rights sales with your publisher. If your publisher is of any size at all, they'll certainly be involved in the international rights fest in Frankfurt and perhaps London, which means they should be able to guide you there.

Do also note that it's by no means certain that if you have a UK book deal – even a very good UK book deal – you will be taken up in the US. It just isn't true. Often enough, a book that seems like an obviously strong book for the US market won't find an American buyer at all, whereas one that seems as eccentrically British as deep-fried Mars bars or Marmite sandwiches sells and sells very well. The British market, conversely, is always open to books by strong American authors.

Finally, before we leave this topic, it's maybe worth picking up a topic briefly alluded to when we were talking about your choice of agent. Some agents work with one and only one sub-agent in New York (or in London, if your home agent is in New York). Others will work with a variety of partners, depending on the nature of the project in question. The latter makes more sense. No agent can really make a sale if they don't believe in the quality of the work they're pitching. If your agent pushes all their clients' work in the direction of one particular counterparty, then – and no matter how good that counterparty may be – there will be times when the wrong agent is selling your work. If, on the other hand, your home agent is working with a sub-agent specifically selected because of their enthusiasm for your work, then so much the better. (Of course, with smaller territories, your agent will use a sub-agent and will almost certainly only use one particular partner for the territory in question. That makes perfect sense given the way those smaller markets operate.)

On the other hand, these considerations are all rather theoretical. Quite likely you didn't have much of a choice of agent in the first place. Even if you did, you probably – and rightly – made the decision on the basis of gut feeling and personal chemistry. These ruminations about how sub-agenting is handled should probably have featured in your initial discussions with that agent, but they shouldn't have determined its outcome. Although it's important that your key sub-agents love your work, it's also important that you work constructively with whatever relationships your agent has built up. The truth is, you're not likely to have any other choice.

FOREIGN-LANGUAGE SALES: WHO SELLS WHAT TO WHOM?

If the allocation of rights in the English language seems strangely complex, the sale of overseas rights is blessedly simple in comparison. If you have an agent, then they will look after foreign sales for you. Sometimes, they'll be working via agents in Germany, France and elsewhere. In smaller territories, they'll probably work directly with local publishers. Very often, they'll be selling at the big international book fairs, but they'll also have a depth of local contacts through whom sales take place outside the set-piece events.

Again, let me stress that many of these sales won't make much money for you. I once sold a book into China that earned me $500 before agents' commissions and tax. Back then, it's true that intellectual property rules in China were so feebly enforced that the $500 was in effect a polite way to say, 'We could have just pirated this book, but look how nice we are – we've paid for a couple of nice meals out for you instead.' These days, those rules are tightening up a bit and advances may be rising a bit, but they're still unlikely to make you rich.

The same goes for most other international markets. Book sales in Germany can be a genuinely nice addition to an author's income. The same goes (to a slightly lesser extent) for Japan, France, Italy and Spain/Latin America. I do know authors whose books largely drowned in the UK but went on to become best-sellers in Germany. In such cases, you'll end up making more money from those overseas markets than from your home market, but such instances remain the exception. In most cases, you'll get most of your sales, most of your exposure and most of your money at home.

KEEPING IT LOCAL

If you sell your work all over the world, it may have occurred to you that you'll end up with a huge number of editors, a huge number of publicists, a huge number of marketers, and so on. This, indeed, is perfectly true. Until, however, you become a genuinely global brand, none of this will bother you too much. If you have an editor in both London and New York, you will get editorial feedback from both places and you'll need to juggle that as well as you can. Apart from that, foreign publishers are buying your book. They're not buying you. You won't get editorial feedback from Seoul and Taipei. You won't be going on Radio Düsseldorf or giving interviews to *Il Giornale*. In short, you may have a dozen or more publishers who have invested in your work, but only one or two of those will make any material difference to your daily life. The rest of them are just there to chip in with the occasional welcome cheque.

HOLLYWOOD AND OTHER ILLUSIONS

Which brings us to the subject of film rights.

Almost certainly, as you've sat typing away at your novel, it has occurred to you – in the most objective possible way, of course – just what a tremendous film you have on your hands. You're not dumb enough to believe Tom Cruise would be *certain* to want the role that you have in mind for him. It's simply that, standing back and being coolly rational about it, you can see that it would be ideal for him. Likewise, it's just hard to see Meryl Streep's agent not being wildly excited about that role which might as well have been written for her. As for directors – well, as you're perfectly well aware, that would never be your decision to make, but you do have a shortlist in your bottom drawer, just in case anyone happens to ask.

Because I don't want to shatter any dreams, and because you are indeed being entirely objective and rational in your assessment of things, let's put your own particular case aside for the time being and consider instead the position that all other novelists are in.

The first point to make is that Hollywood doesn't make all that many movies – perhaps 500–600 in a typical year. Of those, around two-thirds will be based on original scripts, which means that there are around 150–200 adaptations. Of those adaptations, many will be of classic works (Shakespeare, Jane Austen, and so on). Others will be of short stories or comic books or newspaper articles or foreign films. That leaves a very small number of a dozen films which are based on the works of contemporary novelists.

Of that small number, a majority will be the work of people who already have a significant name – Grisham, Pullman, Rowling, Clancy, etc. It's also true that Hollywood, for obvious reasons, tends to prefer US source material to material from elsewhere, no matter how good it may be. Since there are still a huge number of novels being published, simple mathematics suggests that all those other novelists are really going to struggle to get the film deal that they've oh-so-foolishly been dreaming of.

In the second place, there's a curious kind of assumption that the film world just sprays money over all that it touches. No doubt by publishing-industry standards, there's some truth in that, but ordinary commercial logic does play its part, even in movies. As a rough rule of thumb, a movie budget will set aside 2–2.5% for the script or book, seldom more. If there is both a script and a book, the budget might run to as much as 5%, but it would be rare to see more than that in total. These percentages will need to pay for the rights purchase from the original novelist, payment to the screenwriter(s) who will be adapting that material, and all other script-development costs to boot. Though blockbusting movies may well cost in excess of $100 million, a more normal amount for Hollywood would be somewhere closer to $30 million. A British, European or Australian movie would be more likely to cost in the region of £5 to £10 million, or the local equivalent.

As soon as you start to multiply these figures out, you end up with numbers that are attractive but not mind-blowing. Let's say a British company is making a film of your novel. The film will cost £7.5 million, of which 3% is allocated for the total script budget (including rights acquisition). That means that there is £225,000 allocated to the script. Script writers and script doctors will probably eat more than half of that sum, which leaves, let's say, £60,000 left over for you. Now you'd need to be a pretty wealthy individual not to feel lighthearted if you suddenly scooped that kind of money, but you're also unlikely to find it life-changing. I know one author who has a very nice kitchen extension named after a screenplay he sold, and that's perhaps the way you should view things: selling movie rights may buy you a new kitchen; it's not likely to get you a villa in Palm Beach.

It's also worth noting that the film industry is a much less probable taker for your work than is the TV industry. As noted before, there just aren't that many feature films made in any given year, whereas the week-in, week-out demands of multi-channel TV are a monster that needs continual feeding. Because TV budgets are tighter than movie budgets, the payouts to authors are correspondingly lower – a new bathroom perhaps, or a very nice kitchen from IKEA.

Since we're still talking here about other people, it may finally be worth noting that the film industry will flirt with numerous projects for every one it options, and it'll option a good many projects for every one that gets made. Even if you do get as far as selling an option (and most authors never make it as far as that), that option will pay out (let's say) $10,000 on signature and $90,000 on the first day of shooting.

Needless to say, no one spends $10,000 without thinking that they have a realistic shot of going on to complete the project, but the film world is not like any other you've ever encountered. The phrase 'many a slip 'twixt cup and lip' is always a rather baffling one, taken literally. After all, most people are perfectly capable of lifting a glass to their mouths without spilling the fluid inside. In the film world, however, it seems that every market participant suffers from an uncontrollable, violent palsy. Time after time, glasses are filled and raised, in every expectation of taking a long refreshing drink – only for calamity to ensue. In Hollywood, getting from cup to lip is a long journey and one much stricken with accidents.

And since we're having a proverbial moment here, let's close it with a second one. In the film world, more than any other, it's as well not to count your chickens before they're hatched. In the publishing world, if a deal is agreed orally, then a contract will be produced – however slowly – and the money will finally arrive. The film world is not like that. Deals that were absolutely certain to happen have a funny way of disappearing into silence and emptiness. I would therefore recommend waiting until your chickens have arrived clucking in the safety of your bank before you start to celebrate on any scale. Go crazy with the fizzy water if you must. The champagne should wait until the cheque is cashed, cleared and counted.

A QUIET WORD TO YOU ON THE SIDE

Now, as mentioned earlier, all these cautions and caveats are important but, as we both know, they don't apply to you. I mean, sure, Spielberg is a busy man, but quality is quality and some projects simply sell themselves.

The question then is how do you get from here to there. In New York, the studios are fairly closely integrated with the books industry, either because of common ownership or through working relationships that function in much the same way. The result is that, if a New York-based publisher has an eminently filmable book, you can be pretty sure that the book will be looked at by someone in the industry. If your agent is American, they will also have some relationships in Hollywood that may help. None of this means that your novel is going to be thumping on the doormats of the rich and famous. It just means that there will be industry scouts reviewing your material – along with a huge volume of other material.

If you're based outside the US, you still don't need to panic. The film industry is always on the lookout for good-quality work. Local production companies will scour publishers' catalogues for potential material. If they're interested, they'll get in touch with your publisher or agent directly to ask to see it. At this stage, they're still just asking to see it. If that interest hardens into anything serious, you will need an agent to handle things.

Larger British agencies will deal with any such interest in different ways. Some will be able to handle the enquiry in-house. Others will take any enquiry straight across town to a film and TV specialist. You'll end up paying

THAT ELUSIVE ALCHEMY

After twenty-something years as a film agent practising the most elusive alchemy of all – turning either base metals into film gold or, even harder, turning book gold into film gold – my short advice to authors seeking film joy is – don't. Or at least don't try. By which I mean write a book intended to find its way in the world as a book rather than a film prospect.

In some instances, the transition is inevitable. This is when the book or series of books has become such a literary or commercial phenomenon that it is only a matter of time. Some – Harry Potter, The Da Vinci Code – have such a secure readership that the reputation seems beyond damage. For others, you hold your breath waiting to see if a well-loved friend will be mugged (Captain Corelli, Love in the Time of Cholera) or embraced (The English Patient, Lord of the Rings) by their new infatuation.

Sometimes, films really can seem to have alchemical powers, finding film gold from the most unlikely sources. Charlie Kaufman's adaptation about film adaptation called Adaptation from Susan Orlean's non-fiction The Orchid Thief, for example. Or Jason Reitman, who has mined unexpected drama out of two novels Thank You for Smoking and Up in the Air.

These films show the real key difference between selling film rights as opposed to publication rights. Books emerge from the publishers, give or take some editorial discussions, as delivered. Films, on the other hand, are an enormous collaboration, with the book or script only the first link in a long chain towards the screen. Selling film rights involves incessant matchmaking, with screenwriters, directors, actors, producers, financiers, distributors, broadcasters and many other twice over for that agenting (once to the film and TV guy, once to your own agent for making the introduction). It's not thrilling to pay twice for the same thing, but you do need the expertise and you wouldn't even have a book deal if it weren't for your literary agent, so it's only fair that they take a commission on its resultant rights sale.

Once you're in the hands of a professional film and TV type, they'll be able to assess speedily what kind of work yours is. Is it the kind of thing that demands Hollywood budgets and can appeal to Hollywood audiences? If so, you'll find your work scooting fast across an ocean to Los Angeles. There may be yet another fee to pay to an agent there if all goes well, but, again, you need the expertise, so don't begrudge the payment. A lot of contemporary film-making, however, goes on outside the studio system. German

---

breeds. The film agent is always looking for the relationship which will last a production lifetime and often the best partnerships seem the most unlikely.

In the UK and in other smaller markets, television is a crucial industry. It is significant that, whereas television drama producers have flourished in the past years, often creating valuable production houses, it is now almost impossible to forge a career as an independent film producer in the UK. There are some genres where the commercial worlds of film and television seem to disperse – women's commercial fiction, for example, where television often prefers to create its own relationship dramas and comedies. A recurring detective character, however, or a British-based thriller which can be turned into a multi-episodic serial are always in demand.

I have found that, whether aiming for film or television, it has become crucial to bring at least some of the constituent parts together as early as possible. This led us at Curtis Brown to create an in-house production outfit, where we could match books and writers and start the development process ourselves. Our first production was Boy A, funded by Channel 4, written by Mark O'Rowe and based on a spectacular but neglected novel by Jonathan Trigell. I am glad to say the film won five BAFTAs and Jonathan's book was discovered by a whole new audience.

So, although we curse the fickle promises of the film and television worlds, they do remain highly seductive. This is because, although bad experiences should teach us otherwise, when books and film come together and the circumstances are just right, they are always capable of making sweet music.

NICK MARSTON
MD, Media Division, Curtis Brown

investors might work with a British director on an Australian-scripted project that will end up being broadcast on TV stations on two or three continents. Such deals probably don't require the involvement of a Hollywood agent and can still pay very nicely.

The real moral of these ruminations is twofold. The first is that the film industry *is* looking for strong new work. If your work is strong and original and happens to suit the marketing flavour of the moment, then you've got a more than decent chance that it'll be noticed. The second moral is that, if you are noticed, you need to trust your advisors. For the most part, they'll be reactive rather than proactive, but there are very few film agents around with the authority and contacts to make things happen – and, even then, they'll be reacting as often as they are promoting a particular deal. If your literary agent recommends a particular course of action, you will generally need to trust their judgement. Feel free to talk about what lies behind it, of course, but your default position should be to agree with whatever they recommend.

Last, you need to be realistic about both control and screenwriting. If you sell your rights, you are selling them. Tom Clancy has gone on record (on his www.clancyfaq.com site) as saying:

> I have been quoted as saying that selling a book to Hollywood is rather like turning your daughter over to a pimp. I will not confirm the accuracy of that quote.

The book you have in your head is not likely to be the one you see on screen. Doesn't matter. Don't watch the movie, just stay at home and count the money instead.

The same goes for actually writing the script. If you have worked professionally as a screenwriter for major production companies in the past, then fight and fight hard for the right to be named a co-writer on the project. If you haven't, then feel free to offer your services. Feel free to produce a sample script. But don't hold your breath and don't make a scene if people say no. There's an old Hollywood joke about the starlet who was so dumb that she slept with the screenwriter. But that screenwriter is way above your reach. You're source material, nothing more. Sell your work, cash the cheque and wave goodbye.

Part Five

TOWARDS PRODUCTION

WORKING WITH PUBLISHERS

You've sold your book. You've signed your contract. You're an author! Assuming that your book is going to be published in the relatively near future (let's say in the next six to nine months), your publisher will start to work simultaneously on three or four parallel tracks. Those tracks are:

➢ *Editorial*
The editorial track deals with the final completion of your manuscript. There's likely to be a little editorial fine-tuning, and then the whole process of copy-editing, page proofs and proofreading.

➢ *Design*
The centrepiece of the design process is, of course, the development of a cover, but the layout and typography of the text will also play a part, as will any illustrative material included in the book.

➢ *Sales and marketing*
For most books these days, the sales and marketing process is largely about the publisher's effort to secure store position with retailers. The 'sell-in' to retailers is where the most crucial battles are lost or won – and also the area where you will be least involved and least able to contribute. Nevertheless, it helps to understand how the process works, because it'll illuminate the market which publishers are seeking to sell into.

➢ *Publicity*
Although it is part of the whole marketing campaign, the PR effort involves the author so closely that, from an author's point of view, it'll feel like a whole separate element of the publishing process and one that we'll deal with separately in this book.

The precise order in which you encounter the various different ingredients of the entire publishing process will vary somewhat with each different project, but – unless your editor is asleep on the job – the complete publishing pudding is being baked, nevertheless.

THE AUTHOR–PUBLISHER RELATIONSHIP

Before we get to the specifics of any of those processes, it's worth pausing a moment to reflect on a problem almost as old as publishing itself: the difficulty of the author–publisher relationship – a difficulty that arises from the very different perspectives that the two of you bring to bear. You, the author, are rather excited by your imminent publication. You probably believe several of the following propositions, and quite possibly all of them:

☐ *I have worked for months and years on this book, so I deserve to be closely involved in its publication.*

☐ *I have thought long and hard about matters such as title and cover design, so my editor would do well to consult closely with me on such things.*

☐ *I have some unique and excellent ideas on marketing, which any sensible publisher will want to adopt in whole or part.*

☐ *I don't imagine that I'll be part of the core decision-making team as such, but I imagine that I'll be cc-ed in on any really significant emails and be invited to contribute.*

☐ *I will be kept informed of any promotional support from retailers, of intended print runs and of news on sales as it comes in.*

☐ *I will be collaborating closely with my publicist in developing a PR campaign.*

☐ *I will get to see and comment on any press release relating to me or my book before it is sent.*

I'm an author myself. I've certainly held many of the above beliefs at one time or another, and I think some of these expectations are reasonable. To take one simple example: if an organisation is issuing a press release about me, I would expect them to clear it with me first. Partly that's a simple question of common sense. Press releases may contain errors which only the author will spot.

More to the point, though, it's a question of courtesy. How can it possibly be polite for a large organisation to release a statement about you to the national media without running it by you first? Obviously, if there was some major emergency – or you were lost for several months in a jungle, or if you were known to be rude and unbusinesslike in your dealings with PR types – politeness might be obliged to give way to other considerations. But in the typical case, you are not lost in a jungle. Nor is there typically an emergency of the sort where a press release has to be issued by midday or else some PR-hostage is shot dead. Nor do you (I hope) treat your publicist with anything but courtesy and respect. Quite likely, in fact, you're sitting meekly not far from your home computer, only too eager to help if asked.

What's more, you know your book far better than any publicist. Perhaps they've nailed the salient point about the book in their press release. Perhaps they haven't. Since they're expert in public relations but not expert in your book, they'd be crazy not to want you to look at the release before it's issued. That's not to say that you should have a veto, but you bring a depth of expertise on one particular subject – your book – that no one else can offer. It's just not good business practice not to include you.

Yet in the pressure to get things done, good business practice can sometimes take a dent or two. In my publishing career to date, I believe I've only ever seen one press release written about me in advance of its being issued, and then only because I made a point of asking to see it first. In fact, by way of contrast with the list of authorial expectations above, an editor is likely to think:

☐ *We know how to sell books; an author doesn't; it doesn't make sense to involve the author too much.*

☐ *Authors can be notoriously prickly about such things as titles and cover designs. It's better to decide these things in-house, then sell the resultant idea to the author.*

☐ *Authors' views on marketing wheezes invariably involve ways of getting publishers to spend money. The answer is no.*

☐ *It wouldn't even occur to me to copy my author in on key decision-making emails. An author will misunderstand, get upset, require soothing – and in short waste time. The simplest thing is just to get on with the job.*

☐ *I certainly intend to keep my author reasonably up to speed with such things as print runs, retail uptake and so on, but I'm a busy person and these chores don't come at the top of my To Do list, or even close. Quite frankly, I'm likely to forget.*

☐ *Publicists do involve authors as much as they need to; but, again, authors tend to have hopelessly unrealistic expectations of how much interaction is appropriate, and we'd be nuts to waste our time in trying to meet those expectations.*

☐ *As for that press release – heck, as far as I'm concerned, every morning is an issue-the-release-by-midday-or-the-PR-girl-gets-it sort of a morning.*

The gap between the editor's outlook and yours may not always be yawning, but it will usually be there nonetheless. If you approach that gap in the wrong way, you risk riling those you work with and achieving nothing. If you instead adopt an entirely passive 'My Publisher Knows Best' approach, you may also end up disappointed. You need, instead, to aim at a posture which is assertive when it needs to be, sweet-tempered when it can be. You also need to start from a realistic understanding of what your editor can and cannot plausibly deliver. You need, in short, to be able to view the world through the eyes of a publisher.

THE EYES OF A PUBLISHER: MONEY

Publishing is not an industry that floats about on a sea of money. Although there's a media-created image of publishing as being all about long lunches, expense accounts, celebrity book launches, and the rest of it, the truth is much more prosaic. Many small publishers barely break into profit. Even the largest and best-known publishers pay their staff relatively meagre wages, are not lavish with bonuses and scrutinise all expense claims closely. (One editor I spoke to about this told me that he had recently been interrogated about puddings – the bean-counters responsible for checking expense claims had wanted to know whether, at a recent author lunch, it had really been necessary to order a pudding as well as a starter.)

What's more, your book is not a big deal. Let's assume that you've been offered a £10,000 advance for your literary novel – which is a perfectly respectable offer in the current climate. If your book achieves 2,000 sales in hardback and 10,000 sales in paperback, then it'll have done well. Your publisher won't exactly be rejoicing in the hallways, but the outcome will have been a thoroughly decent success.

But just consider that result in a little more detail. Let's suppose that the publisher sold the hardback to retailers at a 50% discount to its £12.99 cover price, then the publisher received a total revenue of £13,500 on its hardback sales. The paperback sums (involving, let's say, a 55% discount on a £7 cover price) yield a total revenue of £31,500 – or a total revenue for the entire book of £45,000. That £45,000 needs to cover your slice of the pie. It needs to cover your editor's time, as well as all the overheads (rent, heating, lighting, etc.) that go with it. It also needs to cover the time and overheads associated with everyone else on the project. It also needs to cover the production, warehousing and transport costs of getting your book printed and into bookstores. If the book has been entered into any retail promotions, the publisher will have paid something for that privilege and the £45,000 needs to cover that too.

In short, and looked at like this, it seems little short of miraculous that the book can turn a profit for anyone. It certainly won't turn a profit for anyone if the publisher starts sloshing money around on advertising and other consumer promotions. It's at this point where authors and publishers often start to part company. Let's say that your book is entitled *Regency Table Manners: A Guide to the Etiquette of Jane Austen*. You think, perfectly reasonably, that the potential market for your book is huge. There are millions of people who have read and loved the work of Jane Austen, millions more who have seen and loved it on screen. You think that it is your publisher's job to find those people and let them know that your product exists. After all, how can anyone be impelled to go out and purchase a title if they don't even know that it's there?

All true and all logical, in a way, yet it's a kind of logic that simply ignores the cold mathematics of costs and revenues. Any genuinely national advertising campaign will have costs running instantly into six figures – far beyond what any publisher could afford. If a national campaign is out of the question, then perhaps you feel publishers need to be a little smarter. Perhaps, for example, you feel that heavy advertising on the London Underground would draw the book to the attention of London's chattering classes, who might then seed a wider interest in your book. Or perhaps highly targeted print advertising could achieve the same effect. Or perhaps clever viral advertising on the internet could deliver a large audience at a low cost.

The trouble with all these ideas is that they want to get something for nothing. They're tricks of wishful thinking, and little more. It is probably true, for example, that advertising in London has a disproportionately powerful effect on cultural tastes at large – but everyone knows this, and ads on the London Underground are priced accordingly. And the phrase 'highly targeted print advertising' sounds good on a page, but is more naked than a ghost in practice. How exactly, after all, are lovers of Jane Austen to be 'targeted'? Is there some print publication to which Jane Austen lovers all secretly subscribe? Are they members of some secret society, or have a code word that they're all trained to respond to? Or is it, in reality, the case that Jane Austen lovers are pretty much as diverse in their interests and practices as human beings at large?

The phrase 'viral marketing' is also, usually, a con. It's easy to create something which *could* go viral on the internet, but eyeballs on the net are as hard to reach as eyeballs anywhere else. Hordes of corporate marketers (most of whom have budgets far larger than those of publishers) are anxiously trying to reach them. Although there are some wonderful stories of internet successes, there are countless more unreported stories of internet-based marketing efforts which tried and failed to make an impact.

In short, when publishers tell you that the budget does not permit a certain investment, they are almost certainly telling the truth and have shown some wisdom in setting the budget in the first place. The simple fact is that most books by people who aren't already celebrities or best-sellers find their readers more or less at random: that is, from readers going into bookshops and browsing titles. The process works in the sense that bookshops mostly turn a profit, publishers earn their crust and you get paid a little too. It fails

in the sense that loads of people go into bookshops and come away without
some books that it would really please them to have found. It fails further
in the sense that loads of people don't even go into the bookshop in the first
place, despite the fact that they might have found something there to delight
them if they had gone in. But that's life. That's life in any industry, and it's
life twice over in the impecunious world of publishing.

THE EYES OF A PUBLISHER: TIME AND TIMING

An important consequence of the low-budget world of publishing is that
time is also strictly rationed. Your book might well be better published if
everyone could spend more time on it. It's also true that, if you're a good
enough writer to have secured a book deal, you yourself probably bring an
obsessive degree of perfectionism to the project. That's just as it should be,
but you, remember, write from passion first and for money second. Your
editor likes your book, but she's got twenty-three others to publish this year
as well, and she likes all of those books too. She also has new submissions to
consider, committees to sit on, book fairs to attend, and so on. She does not,
in fact, have a huge amount of time either for you or your book. If that
sounds harsh, then bear in mind that it is only rigorous discipline about cost
and time which allows publishers the money to pay you anything for your
book at all.

You will encounter the same disciplines at work when it comes to timing.
On the PR front, you will (if all goes well) experience a burst of publicity
activity around the launch of your book and then – nothing. Dead silence.
You'll find yourself thinking of other articles you could write, other interviews you could do, other news stories you could seek to engage with, but,
if you try to contact your publicist to talk about these terrific ideas, you'll
find that it takes longer and longer to get your phone calls returned, until
you give up making them altogether.

From your perspective, valuable opportunities to promote the book are
being wasted. From a publisher's perspective, there is only one 'sweet spot'
for publicity, namely around the launch of a book. (Its first launch, that is: a
launch in mass-market paperback following either a hardback or trade paperback edition isn't news at all. It's a minor alteration to an existing product.)
Because a publisher knows this, they'll focus all their PR efforts on the week
or two when it's most needed and most fruitful. Unless the circumstances
are unusual, any effort beforehand or afterwards will largely be a waste of
time.

THE EYES OF A PUBLISHER: FASHION

Authors are, almost universally, oblivious to publishing fashions and disdainful of them. On the whole, they're right. No genuinely creative act emerges from focus groups and marketing analyses. The best books spring into being because, in the author's mind, they *have* to exist.

But that's authors. Publishers don't and can't and shouldn't think like that. Publishers have to sell to retailers who, in turn, have to sell to ordinary book buyers. The books industry is as prone to fashion, excess, flippancy and illogic as any other industry where the consumer is boss. If celebrity cookbooks are all the rage, then publishers will seek out celebrity cookbooks. If vampire books are selling like holy water and garlic, then publishers will be seeking to sink their teeth into something vampiric.

At the same time, publishers can see further ahead than regular book buyers. As an author, you can only look at what's on the bookshelves. You'll be a year behind the market, as viewed by the publishers who are buying manuscripts now for sale next year. You'll be two or three years behind the market, if you consider the gap between starting your novel and seeing it on the shelves. Those delays are largely unavoidable, but they can be lethal to your ambitions. All fashions, particularly when they're frenzied, will have their turn. If the shops seem crowded with Dan Brown lookalikes (let's say), then it's a fair bet that publishers are already refusing to buy any more Dan Brown-ish manuscripts that come their way.

What's more, publishers have a thousand things to consider that will never cross your radar. What other books are on their release schedule? What books are other publishers releasing? What are the supermarkets asking for? What's the state of play in negotiating promo slots at the major retailers? What's the mood in the rights market? What are important media partners on the lookout for? What are the implications of changes in key personnel at the major retailers? And so on. It's a fair bet that, when an author is stricken by some adverse and apparently random piece of industry decision-making, the decision in question has been carefully thought through and makes perfect sense when all extraneous facts are taken into consideration. That's not to say that the publishers will always be right, of course. They can't possibly be. The market simply doesn't allow for perfect vision. All the same, publishers won't do their job any better if they simply choose to ignore the multiplicity of factors that come together in determining what does and does not sell.

BUT ON THE OTHER HAND . . .

So far in this section I've tended to side with the publisher. Authors are often unrealistic about the extent of advertising support that is possible. They are also often unrealistic about the amount of time that will be lavished on their book, unrealistic about sales expectations, unrealistic about the likely shelf life of their book, and so forth.

And that unreality is not their fault. When I got my first proper job, I was given an 'induction course' which told me what I needed to know to orient myself effectively in an unfamiliar world. The course hardly made me an expert, but it no doubt saved me from a folly or two. Pretty much any competent employer will offer something similar to new employees. Yet no publisher or agent is likely to spend a morning acquainting their new charge with the realities of the business. No publisher that I know of invests any real time training authors to play an effective and useful role in the publishing process. If authors are naive, that's because nobody has ever made the effort to help them be otherwise.

And since authors are never divested of their naivety, their suggestions and desires are often inappropriate, counterproductive or unrealistic. For those reasons, publishers tend to keep authors well outside the publishing process. Decisions are made in-house by people who do indeed know the industry extremely well, and then those decisions are sold to the authors. Indeed, one of the remarkable things about the publishing industry from an author's point of view is how nice everyone is. I've hardly ever met an unpleasant publisher, and all my editors have been delightful. If I'm bothered by something, they're reassuring. If I'm upset, they're soothing. If I'm cross, they're diplomatic. If I'm optimistic, they're politely encouraging.

All this is remarkably nice in many ways, until one starts to notice that one is being treated like a mental patient with a history of impulse-control issues. I remember once having lunch with an editor (and, as it happens, a very able one). We were talking about the books industry. Thanks to my work with the Writers' Workshop, I've engaged with thousands of writers, I know countless agents, and my contacts in publishing are eclectic and extensive. In short, I'm not just an author, I'm an insider. My editor was much more open about the inner workings of the trade than I'd ever heard her be before, or than any of my previous editors had been. After a while, she brought herself up short and apologised. 'I'm so sorry. I'd never usually talk so openly about the publishing industry with an author, but then you're a part of it, after all.'

I don't quite remember what I said in response to that, but I do remember feeling astonished. Not only was my editor saying explicitly that being an author did not in itself render one a part of the industry, she was also saying that she would have censored her commentary if I had been 'only' an author. These attitudes are not specific to that particular editor. They are, I would say, pretty much universal.

They are also, very often, unwise. Authors cannot collaborate effectively in publishing a book if they are deliberately kept at a convenient distance. Now while it's perfectly true that books can be effectively published with the author kept firmly on the sidelines, it's also true that they can be published very badly that way too. It will also go on being the case, much more often than not, that authors know more about their book and their subject than their publishers can do. By keeping authors in the gently padded area reserved for impulsive mental patients, publishers are excluding themselves from properly accessing that special area of expertise.

This book has two primary purposes, one (from my point of view) rather routine, the other (in a mild way) revolutionary. The routine objective is to help first-time writers make a proper, businesslike approach to agents and to navigate all those other opening steps of an authorial career in a professional and commonsensical way. The revolutionary objective is broader and more interesting than that. It's to supply the training that publishers don't. It's to equip authors with the know-how to play their part in the publishing process constructively and creatively and in a way that increases sales for the author and profit for the publisher.

That objective is a revolutionary one, because it means encouraging you to clamber over the red ropes penning you into your area of long lunches and padded sofas, and into the offices where decisions are made and campaigns constructed. No publisher wants you on their side of those ropes. They will – in a thoroughly nice, diplomatic, encouraging way – seek to return you to the sofa. Much of the rest of this section and this book aims to supply a set of escape notes. If you follow them wisely, it's perfectly possible that you will gain a reputation for being an assertive author, but not an imbecile or difficult one. Your book may succeed or it may fail, because life is like that, but either way you'll have done all you can to shape its destiny in a way that makes sense for the book and that reflects your own knowledge, passion and enthusiasms.

ENGAGING WITH PUBLISHERS

The first thing to say about successful engagement with publishers is to recall the lessons from earlier in this section.

➢ Publishers have to sell a series of highly disparate products, few of which will achieve any great revenues.

➢ The fact that publishers succeed in making money at all is because they are disciplined and rigorous when it comes to budgeting for time and money.

➢ Because you care more about your book than anything else, excluding (probably) your children and (possibly) your spouse, these facts are likely to exit your head almost as soon as they enter. They need to stay there.

➢ If you are to engage constructively with publishers, you need to deal with the world as it is, not as you'd like it to be. Almost certainly, that means no advertising, no zeppelins over London, no girls with sashes handing out freebies at mainline rail stations. It means working within a smaller, tighter, narrower budget than you would ever choose.

It also means accepting that your publisher is usually right. They know more about retailers, more about the print and broadcast media, more about printing costs and logistics, and more on a hundred other subjects than you can or ever will. If you start to argue on those fronts, you will instantly prove yourself a dunce and your subsequent efforts to escape those enclosing ropes will become ever harder, ever less likely of success.

It's also important to be a nice person. Publishing is a *nice* industry. If you come over as arrogant (and many authors do), or overbearing (ditto), or aggressive, or demanding, or contemptuous or anything along similar lines, then your editor will deal with you politely and firmly – while unhesitatingly and rightly, keeping you away from anything important. Assertiveness does not mean aggression. It means polite, businesslike focus on the point at hand. It means respecting your publisher's comments, seeking to see the world from their perspective. It means being appropriately grateful for points conceded. It means being generous with praise and niggardly with criticism.

These things matter. I once worked with a publisher one of whose authors was a Very Famous Writer, with loads of best-selling titles to his name. The VFW was on the point of shifting his business to another firm and, far from being upset about this, everyone at the publisher concerned was delighted. They didn't like this individual. Handling his work had been a chore, not a pleasure. When the time came to renew his contract, they duly made an offer – it would have been commercially crazy not to have done so – but the offer was pitched low. The VFW turned it down and went off to another publisher instead. Because he was well known to be arrogant and difficult, it's likely that the winning publisher was also paying less than they might otherwise have done. If you value your arrogance so much that you don't mind getting underpaid for your work, then by all means be arrogant and inconsiderate. Just make sure that you have several top-ten best-sellers to your name before you start to exercise this policy, however, as arrogant debut authors don't get underpaid; they don't get published.

Having said all this, you do need to be assertive, not simply nice. Many editors have perfected the art of soothing words and empty meanings. I knew one author who, for various reasons, was keenly interested in how one of her paperbacks was selling. She knew that the first print run had been 17,000 copies, but she also knew that she needed to sell some 50,000 if her existing level of advance was to be supportable into the future. As she saw it – and probably correctly - the sales of that book bore directly on her ability to continue in her chosen career.

Her editor knew her position. The two individuals had always got on well and had a strong and professional relationship. There was no reason why the editor in question should not have told the author whatever she knew about book sales. And the news that the author received was positive. The publisher had just ordered another print run. Things were looking good. The author went away from that encounter chuffed and happy. Her book was selling! It would need to go on selling strongly if it was to break through that 50,000-book barrier, but after a disastrous previous launch things were looking up.

They weren't. The second print run which the publisher had ordered consisted of just 4,000 copies. The editor knew that when she told the author. She knew that if, the author were to be offered a further contract at all, any advance would be precipitously down from what it had been in the past. She knew all that, but preferred not to tell the author, who would only find out much later after receiving a computer-generated royalty statement which put the news in cold black and white.

This kind of editorial 'niceness' is entirely phoney. It wasn't a kind act to withhold the truth from the author. She was going to find out sooner rather than later, and she'd have much preferred to learn as soon as possible, so that she could plan accordingly. The trouble is that, because editors have been trained to soothe the author away from possible confrontation, they've never learned the art of relaying bad news in a straightforward, timely manner. Indeed, they've never come to think of it as their responsibility to do that.

Since many authors come into the books trade from rougher, franker, more direct professions, the polite evasions of publishing are apt to be disconcerting. In particular, you're likely to come away from a meeting believing that X is going to be done, or Y is an agreed plank of the marketing campaign. You believe this, because you made an excellent case for X or Y, and your editor said something like, 'Yes, it's absolutely that kind of energy and imagination that we need to put to work here.' She might have said a number of other things along similar lines, all of them encouraging and supportive, but none of which precisely amounted to: 'Yes, we are going to do X and then, once we've done that, you can bet your boots we're going to go right on and do Y.' You, naturally enough, heard lots of supportive murmurs and nobody telling you that X or Y was a bad idea, so you concluded that X or Y are, at the very least, firmly on the menu of options. And they aren't. You just won't be told that.

All this makes navigation an unexpectedly difficult business. By the time you find out that X hasn't been done, it's probably going to be too late to do it. You can't get too brusque or too challenging with people, because that will get their backs up – and, remember, you'll be wrong more often than you're right. All the same, you are correct to think that your perspective, if correctly deployed, will add value and, if others don't want to include you properly in the decision making, you will need to overcome their resistance nevertheless.

THE MAGIC FORMULA FOR SUCCESS

There is no magic formula for success. The red ropes are there for a reason, and they're not about to be unhooked just because your editor likes you. All the same, the key elements of your strategy are already plain. You need to learn as much as you can about the industry. This book is your first, best introduction to it, but you need to learn as much as you can from every source. In particular, you need to learn about your own particular corner of the publishing ecosystem. The way things are done at a small publisher of military history books is very different from the way a conglomerate publisher launches a new, big thriller writer.

Next, you need to be businesslike in every aspect of your interaction with a publisher. Don't be late with deadlines – and, if you are running late, talk to your editor sooner rather than later to discuss things. Remember that your publisher is having to print catalogues, negotiate shelf space with retailers, and very much more besides. If you miss your delivery date – and, what's worse, miss it without warning – then you are causing complications that will not be yours to sort out.

Likewise, I recommend that you get into the habit of following up phone calls with a brief email to document what was discussed and agreed. Be courteous, friendly and responsive. The more positive and helpful you are in these routine interactions, the more scope you have to put your foot down on issues that bother you.

Thirdly, you need to see the world from the publisher's point of view, and accept that any proposal you make has to look as good from that perspective as it does from yours – which means, above all, realism and cost-effectiveness.

Lastly, you need to pick your battles. You can't micromanage all the aspects of a publisher's campaign – indeed, you can't micromanage any. You are not a publisher. You are not publishing your book. Nevertheless, there will, from time to time, be issues that you think are being poorly managed or that you care deeply about for some other reason. Focus your efforts on those issues. Engage keenly on those things. Be polite but assertive. Be reasonable. But push. You may or may not get the result you want – and the result you want may or may not make an overall difference to sales – but you will feel better with a campaign shaped, at least in part, around your ideas and convictions.

The rest of this book will focus on a whole series of topics, some of which are highly unlikely to concern you directly (though you do need to know about them to have a balanced picture of the publishing process), and some of which may well concern you deeply. What follows, therefore, is an escapologist's guide, a handbook for ducking under those red ropes and making a break for the office suites beyond. Good luck! You're going to need it.

EDITORIAL

At this happy stage of your career, you quite likely don't need to worry too much about editorial feedback. Your work has already convinced an agent to take you on. A publisher has already been persuaded to get out their chequebook. If anyone had serious reservations about any central aspect of your work, you'd have heard all about it before now.

If you secured your original deal on the back of a book proposal, of course, the position is somewhat different. A proposal is only a sketch of a future work. If you deliver a work that seems to the publisher to fall short of the original intention, then you may well get tougher, more substantive comments.

HOW EDITING WORKS

Even for reasonably major projects, an editor won't have all that much time allocated to editorial work. For each book, they might have about a day and a half at their disposal. Since it probably takes a careful day to read something thoroughly, that leaves about a morning to compile a set of notes sufficient to steer a book from where it is to where it needs to be. If the book that emerges from this round of editing is not yet right, there will not be a further day and a half available to do the same again.

Obviously, no book will be sent to press with any really gross imperfections, but the emphasis at the second-round stage will be on a swift, practical tidy-up – the way teenagers clean up after a party, shoving the most visible rubbish into binliners and not worrying too much about the dark stains on the Persian carpet, or those weird marks on the sitting-room ceiling. If for any reason the editorial problems are profound, a more intensive editorial approach might kick into action, but that's an exception. What's more, since you've achieved a book deal on the basis of the manuscript you already have, you are not likely to find your manuscript being suddenly whisked off to the emergency ward.

In terms of the way you receive editorial feedback, different editors work in different ways. Most often, you'll get a long email. That'll start with praise – almost certainly meant, but also there to comfort your soul for the hardships to follow. You'll then get some paragraphs of general advice. Such-and-such a character seems a little too limp. The plot twist at Irkutsk seems a little contrived. The subplot involving the ghost of Cleopatra seems a little underwhelming at times. The criticisms you'll receive are likely to be on about that scale. Your editor will also suggest remedies. You could talk more about such-and-such's childhood, to help the reader understand why he is as he is. You could deal with the Irkutsk problem by having the protagonist receive a key letter before, not after, she arrives there. And so on.

After you've waded through the equivalent of an A4 page or so of such comments, you'll get to a long series of close notes. 'Page 23, you have Jan included in the conversation, yet it wasn't clear from page 21 that she had entered the room.' 'Page 34, some of the comedy seems a little thin. Maybe cut some of it out?' 'Page 38, you are repeating some of the info contained earlier in the chapter.' And so on.

Different editors will work differently, but I'd say that notes of this sort would be fairly typical. For what it's worth, I've also had editorial discussions which in the first place were entirely oral, culminating in just two pieces of advice. (Beef up two or three chapters, lay more emphasis on such-and-such a theme.) Once these bits of advice were dealt with, I then got a series of page-by-page close notes. On another occasion, an editor I worked with just sat with me in a room, and went through the manuscript page by page. She'd scribbled comments on various pages, and we just spent time talking through those comments in cases where they weren't already obvious. The whole thing took about forty minutes.

PEER REVIEWS

In some areas of publishing – where the publisher is diligent, where the subject and audience are specialist and where funds permit – the publisher may send the draft manuscript out for peer review. The object there is to solicit the views of other experts in the field, in order to eliminate any stray errors of fact and in order to ensure that the tone and argument is appropriately pitched and balanced.

If your publisher is intending to obtain peer reviews for your manuscript, you should welcome them. You most likely won't see the reviews themselves, as they'll be filtered via your editor, but you will have the reassurance of knowing that your manuscript has been crash-tested in privacy before being launched on to the market. These reviews provide feedback, nothing more. Sometimes, you will consider a particular element of feedback and decide that your original statement was fine just as it was, or with only light modification. At other times – which will be in a majority – you'll want to revise or amend your text to deal with the objection. If you stubbornly resist all changes, it is likely both that your text will be weaker and that your manuscript is less happily shaped for its intended market. Feedback is there to help, not criticise, and any wise author will draw the maximum benefit from receiving it.

HOW TO WORK WITH YOUR EDITOR'S COMMENTS

When you get comments from your editor, do be prepared for a certain amount of emotional reaction. Different authors react differently – and over time your skin tends to thicken – but it can be hard to hear anything negative about your work, even if any criticisms come wrapped in plenty of praise (and, if it comes to that, a book deal). If you're a sensitive soul, then just let yourself be. Allow yourself to have that first reaction and then, as it starts to pass, dig back into your editor's report to scrutinise it again. You may need to review it several times over several days to let it settle and to get the fullest possible value out of it.

As you do this, you need to remember that your editor is there to advise, not to order. In particular, though you'd be well advised to take seriously any areas of discomfort which your editor highlights, you certainly don't need to adopt her suggested remedies. Editors are not writers. Some of them may approach your text with something like an author's intuition for how a certain approach would play out in practice. The majority won't. In the past, I've received editorial reports where I understood precisely what my editor's concerns were – and where I thought she was probably right to have them. At the same time, I was confident that, if I'd adopted the specific remedies she suggested, I'd have had a train-wreck on my hands, not a novel.

In that particular instance, the approach I adopted was more or less the direct opposite of the one my editor had suggested. (She had wanted me to add more about X, more about Y, more about Z. Instead, I cut 25,000 words out of the novel, tightening the focus and ratcheting up the intensity.) When I delivered the revised manuscript, she loved it. She wasn't at all bothered that I hadn't taken her advice, because the point was I *had* taken it. She'd indicated the things she wasn't happy with. I dealt with those things. She did her editorial work as she was meant to; I had done my authorial work as I was meant to. Truth is, I doubt if she even noticed that I'd done the opposite of what she'd suggested. She wasn't reading my manuscript to see if I had ticked the various boxes on her notes. She was reading it to see if she still had any significant areas of discomfort.

If you're worried about heading off in a direction different to that recommended by your editor, then talk to him. He'll almost certainly want to know that you've got a plan to deal with any issues that he's drawn to your attention, but, if your plan for fixing those things sounds reasonable, he'll probably just encourage you to go ahead. If you want to run particular chunks by him before you tackle the entire manuscript, then feel free to ask if you can do just that. He'll certainly say yes.

THE ROLE OF THE EDITOR

We hear a lot about the death of publishing and, either by extension or as blame, the death of the editor. And perhaps there's some truth there: agents are being asked to do more editorial work, particularly in the build-up to an acquisition. But I'd argue that what we're talking about is not a 'death' of the editor, but a transformation.

All editors get into publishing because we love books. From the desk editor who works on humour books to the literary editor with a string of Bookers and Pulitzers to his name – we all believe wholeheartedly in the magical power of books to transform, enlighten, entertain, move and educate readers. For me personally, every great moment I've had in publishing has been about the writing.

However, publishing is also a business, and an increasingly difficult one – and editorial love alone is not enough.

That love affair starts at the moment of acquisition. Being an acquiring editor means, among other things, fishing around for interesting books, jumping on them before anyone else does, then convincing twenty or thirty other people in-house that the book in question is unmissable. These days, there is huge pressure on title count – which means we are not allowed to publish as many books a year as we once did – and we're offering much more modest advances than used to be the case.

There is also a great deal of caution about smaller books which, while they don't cost much, often don't do much either in terms of sales, and therefore simply don't represent a good investment. (This attitude is easy to bemoan – and, of course, publishing is littered with tales of books that were roundly rejected, eventually picked up for a song, then went on to sell millions of copies. Perhaps the digital revolution will turn the clock back here, in a positive way.)

In the meantime, we need to be even more discerning that we were. It's not enough to find a book that you like or that you simply find enjoyable. You have to feel completely passionate about it and you have to be able very clearly to imagine exactly how you would publish it, from what kind of cover might work on it, to whom you could approach for advance praise, to which retailers might stock it and in which promotions.

If you as the editor aren't able to see this, you can be pretty sure no one else will either.

But assume you manage to find a brilliant book you utterly adore, everyone else in-house feels equally passionately, and you manage to beat all the other rapacious editors out there to the punch and buy it. You then move into pre-publication, at the heart of which is – from an editor's point of view, anyway – the edit. And the essence of this remains unchanged. I said earlier that I thought agents were playing a larger role in helping to shape material, and this is true as far as material that we receive on submission. But the agent's involvement with the text usually ceases once a book has been bought.

The editorial relationship varies enormously from author to author, agent to agent, and editor to editor. And I think to be prescriptive with this most *nebulous aspect of the entire publishing process — to say it must be one way or another, that it must involve weeks on end of close tête-à-tête — is not necessarily constructive. Some authors like daily conversations, others like to be left along for months on end and get tetchy if you email them more than once a week.*

Once the main structural edit is done and you've ironed out any big issues with the structure, characterisation, plotting and what have you, there are countless other aspects of the book that need to be attended to. Covers have to be briefed; sales, cover and catalogue copy written; copy-edits and proof reads performed; plus any number of other tasks completed, from picture research to commissioning an index.

Interestingly, this role of the editor at this point of the process is also changing. Increasingly at this stage we're now thinking about digital options, whether it's how to generate or integrate extra content for websites, e-books and apps, or whether there are alternative ways in which authors can be published and promoted.

But, eventually, you have your finished text. And at this point — or in fact usually earlier, during the edit — you need to start thinking about 'buzz'.

Obviously we have sales and marketing teams whose entire job is to help create buzz and get people enthused about our books. But their access to and understanding of the book is often mediated by editors.

Don't get me wrong, these are passionate and voracious readers who are incredibly skilled at marketing and selling them — but they have to sell about thirty books a month. And that's on top of reading any books that come up for acquisition. It would take a superhuman to be able to read them all.

And so frequently they rely on the editor not just to supply the samplers and bound proofs and crib sheets that they need to sell-in with, but also to communicate clearly what it is that makes each book special. This phase of the publishing process is all about 'communicating passion' to use a phrase that sounds like it should belong to advertising. But then publishing is partly advertising. We're selling something: your book.

Then, finally, after about ten months of mounting excitement and assiduous polishing of the manuscript, we hit publication and, hopefully, acclaim.

And, in the end, we editors do all this because we believe in culture and we believe in literature as an art, as well as a form of entertainment. And for these things to matter, they have to be relevant to the population they speak to. This doesn't mean lowest common denominator. It means looking at yourself, looking at the world around you, and somehow reflecting it back in an insightful way and communicating this vision to the people you hope to reach. It's this that the editor tries to facilitate.

No editor is infallible, of course. But publishing is an optimistic as well as a pragmatic business and it wouldn't survive if we allowed ourselves to linger too long on the negative. You have to be able to imagine the successes in order to make it happen. And that is the great gamble, the great thrill and I think still the great privilege and responsibility of the editor.

ANNABEL WRIGHT
Commissioning Editor, HarperPress

Now, while it's true that you have plenty of flexibility in deciding how to respond to a given set of comments, you do have to respond to them. That's partly because your relationship with your editor is likely to slide rapidly downhill if you come over as disdainful of their expertise. It's also because editors do know their stuff. If they draw attention to a problem, then there is almost certain to be a problem there. Those problems are most often literary ones: flaws in characterisation, say, or gaps in the narrative logic. Sometimes, though, they'll be market-related ones. A couple of times, for example, I've turned an ambiguous and muted denouement into a more upbeat one, because my editor has insisted that the market prefers happy endings. (Which, sigh, is probably true.) Either way, you need to respond. Your book will be a worse book and a less saleable one if you don't.

When it comes to dealing with the close notes, things are much simpler. The problems mentioned are more minor, the fixes more straightforward. Even with these things, however, there's room for differences of opinion. If you fix 60% of the issues the way your editor suggested, fix a further 20% but in some other way, and leave the last 20% of the issues untouched because you thought your editor was missing the point, then you're probably doing just fine. And at all times, in cases of doubt, just pick up the phone and talk. Your editor will welcome you doing this. It's certainly better to spend fifteen minutes talking things through by phone than spending a day or two fiddling uselessly with your manuscript because you're hesitating over what your editor might think of this or that new idea.

EDITING TO THE MAX

Most editors in publishing houses are decent, capable editors. Most of the time, your editorial relationship will function very much as you want it to. But not always. Various different problems can arise.

Number one, your editor might not be very editorially minded. That sounds almost like a contradiction in terms, rather like accusing a plumber of not being much interested in plumbing. Despite the job title, however, an editor is about vastly more than editing. If I were obliged to choose between an editor who was editorially brilliant but useless at her other jobs, or one who was an editorial dunce but supremely gifted at co-ordinating design, production, sales, publicity and all the rest of it, I'd unquestionably opt for the latter. So would any sane author. Some excellent editors are mediocre editors. It sounds strange, but it's true.

Number two, the level of editorial ambition in a modern publishing house is not very high. Again, that's not a veiled attack on anyone; it's a reflection of the economics of publishing. Modern publishers just don't have time to engage in extensive, iterative, collaborative editing work. They

---

THE WRITER–EDITOR RELATIONSHIP

The writer–editor relationship is at the heart of the publishing business. This is because writers are at the heart of the business, and, however much people might like to pretend this is not so, it is absolutely the fact. The best publishers respect their writers, value those relationships above all others, and feel that their job is to work for them and with them.

No one can predict what will sell. As an editor, all you have is your instinct, your experience and your belief in what you are doing. It is the editor who is the engine that drives the publication of a book. An editor's job is not just to acquire and edit a book. Work on a book is never finished: the editor must oversee the entire publication process, from the content of the Advance Information sheet, the image for the cover, the copy written about the book, finding quotes for the cover, dreaming up the right sales angles, through to the publishing and publicity of the book. Indeed, I feel it is as much an editor's job to publicise a book as to edit the text – both in-house, enthusing colleagues, and then in the outside world, through contacts with writers, journalists and other influential people. This means that it is impossible for an editor to separate their work and their personal lives.

Above all, as an editor, you need to have a great deal of optimism and an ability to take failure. The sad truth is that more books fail than succeed – and it can be the most cherished books that fail and the most unexpected books that take off. Finally, therefore, an editor needs quite a lot of luck.

ALEXANDRA PRINGLE
Editor-in-Chief, Bloomsbury

have too many books to bring out. Time is costed remorselessly. What's more – and this is sad – publishers have worked out that editorial excellence doesn't necessarily buy you success. No one wants to diminish the importance of those old editorial skills, but it remains true that getting the cover right, the launch right, the marketing approach right will all pay larger, faster dividends than tinkering with sentence rhythms or honing narrative structure. The commercial logic therefore tends towards the swift decisive correction of obvious, correctable things, and that's it.

I once had a lengthy editorial conversation by phone with my editor. We'd discussed her general comments, and the several pages of close notes that had followed. We chatted a little further and by this point had been on the phone perhaps 45 minutes. She was getting ready to close the conversation, but I had one last question to ask before we ended. I said, 'But, S——, don't you think that the middle third of the novel is a bit saggy?' She said, 'Oh yes. Yes, it is a bit.' I was gobsmacked. Her other comments had been accurate but fairly minor, yet all the while she'd had a much larger reservation about the work and hadn't even thought it worth mentioning. Her attitude in that conversation wasn't, however, unusual. It's commercially responsible editing. Alas, it's not the sort most likely to bring your work to a state where you'll be enduringly happy with it. (You may ask why I delivered a manuscript that I myself had reservations with, and the answer, I suppose, is that I had done as much as I could, that I knew the manuscript was strong enough to publish as it stood, and that I felt in need of someone else's guidance on how to improve things yet further. If I had been a better author, I wouldn't have delivered something with any degree of sag.)

The third reason why the editorial process might not work as well as it ought is simply that the chemistry might not be right. Perhaps you and your editor just don't see your book in quite the same way. Or he can't get his points across in a way that makes sense to you. Or you find him domineering, or you think he finds you woolly. Sometimes, two people just can't work together well.

If you encounter any of these problems, you'll need to decide what to do. One is simply to make the best of it. Use your own editorial wisdom. Use whatever you can get from your editor. Do the best job you can. That'll be the approach of most authors. It's not perfect, but it's perhaps good enough.

Another alternative is to make full use of whatever other professional resources are available to you. I know one author who doesn't think much of her editor in the UK, and relies heavily on her editor in the US. I know another who rates her agent exceptionally highly as an editor and works extensively with her. If you have access to such resources, then you're lucky. Most authors won't.

One, somewhat nuclear, option is to ask your publisher if you can have a different editor. That's a perfectly reasonable strategy, or would be in most professional situations, but you may well find yourself feeling like the boy who asked for more. I know one author whose first novel had been short-listed for a major prize and earned out her advance. The editor she'd worked with on the book left the firm. She was allocated another editor. She didn't get on with that editor, and wrote a perfectly respectful letter to the publisher suggesting that she would work more successfully with an editor with whom she had better chemistry. (I know the letter was respectful: I saw it.) The publisher was not amused. For a while, it looked as though the author had jeopardised her relationship with that firm altogether. In the end, things were smoothed over, but it was an episode that left its mark on both sides. The author concerned would have been better off to have approached the situation via her agent, but I'm not sure she'd have secured the desired outcome by doing that. She'd just have avoided disaster.

One still further option is to pay for outside editorial advice. That's not an approach I encourage. Authors should not be required to pay for a service that their publisher should be providing to a high standard and without charge. Nevertheless, some authors do end up paying for help. My own agency, for example, works with a small number of professional authors who get from us what they can't get from anyone else. No doubt other editorial agencies have the same experience. As I say, though, I think this will be a last option for most authors. If the industry worked as the industry ought to, it would never be required. Failing that, gritty self-reliance is free and probably does wonders for your soul.

GETTING ON WITH IT

Editing your book is not an endless process. By the time you've got an agent, got that book deal and got your first set of notes, that process is effectively at an end. Address any last changes. Reread your work. Then leave it. Your editor will certainly read your manuscript again. If there are any last niggles, they'll need to be addressed, but essentially you need to take your hand away from the keyboard.

There is, as it happens, a clause in any publishing contract that can make it hard or costly for an author to make late changes to their work, but the issue is more about good professional behaviour than any specific contractual risk.

The point is that your publisher needs a completed text, so they can get on with copy-editing and page layouts and typesetting. If you are constantly seeking to amend the text, all those processes will be disrupted and will be done in a worse way and more expensively.

Some authors, of course, will be only too delighted to drop their pen, stretch their fingers and never look at their manuscript again. Others are dyed-in-the-wool tinkerers, who'll have to exercise a mighty act of will to do likewise. So good: exercise that will. It's good for you. Apart from anything else, bringing an end to the editorial process means you're all ready to leap straight into copy-editing, and how could that not be fun?

THE LOST ROLE OF THE EDITOR

As a literary agent for these past 33 years, I am compelled to express my observation that over the past decades the editorial role has been profoundly devalued. As corporate structures have gulped down and digested independent publishing houses and imprints, their corporate agendas have brought about a slow but steady erosion of reliance on the editor's skill and intuitive vision. In order to release the magnificent sculpture that such an editor may perceive in a stone, the work of editing takes time, focus, sometimes isolation, silence, deep cogitation, and some eureka moments when the objective eye finally perceives the solution to a thorny dilemma. Few editors today are granted the luxury of so much quality time. As a result, most are on a search for near-perfect manuscripts that they can present to their editorial boards, where sales and marketing can immediately perceive the potential for a successful publication. Needless to say, if editors are not encouraged to flex their editorial muscles effectively, the more atrophied those muscles will become, and the safer it seems to reject than to commit.

From where I sit, this has meant that we literary agents are now essentially functioning as editors, stepping into the vacuum and metaphorically taking up the stubby red pencil we had stored as a memento of a bygone age. It is now our responsibility to our writers to polish the gem before it is even seen by editorial eyes. And since most publishers today will not consider unagented manuscripts, over our transoms they come tumbling for us to filter and refine.

I realise with gratitude that for every editor who espouses the fast and furious view there are still some willing to fall in love and to commit. I know who they are. Their names are lovingly breathed within the walls of our agency, their opinions are shared and treasured. We know the editor who knows how to edit without dictating or ruffling the feathers of a sensitive novelist, who grasps the unspoken intent of the author and enables it, who believes in a work before that belief has been endorsed by everyone else, and who is willing to fight for it in a job climate where a lay-off may be a breath away.

So many of the elements of publishing that a writer and agent used to expect of an editor are currently being farmed out as publishing houses downsize. Indeed, many excellent editors and experienced marketing teams are plying their skills outside of publishing houses. Writers themselves are being asked to write their own jacket copy (and this in a major publishing conglomerate), create a national platform, develop a continuing presence in the world of social networks, twitter and tweet and write smart funny blogs to capture a readership before a book comes close to market — and of course to write a book a year to build branding.

Writers are expected to mine their personal brief encounters for blurbs for the jacket. Some have been asked to design the jacket themselves. They are frequently more savvy about the world of digital marketing than their editors are. And no sooner do they feel that they have established a true dialectic with a good editor they like and respect than that editor, as often as not, moves to another house, and the author is left floundering in the grip of a contract that does not take the relationship into account.

Yes, the editor is the negotiating voice as deals are struck, but agents are finding that editors are not given the opportunity for education in the swarm of urgent contractual issues that appear almost on a daily basis at this time of paradigm shift in our industry. Lacking the tools for relevant conversation, they quickly claim corporate policy, pass the negotiation along to others, and are unprepared themselves to deal with the hot issues of the day.

Despite all I have said here, my battle is not with editors. Most of them would like nothing better than to be the writer's advocate they had dreamed of becoming. My issue is with an industry contorting to reposition itself rather than to reinvent itself. No longer valuing editors' work and insights, it fails to trust that an editor may have the vision to find and curate the rough diamond, and provide the insights to reveal the dazzling gem hidden within.

JEAN NAGGAR
President, founder and agent at The Jean V. Naggar Literary Agency, Inc.,
Jean is also author of the memoir *Sipping from the Nile*.
This article first appeared online at The Huffington Post

COPY-EDITING, PROOFREADING AND THE CLAN PEDANTIC

'Copy-editing' and 'proofreading' are sometimes used interchangeably, but the former term implies more breadth than the latter. A copy-editor is there to correct spellings and typos, of course, but also to excise repetitious language, smooth out clunky sentences, ensure accuracy and consistency, make sure that dialogue formatting is done corectly, and so on. Proofreading is more restricted in scope. A proofreader assumes that the source text is fine in all its essentials, and his only task at that point is to correct any obvious mistakes introduced by the typesetting process or neglected by the copy-editor.

You will be involved with both phases, and the degree of your involvement is up to you.

THE LAID–BACK SOUL

If you're not too fussed about the fine detail of your text, then relax. Someone else will do all the hard work for you. A typical copy-editor will find countless little slips of the pen through your manuscript, even if it's well presented, and they'll fix them. They'll deal with it all. They will also compile a short list of questions – perhaps up to a dozen – which they need you to answer. (For example: 'Carly's eyes are described as "smoky grey" (p. 87) and "like the blue of far-off mountains" (p. 254). Is this OK?')

If you are the kind of laid-back sort, who honestly wouldn't be bothered if you were described instead as 'laidback' or 'laid back', and really wouldn't notice or care if the word 'laid-back' was used five times in the same sentence, then you can just answer your copy-editor's questions and go back to burning joss sticks or listening to whale songs, or whatever it is that the truly laid-back spend their time doing. You have an easy life.

THE PEDANTIC SOUL

If you're not that way inclined, you'll want to examine your copy-editor's corrections more closely. If you haven't been sent the entire corrected manuscript, but just those few pages containing the copy-editor's questions, then ask for the whole thing. No one will think that you're being unreasonable in wanting it. This is your manuscript. You have every right to check that you're happy with any alterations.

When you do get the whole thing, your first reaction is likely to be one of shock at the sheer number of pencil marks. You may well feel like the idiot child at school, given a D for English. Most of those marks, however, are of trivial importance. Contemporary manuscripts in the UK use single inverted commas ('like this scrawny pair'), but many authors continue to use doubles ("like these well-fed beauties"). The authors aren't incorrect, however. It's just that fashions have changed (except in North America, where doubles are still preferred). Likewise, many marks will simply be bringing the manuscript into the house style on a variety of presentational points.

Probe a little closer, however, and you may find some more substantial edits that you really don't agree with. For example, copy-editors are eagle-eyed when it comes to repetitious language. Their eagle eyes unquestionably help things most of the time, but often isn't always. Frequently, for example, a repeated word will be excised and replaced with a rough equivalent, thesaurus-style. The trouble is that copy-editors often have a tin ear when it comes to sentence rhythms; and the sentences that result from their often rather mechanical edits can be sentences that sound badly. What's more, some repetitions are deliberate. The repetition of 'laid-back' in the sentence three paragraphs back was an obvious case, but it's easy to think of rather more literary uses too. T. S. Eliot's famous opening to *Burnt Norton* – 'Time present and time past / Are both perhaps present in time future, / And time future contained in time past' – would hardly have been improved by a heavy-handed copy-edit.

Likewise, if your prose style is deliberately rough, casual, free and easy, it's not likely to fare well in the hands of a copy-editor who likes things tidied up in the manner of a 1950s librarian. Maybe you like your sentence fragments as fragments. Maybe you prefer the American 'like' to the British 'as if '. If a character of yours splits an infinitive in dialogue, then maybe you intended to split it, so it'll stay split.

These things don't matter to everyone. Indeed, they matter intensely only to a tiny minority – it's just that authors are hugely over-represented in that minority. If (like me) you belong to the Clan Pedantic, then feel free to express your pedantry to the max. This is your moment! If you have strong views on the Oxford comma, or whether the word 'hoover' needs a capital, or the correct deployment of the semi-colon, express those views to the full. You'll be in good company, because editors and copy-editors care about these things too. Indeed, they may care about them even more than you do. I once had a long email exchange with an editor about a single pair of inverted commas, whose use was certainly optional, and whose function in the manuscript was marginal in the extreme. But she cared! And I did! We were soul-mates! (Or as we'd both, I'm sure, have preferred, soulmates.)

These joys can't, alas, last for ever. Your editor will want your own corrections of the copy-editor's corrections back sooner rather than later. Do what you're told to do. Do it by the deadline. Relish the hour.

DEDICATION, ACKNOWLEDGEMENTS, HISTORICAL NOTE

If you want a dedication, or a page of acknowledgements, or an historical note, or anything else, then (within reason) you'll be welcome to incorporate such things. Your editor may already have asked for them. If not, then you'll certainly be asked for them now.

Acknowledgements these days are fearsomely cool. ('Thanks too to Max the Biker for his immense right hook, to Nadia for showing me her Ingushetia, to M. who didn't want me to mention his name for fear of retribution – and if I've forgotten to mention anyone, then thanks to you especially. The best nights go unremembered.') Personally, I've never mastered the art of the cool acknowledgement, but I understand that a willingness to lie and a hair-raising imagination are useful ingredients in the concoction.

Do also be sensible about what your book needs. A novel does not need footnotes. An historical note should probably not run to more than two or three pages. A dedication should not be pornographic. If you really, really feel the need to explain the background to your work in twenty or thirty close-set pages, then do so and post it on the internet. A book is not the place for such things.

INDEX

If your book needs an index, then you should already have discussed that with your editor, who'll make the appropriate arrangements. The index to this book was compiled by a professional indexer, which is why it works. If I'd been responsible for it, I'd have messed it up. In some publishing contracts, you will be asked either to prepare an index yourself or to pay for the work. You should resist either option. Indexing is as much a part of the book's production as is copy-editing or typesetting. It's not your skill. Don't get involved unless you want to – and have the skills to make a genuine contribution.

(And, if you happen to be the author of an academic monograph, the above paragraph does not apply. The index is your job. If you don't do it – and do it right – no one else will do it for you.)

PERMISSIONS

If you are quoting copyright work or seeking to use illustrations that belong to someone else, then you need to secure permission for them. Work is generally out of copyright only after an author has been dead for seventy years. The criteria in the US are a little more complex. If you're not sure what the rules are in your own country, research them on the internet.

The whole permissions process is a tedious and rather silly one on the whole. If you are quoting a few lines of prose, you will need to locate the copyright owner (normally the publisher) and write to them asking for permission to use those lines. Different publishers require different things from such approaches. Go to the relevant publisher's website and search it, using 'Permissions' as your search term. You'll find a page that sets out what you need to do. Often you need to write a letter saying how many lines you want to quote, what the intended publication is, what the expected print run is in hardback and paperback, and a few other things besides.

Much of this is nonsense. These days, for example, the print run of a work is decided very close to publication date and is, in any case, of little significance as publishers tend to opt for frequent, shorter print runs than in the past. Nevertheless, you need to locate the hurdles you have to hop over, then hop dutifully over them. In the vast majority of cases, no one will ask you to pay for permission to use their copyright material, which means that you've wasted your time and they've wasted their time and no money has changed hands. If you want to quote a significant chunk written by a major modern poet, you will be asked to pay something – perhaps £60 – and quite right too. That money will theoretically come out of your pocket, but you may find that your publisher picks up the tab. Make sure you discuss things with your editor beforehand and work out some parameters that you are both happy to live by.

It's the same deal with any other copyright work – illustrations, quotes from film scripts, and so forth. If you can't trace the copyright holder, then say so in a note somewhere. Say that, if the copyright holder makes themselves known, you will seek to have them appropriately acknowledged in a future edition of the work . . . which in many cases is nonsense as well, since many books never make it into a revised, updated edition.

Do leave plenty of time for all this. You don't need to start the process before you have a book deal – apart from anything else, you won't be in a position to supply most of the information that is asked of you. But, once you've got your deal, you've dealt with editorial matters and you're wondering what else you should be doing, then do this. It can take eight to twelve weeks to secure copyright permissions from some publishers and, if the process proves convoluted, even longer. If you're on a tight deadline to publication, you may even wish to get started as soon as your deal is agreed.

Do also note that, if you do fail to get permission to quote something, any liability arising from that is yours. If you've failed to get permission to quote a couple of sentences from a little-known work that came out a couple of decades back, it's likely that any liability arising is essentially nil. It's likely, in fact, that no one will ever notice or care. On the other hand, you need to be much more scrupulous where your quotations are extensive, or where they are taken from books with obvious current market value.

Finally, if in doubt about any of this, talk to your editor. Your publisher has encountered all these issues a zillion times, and can advise you if you're not clear about anything. And, for all that it can be a headache, there are times when the permissions process works with surprising speed and ease. I once wanted to quote a chunk from *Monty Python's Life of Brian*, and was gloomily wondering just how painful and expensive it was going to be to extract permission from a bunch of millionaire anarchic comedians. In fact, it took a single email, which was responded to within 24 hours, granting me the permission for free. One more reason to love the Pythons.

PAGE PROOFS

From the corrections of the copy-editor and your own amendments of those corrections, your editor (or managing editor) will compile a master document that goes out to be typeset. That process is now, of course, largely electronic, but electronic is not the same as automatic. There are still a host of decisions to be made about page layout, fonts, pagination, and so forth – but these are not your decisions.

The next you will see of your beloved is a set of page proofs. Usually, these will be sent hard copy, but the drift now is perhaps towards sending them electronically. It's likely to be the first time that you've seen your manuscript looking anything like a book, equipped with title pages, and proper layouts, and that page with all the tiny, boring detail at the front of every book. It's an exciting moment, a significant step on the road to publication.

Yet it's not a step that need trouble you too much. The laid-back can simply admire the look of their new book, and flip through the pages if they fancy pretending to do some work. The Clan Pedantic will instantly get to work seeking to see if they can find a double space where there should be a single, and to see who won the War of the Oxford Comma. I gently recommend that you do reread your manuscript attentively, as this is your last opportunity to make any (minor) corrections, but it doesn't matter vastly if you don't.

Finally, don't expect to make significant corrections or write in any major new material at this point. You'll be messing a lot of people around if you do and may even be responsible for bearing some of the costs of resetting the document if you try.

WAVING GOODBYE

And that's it. The journey that began with your opening sentence, that reached its mid-point when you reached the final full stop, has now ended. There is plenty yet to do, but what follows is a marketing challenge, not a literary one. You may holster your pen, wipe down your keyboard and remove the orange plastic troll from the roof of your computer monitor. It has done its duty. The luck and perseverance that you needed have come your way, and brought you the rewards you yearned for. It's time for other things, the things that matter – the things that will sell the book.

COVER DESIGN AND TITLE

At some point, and quite likely overlapping with the processes of the last couple of sections, you will be presented with a draft cover design. You might receive it nicely printed on card. You might get it as a PDF file sent online. You might see it first on A4 sheets printed off from an ordinary office colour printer. Sometimes, the material will simply be emailed or posted. If it works logistically, you'll be presented with the concept when you're next at a meeting or lunch with your publisher.

Mostly, you'll just see a single design. You're being asked to choose from a menu with only one option. Occasionally – very occasionally – you might be invited to air your thoughts about a set of possible options, but those 'options' will almost certainly be variants on a single theme: in effect, the same design concept, but tweaked this way and that for the sake of variety.

The one universal, however, of these moments is a slight air of tension in the room as they happen. You're the author. This is a genuinely nice industry, where people want you to like what they've done. They want you to be happy with the approach to publication. But they also want you to say 'yes'. The image that you're shown has evolved from meetings, discussions, experiments, comments and revisions. It's the version that has the house seal of approval. Your 'yes' will be very welcome. Your 'no' will not be popular.

There's tension in the air for another reason besides. You have no say on cover design. In a typical contract, your publishers are obliged to 'consult' you on the subject, but they would certainly have met their legal obligations in full if they said, 'Here is our cover design,' you said, 'I loathe, despise and detest it,' and they said, 'We note your opinion but are going to go ahead anyway.' In formal terms, you are powerless.

Nevertheless, life is about more than contracts, and so is publishing. Editors will want you to be happy. What's more, while the consensus house view hasn't been arrived at lightly, if your argument against a given design is cogent and persuasive, your editor may well change her mind anyway. Because cover design is an absolutely critical element in the approach to market, all these things matter intensely. This section is here to help you manage them as best as you possibly can.

TA–DAAA!

The best place to start is with the moment of revelation itself.

It's common for editors to turn the unveiling of a cover design into a 'ta–daaa!' moment during a lunch or meeting. The impulse to do it that way is perhaps understandable, but it's also a bad one. The cover design is the most important single decision of the entire publishing process. It should no more be made the centre of a 'ta–daaa!' moment than should a corporate budget or a crucial marketing plan.

In particular, it's fantastically hard for you, the author, to respond sensibly in the handful of seconds after the curtain (metaphorically) falls. That's no way at all to produce a smart business decision. What ought to happen, in fact, is that a draft cover design is sent to you, probably by email, at an early stage. That way, you can be involved when decisions are still malleable, when the timetable still has plenty of room. Because your editor may not play it that way of her own accord, you need to nudge her as far in that direction as you possibly can. You won't move her as far as you'd like, but, if you don't nudge at all, you won't get anywhere. So the first piece of advice is to start nudging, politely but early. Just say that you're bad at thinking these things through quickly, and you'd like to see a draft cover at the earliest possible stage.

If you're lucky, you'll get what you asked for. If you're not, at least you'll have prepared the ground for a guarded reaction when the moment arrives.

In any event, just be prepared in advance *not* to be too nice, too helpful, too quick to say yes to that cover. Everyone around you will want you to do just that. There'll be a gentle but unrelenting pressure on you to do it. Yet now is almost certainly not the moment to make a final decision. So just make yourself say, 'Yes, interesting, do talk me through your thought processes here . . .' Whatever else you go on to say, just be certain that you leave yourself room for manouevre over the next few days, so that, if, on reflection, you think the cover is not as strong as it ought to be, you are able to say so without having to backtrack. Even if you find yourself absolutely loving the cover when you first see it, make sure that you leave yourself wiggle room. First impressions matter a lot (especially with book covers) but thoughtful reflection will often add significantly to that first reaction.

Above all, remember that in a large majority of instances your publisher is looking to secure your agreement, not solicit your commentary. Your publisher doesn't *want* any reaction other than, 'Gosh, fantastic!' Sometimes, of course, that reaction will be absolutely appropriate. Other times, it will not be. When it isn't, you need to do what you can to improve things – while all the time bearing in mind your meagre bargaining position and the importance of not rupturing your relationship at this early stage.

THE IMPORTANCE OF COMMON SENSE

In any debate over book covers, it's easy for an author to be over-impressed by the authority of those who publish books for a living. Publishers know so much more about the attitudes of retail buyers, image libraries, production possibilities and so forth that it's easy for a mere author to defer to the weight of all that superior knowledge.

Yet authors are experts too. Presumably you tend to read the kind of book that you've just written. You've spent hours browsing in bookstores. You know which book covers work for you and which don't. If you're a crime writer, then you'll be decently familiar with the state of the art. That is, you know the 'look' of a Rankin, Cornwell, Reichs, Billingham, Deaver, Rendell, and so on. That doesn't give you more authority than anyone in publishing, but it certainly qualifies you to have a view.

What's more, my own experience has been that ideas that seem to be bad are bad. I don't think I've ever encountered an exception to that rule, either when it comes to my own work or anybody else's. Indeed, it's often been the case that, when a book hasn't sold, at the post-mortem afterwards people will universally point to a jacket design that missed the mark. In the large majority of such cases, the problem was obvious beforehand and was the very thing the author had been uncomfortable about.

In particular, there is an understandable (and laudable) drive in publishing to seek ideas that are new, different, edgy and clever. Apart from anything else, a jacket designer doubtless loves to express his own creativity to the max, and would love to see a design award coming his way at some point. You, however, are not interested in design awards. You are interested in book sales. If the new, different, edgy and clever cover is going to help sell your book, fantastic. If not, you need to do what you can to procure a change. In one case, for example, I knew of a cover designer who wanted to wrap the book's title right round the hardback jacket so that, in order to understand what the book was called, a browser would actually need to unpeel the jacket (including its inside flaps) and spread it out flat. It was dazzlingly clever in some sense, but threatened to deliver no book sales at all. In that instance, I believe the book's editor was rather pleased by the author's opposition to the jacket, because it gave her a chance to combat a design she was deeply uncertain about, but few cases will be quite so extreme.

You also need to use your common sense when it comes to deciding whether a particular design is going to work for your kind of reader. Again, book designers are quite likely to be young, metropolitan, design-oriented, left-of-centre, cool types. Your book might have its natural market among older, conservative-minded, deeply uncool, *Telegraph*-reading types. You need to make sure that the designers are producing a cover that suits the book's target audience, not one that suits their own tastes. Naturally, an editor will make the target audience clear to the designer as part of the design brief, but that brief may not always be followed as closely as you think it should be.

Do also beware the cries of procrastination that you may hear. If you think a particular design is misfiring, then you're very likely to be told that you just need to wait until you see the cover in its completed state, that it'll look so much better with the foil, that they've got new effects technology which looks amazing, but can't accurately be conveyed in the early design stages.

All this is nonsense. It's true that jacket designers do now make imaginative use of the various new technologies open to them. Jacket covers can now have special metallic-style effects, gold foil can be embossed or dimpled, covers can be snipped through allowing you to peep beneath the surface. And so on. But the final copy that emerges from all this cleverness will look almost exactly the same as the one now in your hands, just a bit shinier. It is just not true to suggest that you can't judge the one by the other. You can. The main reason why you are being told to wait is so that, in three or four weeks' time, when you have the cover in its metallicised version, there will be no time left to change it. You need to combat that kind of procrastination by putting your foot down early and firmly.

One last point – the most crucial of the lot perhaps – is that you need to be careful to distinguish between a cover that you like and one that you think will sell the book. It really, truly doesn't matter whether you *like* the cover. No one cares. What matters is that you feel the book will have its commercial appeal enhanced by its jacket. Making that judgement sensibly requires you to put your own feelings aside and view the cover as neutrally as you can.

If you want to use friends and family as a focus group to help you home in on the reactions of others, then do that – though do so with care. If your book is aimed at street-smart twenty-somethings, then the view of your mum and your granny may not be very relevant. Likewise, people will often tell you whatever it is they think you want them to say, so make sure you give them the cover neutrally and ask them for honesty. Even then, you'll have some friends whose opinions you trust more than others. Listen hard to those people, and disregard the rest. Listen particularly carefully, however, if someone rates the cover very highly even if you don't. Perhaps you're missing something.

IF SOMETHING ISN'T RIGHT

If, on reflection, you feel that your draft cover design is not working, then say so. The more calm and businesslike you can be about this, the better. A good strategy is to make clear how you see the target market for your book and how you think the cover is missing that market. For example, let's say you've written a crime novel that includes the compulsory murder or two, but which is fairly light in nature – more Miss Marple, let's say, than Scarpetta. Let's also say that you've been given a cover which is sombre, black and splashed with blood, guns, syringes and the like. You may well feel (and probably should) that the cover and the book are missing each other. The jacket design might well be excellent, but for a book different from yours. You could put together a table, like the one on the opposite page, that simply but clearly makes your point.

You could go on to pick out the kind of covers that you think would work. That will mean a trip to your local large bookshop and an hour or two of browsing with a notepad, but it's time very well worth investing. Come up with a list of the *kind* of jacket designs that you think are more in tune with your book. At the same time, be alert to changing your mind. If you

Target market for book	Cover likely to appeal to
Mostly women	Larger male balance
Somewhat older	Somewhat younger
Times / Telegraph reader	Not *Telegraph*!
Wanting crime without much violence	Wanting darkness/violence
Gentle	Gritty
Likes nature, antiques programmes	Likes thrillers
Likes Agatha Christie, P. D. James etc.	Likes Cornwell, Reichs,

notice that, in fact, all the writers you thought you were similar to have got covers very much the same as the one presented to you, then your jacket designer has more than likely got it about right.

Once you've done all this, you probably want to phone your editor and talk through your thoughts in a calm and businesslike way. You can't veto any design, so don't even try to do so. Just raise objections in the most rational way you can. Be persistent, but forceful. Follow up that phone call with an email that summarises things. Be very careful to praise what is good – and, if you can't think of anything, then invent something. Then go on to point out what you think the issues are. But remain reasonable and unemotional. Your email needs to be the sort of thing that could be forwarded to the cover designer himself, if need be, without creating a stir.

TITLE

As an author, you probably think of your title choice as part of the manuscript itself: an aesthetic choice that shines its light over the book as a whole. As you approach publication, however, you need to lock such thoughts firmly away. Your book title is really no more than an aspect of cover design. The title needs to be part of a package which instantly intrigues and attracts your target audience. From that point of view, it doesn't really matter if the title neatly encapsulates the book or not. Nor does it matter whether you have to rewrite the book a little to accommodate a title (something I did with two out of my five novels). All that matters is that the cover design, together with the title, form an instantly attractive package for the potential reader. If your publisher tells you that your chosen title isn't working, then they're more often than not right.

That last sentence may strike you as inconsistent with the tone of this section. When it comes to cover designs, I've argued that your publisher may well be wrong and that you have enough expertise to be confident in identifying those errors. When it comes to title, however, I'm telling you that you need to trust your publisher. The underlying logic is actually the same. When it comes to cover design, it becomes very hard for a publisher to avoid group-think – that process by which dissenting voices are unwittingly choked off. It can also be hard for a design team to rip up the best first idea they had and start again from scratch. The issue here is that it is hard both to create something and not be over-attached to that creation.

The same goes with you and your title. You love your title. You've lived with it. You got excited when you thought of it. You love the tune of it in your head. It just strikes you as implausible when your editor tells you that it's not working with the design concept that they have. Nevertheless, you'd mostly do well to listen. My fourth novel, a book about flying in the 1920s, ended up being entitled *Glory Boys*. I think I had wanted to call it *Heaven and Earth*, or something of that sort. I liked my title. I hated *Glory Boys*, which I thought sounded camp and underwhelming. Nevertheless, I was wrong. The designers were right. The design they chose just worked with that title. The title *Glory Boys*, in fact, became part of the look of the cover, which was attractive and buyable.

Occasionally, publishers will actually suggest a title to you. Mostly, however, they'll ask you if you have any other suggestions. If they don't like those other suggestions, they'll ask you for more. And so on. The best way to generate a good list of possibles is to use the method discussed on pages 70–1: essentially just force yourself to compile a list of some hundred or more options, the good and the bad all together. From that long list, strike out the obvious bad ones, then give the remaining ones ample time to call to you. Sometimes, the best titles are ones that you thought of immediately and dismissed.

Give yourself as much time as possible for this process. It takes time for the subconscious to generate titles, and it can take further time for the best titles to make their virtues apparent to you. And don't skimp on giving the matter your attention. The title is a crucial part of the jacket, and the jacket is crucial in selling your book. A title may only be two or three words long, but they're the most important ones you'll ever choose.

SHOUT LINES AND SUBTITLES

Another important ingredient of some book covers is a 'shout line' or subtitle. A subtitle is more for use in non-fiction, and expands or explains the meaning of the title. Thus, Steven Pinker's best-selling *The Language Instinct* was explained and amplified by the words that followed the title in smaller type: 'The new science of language and mind'. With non-fiction, you're more than likely to have developed such a subtitle already. If not, you can do so in collaboration with your editor.

Pinker's subtitle is a good example of the genre. Non-fiction mostly sells itself on the basis of its subject matter, so simply advertising that this is a book about the science of language and mind is a very good start towards attracting your audience. At the same time, do note the importance of that word 'new', which functions in this subtitle in much the same way as it does when stuck on to a new formulation of washing powder or a rebranded mortgage product. The word teases and attracts. It teases, because its coded message is, 'You may think that you know this subject, but you really can't do because everything you thought you knew is out of date.' It attracts because it promises to let you in on something that others don't yet have. If you can find a subtitle that sends similarly attractive messages while at the same time straightforwardly conveying the book's subject matter, then you're on to a good thing.

A shout line does something rather similar for fiction. You don't often see such shout lines on the front covers of best-sellers, simply because best-selling authors are normally sold first and foremost on name recognition and prior reviews ('The best writer since Shakespeare' – that sort of thing). With first novels, however, you have neither of these things to help you, so a shout line is sometimes introduced instead. The shout line on my first novel, for example, read, 'The legacy of Bernard Gradley: three sons, one fortune, and a winner-takes-all race to inherit'.

Sometimes your publisher will come up with such a shout line. Sometimes they might ask you. Either way, it's useful to get involved. Do note the need for extreme brevity. That shout line on my novel, for example, ran over three lines and it would probably have been better if we could have squeezed it into just two – or about a dozen words, all told. Don't worry about being *precise*. Of course, you can't encapsulate your novel in a dozen words. All that matters is you sell your novel's concept or hook as hard as you can, without misrepresenting anything crucial. Do also note that this is not a game where subtlety will come away the winner. You need to think not as a novelist, but as an advertising exec. The sharper and stronger your shout line, the better.

TIPS FOR GOOD JACKET DESIGN

They say that you can't judge a book by its cover; but the fact is that the jacket is the first thing that a buyer will see. If it catches the eye, then that's half the battle. So how should designers set about creating such a look? In a perfect world, you would read the book to get a feel for the content and style. Unfortunately, now that everything is needed yesterday (if not earlier), this is rarely possible. But you may be able to get a synopsis, either from the author or elsewhere. This information should be included in the design brief; and, if it isn't, it should be requested!

Let's assume you've got a reasonable idea of the content. The next step is to think about the buyers. Who are they? How old are they likely to be? Knowing the demographics of the readership will allow you to craft a cover design which will combine type, graphics and layout and reflect the content in a way which will be visually appealing to your target audience.

What will be the most prominent feature on the cover? There are various routes that can be taken, but a lot will depend on the book itself. Fiction books typically have the author's name as the largest element, but with a reference book the title is usually more dominant.

Other things to consider are whether the book is a one-off or part of a series. If the latter, you might want to design each book as part of a brand, thereby making each volume instantly recognisable. This approach could include using the same typography, similar illustrations or photographic style, etc.

You'll also want to organise the size of elements on the jacket in order of their importance, selecting colours which are appropriate and harmonious and which will ensure that features flow through the visual story and allow the reader's eye to move effortlessly between them.

If you do all that, you'll be well on the way to a cover which will present the book in the very best light.

PAUL MARTIN
MD, The Page Design Consultancy

A FINAL WORD

As you mull over these thoughts in the context of your book and your draft cover design, you need to bear two things in mind.

First, nothing matters more than the jacket. It quite possibly matters more than the content of the book itself – not in building a word-of-mouth best-seller, but in giving you an initial sales platform that could support such a best-seller. That early sales platform does not and cannot come from your book's content, simply because people have not read your book at that stage. It will not come from book reviews because you are unlikely to have many, and in any case book reviews can be not particularly timely or generative of sales. And, if the initial sales platform is lacklustre or worse, your book will vanish from the promo slots so quickly that any word-of-mouth sales momentum will never have the chance to take off. So the jacket matters. It matters hugely. Your success as an author depends on it.

Secondly, you have no right of veto. Publishers aren't, on the whole, looking for you to play a constructive and collaborative role in determining the look of the jacket. On the contrary, in most cases, they'll be pressuring you (nicely, but persistently) to approve the design that is put in front of you. Mostly the draft design will be either excellent or good enough. Sometimes it won't be. In those instances where the design is poor, you need to do something – and that means leaping over the hurdles that are put in your way, whilst also doing so with enough grace and humour to avoid destroying your relationships before they've even begun.

That isn't, I know, an easy brief, but then, if you had been after an easy task, you should never have become an author.

THE BLURB

The novelist and playwright Michael Frayn once created a character who, in theory, was hard at work writing a novel but who, in practice, spent his whole time writing and polishing the blurb. Frayn was making a joke, not recommending a strategy, yet there are things one could learn from his character all the same.

The previous section talked extensively about cover design. The combined visual and associative impact of a book's title and look should, you hope, be strong enough to make a potential reader reach for the book and pick it up. Their very first movement after that is to turn the book over, to learn more about it. Just as the cover image is crucial to securing the reader's attention, then the blurb is equally critical to the putative reader's next decision: whether to open the book and start exploring its content, whether to pop the book under an arm *en route* to the tills at the front of the shop. In short, the blurb matters and it's worth putting in plenty of effort to get it right. Just make sure (unlike Frayn's character) you've written your book first.

DESIGN ASPECTS

The main themes of the cover design will continue on the back of the book. There'll need to be room for an ISBN number, barcode and a website address or two. As a debut author, you are unlikely to have any book reviews or usable book puffs (more about those in a moment), but it's quite likely that your jacket designer will want to make the book look a little as though you have such reviews, by setting opening and closing phrases in a different colour, font, size or style from the rest of the text. For example, the (UK) blurb of John Grisham's first novel, *The Firm*, has as its opening sentence: '*The job of his dreams is about to become his worst nightmare.*' It closes with: '*Now Mitch was in the place where dreams end and nightmares begin . . .*' Both those phrases were picked out in a font and colour to separate them from the remaining text. If the phrases had been set in exactly the same way – and at the very outset of his career before the positive reviews started to pour in – then the back of the book would have looked rather bland, no matter how spicy or interesting the text.

These thoughts are worth bearing in mind, because whoever comes up with the blurb needs to ensure that the cover designer has material to work with – notably a very 'sales-ey' first and last sentence. Again, it matters less that these sentences accurately describe your book. They need to describe it roughly, of course, but, more than that, they need to sell it. Brevity and punch are your watchwords here.

WHO WRITES THE TEXT?

On the whole, publishers write the blurb, not you. I've seen some excellent publishers' blurbs in my time; I've also seen some limp ones. At the same time, writing blurbs is a chore for your editor, and, if you volunteer yourself for the task, they're quite likely to be responsive. Better still, if you simply offer them some text, then – if it's strong enough – your editor will most likely be only too happy to accept it.

If you care to write the blurb yourself, then do so early and email it to your editor sooner rather than later. If your editor has already composed some text, and got approval for it from the sales and marketing types, and from the folk over in design, then that text has a huge, maybe unassailable lead over yours, irrespective of which one is actually better.

GETTING THE TEXT RIGHT

Writing blurbs is an utterly different art form from writing a novel or non-fiction manuscript. Everything you so painfully learned about writing over the last few months and years needs to be forgotten, or at least ruthlessly suppressed.

For one thing, a book blurb is extraordinarily brief. It's worth going down to a bookshop to examine the length of blurbs in comparable works. You're likely to encounter a going rate of about 100 words, including header and footer text. You just can't say anything detailed, or layered or complex in such a space. You need to set up the premise. Throw in a dash of intrigue. Maybe a dab of self-praise ('this moving and beautifully told tale . . .'). Then quit.

If your blurb leaves lots of questions unanswered, then fine. Unanswered questions are a reason for someone to buy a book. If your blurb isn't quite accurate in setting out the premise or developing its implications, that doesn't matter either. Readers know perfectly well that the back of the book is not some legally sanctioned summary of the content. Think of the blurb like a movie trailer. Those trailers don't even pretend to convey story; they are just there to advertise a taste of all the action and excitement to come. Your blurb can't be quite as disconnected as a movie trailer, but it functions nevertheless in much the same way.

Finally, don't try to write the blurb in a single sitting. You won't succeed like that. You need to work more the way that a poet might: cutting out unnecessary words (you've only got 100 to play with!), honing phrases, trying out different strategies. Spend several hours on the project over several days. If you end up with more than one version that appeals to you, then (if they're highly similar) toss a coin and pick just one. If the rival versions offer something rather different, offer both to your publisher. With a little luck, one of the versions will appeal, and you'll be on your way.

PUFFS

Because you are a debut author, your book will emerge into the world with no book reviews to garnish it. There'll be nothing reading, 'Praise for Joe Schmoe'. Nothing promising that you're scarier than P. G. Wodehouse, funnier than Virginia Woolf, wiser than Paris Hilton, more up-to-the-minute than Homer.

Without these things, however, your book risks looking a little naked. A little clever blurb-writing combined with some sleight-of-hand typography will help a little, but ideally you want more. The theoretical solution is the 'puff'. A puff is an authorised comment from some celebrity endorsing your book. *'I laughed till I cried'*, *Oprah Winfrey* – that sort of thing. The quotation doesn't need to have appeared in any publication or any media outlet at all. All that matters is that the celebrity is happy to stand by the words in question.

The huge, almost insuperable, challenge is how to get the darn puff. The starting place is likely to be a bound proof. A bound proof is simply a proof (i.e. unfinalised) copy of your work, quite possibly just encased in plain covers. The plainness doesn't matter. The book is never going to go on sale, it's simply going to be used as something that can be introduced to the trade more feasibly than a bundle of loose-leaf paper. Not all books will ever see a bound proof. A major launch for commercial fiction certainly will. A minor launch for a niche book certainly won't. The decision on whether to commission a bound proof won't be yours, and it'll be driven by whether the good folk of marketing feel they need it as a selling tool.

But let's say that your book is going to experience life as a bound proof. You've therefore got the kind of thing that could be sent out for a celebrity endorsement. Often enough, I've witnessed my editor diligently compiling a list of people who could be asked for plugs. For my book on British history, for example, I believe we approached upwards of thirty people. I don't know if any of them ever responded (because it was my editor who sent out the letters, not me). I do know that we drew a total blank.

The issue was not that we sent the book to inappropriate people. For example, I recall that we sent the history book to Jeremy Paxman, a well-known TV journalist who had written a book on a similar theme himself. If he'd responded with a puff, it would have been a valuable selling tool. If he'd read the book, he might well have been interested in it and willing to boost its chances.

Inevitably, though, there aren't all that many names whose endorsement is going to prove useful. You need to have a realistic threshold of who will and will not help. An Oprah Winfrey/Jeremy Paxman/Brett Easton Ellis/ Bill Bryson level of endorsement really adds something. A plug from Obadiah the Obscure or Fi the Forgotten will not. Because everyone knows that, the Winfrey/Paxman/Easton Ellis/Bryson mob receive a vast number of books, some of which might really appeal to them, but few or none of which they are likely to read.

I don't have an answer here. I once got a useful puff from someone. He's little-known himself, but has co-written a worldwide best-seller. He lives round the corner from me, and we both go to the same pub. Your optimal strategy therefore – the only one you can have any confidence in – is to make sure that you drink in the right pubs and with the right people. If you have failed to take this elementary step of authorial self-promotion, then I don't know what to advise except that I advise you to be ruthless.

Did your brother-in-law go to school with Jerry Seinfeld? Can your mother wangle a comment out of Michael Palin? If you notice that Jeremy Clarkson is coming to open a village fete near you, can you get close to him and offer him a copy of your book?

As you scour your address book, do make sure that you keep a firm eye on relevance. It's simply no use coming back to your editor with a worthy but unflashy name to endorse you. Marketing is about glitz, not worthiness. Look at other books on the same shelves as yours. Look at the puffs they've accrued. You need names of that calibre. Nothing else will do. If you can track down any such names, then do so, and, if you need to be a bit embarrassingly crass in your approach, so be it. Crass is good. Chutzpah is good. The worst that can happen is that they'll say no.

Do also talk to your editor. If she's about to fire off a batch of books to a list of standard-issue celebs, then talk about whether you can do anything to personalise those missives. If, for example, you're a crime writer and you've always loved the work of Mark Billingham, then why not send out the book proof with a note from you? Perhaps a handwritten one, if your writing is legible in a nice artistic sort of way. In any event, discuss these things. Two people putting their heads together collaboratively for twenty minutes will come up with a better plan of action than any one person will, no matter how long they spend on the challenge.

And if you draw a blank, you draw a blank. There's nothing to be done about that. At least you tried.

Part Six

PUBLICATION

SALES AND MARKETING

You've now got a text that everyone is happy with. You've got a jacket design that you have pasted above your computer and that you look at about three dozen times every day. You have lit candles to St Francis de Sales who, let's face it, isn't exactly a heavy hitter among the company of the blessed, but he is the offically appointed patron saint for authors and (less flatteringly) journalists, so he's the chap you need to light candles to. If you are slightly more New Age about things, then you have probably consulted fortune-tellers, enjoyed a Reiki healing, placed crystals under your pillow, rubbed the right kind of essential oils into the soles of your feet, gone macrobiotic and completely redecorated your house in line with state-of-the-art feng shui. That's all excellent. All the more so, because the single most important element of the publishing process is about to take place – and it's about to take place out of your sight, and beyond your control.

THE HOLY QUINTET

A recent issue of the *Bookseller* described a seminar held by Waterstone's – the UK's premier quality book chain – for the benefit of agents, the purpose being to tell agents directly about all the good things that the group was up to. Agents were generally impressed and came away with a positive view of developments at the group, but the *Bookseller* article did carry a nasty little sting:

> There was widespread consternation when the seminar revealed that the four key considerations when ordering a book were its track record, support from the publisher, market context and pricing/cover. 'Half the people in the room put their hands up and said "What about the writing?",' said an attendee at the event. '[Waterstone's] reassured us, but for [them] not to mention content as a key consideration was a shock. They are not Tesco.'

I don't want to make too much of this. Of course Waterstone's and any half-decent chain will care about the quality of the books they are placing on their shelves. I wasn't present at the seminar, but I imagine that Waterstone's reassurances about the importance of content could be taken pretty much at face value.

Nevertheless, the anecdote is telling about the importance of all those other things that you, the author, do not have control over. We'll take them in turn, splitting the last of Waterstone's criteria into two – a holy quintet:

➢ *Track record*
If this is the first time you've been in print, then you don't have a track record. If, on the other hand, you're launching a paperback when your hardback has already been launched, or if you've published broadly similar work before, then you certainly have a sales track record and you will be judged on it.

➢ *Support from the publisher*
This criterion translates roughly into an assessment of how much money the publisher is putting into the launch the book. The more money he is spending, the more the retailer is likely to promote the book themselves.

➢ *Market context*
Naturally enough, retailers are selling to a market, and they need to respond to its fashions and its quirks. Misery memoirs are all the rage one year; they may fall away drastically the next. Dan Brown knock-offs may be huge sellers in one season, impossible to shift the next. Retailers have to take these things into account when placing their orders.

➢ *Pricing*
Pricing, here, means two things. First of all, the cover price the publisher has placed on the book; and second, the price at which the publisher is prepared to sell your books to the retailer. If a supermarket is being offered two books of similar quality and appeal, and they can get one at a 65% discount to the recommended retail price, and the other one at a 55% discount, then they will go for the former every time. Indeed, even if the writing in the latter book is certainly stronger, they will go for the first. And so they should. They are there to make money, not advance the cause of literature.

➢ *Cover*
If you don't have an established name, readership and critical reputation, then in most cases readers will have to judge a book by its cover – and perhaps an inside page or two – because they have nothing else to go on. Again, retailers are absolutely right to care about the quality of your cover.

These thoughts are sobering ones for any author, because you start to realise how much of your destiny lies in hands other than yours. You remember the time you read through your entire manuscript, concerned that some of your sentence rhythms were a little abrupt? Well, good for you. You sound like the right sort of author, meticulous and perfectionist. But none of that matters at this stage. No one cares, or at least there are other much more important things in play right now.

TRACK RECORD

Of the holy quintet above, perhaps the only element that calls for somewhat fuller explanation is the concept of track record.

Many readers of this book will have no track record. (Academic, business or other specialist publications don't count in this context.) That doesn't matter – indeed, it may even be a good thing. Debut authors are recognised as such, and the trade will be perfectly open to promoting – and promoting heavily – really strong contributions by complete first-timers. (Retailers will, of course, be able to look at the track records of books on similar subjects or in similar genres, so they aren't entirely in the dark when it comes to guestimating possible sales.)

On the other hand, as soon as you get into print, you do start to accumulate a sales record. If your novel came out in hardback before it came out in paper covers, your hardback sales will be assessed. If this is your second book, the sales of your first will be closely scrutinised. Because most authors do not clamber straight on to the best-seller lists and stay there for weeks on end, there will be many pro authors who'd rather prefer it if they could relaunch themselves with the virgin whiteness of an unspotted sales record.

If you have been in print before and your sales were mediocre, you can to some extent escape that history by reinventing yourself: jumping from fiction to non-fiction, from literary fiction to crime fiction, perhaps even changing your name.

But those sales records do matter, and they matter more now than they ever used to in the past. Whether you're completely new to publication or have a long history of books behind you, you'd do well to push as hard as you can to maximise the sales of every book, in every edition. It's not simply that you may earn out your advance and achieve some royalties by doing that. It's that you are working to build the foundations of a career that will sustain you long into the future.

A DECENTLY SIZED PEOPLE CARRIER

Important as the issues dealt with in this section may be, the crucial discussions will take place where you can't hear or influence them. You will not even be told – except perhaps in extreme summary form – the upshot of those discussions. Still more scarily, perhaps, the number of key buyers has greatly diminished over the years. Some years back, publishers would employ local reps to chase round all the bookstores in an area, pressing shops to order titles from the current catalogue. The system had its inefficiencies, of course, but from an author's point of view it did at least mean that your own sales outcome would be determined by a large number of one-to-one conversations.

These days book buying has become very much more centralised. Those old-fashioned sales reps do still exist, but their importance in the overall retail ecology has declined significantly. To a large degree, your fate will be determined by a group of buyers who could comfortably fit into a decently sized people carrier. That group of people will all be avid and eclectic readers, but they aren't superhuman. They can't read every title that publishers are pushing at them. They can't even come close.

When publishers are seeking to sell their wares to retailers, the conversations will not simply be about how many books are being ordered. Indeed, because printing technology has become much more flexible than it used to be, print runs have become shorter, orders smaller, and reprints and reorders more frequent than of old. Now, it's easier to think of those sales conversations as being multi-dimensional, and interlocking. What discount is the publisher offering? How much consumer advertising? What kind of PR effort is being made? Is the publisher willing to pay for promotional slots, and, if so, how much and for how long? And what other competing books are out there at the same time? And what are *their* publishers saying about discounts, and promotions and all the rest of it? For your book to achieve a strong sales platform, retailers will need to be impressed by the entire package and be relatively more impressed by your package than by any comparable offerings from rival publishers. It is in discussions of this kind that many a crucial battle is lost or won. And you're not there to fight them.

THY REFUGE AND THY STRENGTH

So what can you do?

The first, best, most certain answer is a simple one. You need to sell your book for the highest possible advance in the first place. The more money a publisher has riding on a book, the less he can afford to see it bomb. There are no guarantees, but this remains your best protection by a country mile.

If, like so many authors, you don't really care about the money but just want a decent career and a committed readership, then you would do well to chase the money anyway. That doesn't mean that you need to write commercial fiction instead of literary fiction, or mass-market non-fiction instead of your own cultured highbrow work, but it does mean that you need to be attentive to the market for these things. There's highly saleable literary fiction, and there's highly unsaleable literary fiction. If you are determined to write the latter, don't be surprised if your publisher finds it hard to shift it.

While securing a strong advance is, for sure, your best bet, it remains a bet, a gamble. A little while back, when the power of publishers vis-à-vis retailers was greater than it is now, the hierarchy of titles was both explicit and effectual. A really big book would be granted 'super-lead' status, meaning that publishers jolly well expected retailers to push it hard. A big, but slightly lesser title might come out as a 'lead' title. The rest – well, they'd just be titles. Retailers generally responded to these signals, giving publishers some degree of control over how to deploy their resources.

These days the old terminology of lead and super-lead still exists, but power has shifted from publishers to retailers. If a retailer just doesn't like a particular lead title, it won't feel obliged to give it significant promotional support. If it loves a regular title, it may (for a price) offer quite extensive support. Because publishers will be having at least eight or ten important conversations with key buyers at the same time, predicting the end result of these is like determining the answer to a set of simultaneous equations with eight ever-shifting variables. In the best case, all retailers will think positively about the same title. That means that the publisher can be confident of offering strong support for the book, knowing that it will be sold with sufficient prominence through enough outlets to justify the investment.

But suppose that one really important buyer suddenly withdraws support – and there could be a million reasons why they might – then the publisher will have to reconsider their overall level of investment in the book. That reconsideration may nudge other retailers into reducing their degree of support. In the worst case, two or three major abstentions from key buyers will be enough to force your publisher to scale back severely their intended support for the book. That outcome may well be heartbreaking for you, but it is rational and necessary on the part of the publisher. It may or may not help you to know that the buyers who abstained from supporting your book quite likely never even read it.

GETTING DRUNK WITH THE MONEY

At my very first meeting with a publisher, I was introduced to various people: the editor, the publisher, the publicist – and the sales guy. It wasn't too hard for me to understand all those other jobs but, maybe because I was being a little dim, I didn't quite understand the task of the salesperson. Publishers print books. Retailers buy them. I could see that you needed a catalogue and some discussion over what that catalogue contained, but a bookseller was no more likely to stop ordering books than a supermarket is likely to stop ordering baked beans. I didn't quite get it. My bafflement must have been obvious, because the sales guy was patient with me.

'I talk to buyers about the book. I get them excited by it. We get our reps to spread the excitement. We want to have your book as strongly positioned as we possibly can.'

Ah! I was beginning to get it now. There'd be earnest conversations about the market for adventure fiction (in my case), discussions of trends, a committed pitch for my style and approach – like a college discussion about literature, only played out for real. I started to nod my understanding, but the sales guy was still talking.

'Basically, my job involves getting drunk with buyers.'

Ten years on from that conversation, I've grown increasingly sure that the sales job involves more than just strategic alcohol abuse, but there's no question that (erm) informal sales techniques play their part in the books trade, just as they do anywhere. Many authors will see out plenty of book deals without ever encountering trade buyers, but many is not the same as all. If you do get the chance to meet the trade, then make the most of it.

The evenings I've attended have involved buyers from the supermarkets, from WH Smith and from some of the wholesalers and other operators. If your work is more literary, you'd be meeting a group with a more upmarket bias. Other than that, the exact shape of the evening will depend on the way your publisher happens to arrange it. Quite likely, however, your publisher will have arranged a get-together at some nice hotel somewhere. Quite likely, there will be an opportunity to show that you know how to find the bottom end of a glass. You will probably be called on to make a brief speech – a few minutes long, no more – but the real business of the evening will simply be socialising with the people who have the power to buy your book by the thousand, or reject it altogether. You won't be the only author there, but there will only be a few others present. You're lucky to be asked.

So be nice. Be as interested in them and what they do for a living as they are in you and what you do. As a matter of fact, what they do is not simply important to your future career, it also gives you a precious opportunity to understand how they think, how decisions are made, how the retail end of the trade thinks about consumers and buying habits. That's scarce information and you should squirrel it away (before, of course, you become so drunk that you've forgotten where you keep your head).

After the evening, and after you've crawled miserably down from Mount Hangover, send a 'nice meeting you'-type email to the people you met. It's so easy, at these things, for authors to come across as snobby and pretentious. That's almost certainly a misleading impression, yet it's worth combating anyway. A short, friendly email that touches on some aspect of the previous night's conversation is easy to send; it's personal; and it'll help you to stand out from the crowd. Don't allow these things to stay on the bottom end of your 'to do' list. Retail buyers are, by far, the most important people in your life right now, so take them seriously.

MARKETING

Ten years ago, marketing meant marketing. My first book saw large adverts at mainline rail stations in London. There were posters on the tube. There were girls with sashes handing out little pamphlets that contained the first chapter or two of my novel. One marketing whizz wanted to have a 'Win a Million' contest that you could enter by buying a copy of the book. That particular plan folded, but the publisher was genuinely serious about it for a while. (And not because they would have been happy paying a million quid out in prize money. There are, apparently, ways around such things . . .)

But that was then. In the intervening years, the book trade has evolved, and not necessarily for the better. Retailers started eyeing up the money that publishers were splurging on consumer marketing and thought that they'd quite like some of it. So retailers started to charge for in-store promotional slots. That didn't mean they abandoned any notion of quality control – they are still careful about which books are offered those slots in the first place – but they realised that an advantageous store position was something that they could charge for, and so they went ahead and did just that.

You might think that this was an excellent move by retailers and one that would ensure them a prosperous and contented future, but it wasn't long before retailers had competed that lovely new money away by offering discounts to customers. The result is that the book trade has denuded itself of the cash with which to promote new authors and books. (Celebrities and

BUYING FICTION

As one of Waterstone's fiction team, my job is to select the new titles that we order centrally, as well as selecting backlist titles for promotion and managing the core range for our stores. As we have over 300 shops of all sizes, and with store teams that buy titles and tailor their local range themselves, this is never straightforward!

However, at the end of the day it's all about books. I've been a keen reader as far back as I can recall, and a bookseller for over fifteen years, working in or running bookshops in many towns across the country. I have been lucky in that in all the stores I worked in, as bookseller or manager, I was able to be a part of the buying process, and have seen how important it is to be able to get the right books for the market the store operates in.

I look after several areas of fiction for Waterstone's. Of those, I'd argue that literary fiction is one of the most difficult areas to buy for — it's an almost indefinable genre that is under intense scrutiny from the critics and that can offer incredible successes, but we all know there is no such thing as a 'sure thing'. Every genre has its challenges and my job is to make sure we have a mix of titles that suit every taste.

I get shown around 500 new books a month — firstly when the publisher visits us to show the whole team their highlights for the next four months (people often think publishers show us everything they publish, but with over 100,000 titles every year they have to be selective, as do we).

Following these meetings, we will have further individual meetings to select titles — sometimes discussing a range of books, occasionally focusing on just one 'event' title. Proof copies appear every day, and I read as many as I can — if not the whole book then certainly a sample. These advance copies are a blessing and a curse — I am privileged to get them, but it does mean that I never get to catch up on older books I've missed out on, as I'm always trying to stay ahead, figuring out what authors or genres are popular now, and what will be happening several months down the road.

When buying, I look what the author has achieved in the past, how the market is treating similar books and our own sales data. Does the author have a backlist and, if so, what should we do with that when the new book comes out? I look at the cover, the format, marketing and event plans and the price — collectively known as 'the package' — and think how these things will affect sales. Format is more important than ever — everyone loves the look and feel of a hardback, but they are the toughest format to sell. 'Is there an e-book?' is a question I have to ask now which I didn't a couple of years ago. And of course my own opinions come into play — did I think it was good or do I think other readers will enjoy it? We all have different tastes and what one person hates another loves, and vice versa.

Finding new talent is crucial. Waterstone's can and does help launch new writers to readers in a way that our biggest competitors can't. When a new writer we have supported becomes successful, other outlets will take them up, and we will of course lose some of our sales to the competition. And so we need to keep finding new writers to build – it's a never-ending process.

Lastly, none of us buys in isolation. Every decision has to take into account what else is going on in stores and online. I'd like to put all my favourite books into our windows and on the front table in every store, but space is limited and tastes vary. All the buyers want to make the most of their books, and in our stores the booksellers have titles they want to highlight – it's a constant search for balance. Obviously I want to make sure that the books I buy are ones that our customers will love, and that our booksellers will love selling. It's not easy, it's hugely disappointing when we get decisions wrong, but intensely satisfying when I see a book, a really good book that I love, at the top of our charts and can think that I had something to do with getting it there.

JANINE COOK
Fiction Buyer at Waterstone's

existing best-sellers are in a different category, naturally.) This outcome isn't anybody's fault. It's just what happens when you let capitalism do its stuff. And as always with capitalism made flesh, there are beneficiaries too: in this case, all those customers buying books at ever cheaper prices.

From your perspective, however, none of this is good news. You don't particularly care that consumers are getting cheaper books, and you jolly well do care that the old-fashioned marketing lolly isn't going to come your way. Nevertheless, although the news isn't good, it's not awful either. At their worst, publishers are inert when it comes to marketing your work. At their best, they're imaginative and resourceful at making their slender marketing budgets stretch.

SQUARING THE CIRCLE: SPECIALIST BOOKS

Marketing highly specialist work is perhaps rather easier than marketing more broad-spectrum material. There will be, presumably, a tightly defined target audience. You will also presumably have some expert knowledge of that audience and, quite likely, a number of useful connections. Any sane publisher will want to make as much use as possible of your expertise and connections, and you will most likely find that the marketing conversations are genuinely collaborative and productive.

Let's say, for example, that you are a motor enthusiast and have written a book about racing cars of the 1950s and 1960s. You are working with a publisher that specialises in such books. You yourself are the head of a vintage-car racing association. Between you and your publisher, you almost certainly own a number of websites, possess some highly targeted mailing lists, and possibly operate online communities, or are closely involved with other membership organisations.

Marketing your book becomes a question of how to make use of all these assets in an effective but professional way. You want to ensure that everything you do is carefully co-ordinated with things that the publisher is doing. You also want to make sure that your approach is nuanced and helpful, not crass and annoying. Thus, if, for example, you have access to a mailing list, use that list in a way that you yourself wouldn't find annoying if you were the recipient of the relevant emails. Use a touch of humour. Don't go overboard.

Equally, you should have your eye on events or festivals where you can promote yourself. It's unlikely that you will achieve enough sales at any one event to justify the travel and accommodation costs of getting there – but, with luck, your position is such that you were intending to be at the event anyway. You may want to print up (cheaply!) cards that you can give out. Publishers may well be able to supply you with flyers, if you ask them nicely. You may want to adjust the signature footer of your emails to promote your book.

You should also talk to your publisher about any promotions that make sense. If you do introduce the topic, introduce it lightly. For a publisher to offer £5 off a book may sound easy to say, but it's the kind of offer which can quickly rip into their profits. Attractive, short-duration price promotions around launch date may be the best way of achieving good results for relatively little outlay. (And do bear in mind that, as well as the sheer profit impact of the price reduction, there will be a host of logistics issues to be sorted out as well. Publishers aren't set up as retailers, so even the management of promotions can be difficult to sort out.)

Lastly, most specialist books have relatively long sales curves. You don't need to sell fast and furious to achieve success. Indeed, most specialist non-fiction successes are the ones that sell a smallish number of copies week after week, and year after year. The *Writers' & Artists' Yearbook* recently celebrated its one-hundreth anniversary and its accumulated sales have been extraordinary – enough to rival all but the most successful best-sellers. All the same, in any single week its sales are good but unspectacular. If your book can achieve even a tenth as much, then you'll be doing well. Steady, well-judged and committed marketing will help you get there.

SQUARING THE CIRCLE: NOVELS, MAINSTREAM NON-FICTION

Circles can't be squared. That's the point of the phrase. And when it comes to novels or to non-fiction of broad appeal (the kind that, at least in theory, might be found on a best-seller list), you're going to find that the charges levied by retailers for inclusion in in-store promotions will have swallowed most – but not all – of your book's marketing budget. (All books do have a budget attached to them, usually calculated as a percentage of sales, though it would be unusual for you to know what that budget is or how it's been arrived at.)

Nevertheless, and despite a climate that has become more hostile to direct consumer marketing, some low-budget ways to promote your book may well exist. Let's say that you have written a historical novel about the Georgian navy. There will certainly be associations for people who care about such things, there will be events and anniversaries to think about, there will be websites and so forth. Your publisher will certainly have a look into such things, but the more you can do to help them the better. You are looking to make talks, do e-interviews, access mailing lists and the like. Perhaps, if your publisher is feeling reckless, they might engage in some click-through-type banner advertising on websites that bring a sufficient focus to bear.

With all such things, do as much preparation as you can. Bear in mind that the publisher has a limited amount of time and money to put behind these things. Be enthusiastic about good ideas. Be realistic about budgetary limitations. Be as helpful as you can be.

And finally, if your book has sold for a decent advance and if your publisher is ambitious to do well with it, then their sights may be raised just a little. They might run a competition, perhaps in association with a relevant magazine. For example, if you are a thirty-something author who is writing chick-lit for thirty-somethings, then a women's magazine with a similar demographic in its readership might want to run an interview that combines with a competition and a promotion for your work. In cases like this, by all means engage as actively with your publisher's marketing folk as you can, but the big decisions are theirs, because they are the ones waving the chequebook. And if they do wave it, and wave it actively and well, then consider yourself fortunate. These days, you're a rare and fortunate author.

PUBLICITY

Publicity, publicity, there's nothing like publicity.
It's the goal of every writer, it is market-electricity.
You may find it in the papers, you may find it on TV,
But you must not fail to find it, for publicity's the key.
And should you find an author with a suicidal air
Unshaven and unwashed and with an alcoholic glare,
Then his sickness is a fatal one; its cause, alas, too clear –
When his book came to be published, the publicity wasn't there!
With apologies to T. S. Eliot, publisher and part-time poet

Publicity matters. For a book to succeed, it needs excellent content. It needs a strong, clear, attractive cover design that is appropriate to the target audience. It needs an excellent retail platform (that is, it needs to be in the promotions of chain booksellers and have a good uptake from supermarkets). And it needs the oxygen of publicity, because publicity is likely to be the only means by which potential readers have their attention drawn to your book.

All larger publishers have in-house PR specialists. In my experience, these people are usually good and often excellent, but it's also true that your book will constitute a small part of their overall workload, that you won't have their concentrated attention for more than a limited period and that effective collaboration is crucial to a successful outcome. Whereas no author can have more than a limited influence on the sales and marketing process, an active author can make a huge and potentially vital difference to how the publicity pans out. It's the purpose of this section to ensure that you make as much of this process as you possibly can.

HOW PUBLICITY WORKS

Ideally, you'll meet your PR person a fair few weeks before publication – perhaps twelve weeks beforehand. You need this advance preparation because different media outlets require very different amounts of lead-time. The flagship *Today* programme on BBC Radio 4, for example, will make its crucial editorial decisions the day before the show goes out, and perhaps on the very morning of the show itself. At the other end of the spectrum, a glossy magazine needs weeks and often even months of lead-time. Because you want all of your publicity to fire in one concentrated burst around publication date, you need your own PR team to juggle all those different lead-times and launch dates as best they can.

In the best of all possible worlds, that meeting with your publicist will be one-to-one; it will not be time-limited; it will be discursive and collaborative and allow plenty of room for brainstorming and lateral thinking. Those kinds of sessions work best because the best ideas don't always emerge first. Curious little facts about you that you've never seen to be of much consequence can come to make all the difference to the PR opportunities available. Larger ideas can grow out of casual comments. A campaign can take shape in a way that it never could have done had the meeting been brisker and more agenda-led.

Alas, you are unlikely to have such a meeting. Most meetings are time-limited and not one-to-one. In most cases, your publicist will approach things with something like a plan of action already sketched out. That plan will certainly be based on your book. It will also have been based on some discussions with your editor over strategy. It may also be based on a questionnaire about yourself that you've been asked to fill in and return. The result, most likely, will be a pretty decent set of ideas about how to proceed. The purpose of the meeting with you will be in order to check that you are available to do what needs to be done, and that there is no obvious impediment to the ideas under consideration. You are there to respond, not to initiate; to approve, not to instigate.

Either way, you'll end the meeting with a list of ideas to explore. If you are a novelist, those ideas are likely to centre on you rather than on the novel. You may well find that somewhat disconcerting – after all, it's the book that's meant to be the star of the show, not you – but the truth is that the publication of yet another novel by yet another debut novelist is not, in itself, a particularly newsworthy story. On the other hand, if there is a good human interest tale in the making of the novel, then there's plenty of scope for publicity there

For example, I turned to writing when my wife became seriously ill. I gave up my job as an investment banker to look after her and, in the process, wrote my first novel. That story, thoroughly feeble as it may appear, lay at the heart of a highly effective PR campaign. Indeed, as far as I can recall, we achieved absolutely no publicity for the book itself. Every single element of the campaign centred in one way or another on my own personal story, and that story achieved a considerable degree of publicity.

If you are writing non-fiction, then, of course, any strong personal stories are still available by way of ammunition, but you can also look to your subject matter to generate news coverage too. Thus, if you happen to have written a book about (let's say) the experience of mass unemployment in the 1930s, your publicist will want to think about ways in which you'd be able to use your expertise to comment on similar issues in the media today.

Once you have your list of ideas, it will be your publicist's job to go away and see how many of those can be made to happen. You should be on stand-by to do whatever is asked of you, but it's your publicist who has the contacts and the authority, so your role is supportive at most. On some occasions, a newspaper or magazine will want to send someone to interview and photograph you. On other occasions, the newspaper or magazine will want a 'first-person' piece, authored by you, and written to a particular brief. Whenever you write something for a newspaper, you will be offered payment and you should certainly take it. If you are asked to write something and no one mentions payment, then ask. You're a writer. You are supplying content for someone else's commercial enterprise. Don't feel embarrassed to demand payment.

When it comes to the broadcast media, you're not likely to achieve significant national exposure unless your story is particularly remarkable, or your book particularly topical. Nevertheless, if you do have something special to offer, there are opportunities for you and you should gladly take them. In most cases, TV appearances will require you to travel to London. Radio appearances can usually be handled either by phone or (better still) by hooking up from your local radio studio. You'll be told what to do if this latter option is available to you.

Writers are often somewhat nervous of the whole PR enterprise, but it's generally a fairly pleasant experience. For one thing, the kind of journalists who come to interview writers are a very different breed from the sort of journalists who hound politicians, expose celebrities and write scathingly about whatever happens to fall beneath their withering scrutiny. I've done a lot of stories with journalists specialising in 'human interest' stories, and on the whole they've been a warm, lovely, sympathetic bunch. If you have specific concerns – things you do or don't want to talk about, for example – then just talk to them. I've never once had a journalist betray a confidence or ignore any reasonable request for discretion.

Photographers are likewise easy to deal with. Any photographer who comes your way will specialise in features, not news – the basic difference being that a news photographer specialises in subjects who are running away from the camera; a features photographer is dealing with someone happy to stand and look at it. Photographers won't be expecting you to be the world's most beautiful or glamorous person. (If you are, then so much the better.) Nor do they need you to know what you're doing. Nor will they need you to sort out the lighting, or anything else. Your job is to make the tea and smile on command.

When it comes to interacting with the news media, it remains true that no one will be out to stitch you up, make you look bad or interview you aggressively. Your book simply doesn't constitute that kind of story. At the same time, any relationship with the news media is apt to be a little jumpy, rather like dating somebody who suffers from attention deficit disorder combined with an inability to maintain lasting personal relationships. You may talk enthusiastically with a radio editor on Tuesday about your pro-jected contribution to their Thursday show, only to find out in the course of Wednesday evening that their attention has moved elsewhere. Or you may have been commissioned to write an article on your specialist subject for inclusion in a Sunday newspaper only to find that your article has been ditched at the last possible second and without anyone having had the courtesy to let you know. Don't take these things personally. It's not you; it's them. The pace of the modern rolling news cycle is so frenetic that these abrupt switches of attention are commonplace. All you can do is do as you're told and hope that you can ride the rollercoaster for long enough to get something of what you want from it.

TIMING

The ideal timing for all these things is simple. With non-fiction, you'd hope to be serialised in a newspaper a week or two before publication. (Serialis-ation, by the way, doesn't usually mean that a *series* of extracts will appear. If you're not already famous, then serialisation is almost certainly going to be a one-off.) The newspaper is partly purchasing your serial rights, because it loves your book so much that it wants to bring your work to the attention of its readers, but it also – in true industry fashion – is buying the rights because it wants an exclusive. That means that your publisher won't allow any other publicity to go out prior to that serialisation, but will seek to gen-erate as much publicity as possible thereafter.

Fiction is very seldom serialised, so there's not quite such an obvious kick-off point, but you'll find that most PR concentrates around publication date or just a little before. Either way, the aim of a strong campaign will be

NEWSPAPER BOOK REVIEWS

As a books editor, I am often asked how I choose which books to send out for review. I answer, only slightly abashed, with the truth: 'By their covers.' Nor could it be otherwise. It's not a question of high-handedness: it's a question of maths.

Let us say that the average newspaper books desk gets 300 books a week sent for possible review. Coping with that avalanche, the Daily Telegraph books desk has – including me – a staff of three; a figure roughly half what it was ten years ago. Between us, we need to commission and edit full-length reviews of roughly eight non-fiction and four fiction books a week, seven capsule reviews of paperbacks and a handful of genre reviews, as well as overseeing columns, a weekly feature or interview, and a great deal more. The job is fun, a privilege, and one that we take very seriously.

The two chief grievances authors tend to have with books desks are being reviewed badly, and not being reviewed at all. Let's start with the first. The instinct of many people in receipt of a bad review is to assume either that the reviewer hasn't read the book, or that they are the victims of a conspiracy. This is understandable – egos are at stake and it must be mortifying to conclude that an intelligent person has open-mindedly read your work, and found it bad. But that, nine times out of ten, is what has happened. If I ever found conclusive evidence that someone writing a full-dress review for me had not read, and read properly, the book in question, I'd never use them again.

Second, we never 'commission hatchet jobs'. That is not how it works. Any self-respecting critic would regard it as a bloody cheek if I told them what to write. Indeed, I often find a book I reviewed favourably in another organ comes in for a kicking in my own, or vice versa. I admired J. G. Ballard's Kingdom Come in the Literary Review, for example, only to see Lionel Shriver attack it in the Daily Telegraph.

The idea that a books editor controls who gets a good and who a bad review is naive, but there is a more sophisticated question about the propriety of the commissioning process to be answered. Should people be allowed to review the books of their friends, of their enemies, or of their rivals? Broadly, the answer is no. If I have reason to believe a critic has more than a nodding acquaintance with an author – or, having been reviewed in turn by them, reason either to detest or be grateful to them – I won't make the commission.

Sometimes, however, there is a trade-off between finding a writer qualified to do the review, and one who can claim to be disinterested. If you're a British specialist in Indonesian politics, you are likely to know the author of the big new book on the subject, or to have a competing book out yourself. I have to decide: do I give the book to someone who knows nothing about the subject and risk doing the author a disservice that way, or do I give it to someone who may have an axe to grind?

Often we'll go for the generalist. Our pages are, after all, aimed not at academics but at intelligent average readers, who want to know whether a book is boring, what they may learn from it, and whether it justifies its cover price. John Irving once complained on air that his latest novel had been panned and asked, in effect, what right has a critic, who spends a few hours reading the book, to pronounce on it when it took Irving hundreds of hours to write it? The answer is that Mr Irving is offering it for sale to a public each member of whom will only spend a few hours reading it. The critic is entitled, as their representative, to say whether it's worth their money and their time.

A vicious review can be entertaining to read. But we don't seek them out. Ideally, we try to find a reviewer who will be in sympathy with a book's project, and will find in it something to praise. Given the number of books published, it makes more sense to highlight the good ones than to warn people off the bad. And we purposely don't attack first novels: if our critic thinks they aren't any good, we ignore them.

It is annoying that the area where we could arguably make the most difference – in picking out the best debuts and giving them a huge show – is the one in which it is hardest to do so. Why, people ask, are we lavishing a big review on already-famous Zadie Smith when still-unknown Jody Smith is the one it would make a difference to? They have a good point.

In part, it's because our readers will want to know about Zadie's new book; and in part, it's because if we're getting twenty Jody Smiths a week, we can't commission reviews of them all. We can only listen out for publishing buzz (often very deceptive), skim pages and hope that the one Jody we do pick out turns out to be the coming superstar. Our record in this is very mixed, and often downright dismal.

Are we prejudiced against self-published books? Dogmatically, no. Snobbishly, no. But if I'm asked, as I am daily, to guess quickly which of two books is most likely to be good – one of them self-published and probably much rejected; the other having won the approval of a reputable publisher and having benefited from the attentions of an editor – I'm likely to plump for the second. And though there are self-published books that shine out like diamonds in a dunghill, I'm more often than not going to be right.

And I am, sincerely, trying to give everyone a fair crack of the whip. If I fail, all I can plead is that I fail in good faith. You'll think so, next time round, when your book is the lead review.

SAM LEITH
Adapted from an article first published
in the spring 2008 issue of *The Author*

to have as much publicity as possible appearing within two or three weeks of the book's launch. In practice, there'll almost always be a certain amount of compromise required here. If, for example, a major women's magazine wants to run a feature on you in their November edition (which will go on sale in October), but your book comes out in early September, then you'd be nuts not to agree to the proposal, simply because the dates aren't ideal.

You should also be aware that media folk are very touchy about priority and exclusivity. If *The Daily Yadda* has profiled you for their health page, then *The Morning Blah* won't even think about using your story for its health page three days later, no matter that the *Yadda*'s readers don't overlap with the *Blah*'s. Having said that, a major regional newspaper won't feel upset if a national has previously run a piece on you, and a minor regional newspaper won't care if the entire world has already run a piece. Equally, the women's magazines see themselves as distinct from the newspapers, and the tabloids to some extent regard themselves as different from the broadsheets. To human beings of normal sanity, these prickly feelings of jealousy and precedence are all rather hard to understand – but it's not your job to do so. You have a publicist whose job it is to enter the jungle and deal with the beasts that lurk therein. Your job is to do what you're told.

Finally, if you're concerned that two weeks after the publication date everything seems to have gone quiet, you needn't be. It certainly will have gone quiet, but it's gone quiet because by this point your book is no longer newsworthy and neither the *Yadda*, nor the *Blah*, nor the *Women's Chitterchatter*, nor even your reliable friend the *Barchester Bugle* has got time for you any more. Your book may or may not be selling at the tills, but the good ship publicity has now steamed on by. You may bid it farewell.

SUPPORTING THE PROCESS

For all that the media game is best played by specialists, you can do a lot to help. Sometimes – in the best cases – you'll find that your publicist spends real time with you, collaboratively working out a plan of action. This, however, is unlikely to happen. It's much more likely that the meeting with your publicist will be relatively cursory and non-collaborative. But if you are very well prepared, you may end up coaxing a genuine (albeit temporary) partnership into being or, at the very least, tabling some ideas which wouldn't have been there otherwise.

One first strong tip is that you should try to arrange your meeting with the PR person so that you have real time with him or (more probably) her.

If you are trying to discuss a PR campaign when your editor is in the room, along with someone from marketing, someone from the rights department and someone else called Becky who seems really smiley but whose job function you didn't quite catch, then it's not likely that the meeting will have much patience for a long discussion. Therefore, either ask beforehand if you can book an hour or so's slot with your publicist, or politely suggest that the person from marketing, the person from rights and Smiley Becky all feel free to make a move, because you want to focus for an hour or so on PR. (Your editor will probably stay whatever, but it's their call.)

Second, the more you can do to generate ideas, the better. The trouble with most authors, of course, is that they're deeply ignorant. Not ignorant of the important things in life – mass unemployment, Victorian parlour games, the life and loves of Freddie Mercury, or whatever else it is you've written about – but ignorant of the media world. The key to success in PR is to find the right intersection between what the media wants and what you have to talk about. The more realism you can bring to what the media are interested in, the more usefully creative your ideas will be. It's difficult for a book like this to suggest the sort of ideas which will work for your particular situation, but the following list should at least get you thinking on the right lines.

Human interest
If there is a human interest story that lies behind your writing, then it's a very strong angle for publicity. For example:

➤ You have two children with learning disabilities, a subject that lies at the heart of your novel.

➤ You suffer from a rare but colourful condition. Writing a novel has been the only thing that kept you sane.

➤ You ended an abusive relationship after being hospitalised by your husband. You found that only through writing could you deal with your experiences.

➤ You competed in the Olympics, but realised that you are a writer first and foremost and gave up sport to focus on your art.

➤ You have breast cancer; you've been treated for it; you're in remission. While undergoing tests and surgery, you started to plan and write your novel.

You'll notice that there's a certain mawkishness in most of these examples, and it's perfectly true that 'human interest' normally involves an illness, a disability, a lousy relationship or a Triumph Over The Odds. It's also true that you may well feel that, when your story is condensed to a soundbite, the truth has somehow evaporated away in the process. For example, perhaps your breast cancer had damn all to do with the novel. Perhaps you always wanted to write a novel and it so happened that you had just begun on Chapter One when you were first diagnosed and treated. You never connected the two; you don't see why anyone else should either.

It's important, however, that you don't worry about such details. No one else will. Really, the template for your story has already been written. It is the job of the PR industry and the feature-writing media to find subjects to fill that template. If they can shove you into it, then smile gracefully and let yourself be shoved. It's the publicity that matters. The truth can take care of itself.

A corollory of these comments is that you shouldn't be too shy about volunteering information that might be relevant. You are white but have a West Indian partner and your book deals with race? Then that is a relevant fact. You once played for Leeds United Football Club? Then that's of interest. You nursed your father as he died of Hodgkin's? Then say so. Your mother was a noted parliamentarian? Mention it. Depending on the exact circumstances of your situation and your book, these things may or may not be relevant, but it's not for you to decide. Your job is to give your publicist the fullest possible view of the available materials and let them pick the ones that work for them.

Features

Somewhat widening the net, you should muse about what kind of features you could write. Ideally, those features will be clearly related to your book. If you have written about a tropical paradise, pitch a feature which looks at the environmental degradation that's currently threatening the area. If you've written a book about life in a northern mining town in the 1980s, pitch a feature talking about your culture shock at moving to the Thatcherite south-east.

You needn't, however, be too hung up on relevance. I was once seeking to promote a novel that dealt with aviation in the United States in the 1920s. Quite separately, the *Financial Times* asked me to write a travel-style piece for them covering a ceremony in St George's Chapel in Windsor Castle. The *FT* article had nothing at all to do with my novel, but the opportunity was too good to turn down. I wrote the piece. I stuck in a section at the end that linked the (rather elderly) Knights of the Garter who had just processed down the aisle with the (rather youthful) fighter aces of the First World War. The connection was forced, but the article read well and it got something about my novel across to numerous readers who would have known nothing about it any other way. Any publicity is good publicity.

In coming up with ideas for possible features, don't try to make a list in a single twenty-minute session at your computer. Ideas will bubble up over hours and days. Make a list of possible ideas. Discard ones that sound awful, but leave the rest. Also, try to broaden your media consumption, at least for a while or until insanity beckons. The *Daily Yadda* will have specific slots on a Tuesday that they don't have on any other day. The *Morning Blah* will have openings that the *Yadda* wouldn't consider. The *Sunday Tree-Destroyer* will have a host of regular features that need to be filled every week ('Me and My Pet', 'Like Father, Like Son', 'My First Car', What's in My Wallet', etc). Identify the slots that exist, then check to see if you've got anything that might plausibly fill them.

When you've assembled your list of ideas (which will, ideally, be as specific about possible media slots as possible), you should show them to your publicist. She may well leap on ideas that you think are fairly weak and discard ones that you thought were strong, but that's her job. Don't feel injured by rejections. Your job is to be bountiful with ideas. Her job is to be selective. If none of your ideas is rejected, then you haven't come up with enough of them.

The news

Not often, but occasionally, it is possible to shoehorn your book into an existing national debate. Let's say, for example, that the media is abuzz with some story about declining standards in schools. You just so happen to have written a memoir describing your schooldays in the late 1950s. If you can find a way to tie your memoir into the national debate, then so much the better. You need to watch the news story as it develops day by day. Propose ideas to your publicist. Don't just say, 'I could write something about my memoir.' Say, 'I could do a 1,200-word piece for the G2 section of the *Guardian* looking at the best and worst of old-fashioned education.' That gives the publicist an outlet and an angle. All she needs to do is make the call.

Still better, it sometimes happens that you can – in a very modest way – seek to *create* a news story. You won't be able to create one from scratch, but let's say that a senior politician has called for a return to the values of the 1950s in education. You could perhaps write a direct attack on that politician and seek to place the piece in a newspaper where it will attract the very maximum degree of attention – the *Sunday Times News Review*, for example, or Radio 4's *Today* programme. Your attack then becomes fodder for rejoinder, for debate or discussion, and all of a sudden your book has become the centre of something larger than the PR campaign alone. Articles may start to appear that you and your publicist did not yourself initiate. This is the sweet spot of all PR. It's rare that a particular book and a particular news story coincide well enough to achieve this happy outcome, but it's worth reaching for if you possibly can.

Special interests in mainstream publications

The appetite of newspapers for content is never-ending. The property sections need to create new features on property every week. The motoring sections need something on cars. The money pages need their column inches filled, as do the travel pages, the health pages, the science and technology pages, and so forth. If you can engineer some kind of link between your book, yourself and one of these specialist sections, then engineer away.

One of my books was promoted by, among other things, a front-page article in the property section of a Sunday newspaper about our impending house sale. Most of the article was about the house, but there was a column inch or two in which the journalist gushed about what a wonderful place it had been for me to write my novels. At the end of the article, there was a little bit of blurb in italics giving the title and cost of my latest book. The article hardly constituted the world's most accurately directed publicity, but who cared about that? It was on the front page of its own newspaper section and landed on the brunch tables of 1.2 million readers. If you can achieve something similar yourself, then go for it.

Again, the way you need to operate is by generating ideas for your publicist to amend, use or discard as she sees fit – but, if you don't mention that you are selling your beautiful home, or restoring your beloved 1920s Harley Davidson, or have learned Balinese cookery from an acknowledged Balinese master, then she won't even be able to get started.

Specialist journals

One of the reviews I've had which gave me most pleasure was a small piece in *Accountancy Age*. The review gave me pleasure not simply because it was gently flattering, but because it was there at all. No one ever thinks to give interesting books to *Accountancy Age* to review. They review books all right, but the majority have titles like *New Approaches to the Pricing of Untraded Securities*, or *FIFO vs LIFO: The Everlasting Debate*. My book wasn't about accounting, but it was a financial thriller and either my publicist or I had the bright idea that maybe, once in a while, accountants would like to read a financial thriller as well as the dramas attendant on inventory accounting techniques. So we sent them my novel and asked them to review it, and review it they jolly well did.

To be sure, such publications hardly have readerships that number in the millions, but you can pick your target audience in a way that you can't with mass-market publications. What's more, you can bet that any accountant trailing his weary eye over a list of new publications in the accountancy field would be rather perked up by having his attention drawn to a financial thriller instead of an accountancy textbook. In the din and clamour of a Sunday newspaper, you just won't find yourself standing out all that much.

So think laterally. Specialist journals exist for almost every branch of human endeavour. Think about possible linkages between your book and some of those branches. If you can also assemble contact info for the journals in question, it makes your publicist's job very easy. All she needs to do is pop a book and a press release in an envelope and bang it off with all the others that will be going out at the same time.

Novelty items and the internet

Newspaper readers, being predominantly human, have an almost endless appetite for fun, foolishness, quizzes and novelties of every sort. The expansion of newspapers on to the internet has increased the possible number of outlets for such things. 'Top Ten Xs to Visit.' 'Five Things about Y You Never Knew.' 'The World's Oldest Z.' Or what about a jokey article on doing X à la Zen Buddhism? Or seven reasons why you should be proud about your Y? And who was the world's first Z-ist?

The X, Y and Z will need to have some relationship with you or your book, since otherwise the articles will be just too random, but the relationship doesn't have to be the strongest one in the world. In PR terms, one of the most successful articles I wrote in support of *This Little Britain* – which at its core was a fairly serious book about British history – was a silly novelty piece about English spellings, and how you could spell potato 'ghoughpteighbteau' if you took the 'gh' from 'hiccough' and so on. I wrote that article for one newspaper, which syndicated it to another, which put it on the internet, from where it went (in a modest way) viral, finding its way into all sorts of nooks and crannies of the ethersphere. No serious article would have had quite that viral afterlife.

Local outlets

Lastly, don't forget your local newspaper and local radio stations. These outfits love local authors. The papers will come and interview you for every book you release. The radio station will happily give you a fifteen- or thirty-minute slot chatting with Radio Nowhere's favourite DJ, and the only slight injury you're likely to sustain will be from low-level exposure to a number of easy-listening tracks that will intersperse your musings. These outlets aren't going to make a vast difference to your book sales, but they may make some. The engagements are also both fun and local, a good combination. Your publicist will probably be happy to set these things up herself, but, if she's reluctant, just make the calls yourself. Don't be shy. Local outlets are hungry for local celebrities and, if you're not much of a celebrity, you can comfort yourself with the thought that they're not much of a newspaper or radio station either. The two of you were made for each other.

These suggestions should certainly be enough to set you on your way. Above all, bear in mind (1) that you are the story as much as your book; (2) that you need to be proactive in developing ideas; and (3) that you need to shape your suggestions around the needs of different media outlets and the existing slots that require daily or weekly content.

MEDIA FOR THE LONG TERM

Your publisher will think about how to publicise your book. You will have their attention intensely for about four weeks, then lose it completely. Thereafter, your publisher's PR department won't even think about you until your next book is on the point of publication.

From your point of view, this inattention is unhelpful. Best-seller lists are increasingly dominated by writers (or celebs) with a strong pre-existing media profile. It's not a coincidence that *Bridget Jones' Diary* grew out of a newspaper column. Nor that Ben Goldacre's *Bad Science* books grew the same way. Nor that Malcolm Gladwell was a journalist before he was an author. Nor that Lynne Truss was. Nor that Thomas Friedman was. And so on. The stronger your media profile, the more likely it is that your books will sell. If you had to choose between launching a mediocre book from a strong media platform or an outstanding book from a non-existent one, then you'd be well advised, commercially speaking, to choose the former every time.

In short, if you can clamber your way towards any kind of regular national media exposure, you should strain every sinew to do just that. But it ain't easy. The slots available are few. The competition for them is intense. Journalists tend to know and trust other journalists rather than outsiders. Even if you do think you've secured some kind of privileged relationship with a features editor, you are likely to find that the jumpy attention spans of a journalist and the short horizons of the newsroom combine to make that relationship worth rather less than you'd initially hoped.

These days, of course, the net offers a public platform which you can use as a stepping stone to the joys of a regular column. Ben Goldacre, for example, proceeded in exactly that way and the combination of his blog and his newspaper work means that his PR requirements have been amply taken care of long before his publisher has even received a manuscript.

The proliferation of free newspapers has also created a need for low-cost attention-seeking journalism, which provides a platform of its own. Geraint Anderson's book *Cityboy* was launched off a column in just such a news- paper. Almost regardless of quality, the media exposure was enough to ensure strong sales in hardback, paperback and with a follow-up novelty title to boot. It's perhaps also worth noting that, although Anderson's column appeared in a London-only newspaper, the metropolitan bias of the national news media is strong enough that London journalism 'counts' as national, in a way that is true of no other British city. The same goes for the strongest regional papers in the US, and so on.

THE INTERNET

You'll often see advice to the effect that you need a website, you need a blog, you need to launch yourself on YouTube, Facebook, Twitter and what- ever other voguish websites happen to be making headlines.

I don't think that such advice is wrong exactly, but it's often unduly credulous as to the ease of achieving real exposure. There are, at the time of writing, more than 100 million websites in existence, over 25 billion index- able pages, and perhaps as many as 550 billion documents in total. It's easy enough to put material on the web – though time-consuming and expen- sive, if you don't have HTML skills yourself – but securing eyeballs is no easier online than it is anywhere else. My own consultancy, for example, has a thriving website with about 12,000 unique visitors each month, but we spend £3,000 a month on securing those visitors. If we didn't spend the money, the website would fall into immediate decline. While there certainly are bloggers and Facebookers who have built audiences without any kind of cash investment, there are many, many more who have not.

In short, if you do want to launch an online strategy, you need to be realistic about it. Be realistic about how much investment you'll need to make, not simply in terms of cash but in terms of your time and attention. Ask yourself what you have which is genuinely unique. Work out how you are going to get other sites and other bloggers to link to you. Then ask yourself how much return you're likely to get for your effort. If even one in a hundred site visitors end up buying your book when it launches, you'll have done very well indeed. Just think to yourself how many web pages you view for every one that actually encourages you to get your bank card out.

Needless to say, if you enjoy blogging, YouTubing, and the rest of it, then blog away. If you enjoy what you do, then any further rewards from book sales are the honey on the crumpet. And if you don't simply enjoy blogging, but find yourself slightly addicted to it, so much the better.

What's more, the truth is that online networking is gradually becoming a core part of most writers' workloads – an addition that will, in many cases, make only a marginal difference to sales, and one for which you will receive no direct compensation at all. Nevertheless, increasing numbers of professional authors (and perhaps especially those who boast strong sales and brand recognition) have come to regard blogging, twittering and the rest as simply essential. At a recent writing festival I arranged, I spoke to three different best-selling novelists about their online practices. 'It's got to be done,' they told me – and sure enough, there they are online, tweeting and blogging away. I've now, rather reluctantly, joined their ranks.

If you decide to do the same, then start now. It's no use thinking about these things a month or two before publication. It takes time to build a following. It takes time to build a brand. So start now, build patiently, and remember that your investment of effort may take a long time to bear fruit – if it ever does so at all.

TOP TIPS FOR A SUCCESSFUL LAUNCH
OR HOW TO CREATE A SUCCESSFUL CAMPAIGN

DEVELOP KEY RELATIONSHIPS. *Working closely with and understanding the needs of the author (as well as the editor, literary agent and sales and marketing teams) is essential to a successful book PR campaign.*

UNDERSTAND YOUR MARKET. *Read the book and research other books in the same market – then think carefully about how to position it and how to make it stand out.*

CLEAR AND ACHIEVABLE GOALS. *Devise a clear and targeted PR strategy, liaising with the publishing team and working out how best to promote the book to drive sales; always aim high but always be realistic – this is a very competitive business.*

PRESS RELEASE AND OTHER WRITTEN MATERIAL *should always be clear, informative and persuasive; it provides an opportunity to sell-in ideas and to grab the attention of journalists and literary editors in a very competitive market.*

MEDIA CONTACTS. *Exceptional relationships with the literary press and the full range of media are key. Use contacts wisely – intelligent pitching and delivering the right authors for the right interviews and the right features helps to build trust and reputation.*

HIGH-PROFILE AND HIGH-IMPACT PUBLICITY. *While a broad range of coverage is important, it's the major interviews and headline-grabbing features that will seal a campaign.*

BE CREATIVE AND BE BOLD. *Spotting trends and a good story can drive a book into the news agenda (and sometimes it will become a phenomenon); it not only sells more books, but also builds the reputation of the author, publisher and publicist.*

THE FUTURE IS DIGITAL. *While the publishing industry is embracing the digital age, markets are shifting and so too are the traditional channels of communication. Engaging with the blogosphere, social networks and top literary and cultural websites is an important part of any book campaign.*

ANNABEL ROBINSON
Account Director, FMcM Associates, an award-winning book PR agency

THE DAY OF PUBLICATION AND AFTER

➢ *A Very Short Section* ◄

When your book is published – nothing happens.

You may just possibly get a bunch of flowers from your publisher, which is surprising and nice. There will not be a launch party, unless you have had the wit to arrange one for yourself. (Which I heartily recommend that you do. They're fun.)

More surprising perhaps, you won't even find that your book necessarily appears in bookshops on publication day. Some retailers may have taken it a few days early. Some won't be taking it yet. Others won't be taking it at all. Or perhaps a major retailer has taken your book and entered it into one of their major promotions . . . but, when you actually try to find your book in its appointed position in store, you may well find that it's nowhere to be found.

You can try speaking to the shop staff, or you can let your publisher know and they'll chase it up themselves. Alternatively, and better still, if you happen to be in possession of a mother, then my experience is that letting her loose on any rogue bookshops (in very loud voice: 'WHY HAVEN'T YOU GOT THE *excellent* NEW BOOK BY THE *fabulous* AUTHOR ——') will do vastly more to procure change than any publisher's rep ever will.

And that's it. Your publisher will know how many books have left their warehouse, but they won't usually think to tell you and will be vaguely annoyed if you keep asking. In any event, books leaving a warehouse is not the same as books being sold at the till, and, although your publisher will have access to Nielsen sales data (which is collected at the point of sale itself), they may not be checking on the progress of your book week by week.

As a matter of fact, publishers will often more or less stop communicating with you once your book is launched. That's not intended to send you a message, it's just that their interest has always been with the book rather than with you and, once the book is launched, it's launched. If the book does well, there will be more to be done on the publishing side – negotiating with retailers for an extension of the book's time on the promo tables; further marketing assistance; sorting out reprints and the like. There may even be bits and pieces that involve you – a gig at a literary festival, for example, or a book-signing, perhaps. Mostly, though, your involvement is over. More than likely, the first time you have any firm information about book sales will come through when you get a royalty statement. Because that statement will take account of any returns (that is, books that have been taken by retailers, then returned to the publisher unsold), you may find that you've sold fewer books than were orginally shipped from the warehouse.

If you do get invitations to address festivals or go to book-signings, then accept by all means, but keep your expectations firmly anchored in reality. Salman Rushdie and Jeremy Clarkson can draw enormous crowds to these events. You most likely can't. If a literary festival asks you to talk but doesn't offer you any cash, feel free to ask about payment. If it's travel expenses and a sandwich only, go if you want to, but don't expect to sell so many books that you'll make your money back that way.

Quite apart from anything else, book sales will only benefit you if and when you've earned out your advance, which may well be never. I once drove seventy miles to a literary festival to find that I was talking to the local library society. I must have spoken well, because after my talk a number of people came up to me and promised me faithfully that they'd be searching out my books in the local town library. Which was nice, but you don't pay the heating bills that way. On the whole, though, if you can find a way to cover your time and travel, then these events are enjoyable, no matter how humble. You also get to feel in your own tiny way like a star. Which, indeed, you are.

Lastly, you should call to mind my earlier comments about the shelf life of your book. By around six weeks from publication, your book's destiny has most likely already been determined. If it's selling strongly, it'll stay on those promo tables. It'll rise up the charts. It'll gather attention. It'll stick around long enough for word of mouth to do its bit. If (which is much more probable) your book hasn't sold in any great quantity, then it'll creep from those promo tables to the shelves round the side of the shop. It won't appear on the charts. It won't get any further media exposure. Any nascent word- of-mouth muttering will be stillborn. Your book will sell a little from the side shelves, but the time will come when the bookshop is restocking and your book will need to be cleared away and returned to the warehouse whence it came.

AIMING HIGH

How many do you want to sell? Sales of the Bible, the Koran and Chairman Mao's little red book dwarf all regular best-sellers. But if you aren't either a deity or a communist dictator, you might want to calibrate your ambitions according to the list below. All numbers are guestimates only and the list is not comprehensive.

A Tale of Two Cities	Charles Dickens	200 million
The Lord of the Rings	J. R. R. Tolkien	150 million
And Then There Were None	Agatha Christie	100 million
Le Petit Prince	Saint-Exupéry	80 million
The Da Vinci Code	Dan Brown	80 million
The Catcher in the Rye	J. D. Salinger	65 million
Baby and Child Care	Dr Benjamin Spock	50 million
Black Beauty	Anna Sewell	50 million
The Name of the Rose	Umberto Eco	50 million
Harry Potter and the Deathly Hallows	J. K. Rowling	45 million
War & Peace	Leo Tolstoy	>36 million
Kane and Abel	Jeffrey Archer	34 million
Gone with the Wind	Margaret Mitchell	30 million

J. K. Rowling's agent claims that her total book sales have topped 400 million all told. Stephen King has sold more than 350 million books. Agatha Christie, however, has outsold both authors several times over: it's reckoned that her books have sold around 4,000 million copies.

Part Seven

LIFE AFTER
PUBLICATION

FROM HARDBACK TO PAPERBACK

Fifteen or twenty years back, there was an industry rule of thumb which suggested that a typical book would sell five times as much in paper covers as it had done in hard ones. Still further back, it was common for hardback publishers to be quite distinct from paperback ones. The hardback crowd would buy a book and then sell the paperback publishing rights to a wholly different company.

These days, naturally, things have changed. Your paperback publisher will be the same as your hardback publisher, though the imprint will change. (If you are published in hardback by Viking, for example, your paperback will be published by Penguin. If you're published in hardback by Macmillan, your paperback will come out as a Pan book. And so on.) The rules of thumb have become less certain too. A book that sells 7,000 copies in hardback (an excellent result for most books) might sell just 15,000 in paperback or it might, like Jennifer Worth's *Call the Midwife*, go on to sell more like 350,000.

Your own involvement in the paperback launch will be like a small-scale reprise of the hardback launch. It'll all be on a smaller scale because, whereas the launch of a new book has some news value, the re-emergence of that same book with a somewhat bendier jacket isn't news at all. (This comment and the rest of the section assumes, of course, that you were published first in hardback. If you came out first in paperback, this section isn't relevant to you.)

If you can find a genuinely new angle for the publicity, you can try to get your publisher's attention for it, but be aware from the start that you will be fighting uphill all the way. The assumption among publishers – and in most cases a correct one – is that hardbacks have news value, paperbacks don't. There may be bits and bobs that your publisher looks to do for the paperback launch – an online thing here, an interview there – but it'll all be minor stuff in comparison with what was done for the hardback.

The jacket, likewise, is more than likely going to be a reprise of the hardback jacket. Perhaps a designer will play a little with the fonts and spacing. Perhaps there'll be an icon included, or something surplus removed. On the whole, though, no one will be inclined to invest much time and attention at this stage. The fate of the hardback looms over the paperback like a prophecy. If your hardback sold poorly, your paperback won't have secured significant promotional slots, and without a strong retail platform your paperback won't sell in any quantity. Therefore, it makes no sense for the publisher to fuss too much over it.

Conversely, if your hardback sold strongly, that retail platform will exist, but your publisher is likely to conclude that their sales strategy for the hardback must have been a good one, so they'll simply redeploy it as appropriate for the paperback.

To my mind, publishers have a tendency to take this inattention a little too far. If a hardback was orginally sold into a Christmas market, for example, the blurb on the paperback is unlikely to feel right if it's coming out in July. More generally, if the book sold below expectations in hardback, the paperback edition should provide an opportunity for second thoughts and a second assault on readers' wallets. Nevertheless, if your publisher doesn't happen to share this attitude, you're going to find it all but impossible to procure any shift in their stance.

It's worth mentioning here that, in theory, your original editor is still your editor. In some houses, you'll find that the same person is in charge of both hardback and paperback editions. In others, you'll have a separate editor for the paperback, though your original hardback editor is still your main and most important point of contact. The publishers who most firmly separate hardback and paperback publishing like to say that it allows them to publish with a fresh eye and an undogmatic attitude. And that may very well be true, though, since your paperback editor may have had nothing to do with the acquisition of your book, she may be that much less committed to achieving success with it. My own preference would be to have the same editor all the way through, but, since the decision won't be up to you, it's not one you need to fret about.

Overall, my advice to authors would be to review blurb and jacket carefully. If there are things that could be tightened or improved, then press diligently (and always politely) for them to be altered. When it comes to jacket design, you're likely to achieve some success. When it comes to procuring publicity for the paperback, then you'll do well to get anything at all.

THE NEXT PROJECT

Alas, most authors sense a kind of low-level disappointment around the time of publication. When you're writing a book, it seems like the most important thing in the world to you. When it arrives on the shelves, and after a flurry of PR activity, it seems like no one really cares.

And they don't – or at least in nothing like the way you care. Your agent and editor both genuinely like your book, and probably like you too. But they handle numerous books every year and, in the end, the publication of yours is just business. The best solution for most authors is to live in the warm bath of future hope, not the chilly waters of present reality. Be diligent and persistent in doing what you can to guard the welfare of your babies, but be aware that you can't do all that much for them. You should, by now, be hard at work on your next project. Bid farewell to your firstborn, rejoice in its successes and don't take its failures to heart. After all, they're not really failures at all. I once spoke to my agent about a book of mine that had sold below expectations. The question I wanted answered was, *why*? Why hadn't it sold? Was it the cover? Was it the blurb? Was it the content? Was it the PR campaign?

Her answer was a wise one, namely that a failure to do well at the tills is the default outcome. When a book doesn't sell as many copies as it could do, no publisher sits around asking why. It hasn't sold in shedloads, because books mostly don't. The question *why* is usually only asked in the exactly opposite situation, when all of a sudden a book starts selling in huge volumes at the tills. Was there something about the cover that appealed to the public? Some trick of the author's media profile? Some clever bit of positioning? Publishers are keenly interested to understand the magic, in the hope that they can bottle and re-use it. When they reckon they've found that bit of magic – the pale, mawkish covers now de rigueur in the misery memoir market, for example – everyone uses it, everyone copies it, and the magic vanishes.

But not for you. You came to writing from a passion for a story or a subject. Huge sales would have been nice, but they were never your major motivation. So work hard on your new project and remember why it was that you became a writer in the first place.

And as for that project, we'll deal with the second book and your subsequent career very shortly. First, though, a couple of sections on smaller publishers and on self-publishing. If you've been published by a major-league publisher in the first instance, these sections aren't so important to you and you can move straight on.

WORKING WITH SMALL PUBLISHERS

Thus far, the entire discussion of the publication process has quietly assumed that you are working with a major publisher. That assumption hasn't been explicit, but it's been there nonetheless – lurking in the discussion about promotional slots, the notion that you'll have a dedicated publicist, the idea that there are enough staff knocking around that you might attend a meeting with Smiley Becky not actually knowing who she is or what she does.

Smaller publishers are unlikely to get access to the promotional slots of major retailers. Even supposing that those retailers entered into discussions in the first place, smaller publishers are simply unlikely to have enough cash to buy their place in the sun. Equally, they may not have their own PR department. They certainly can't afford a floating array of Smiley Beckys.

If your publisher is smaller, then you're likely to find that all the foregoing discussion is simultaneously true and false. It's true in the sense that smaller publishers have to deal with all the processes of normal publishing – design, production, publicity, sales, marketing, and so forth. Everything that was said on these topics is, broadly speaking, just as relevant to you. It is, however, false in its implication that your publisher will have abundant resources to promote your book. It won't. These days, a smaller publisher is doing well to get decent uptake from retailers. Any publicity is likely to be scanty. Those three-for-two tables are likely to seem a long, long away from your book.

Yet there's good news as well as bad in all this. The bad news is something you already knew: namely, that huge sales are unlikely for your book. The good news is everything else. Because your publisher is low on resources, they're quite likely to be amenable to real input from you. Indeed, they may even have approached you to write the book in the first place precisely because of who you are. What's more, if your book is a subject-led book of some description – a how-to book on parenting; a memoir about mental illness; a book on flower identification – then you almost certainly have access to certain micro-communities that your publisher very much wants to reach. For example, if you're writing about flowers, then perhaps you're a member of a botanical society, or are involved with some local botanical gardens. More than likely, you know someone who edits a newsletter, runs a website or arranges lectures and garden visits. Those contacts are precious, and your publisher is likely to make the most of them. The marketing exercise can almost become collaborative, in a way that just isn't true for authors working with the larger houses.

THE INDIE PUBLISHER: ALWAYS ON THE LOOKOUT

Not all independent publishers are as small as the seven-books-a-year Tindal Street Press. Imprints such as Faber, Atlantic, Granta, Quercus and Canongate (all members of the Independent Alliance) are also independents. But it's sometimes true that authors with independents can feel more supported and more involved in the publishing process than if they were an unknown amongst the big publishers' star-name authors. Small size isn't necessarily a bar to achievement, as Tindal Street's record of three Man Booker and two Orange listings, plus two Costa winners, demonstrates. One odd, special manuscript ignored by the mainstream can, through an independent publisher, find success: that's the romance of publishing.

The reality is that independents specialise. The Independent Publishers Guild has 550 members who account for a combined turnover of over £500 million. I discovered at an IPG conference how many specialist fields this sector covers: sports, travel, food, law, education, culture, computing, country matters, poetry and fiction. Imprints such as Arcadia, Alma, Aurum, Beautiful Books, Bloodaxe, Duckworth and Honno all have their specialist strengths and particular interests. We happen to specialise in English regional literary fiction and nothing else – no children's, no sci-fi. Carcanet's list favours some kinds of poetry more than others; Salt's has a different flavour. Writers wanting to work with independent publishers need to study a publisher's list and website with great care.

But just like the editors in the big houses, we are always on the lookout for something surprising, assured, beautiful, utterly itself; something we hope will stand up there with the best. But our selection process entails reading more than 500 unsolicited submissions and agented manuscripts a year, inevitably rejecting 99% of them. Covering letters which hint at a track record of publication or author recommendation may make us better disposed, as will three impressive chapters to make us ache for more; and when the full manuscript arrives we want the story to live up to the initial promise, and spring some fresh surprises too. The same high expectations as a big publisher, really.

ALAN MAHAR
Publishing Director, Tindal Street Press

SO YOU WANT TO BE A PUBLISHER?

Publishing is easy. All you need is one great idea and you are off like a barracuda, gliding past the big corporations, with their strategy teams and towering offices and pie-charts.

You don't need any qualifications or an office, or even an awful lot of money. When I started out, almost twenty years ago, I worked on my own in our spare bedroom. Half the time I'd be baby-sitting for the kids as well as calling up printers and doing deals with authors. It was the loveliest time, and the most fun.

What you do need, though, if you are to make it as a publisher, is a really good new idea about the kind of books people want to read. It may be you feel that we are long overdue for a science-fiction revival. Or, maybe, a really good picture book about Labradors, Britain's most popular dog, is what middle England is just waiting to rush out and buy.

In my case, in the beginning I plumped mainly for rock'n'roll and true crime. I even persuaded a virtually unknown hack called Piers Morgan to write one of my first four books. Astonishingly all those first books were hits. One of them – Hell Hath No Fury – went to number three on the Sunday Times best-seller list.

Don't worry too much about all the boring production stuff. There are printers out there who are desperate for work, and who will be delighted to give you a helping hand. To be honest, when I began I just showed a printer someone else's book I liked the look of, then asked him to use the same type-face and layout. It worked like a dream. Unless you are spectacularly talented, you will, however, need to hire a good designer to produce your covers.

The shops decide which books they will order, and in what quantity, simply by looking at the cover and an advance information sheet. I have yet to meet a buyer who has the time or inclination actually to read a manuscript. As a former writer, I was rather shocked to discover this bleak first fact of publishing life.

The difference a spectacular title and cover can make is quite extraordinary. In the early days, when I used to sell my own books into the trade, I would be constantly amazed when a buyer would order fifty copies of a book I loved, and had high hopes for. Then, in the next breath, he would order 10,000 copies of a book I was not particularly confident about.

One piece of information it is helpful to factor in to your calculations is that the unit cost of books drops dramatically according to how many copies you print. We generally find that printing less than 3,000 copies of a new book these days is not really financially viable.

Why not give it a whirl? The average credit card would more than cover the costs involved in producing your first book. Then it's just a case of move over, Lord Weidenfeld! Good luck.

JOHN BLAKE
Managing Director, John Blake Publishing Ltd., London

What's more, because your initial advance is likely to be low (or perhaps even non-existent), every book you sell will end up putting a little cash in your pocket. Small change, maybe, but a nice sensation nevertheless, and one that countless authors with mainstream houses never experience.

Indeed, though the three-for-two tables host the fastest sales, they seldom host the longest. A book on (let's say) working through your tax returns, negotiating divorce or caring for cats can sell year in, year out. If there's material that needs updating from time to time, then you'll be asked to do just that, but the book itself can endure.

This book, as it happens, is a prime example of just this phenomenon. It will never sit on a three-for-two table, nor is it likely to be entered for any promotion with any retailer. It is likely to be found somewhere towards the back of a larger shop, along with the how-to-write books, the *Writers' & Artists' Yearbook*, some dictionaries and other language-based reference texts. In a large and busy bookstore, entire weeks may go by without anyone buying the book, but it'll sell steadily all the same, year in, year out. An attentive publisher will work hard on supporting backlist sales, through steady marketing, cosmetic changes to the cover, updating the material, repeat marketing to existing buyers, the creation of websites and other online promotional tools. These things don't have the glamour of a big three-for-two instore promotion, but such promotions aren't appropriate or necessary for such titles – and that constant flow of sales will be something few novelists ever get to experience.

Amazon and other online sellers will also provide a much longer stream of income for your title than is likely to be true of all but the most successful novels. If your book is sensibly titled – *A Field Guide to British Flowers* or *Breaking Up: How to Manage Your Divorce* – then it will pop up when suitable search terms are entered on Amazon. Direct, practical blurb text is generally useful for this reason. Anyone searching Amazon for a subject-related book is seeking to fulfil a specific need, and the more your book can address that need in clear, concrete terms, the better.

You can make the most of this longevity, by stitching your book into your regular life. Work your contacts to sell your book. Use any online presence you have to market it. Don't go crazy, but be persistent. Again, this book is a prime example of how this can work. I happen to run a writers' consultancy. That position both qualifies me to write this book and helps me to sell it. I'm not going to dedicate my life to selling it, but I'll make darn sure that the mailing lists and the web presence which I already have are deployed, in part, to create book sales.

From the point of view of authorial satisfaction, this longevity can be welcome. A smaller, subject-led book won't have the brief, beautiful existence of a mass-market thriller; but it can aspire to a slow, dependable one instead. And the book may even make some money. I know a couple of authors who sold subject-led books to niche publishers for peanuts, but who sell a few thousand copies each and every year, thereby earning them enough to buy a nice holiday per year for the forseeable future. What's more, if you have a few such titles to your name, if you keep the materials refreshed and up to date (generating a fresh advance and a fresh sales impetus each time you do), then that nice annual holiday might, in fact, transmogrify into a pleasantly steady income, of the sort that allows you to pay mortgages, clear heating bills and even fill your glass with a drop or two of wine.

That's not the kind of outcome which will make a hedge-fund manager sick with envy, but then, if poisoning hedge-fund managers is your goal, you took a wrong turn by becoming a writer.

SELF-PUBLISHING

Writing a single section on self-publishing is something of a fool's errand. In a single section I can't hope to tackle every issue of importance in self-publishing. Nevertheless, as the gates of regular publishing are becoming ever harder to prise open, no book on getting published is complete without at least some overview of the subject, so a book like this needs to cover the topic, however cursorily. What's more, a small number of capable and committed self-publishing firms are starting to behave a bit like 'real' commercial publishers, while a number of smaller commercial publishers are beginning to borrow a few tricks from the self-pub trade, so that the boundaries between the two worlds are blurrier now than they've ever been in the past.

GOALS AND DEFINITIONS

Let's start with some definitions. A book is commercially published if the author never pays a brass cent to the publisher. No production subsidy. No marketing package. No editorial fee. No commitment to buy a single book. Nothing. Just to be clear, this is how 'normal' publishing works. I have never paid a single penny to my publisher ever for anything. That's not because I'm tight. It's because I'm an author.

A book is self-published – or vanity published, subsidy published, or whatever other term you care to apply – if the author pays an upfront fee or if the author is committed to purchasing a minimum number of books at a minimum price. Plenty of self-publishing firms are not anxious to describe themselves as such, but, as soon as any publisher suggests that any money has to flow from you to them as part of the contract, they've revealed themselves as self-publishers.

There is nothing wrong with self-publishing. Virginia Woolf self-published her work. So did Walt Whitman, William Blake, James Joyce, Deepak Chopra, Mark Twain and many others. The issue is not whether you have a moral or artistic right to pay for the publication of your own work; the issue is simply whether you are likely to achieve your artistic or commercial goals that way. If you simply want to print up a memoir for your family's consumption, good for you. More people should do just that, and a printed memoir will be a wonderful monument for years and decades to come. It'll be a living, precious object like no other. Similarly, if you want to print up some fantasy fiction that you've previously been sharing haphazardly with your friends, the same thing applies . . . except that, just to be on the safe side, you may wish to divide the 'years and decades' comment by a factor of five or ten.

Let's assume, however, that you wish to sell your book. You want to make some money, build a reputation, launch a career. Aside from the memoirists, those motivations are, in my experience, the ones which brings most writers to the world of self-publishing. As a professional author myself, I respect those motives entirely. I write because I love it, but I also write to pay the heating bills. Nothing wrong with either objective.

The million-dollar question, however, is what you can realistically hope to achieve through self-publishing, and whether the outcomes are worth the investment. There's no simple answer here, as every situation is different, but it is possible to offer some broad guidance, nevertheless. (I should mention that I've got some pretty harsh things to say about the industry in what follows. But bear with me. There are some good guys too, and we'll get to them at the end of the section.)

MATHS AND ETHICS

A typical self-published book will sell a few dozen copies. Those few dozen will comprise the author's family and friends, any people he or she has succeeded in marketing to directly, and perhaps a handful of others who have stumbled across the book in one way or another. A successful self-pub book will sell two to three hundred copies. Any book that is selling in those volumes is no longer selling only to family and friends; it's selling also to people who are buying it because they love the look of it and want to read it. They are, if you like, 'real' sales and count every bit as much as the sales achieved by regular publishers – rather more so, indeed, given the hurdles that any self-pub book will overcome.

And every now and then a self-pub book will be a triumph. I know one self-pub novelist who sold 500 hardbacks at £17.99 and 1,500 paperbacks besides. That's one heck of an achievement and she had cause to feel justly proud. I know another self-pub author who sold 4,000 copies in four months and whose book is still selling strongly. These are, nevertheless, still relatively small numbers and they are highly unusual ones. The simple fact is that self-publishing companies do not, on the whole, achieve strong sales for their authors.

That's where ethics come in to it. You'd think that, if self-pub companies were proud of what they did, they'd be upfront about how the publishing industry works, they'd be upfront about their own role in it, and they'd be candid about likely sales outcomes. Alas, I could name five companies who are anything but candid in these regards for every one I could name whose ethics I admire.

To take one simple example, when researching this section I thought I'd ask a major self-pub company what sales they actually achieved for their authors. Simple, no? Just ring up and ask. So I did. I didn't say I was researching a book for A & C Black, I posed as a potential customer. 'Please tell me,' I said, 'the average number of books you sell per title published.'

Aha, I was told, there's no such thing as an average book. Each package is individually designed around the author's own personal goals. Perhaps I would like to discuss those goals now?

I persisted. I said I'd be very happy to discuss individual packages, once I had a handle on roughly what sales I might expect to achieve.

Well, came the answer, one of our books is selling almost 2,500 copies per quarter. That's nearly 10,000 a year!

That was nice to know, and nice for the author concerned, but it wasn't an answer to my question. I persisted and persisted. Every time I asked my question, I marked my pad with another stroke of the pen. I had made eleven pen marks and my salesman had had to go to discuss things with his supervisor, before my question was answered. The company in question – one of the largest and best-known in the market – sold approximately 100 copies per title published. That 100-copy figure represents a mean not a median amount. (That is, it was biased upwards by the occasional success story, like the book that was selling 2,500 copies a quarter). The median number of book sales was probably closer to 50 or 60.

If you are thinking of entering into any sort of contract with a self-publishing company, make absolutely certain that you ask this question, in just the same way as I did. If you don't get an answer, then persist. If you persist and still don't get an answer, then the company is not to be trusted and you should have nothing to do with it.

SNAKES

While on the subject of ethics, let's deal with a few other snakes in the woodpile. Perhaps you've sent your book off to a publisher which advertised itself on the internet or in the classifieds somewhere. As far as you're aware, the publisher is just a publisher. It's not calling itself a self-publishing outfit, still less a vanity publisher.

Then you get a letter back that praises your work in no uncertain terms. An editor – and perhaps a reader too – have read your work. They love your sensitivity. They think your story is terrific. They'd love to take you on. The cost of their services will be anything up to £12,000. You'll sign a contract and be entitled to royalties in the regular way. It's a gamble, but you're tempted.

Don't be. I once received an enquiry from a woman who was dying of cancer. She had written eight poems. They weren't, to be candid, very good poems, but they were from the heart and they were perhaps the most important creative act of this woman's life. They deserved to be cherished for that reason alone. She had sent her work off to a publisher and got back a letter precisely as described. The author of that letter commented that he had been particularly moved by this woman's poems, because he had been very sick himself once. He said that the market for poetry was tough, but that there could well be strong demand in the UK, America and Australasia. This woman, who was not rich, was being asked for £8,000. She was flattered by the praise and tempted by the proposition.

The truth is that everything about that letter was deceitful. You can't plausibly publish a poetry collection of eight rather short poems. A poetry collection needs to be as much as ten times longer than that. What's more, even the very best debut collection is unlikely to sell more than a few hundred copies. The market for poetry is almost vanishingly small, and this woman's poems weren't remotely right for whatever market does exist. The simple, nasty truth is that somebody consciously sought to deceive a dying woman out of £8,000. The deceit might technically have been lawful, but most muggers have superior ethics. The company was loathsome and it's still in business today. The company probably sends out a letter like that several times a week – and, if you happen to be the recipient of one such letter, then tear it up, throw it away and give it not another thought. These people will say anything to get their hands on your money. You can't trust a single word they say.

Let's also deal with the claim, made rather widely by some outfits which should know better, that your book will be available through over 25,000 stores worldwide. If that were true, then I should be suing my agent and publisher, because no book of mine has ever been available in 25,000 stores worldwide or anything like it. Indeed, if the second half of this book has taught anything, it's that achieving a decent retail platform is a vital, plaguesome and uncertain business that challenges even the biggest and best publishers in the world.

So what does that claim actually mean? It means, it turns out, that your book will have an ISBN number. That means that any customer armed with your ISBN number can go into any bookstore anywhere in the world and order your book. Indeed, they can go to any computer in the world and, if the machine is plugged into the internet, they can order your book online, thereby making your book 'available' through about 500 million more outlets besides. The trouble is that counting outlets in this way is meaningless. When was the last time you bought a book by marching up to a desk in a bookstore and giving them an ISBN number? That's not how books are bought. In any case, the challenge is to get the ISBN number into the punter's hand and the desire to make a purchase into his head in the first place. That's the hard bit; the physical delivery bit is and always has been child's play.

Which brings us to another dodgy assertion: namely that Amazon has changed everything. It's levelled the playing field. It makes your book as accessible as anyone else's. Not true, not true and not true. First of all, an overwhelming majority of books are still bought through bricks-and-mortar outlets: bookshops, supermarkets, gift shops and the like. Amazon and its peers have taken a big bite out of the market, but it sells many fewer books than the supermarkets do. The bookshops proper are bigger again. What's more, no one goes on to Amazon and just types a random author's name into the search engine. They either type the name of an author they've heard of and like (Dan Brown, J. K, Rowling or whatever) or they type a subject-related search term ('Getting Published', 'Amateur Fishkeeping', 'Simple Bombmaking', or what have you). Amazon is good at selling books of these sorts. It is lousy at selling books with unknown titles by unknown authors.

THE FALLOUT

Unsurprisingly, countless writers are caught out by what are – in my opinion – nothing more than scams that happen not to be illegal, by gross deceit that manages to teeter on just the right side of the law.

It's easy to see how all this happens. Real agents and publishers don't advertise, because they don't need to. They just make sure that they're listed in the *Writers' & Artists' Yearbook* and the rest will take care of itself. Consequently, when people who know nothing about the industry go to the internet to research it, they are rapidly exposed to a plethora of advertisements from a collection of self-publishing firms. These firms have almost nothing to do with the regular publishing industry that chunters away signing up authors, printing books, getting them into bookshops and making sales – but there's precious little information available to tell people that. So writers make ordinary, businesslike contact with what appear to be ordinary, businesslike companies. They believe what they're told. They make their decisions, sign their cheques, hand over their manuscripts and trust to the future.

Some of those people will be perfectly well aware of roughly how many copies they can expect to sell and will be perfectly content with that result. Good. I have no issue with that (although I do have some recommendations, in a moment, for improving your expected outcome). Others are baffled and confused. We receive a regular stream of emails from people saying, 'Hi guys, I've just published my book and am now looking for an agent to help me promote it.' If you've read to this point in this book, you already know how wrong-headed such emails are. Agents are there to sell manuscripts. They are not there to promote books. Even if they were there to promote books, their job would have been largely complete by the point of publication. Even if the writer were emailing well prior to the publication date, no 'promoter' of a book could do anything useful for it unless a strong retail platform existed from which to promote it. And few self-publishing companies can ever create a strong retail platform for their products, because few of them exert any quality control over the manuscripts they take on, aside from checking that writers are sober enough to find a cheque and literate enough to sign it. Unsurprisingly, that's not a procedure calculated to entice retailers into doing business with them.

For what it's worth, my consultancy probably encounters ten people who feel baffled, hurt and disappointed by their contact with the self-publishing industry for every one person we meet who feels delighted and positive. It's true that we tend to act as a refuge for writers in distress, so that ten-to-one ratio may exaggerate how badly the industry fails its clients, but you'll understand that it's not an industry I hugely admire.

THE GOOD GUYS

There are, however, some really excellent self-publishing companies.

First of all, there are the cheapies. Firms that allow you to upload your manuscript, click a few buttons and have your manuscript printed. Some companies have offered rates as low as £50 or £100 for a very basic service. If you've gone to all the trouble of writing your manuscipt, it surely deserves at least that level of love and attention once you're finished, even if you haven't been able to find a commercial publisher. Your work will be preserved. It'll be something for you and loved ones to look at in times to come. And heck, it's only £50. Why not go for it? The cheapest print-on-demand services can also offer excellent value. If you go for this sort of option, you can think of it as cheap printing rather than publication of any sort. After all, the word 'publish' has at its heart the sense of making public. Just printing your book up won't do that. But public exposure isn't everything. Creating something you love and sharing it with others is an utterly valuable exercise in its own right. Most people never write a book. You have done. Feel proud.

Secondly, there are the deluxe vendors. If you've written a memoir, that book is perhaps deeply precious to you. It'll be something that your kids and grandkids and great-grandkids will treasure. That's not sentimentality speaking.

We receive a good many enquiries from people who have unearthed a diary or memoir dating back to Edwardian or Victorian times. They're enchanted by its antiquity and seduced by the fact that it is an ancestor writing. These books have no commercial value now, but they delight those who find and read them. Your book has every right to do the same, possibly a century or more down the line.

Since this is the case, perhaps the cheapest possible internet deal isn't the very best way to go. There are a number of self-publishers who specialise in hand-tooled leather bindings, creamy paper, marbled endpapers, thoughtful font selection, and so forth. They will turn a manuscript into a thing of physical beauty – and also something sturdy enough to last for any number of lifetimes. Publishing that way doesn't come particularly cheap, but £3,000 should buy you a dozen or so genuinely beautiful books.

WHERE SELF-PUB AND COMMERCIAL PUBLISHING MEET

Third, and most interesting, are a new breed of self-publishing companies which offer authors a kind of halfway house between conventional self-publishing and the commercial kind. Of these, the company that has gone the furthest is Matador, though Amolibros is a strong contender too. The thing that distinguishes these companies from their peers is that *they actually try to sell the books they print*. That is, they act like real publishers! They print books and seek to sell them! You'd think that this was precisely what all those other companies would be doing too, but, as we've seen, those other companies act more like production co-ordinators: bringing together typesetting, cover design, printing, and ISBN issuance under one roof. Indeed, if a publisher isn't *actively* seeking to sell its wares, it isn't really a publisher at all.

The activist self-publishers differ from the competition in a number of respects. For one thing, the big, bad self-pub companies never reject any manuscript, ever. Why would they? All they care about is climbing inside the author's wallet and helping themselves to whatever they find within. If, on the other hand, you are an activist self-publishing company wanting to sell real products to real people, you simply can't take any old rubbish without destroying your reputation. If, therefore, a manuscript is of unsaleable quality, it'll be rejected. To be sure, their standards are much less demanding than those of agents and mainstream publishers, but so they should be. There are countless memoirs, for example, which aren't of huge literary merit and which won't set the best-seller lists on fire, which do nevertheless record a real story in a touching and memorable way. Such things deserve publication, and, if self-pub is the only option, then so be it.

At this end of the market, of course, none of these books would be commercially viable without the author's financial support, so the author is asked to pay upfront – just as with any other self-publishing venture. The difference, however, is that this new breed of self-publisher works closely with wholesalers to get the books shipped out to retailers and sold. Matador, for example, prefers its clients to order print runs of 500 copies and almost half the time it manages to sell out this print run completely. Some books go into second editions. These outcomes are still hardly going to blow the socks off the mainstream publishers, but by self-pub standards they're a whole order of magnitude better than the competition.

Furthermore, at this level of the industry, the dividing line between self-pub and commercial publishing is becoming increasingly blurred. Much of the challenge of small-scale publishing has to do with simple mathematics. Most of the costs involved in publishing are fixed. If you can nudge your expected sales from (say) 500 units to 2,000, your cost per unit doesn't quite fall by 75%, but it's not that far off. This unit-cost reduction can make a huge difference to the viability of the project. Whereas a nicely presented paperback isn't going to sell at £25, but might well do at £9.99, a longer print run will mean lower unit costs, thereby allowing a lower retail price . . . thereby encouraging higher sales in the first place. A virtuous circle is born.

To benefit from that virtuous circle, however, you need to be confident of achieving those sales, and I've come across a couple of smaller commercial publishers who are offering book deals to authors on condition that those authors purchase a certain number of units. For example, one company took on a business-related book from an author who was a management consultant in the field. He agreed to buy 2,000 units for on-selling to his clients (something he achieved in just two weeks, apparently). Meanwhile, the company was able to order a total print run of 5,000 copies. The company benefited from the lower costs of a longer print run. The author benefited from having the support of a proper commercial publisher – and made a packet from the profits of selling his 2,000 books to his clients.

In effect, this (somewhat convoluted) tale is nothing more than the story of a nimble commercial publisher purloining self-pub financing techniques to achieve a win-win outcome for all concerned.

HOW TO CHOOSE YOUR SELF-PUBLISHING COMPANY

In choosing a self-publisher, you need to work out first and foremost what you're after. Are you, in fact, just looking for a cheap form of printing? If so, just browse around online and choose a low-cost package that looks right for you.

On the other hand, perhaps all you want is production co-ordination done for you, but you want this done professionally and well. In that case, you'll need to pay a little more. You'll need to quiz different companies about how cover design and so forth is managed. You'll probably want to see some sample products. You'll want to weigh up total costs, and you'll make your decisions accordingly.

If, on the other hand, you want to *publish* your book — that is, have a professional company actively seek to make sales on your behalf — then you need to interrogate companies hard about what efforts they make in that regard. The dodgy companies will, of course, have their patter and it can often sound perfectly plausible. You, however, have an advantage. You've read this book. You know more about the industry than the average punter, so that you'll see straight through some of the nonsense that is thrown at you. Even more important, you know the million-dollar question: *what are your average sales per title published?*

Any fair self-publisher will think that a perfectly reasonable question to ask. (They may want to exclude print-on-demand books from their calculations, as such customers are only after very small print runs in the first place. It's fair enough to exclude such works from the totals.) Otherwise, don't allow anyone to evade the question. If they remain evasive when you press them, don't do any business with them. It's an easy question for them to answer. They will know how many titles they published in the previous year. They'll know how many unit sales were made in the year. Take the second number. Divide it by the first number. That's your average right there.

Because the average will be skewed upwards by a small number of books that sold exceptionally well, you might want to downsize the average you've just calculated by about 60% to get a reasonable guestimate of the median (or 'man in the middle') book sales. Almost all self-pub authors will feel confident that they can exceed this median number — or, at least, all the ones I speak to feel they can. But they can't all be right. Half of all authors will sell fewer copies than that median number. The other half will sell more. That's what a median is.

Once you have this number, some self-pub companies will clearly seem superior to others. Then ask the ones that remain to send you some sample products. Look at production quality. Look at the prices at which these books are selling. Ask yourself who seems best to deal with on the phone. (And beware if you're only dealing with a salesman. Those folk are always friendly.) Do also ask how long a company has been around and how many titles it publishes each year. Self-pub companies do tend to come and go fairly quickly, and you've a better chance of a longer-term relationship if you are dealing with a strong, established company.

Then compare the costs of your various different options. Take your pick from there.

TOWARDS A PROFESSIONAL PRODUCT

One of the most entertaining literary bloggers around is a chap called Scott Pack. Scott used to be the Chief Buyer at Waterstone's, and in that capacity could make the most senior commissioning editor from the most prestigious publishing house quiver in naked terror. He then quit to set up the Friday Project, an innovative small publisher which ended up being swallowed by HarperCollins. Scott's is an interesting blog to follow, because he has some strong and well-informed opinions on various subjects, including self-publishing. His blog, 'Me And My Big Mouth', once published an open letter to self-published authors which I'm reproducing (with his kind permission) below. Before you read on, you should probably know that his blog's subtitle is 'contains wrong language from the start'. He's not kidding. The letter runs like this:

Dear Self-Published Author,

I can only assume that you are a reasonably intelligent individual. You have, after all, written an entire book from start to finish. That is no mean feat. It takes courage, perseverance, patience and huge slabs of self-belief. It also requires a certain amount of skill, no matter how good or bad the end result may turn out to be.

If you have managed to write a book then you must have a brain.

So why, oh why, does that brain stop functioning when it comes to selecting a cover for this magnum opus of yours?

You have slaved for hours, weeks, months, years over a hot keyboard. You have poured your heart into your work. You have honed, tweaked and crafted away. The least you can do is put a decent jacket on the bloody thing.

I receive a fair amount of self-published books to review. In my former life as a retailer I was sent even more. At least 90% of them have unspeakably bad covers. Utter shite.

How does this happen?

Have you ever seen a book before?

Did you not notice that your cover looks completely different to every other book in the bookshop, and not in a good way?

If you have opted for the self-publishing route then you have almost certainly invested a decent chunk of your own money in order to see your work in print. Why not spend a bit more to make your book look like something someone, anyone, may actually want to read?

A good freelance designer will charge between £500 and £750 for a book cover. Hardly pocket money but, trust me, it could make the difference between selling a few hundred copies and, oh I don't know, *selling fuck all*!

And no, your cousin Dave who knows a thing or two about Photoshop will not be able to do you a favour and knock something up for free. He will produce a steaming turd of a design that will make it look like a school textbook or a *Top of the Pops* album cover from 1974.

Now, to be fair, 90% of self-published jackets being shit is merely representative of the fact that 90% of self-published books *are* shit. But don't feel bad. At least 40% of books published by 'proper' publishers are shit as well. My point is that some of the 90% with crap jackets are actually quite good. And yours might well be one of them. Only no one will know as you have successfully put them off ever picking it up.

So there you have it. Spend a bit more time and money on making your book look a tad more normal and then perhaps, just perhaps, a few people may read it. And some of them might not even be related to you. Result.

Yours,

Scott Pack

P.S. Oh, and while you're at it, do us all a favour and get someone to copy-edit the bloody thing as well.

Now, we should say straight away, for any children or Southern Baptists who may be reading, that Mr Pack uses very bad language and should probably wash his mouth out with something astringent. But he has a point, no? Like Scott Pack, I get to see a lot of self-published book covers and the large majority are immediately identifiable as self-published book covers – and, as he says, not in a good way. Professional cover design makes a huge difference. So does a quality, appropriate blurb. If in doubt, pay someone competent. Compare your drafts against commercially published books in a similar genre. Put your own preferences aside and be as objective as you possibly can.

The same goes not just for copy-editing, but for structural editorial work too. Commercially published books have been through the following processes before they land in a bookstore:

☐ The author writes a first draft.

☐ The author revises that draft numerous times, possibly or possibly not with outside assistance. The 'final' version is likely to be very different from the first draft.

☐ The author is the one in a thousand whose manuscript is strong enough to get an agent. The agent suggests alterations. The author makes them.

☐ The agent gets a book deal. The publisher's editor comes up with a detailed list of changes, some larger, some smaller. The author makes those changes.

☐ The editor may or may not request some further minor changes on seeing the revised MS. If she does, the author makes them.

☐ A copy-editor goes through the book and makes countless edits and corrections. The author may check the copy-editor's work. The editor will assemble a 'master copy' from the combined versions.

☐ Page proofs are prepared. Those are proofread by the editor, the author and perhaps a proofreader.

☐ The book goes to press.

Please note, that is not an unusually long series of processes. It is what happens for every single book that you find in a bookshop – and, please recall, those are the books and the authors strong enough to have secured an agent and an editor in the first place. If you care deeply about the quality of your self-published work, it would be sheer folly to try to take shortcuts with the content.

Doing things right certainly means that you'll need to pay for copy-editing. The cost of that service will depend both on the length and the presentational quality of your manuscript, but if you budget £500–£600 for a manuscript of normal length you should be OK. Ideally, it also means working with a professional freelance editor, who will charge somewhere closer to £400–£500 for a normal-length manuscript. For that kind of money, no one is about to start rewriting your book for you, but you will get detailed advice about what needs to be fixed and how to go about it – in other words, you'll get exactly what any professional author gets from their in-house editor. If you feel particularly flush, or particularly anxious to get the manuscript to a very high degree of polish, you can pay a professional

---

SELF-PUBLISHED DOESN'T HAVE TO MEAN BADLY PUBLISHED

Authors come to self-publishing for many reasons, and, though the general assumption is that most want to be best-selling authors, the reality is that most don't. Yes, many want their work to be widely read, but few now expect their book to top the best-seller charts.

Of authors published by Matador, about a third publish for personal reasons and are treating the costs as part of their hobby. A third want to publish a book as part of their business: they are an 'expert' in a specialist field or they want to record some important local event, usually historical in nature. And about a third want to get their work out there in front of readers and get noticed, as a step on a career as an author.

As a self-publisher, your first question must be, 'What do I want to achieve?' Then set your goals realistically, and publish accordingly. The above options will all have differing cost implications, of course, and you may have to compromise to suit your budget. But one thing you should not compromise on is quality . . . of production, of service and of marketing and sales.

Even if your book is for personal use only, why publish something that you're not proud of? If you're publishing a book for a specific audience, it still has to appeal to them, so quality must be at least comparable to commercial books. And if you're trying to sell through wider retail, then you must have a product that is at least as good as something by one of the mainstream publishers. And quality doesn't have to cost any more than something produced poorly with no marketing.

Research your market, set your budget, quiz potential self-publishing companies and make a choice.

JEREMY THOMPSON
MD, Matador (www.troubador.co.uk/matador)

author to go through the whole darn thing tightening sentences, fixing scenes, deleting surplus material, and so forth. This is an expensive business – allow anything from £2,000 upwards – but it can make a huge difference to quality.

Needless to say, you need to do any structural work on the text before you get a copy-editor involved, otherwise you'll in effect be trying to paint a room before you've plastered it. Naturally, you need to be careful about your budget and realistic about your sales expectations, but far too many self-published works are let down by serious shortfalls in editorial rigour, copy-editing and cover design. If you want to create a quality product, you should at least make a stab of going through the same processes that all commercially published books go through themselves. If you don't, then don't be surprised when the quality isn't there.

SELLING YOUR BOOK

You've already chosen a self-publisher. You've ensured that your product quality is bang on the money, as regards both content and appearance. Now comes the job of getting it sold. By choosing the right self-publisher – that is, one driven by selling books rather than simply taking bundles of bank-notes out of your wallet – you've already done yourself a huge favour in accomplishing that goal.

Nonetheless, at this level of the market, your own individual effort, resourcefulness, chutzpah, creativity and diligence can make a huge difference. How you direct your efforts very much depends on you, your book and your set of contacts and resources. You might, however, be able to draw some inspiration from how various successful self-published authors have done it:

> EMMA. Emma's book was a racy, sexy romp, aimed at the Jilly Cooper market. Emma had a background in marketing, and felt that she didn't have anything all that distinctive to offer book-shops. Consequently, she decided to sell (i) through women's outlets such as beauty salons and hairdressers, and (ii) via the racetrack, as her book was set in the world of racing. She pack-aged her book (called *Racy!*) in a glamorous black lacy bag and persuaded retailers to keep it by the till. She sold over 2,000 copies in both hardback and paperback editions, and her success was sufficient to get at least one top agent seriously interested in taking her commercial.

WATERSTONE'S AND THE SELF-PUB COMMUNITY

As Independent Publisher Coordinator, I deal mostly with self-publishers and smaller independent publishers, especially those entering the market for the first time. There's no set definition as to what a small publisher is, but by and large, if you find yourself with a book and don't know what to do next, I'm your first port of call at Waterstone's, and approaches are made by all the usual methods – emails, phone calls, at conferences, even handwritten letters.

A lot of what I do is give advice – pretty much all of which can be found in this book and/or its companion, the Writers' & Artists' Yearbook. *If someone is unwilling to invest in these invaluable tools, then I think they are doing their book a disservice, but I can try and get some key messages across.*

The most important things I talk about are how, however small your operation is, your book is going to be competing with the biggest publishers around, and the customer will make no allowances for your lack of experience or budget. Your cover needs to look as professional as any on our shelves. Your RRP (recommended retail price) needs to be sensible – £20 for a B-format paperback may mean on paper you will recoup your budget quickly, but in practice will kill sales. We need to be able to order – and if necessary return – your book, so you'll need to be set up to supply us properly, ideally through a wholesaler. You need an ISBN *and barcode – that's a fact of life. And you will need to market your book, and tell us how that's going to happen.*

A lot of it is about managing expectations as well as economics. Putting a book into 300 stores and a website means a massive outlay for a publisher, with no guarantee of sales. I discuss titles that are sent to me with the relevant buyers, and we discuss what we can do with each title. If we think there are customers out there who will buy it, we think about where they may be and what the right way to reach them would be. Sometimes the answer is obvious – a publisher with a local book will have already identified the best stores to stock it, so it's just a matter of making that happen. Other times we will be able to advise on which stores may be the best ones to stock a title for reasons of size, location or local interest. Often local authors and publishers will have a relationship with their local store so all parties will have ideas about how best to sell a title.

It's very satisfying to see a title from one of these publishers take off in Waterstone's, and they can have considerable success. Recent books to do well include 4 Ingredients, *brought to the UK by two Australian mums – our sales are into five figures for this book alone – and* The Dealer *by Tony Royden. This crime novel has sold over a thousand copies in only a few months through publisher persistence, events and store support.*

PETER NORTH
Independent Publisher Coordinator for Waterstone's

GLENDA. Glenda's book told a true story about two sisters (her aunts) who loved the same man, but were brought closer by their love rather than driven apart. All the parties concerned lived in and around Swansea in South Wales. Glenda procured a good deal of local press interest in her story, arranged signings in local bookshops and secured excellent local distribution. She broke even financially, and received a large number of phone calls, emails and other messages praising her work. Her initial print run sold out completely, but alas her publisher went bankrupt, so she was unable to order more copies to satisfy unfilled demand.

AIDAN. Aidan is a network marketer (whatever that is). He wrote a book on network marketing. He signed up a self-pub company to handle production and distribution mechanics, but he always saw himself as the person most likely to achieve sales for it. He marketed hard, working the contacts that he had from his existing business. He sold 4,000 copies in a few months and was looking to go mainstream, in part because he felt that he'd be able to access overseas markets more effectively that way.

Notice that a theme common to these success stories is that the authors side-stepped the conventional distribution routes of mainstream publishers. You are highly unlikely to get one-to-one time with a senior buyer at any major national book chain, so you may as well not even try. But you can talk to local bookshops. You can talk to other local retailers who may be interested in your work. You can certainly whip up local PR, and arrange signings in local venues. If your book is subject-led (e.g. *Caring for Your Moustache*) and you are at the centre of a relevant membership network (e.g. you're the Lord High Master of the International Moustaches League), then work that network as hard as you can.

Notice a second point as well. The internet is not the answer. Sure, build a website if you want to. Sure, go on Facebook and Twitter and all the rest of it. By all means seek to get as many links from other websites to yours. But don't for a moment think that any of that constitutes sufficient, effective marketing. It doesn't. You will certainly sell a few more books if you have a website and so forth than if you don't, but the internet is not some magical genie that showers money over all who participate. Funnily enough, life – even cyber-life – ain't like that.

SECOND-NOVEL SYNDROME
AND OTHER AFFLICTIONS

Writing is an unusual profession in a number of ways, but here's one more way in which it's strange. If you choose to become a baker or a banker or a footballer or a call girl, you are probably expecting to bake, bank, kick balls and – er – make calls every day of your professional life. That's presumably why you entered the profession in the first place. Writers, on the other hand, normally feel impassioned by the particular story which drove them to pick up their pens in the first place. They complete their manuscript, find an agent, make a sale and proceed happily towards publication. Then, blow me, the publisher wants another book!

The writer often receives this news with an inner amazement. The first book begged to be written. It was an obsession that captured your waking thoughts and often your dream worlds as well. For most writers, the second book just isn't like that. It's a contractual obligation. It's a matter of craft as much as passion. For sure, you would like to be a writer, so writing another book seems like just the right thing to be doing, but this second assignment simply doesn't *feel* anything like the first one did. Unsurprisingly, this is the point at which many authors foul up badly.

THE TWO-BOOK DEAL AND VARIANTS

If you are a novelist, more often than not you've been given a two-book deal. The publisher's logic is fairly straightforward. Very few first novels make money. New authors are expensive to launch. If all goes well, a first book might break even, or turn a small profit. The publisher can then hope to make some real money on the launch of book two.

Relatively few deals for debut novelists run beyond that two-book period. If agents think you have a huge career ahead of you, they'll be wary of selling you off too cheap at the start. Conversely, most publishers are well aware that more careers run into the sand than otherwise, so they're hardly falling over themselves to make long-term commitments either.

That's not to say there can't be any exceptions to this rule. If you've written a trilogy (and yes, fantasy authors, I'm looking at you), your publisher may agree that it makes sense to sign you up for three books, not two. If you're not entirely a debut author and have a very strong proposition, it may be possible to sell runs of more than three books. For example, I know of a pair of historians who decided to turn their hand to historical fiction, and developed a proposal for an entire sequence of historical novels. The proposal was strong enough that a publisher was persuaded to buy the complete run. Such things, however, are rare.

On the other hand, literary novels are quite often sold in single-book deals. The publisher is keen to avoid too extensive a commitment to what is quite likely a financially perilous undertaking. The agent, on the other hand, may want a deal that establishes the author and positions her for a larger subsequent deal thereafter.

For non-fiction, single-book deals are more common, depending on what kind of book it is. For a strictly subject-led book, single-book deals are very much the rule. Where the work is rather more broad in appeal, and where the author is looking to build his identity as a 'voice' who might explore or comment on any number of subjects, then two-book deals are the rule. Thus, this book (very much subject-led and appealing to a very specific audience) was bought in a one-book deal. My much more general non-fiction books (with a much broader audience, more likely to claim a place in retail promotions, more 'voice'-led, and not nearly as audience- or subject-specific) were bought in a two-book deal.

If you're a memoirist, you should almost certainly say everything that you have to say in a single volume. If you are absolutely certain that you need two or more volumes to say it all, you will almost certainly only be able to sell your work in single-book deals, and there's no certainty at all that, if you do sell your first book, anyone will want the second.

A CAUTIONARY TALE

Because it's mostly novelists who have a two-book deal, and because second-novel syndrome is most acutely suffered by them, I'm going to talk about novelists only in what follows. But if you're a non-fiction author with an alarming two-book deal to satisfy, what follows is for you as well.

Once upon a time, there was an author – let's call him Harold Bingley – who wrote a novel, found an agent and got a nice fat deal from a well-known publisher. He hadn't found that first novel particularly hard to write. Everyone told him it was terrific. He was confident that he knew what he was doing.

Then he was asked to write a second novel. Fine. This author, a friend of mine, wanted to write a second novel, but he had no idea what he was going to write about. There simply wasn't a story clamouring to be written the same way the first one was. But still, he was good at this, right? The first novel had come out easily enough, so the second one would presumably come the same way.

Alas, it did not. The first draft of that second novel was horrible. It was a car crash wrapped in a plane wreck. It did not please Harold Bingley's publisher. They were very nice about it, but they were very clear that the book needed major surgery. Surgery that probably involved the Ctrl-A ('select all') function followed by a simple little tap of the Delete key. That wasn't quite how the publisher put it, but Harold Bingley at this point was back on the straight and narrow. He went back to his computer, opened his novel, hit Ctrl-A, then Delete. He rewrote that novel from scratch. It still wasn't as good as the first one, but it was a solid, professional, dependable piece of work. In effect, it was his third novel, not his second.

He never encountered that same problem again. From there on, his novels were either born of passion and craft working together, or a disciplined, worldly wise craft working alongside enough joy and pleasure to substitute for true passion.

Harold Bingley's travails were perhaps a little more extreme than normal, but without trying very hard I can think of half-a-dozen novelists of my acquaintance who experienced something fairly similar. And the truth is that such experiences come with the territory. First novels aren't asked for. They arrive. Your fingertips burn with the desire to set them down on paper. Second novels are seldom as insistent. You have to jump from an art informed by desire to one informed by excellent technique. What's more, though it's easy to believe that your technique must be good enough, because that first novel came out all right, you are still very much learning the ropes – a phrase which has its origins in the Georgian navy, when the ropes in question might stand a hundred feet above a storm-tossed deck, so falling off had ugly consequences.

NOT FALLING OFF

The most important lesson from these meditations is simple. You need humility. You need to remember that you are still a relative novice, that you haven't proved you can do anything until you can do it twice in a row, that you still have an abundant amount to learn of the novelist's art.

Following straight on from that, you should feel free to get as much help as you can. Your agent and your editor will be perfectly familiar with second-novel syndrome. They're there to help. Even if you have a high degree of confidence in your second novel, I'd urge you to put together a detailed proposal for it. A detailed outline, plus the opening 10,000 words or so. There's no particular format that the outline has to take. If you shun detailed plot outlines in advance of writing (as I do), then you can still say plenty about the overall shape of the plot, the nature of the action, where the narrative drive comes from, who your characters are, and so on. Put down everything you know about the book and everything you think that someone else would need to know to make sense of it.

Don't allow yourself to think of this as a working document, in the sense that you can be at all slipshod about presentation or salesmanship. Agents and editors are all fine people, bless them, but they are not authors. Whereas authors know all too well how slow progress can be from first draft to final draft, and how sloppy things can look in between, agents and editors are not similarly inured. If you send them something that feels first-draftish, they're more likely than not to feel terrified by your sudden loss of form. It's not helpful to generate such reactions, as you won't get the kind of feedback that you most need at this stage.

So take time with that proposal. Work on it at least as carefully as you would if you were submitting work to an agent for the first time. In one sense, this is wasted effort, in that you yourself don't need anything more polished than a first draft at this stage. Yet the act of polishing will in itself teach you something about your projected novel, and you won't get useful advice on roughly sketched work.

Once you've sent out this proposal – either to your agent or to your editor or to both at once, depending on your own particular pattern of working relationships – wait for feedback. When it comes, it'll be the usual combination of illuminating and frustrating. The illumination will come from insights that you needed and hadn't yet reached. The frustration will come from comments that you know to be true and don't know how best to take on board. You should, in particular, listen very attentively to any feedback you are given about the market.

Such comments are often the most annoying. If you're being told that you need to do X or Y to satisfy the current market for this type of book, you are probably able to list half-a-dozen well-known, best-selling authors who have succeeded while doing no such thing. All the same, you can be absolutely certain that, when those famous authors made their names, they were doing precisely what was required of them by the market of the time, and, once their names were made, the same rules no longer applied.

You don't need to treat this feedback process as a one-off. It doesn't need to be. Your second novel *matters*. Yes, for sure, you've got a contract. Unless you make a real pig's ear of it, the novel will be published and you'll be paid. But, if the second novel stinks, it'll be much harder to sell, your sales history will be trending downwards not upwards and, if your career is not quite doomed, the smart money will be moving rapidly away to other authors.

Your agent and your editor know these things very well. If you need an extended process of groping towards a successful concept for that next novel, then help yourself. You'll be given the assistance that you need. You may also find that all those books on writing technique, which seemed irrelevant to your first novel, are suddenly feeling rather valuable now. You don't have to agree with all that they recommend; the process of disagreement can be a mighty enlightening one. If your agent, editor and written resources aren't enough, then there are third-party editorial resources available too. The use of external third parties is not something I encourage. Professional authors should be getting these services delivered properly and for free from their publishers. But publishers aren't always as good as they ought to be and, if you do find yourself needing help that your agent or editor isn't giving, then reach out to others. My consultancy helps a handful of professional authors every year, so you will not be alone.

Finally, once you have a concept that works, feel free to stay closely in touch with your agent or publisher as you proceed. They will (or should) prefer to offer more input at this stage than have to tidy up a car crash at a later one. My earlier advice about not showing unpolished work still applies (and, indeed, will apply at every future stage of your career), but, as you start to build up an editorial understanding, you'll know what does and doesn't work. And with just a little luck, your second novel will be at least as good as your first and, perhaps, even a little better. Harold Bingley wishes you well.

ARE LITERARY PRIZES RELEVANT TODAY?

In 2011, the Costa Book Awards celebrate their fortieth birthday. (Strictly speaking, it's the fifth anniversary of the Costa, but it's the fortieth anniversary of the Whitbread Literary Prize, now the Costa Book Awards.) So this is a timely moment to ask whether literary prizes such as this are still relevant in today's world. The winner of the 2008 Book of the Year, Sebastian Barry, would probably say yes. His novel The Secret Scripture *became Faber's fastest-selling book ever and has, to date, sold over 350,000 copies.*

However, it's important to be realistic. Let me blind you with figures. Currently there are around 90,000 new titles published in the UK each year. More than 90% of these sell fewer than 3,500 copies, a horrendous statistic. And a disproportionately large number of these sell an average of just eighteen copies.

The UK book market is clearly saturated. And all potential readers – young ones especially – are assaulted with a cornucopia of alternative distractions, technological and otherwise, in their many glorious and different forms. So anything that can promote the importance of reading and raise public awareness of books – getting people to discuss them and, even better, buy them – surely has to be a good thing for everyone within the publishing industry (authors, publishers, booksellers), itself an important part of our fast-changing economy. So we applaud all the UK's glorious and different book prizes – over 300 of them! – and book clubs of every variety (television or otherwise), whether Richard and Judy or Gok Wan.

The Costa Book Awards are unique because they pit five different literary genres against each other, effectively saying that each genre is as important as the other. We would like to claim – although we can't – that all sales of our shortlisted and winning books are solely down to them winning a Costa Award. But our most recent overall winners are all well represented in the recently published list of the last decade's best-sellers in The Bookseller *(statistics provided by Nielsen).* The Curious Incident of the Dog in the Night-Time *came third behind two Dan Browns, selling over two million copies; Stef Penney's first novel,* The Tenderness of Wolves, *the first overall winner of the Costa Book of the Year, sold 362,000 copies. Claire Tomalin's biography of Pepys sold 312,000 copies; and the only children's book ever to win the overall prize,* The Amber Spyglass *by Philip Pullman, was at number 32, selling over 1.1 million copies. If you refer back to the sales statistics I quoted earlier, you'll see just how remarkable these figures are.*

Whether this year's winner, Christopher Reid, will reach such giddy heights for his volume of poetry, A Scattering, *is as yet unknown; but he will undoubtedly sell far more copies than he would have done had he not won the 2009 Costa Book of the Year.*

So yes, we believe that literary prizes are still relevant today – in fact, possibly more important than ever.

BUD MCLINTOCK
Director, Costa Book Awards

TAXES, MORTGAGES AND OTHER PLEASURES

One of the most excellent and wonderful things about being a writer is the ease with which you can minimise your tax bill. The steps involved are threefold. They are (1) become a writer, (2) have very little income, (3) have very low tax demands. These simple rules should suffice for most writers. Indeed, the only possible room for error comes if you foul up on step 2. It's possible to think of writers who have managed to make a mess of things here – J. K. Rowling, Dan Brown, Barack Obama, Jordan – but the vast majority of writers will be able to negotiate this stage without undue difficulty.

Because of the ease and simplicity of this strategy, the amounts of money involved in step (3) are not great. Nevertheless, there's no point in giving more money to the taxman than you really need to, so do bear in mind the following points.

➢ All your income is taxable. Not just income from writing books, but income from journalism, income from speaking engagements and the like. Don't forget these additional items as the taxman is likely to feel narked if you do.

➢ You have plenty of expenses that are allowable for tax purposes. Agents' commissions, travel and subsistence, research materials, computers and printers, phone calls, and so forth. Because writing seldom feels quite like work, many of these expenses may feel to you like cheating. The cost of travel to London for a publication lunch with your publisher? Buying a few crime novels as you contemplate your next book? Poking around the Viking museum at York as you contemplate a historical novel? These things may be fun, but they're work. For you, they really, truly are. You're not conning anyone by claiming for these things. You're just lucky enough to have a job that you like.

➢ In addition, and most importantly, if you work from a home office, the costs of that office are offsettable against tax. An office is the place you work from. Doesn't matter if that room is also a place that your husband uses to watch late-night wrestling or a place that your teenage daughter wrecks every few weeks when she has one of her parties. If you use it to work in, you have costs that are perfectly allowable for tax purposes.

➤ You need to check the rules of your own tax jurisdiction as to exactly what costs are offsettable, but a normal approach would be to work out the total costs of running the house: rents or mortgage payments, power, water, insurance and so on. In the UK council tax is not an offsettable cost. If you live elsewhere, then check the rules that apply to you.

➤ As a next step: (A) calculate how many rooms you have in your house, excluding kitchens and bathrooms, (B) work out how many rooms you use as an office, (C) work out how much of that room's usage is accounted for by work.

➤ The amount of your house's overall running costs that are deductible as a home-office expense can be found by the following sum: (B × C) divided by A. So if you have five rooms in your house (plus kitchen and bathrooms), you use one of them for work, and that room is used 90% for work, then you would take 90% of 1 (which is 0.9, as I know you knew) and divide by 5, to give 0.18. Multiply your house's overall running costs by the figure you've just calculated, and bingo. You have your main taxable expense.

In a number of jurisdictions, including Britain, there are special rules available for creators of artistic works. The idea is that you may find yourself with significant income in one year, and much less in another. If you rise into a higher tax band in the first year, then the amount you pay in tax is likely to be higher overall than if your income had come in steadily over the two years taken together. For this reason, authors are often allowed to average their income when it benefits them to do so. If any of that applies to you, you probably want an accountant to run their slide rule over the numbers. You don't need to go to any fancy-pants accountant to do this. It's basic stuff from their point of view. You'll need a fancy-pants accountant when you stumble blinking to the top of the best-seller lists in four continents. Till then, I'd recommend a lower-budget solution.

Likewise, if your accountant recommends that you incorporate as a limited company, register for VAT, re-categorise your grandmother as a special-purpose vehicle based in the Netherlands Antilles, or that you indulge in any other exotic financial manoeuvre, then stay sceptical. If you completely understand what you are letting yourself in for, then make the best decision you can. If you don't – and you're a writer, so numbers terrify you, remember? – then keep it simple.

The one exception worth mentioning here is that, if you make a sale into the US, you will need to obtain an Individual Tax Identification Number from the IRS. Obtaining this number will help you minimise your taxation, and your agent will tell you what hoops you have to jump through to obtain your ITIN. (When I secured one, it was all relatively straightforward and nothing to worry about.) If you don't have an agent, you are unlikely to need an ITIN, but a Google search on 'ITIN numbers' will tell you most of what you need to know in any case.

MORTGAGES

If the matter of taxation can seem to have a blissful irrelevance about it at times, the same happy claim cannot generally be made about writers and their mortgages. If you are a self-employed writer, and you don't have a steady part-time job or (better still) a steady full-time spouse of the income-earning variety, conversations with mortgage companies are apt to be a little disheartening. They run a bit like this:

BORED MORTGAGE CLERK: So are you currently in employment?

WRITER: No.

BMC: Self-employed?

WRITER: Yes.

BMC: Nature of the business?

WRITER: I'm a writer.

[*First pause.*]

BMC: I'll put writing. The name of the business?

WRITER: Well it's not really a business, as such. I'm a writer. I write novels. You know. Novels. So I suppose the name of the business is me.

[*Second pause.*]

BMC: Do you have audited accounts for the last three years?

WRITER: Well, not as such, no.

BMC: I mean, are you able to verify a steady income from self-employment for a three-year period or more?

WRITER: *Steady* income? Erm.

[*Third pause.*]

I've got this amazing idea for a screenplay . . .

I don't exactly have a solution to offer to these conundrums, except to remind you that they exist. In the happy days before 2008, you only needed to prove that you weren't Osama Bin Laden and there'd be someone out there who'd be happy to lend you money. In the colder realities of the post-2009 world, lenders are a little more demanding of their borrowers and you'll need to factor that into your calculations. If your family is largely dependent on writing as a source of income, then I'd gently suggest that a fairly flexible mortgage is likely to suit you better than the kind designed for those tedious folks with their jobs and their monthly paypackets.

In the same way, when it comes to pension planning and the like, you probably want to make your plans more rather than less prudent. I've no doubt at all that your screenplay concept is the most wonderful idea since someone had the brainwave of combining nuns, Nazis and singing in *The Sound of Music*, but it's still not the kind of pension plan you should be looking at to keep you warm in old age.

STAYING ALIVE AND STAYING PUBLISHED

You've written and published your first novel. You've written and published your second. If you first bought this book when you were thinking about your agent letter, then it's now a dog-eared copy knocking around your study with some out-of-date *Yearbook*s and some Bulgarian royalty statements (which are, it has to be said, only slightly more bewildering than those that come from your home publisher).

Now what?

That's not an easy question. Of course, if your first books have sold hugely, your publisher will be hurling large bundles of money at your head and it's easy enough to know what to do. You say thank you very much and pick them up. But few authors will find themselves in this position. For most of us – whether we're talented, average or plodding – writing is not an easy way to make money. Several options offer themselves, and you need to think hard and be fiercely realistic about how to proceed.

MOTIVATIONS

This book started with a discourse on motivations and it needs to end that way too. Why do you write? Did you have a story to tell – a story that is now told and done with? Did you have a passion for writing? Did you want to make money? Did you want fame?

The questions may be the same now as they were at the start, but your answers will have changed. You know more about the industry. You know more about yourself. All good writers are driven by passion, but that passion can take several forms. Here, for example, are some of the forms it can take. (As always, the stories are true, though some of the details have been altered to protect privacy.) I should say as well that all these authors are talented and have, between them, won or been shortlisted for a number of serious literary awards.

ANNABEL wanted to tell a story. Her first novel was stunning, her second novel – written in fulfilment of a two-book deal – was no better than careful. She stopped writing, moved house, got married, had kids, thought about other things. Years after she laid down her pen, another story began to nibble at her, and she was happy to let it nibble. She started to flesh out her ideas, she talked to her agent, and things started to get moving once again. Annabel never wrote for money in the first place, and isn't writing for money now.

BERTRAND is a writer. If he isn't writing, he isn't complete. He has never made much money from his 'proper' writing – though it's always been critically acclaimed both in London and New York – but he's managed to secure himself regular work with various children's educational publishers, writing historical and other books for them. He also does bits of editorial work, various teaching gigs, and the like. None of this pays terrifically well, but it's all writing-related and satisfies him. His 'proper' work fits in around the rest.

CATHERINE wrote women's fiction. She's had best-sellers to her name in more than one country. She's had a decent TV deal for one of her books. She loved writing more than anything else she's ever done. And she's given it up. The money, at its best, was good, but it was utterly unreliable. What's more, though she loved the writing process, she wasn't a particularly speedy writer and found the work more exhausting than anything else she'd ever done. In the end, she decided that she'd do other things. She now mostly lives off the income from property investments she made from her brief sojourn in the big time. She keeps her literary muscle alive by doing freelance editorial work and the like, but mostly those muscles have been allowed to lose their fitness. She's happy to let them.

DANIEL is a literary author who simply has to write. He's migrated from large, prestigious publishers to small, passionate ones. He makes next to no money from his literary work, but is fiercely committed to it. He's an immaculate stylist who can turn out maybe 250 words on a good day, so he's not merely working for very little money, he's working slowly for very little money. Daniel also finds other minor sources of income to keep body and soul together – a little journalism, some translation, the odd ghostwriting job – but mostly he's adapted his life to need very little money at all. He lives in a self-build home that is little more than a fancy shed. He gets his electricity – such of it as he uses – from a solar panel. He grows his own veggies. Every now and then, he finds himself dining off fresh air and sunshine.

EDIE has taken a classic authorial route. She writes novels and teaches creative writing. It doesn't matter too much if the novels sell or if they don't; they've always been more of a decently paid hobby than a real profession. She likes writing and expects to go on doing so, but it wouldn't kill her if her publisher stopped taking her books (and nor would it bother the authorities at the university where she teaches). She admits that there's something a little weird in teaching others how to write when her own relationship to that profession is a little ambiguous, but she enjoys her students, enjoys her teaching and enjoys her writing. For her, the combination works.

Those are their stories. Here is mine.

AN AUTHOR'S TALE

I wrote five novels for HarperCollins. Those novels were broadly in the same genre – old-fashioned adventure yarns, in which there were no vampires, no violence, no trays of dissected body parts, just flawed heroes and heroines struggling to meet their goals. The novels morphed gently from financial thrillers to historical dramas, but the tone and approach was broadly similar. It's true that with my last book (a historical romance) my German publisher wanted to change my name to a woman's name because they reckoned it had strayed too far from my original brand identity, but on the whole I played by the rules of the marketing game.

The sales of my first book were excellent. The sales of my second book (which was less good than the first, and had an ineffective cover design) were lacklustre but OK. The third book was all set for a major launch, when a critical wholesaler went bankrupt, knocking out a swathe of potential sales. At the same time, a major chain retailer underwent a violent series of corporate upheavals, in the course of which I went from being one of their most heavily promoted authors to one they weren't even going to stock at all. This abrupt reversal had nothing to do with my book; it was simply that the new person had only just got his feet under the desk and hadn't yet had time to survey his new domain. Not his fault, not my fault, not my publisher's fault; just one of those things. My publisher, who had planned a major national launch campaign, withdrew the whole thing because of the sudden gap in the retail uptake.

The sales of that book – perhaps my best novel to date – were shocking. Two more novels followed. My sales were still decent, but I'm not an author who's happy to accept a meagre income and the advances I demanded were more than my publisher was ever going to pay.

So I switched tack. I put together a non-fiction proposal. The proposal had nothing whatever to do with anything I had written before. My existing agent liked it, was happy to continue representing me, but told me that this kind of non-fiction wasn't her main enthusiasm or strength and said that, if I wanted to move elsewhere, then I should feel free. So I did. That proposal was reshaped under the beady eye of my current agent, and we ended up selling that proposal for a lot of money to Fourth Estate – effectively a different department of HarperCollins. The fact that I still happen to be published under the same lofty Hammersmith roof is pure coincidence. The editor at Fourth Estate who offered for my book hadn't even spoken to my former colleagues in mass-market fiction before she made her offer.

I'm still in the middle of the two-book deal I signed at that time. To be precise, I've delivered my second manuscript but am still nine months or so off hardback publication. Exactly how my non-fiction career pans out will depend very much on book sales. I'm confident in my writing abilities, but I know by now that there are plenty of other factors in play as well.

Even if I can't read the future, there are some things that have become clear to me. First, I don't want to live in a yurt, eating sunlight. I don't want to struggle to pay the mortgage. I want a certain amount of income that's independent of the vagaries of publishing. At the same time, I prefer a life that centres around writing to one that doesn't. Creating the Writers' Workshop has gone part way to meeting both goals, and in a way that satisfies my need to be in charge of my own affairs.

This book is also a response to those two goals. Creatively speaking, I've thoroughly enjoyed writing this book, but it hasn't satisfied a soul-need the way some of my other books have. Nevertheless, I prefer writing to most other activities, and writing a book about my profession has been a logical move for me. A & C Black did not approach me to write this; I approached them. I didn't do this via my agent, I just did it. When Jenny Ridout, my now editor, responded positively, I trotted over to my agent with her expression of interest, like a cat coming in from the garden with a dead bird in its mouth. My agent removed the dead bird and turned it into a contract. I'm hoping that in due course other similar books may follow.

But I also want to return to fiction. If I tried to go back to my old haunts – old-fashioned adventure yarns on historical themes – then I wouldn't get the kind of advance (especially in today's terrible market) that would make it worth my while. So I need to think laterally. I've got a few ideas of things I'd like to write in different areas, and am beginning to work them up now. I'll work closely with my agent, to make sure that my crazy ideas aren't too crazy for the market. (Or perhaps to make sure that they're crazy enough.) Although I know an awful lot about writers and writing, only agents and publishers are in the market, day in, day out, buying and selling manuscripts. Consequently, those folk know the market as no writer ever can, and I'm wise enough to know what I don't know.

As I say, I don't know how these things will pan out. Maybe my non-fiction career will take off. Maybe a new fiction career will take off. Maybe neither will. If things don't work out, I won't knock for ever at the same door. If and when I stop making money from writing, I'll stop writing. I'll do something else. I'll miss it – and may always dabble by way of a hobby – but I'm not the yurt-dwelling sort and never will be.

YOUR STORY

Your story is still to be written. There's loads you don't yet know about yourself, about your sales figures, about what really propels you. Here, nevertheless, are a few suggestions that you may find helpful.

➢ *Don't give up the day job*
The oldest adage and still the truest. You won't really know how your career is progressing until you've completed your first two-book deal and have

started to talk about advances for the second. Even then, of course, huge uncertainty lies ahead of you, but, if your sales and advances are nudging upwards, at least you've avoided your first opportunity to sail straight on to the rocks of calamity. Writing (especially writing fiction) is hard to do alongside a day job. If you have the kind of job that can be a part-time one, then go for it. If you need to, adapt your career to one that more easily permits writing. But that job, the real job – the one with things like payslips and pension provision and sickness and holiday pay – is a precious thing. It's not simply a safety net. It's a safety net you're likely to be falling into sometime soon.

Even if your writing career flourishes and does well, it may well have gaps in it, caused by oddities in your publication schedule or anything else. If your publisher puts back the publication of your book by six months to avoid clashing with Dan Brown or whoever else, they won't even think about asking if that is going to cause difficulty for your finances, so your finances need to be robust enough to take the strain. Go on Oprah, then give up the day job. Never the other way round.

➢ *Marry for money*

Not everyone is fortunate enough to have the kind of day job which can easily accommodate writing. In such cases, you need to give even greater thought to creating that safety net. If you haven't already been foolish enough to throw your life away for love, then I'd urge you to marry someone obscenely wealthy. Choose someone whose personal habits can be endured for just long enough to accrue some decent alimony, then take the cash and enjoy the rest of your life. That's a safety net.

If you're soppily romantic about these things, then you'll need to be a little more creative. You can think about all those classic writerly dodges – teaching, editorial work, journalism, translation, copy-editing and the like – but bear in mind that these things are almost always poorly paid, because there's always a plethora of amply qualified writers queuing up to do them.

Better still, therefore, think more broadly. Think of an occupation which suits your skills and your temperament and which can happily sit alongside your writing. Don't diminish the importance of this decision simply because you happen to value your time spent writing more than anything else. There may come a point at which your publisher no longer wants a book from you, your agent isn't returning your calls, and you have a gas bill sitting on the mantelpiece, shouting across the room at you in bossy red capitals.

➤ *Be promiscuous*

Perhaps you see yourself as an author of women's sagas. Fair enough. If that's what you are, then plough that furrow to its end. But let's suppose your sales and your advances shrivel. Not your fault, just one of those things. Do you want to quit writing, or do you want to reinvent yourself? There isn't a right or wrong answer here. Different people will have different responses. But be aware that you *can* reinvent yourself if you want to.

The reinvention needs to be a real one. That is, if you wrote women's sagas under your own name, you can't simply delete that identity and write the same kind of work under a different name. You need to write in new territory altogether, probably using your existing name, though your agent or publisher will tell you if you need to change it. Thus, I know an astrologer who also writes cookbooks. I know a literary author who also writes picture books. I know a screenwriter who also writes novels. I know a crime writer who also writes erotica. These different spheres of activity produce their own challenges, their own rewards. And the biggest hurdle to this kind of reinvention is always the same: a rigidity in the author's own view of who they are. Play with that view. It may be right. It may not be. You won't know until you start to experiment.

➤ *If you see a door, kick it*

A common outside view of the industry is that what matters is who you know, not what talent you have. I hope it's clear to you by now that that view is wrong. Talent is and has always been the single most important element in gaining access. Without it, you'll get nowhere. All the same, connections help, because you never quite know what they may lead to. My friend, the screenwriter-who-also-writes-novels, was working with a major international TV director. He was hungry for new projects and (because this is the film industry) needed them the day before yesterday in order to impress some affluent German investors. He asked her for ideas. She suggested my novels. He asked me for a treatment. I worked late that night and gave him three.

So far, nothing has come of that interest. There's at least a 95% chance that nothing ever will. All the same, a connection was made that wouldn't have been made had it not been for my friend. Equally, if you happen to know journalists, publishers, authors, agents, celebrities, film-makers, BBC types and the rest, then nurture those connections. That doesn't mean getting creepy about it, but it does mean keeping some kind of inner Rolodex. It also, unquestionably, means being willing to push hard at doors, even if they're barely open to you. Often enough, you'll find yourself being welcomed once you're through – and it's most unlikely that anyone will be upset with you for trying.

It should also go without saying that one good way to nurture connections is to be as helpful as you can to others. If you can help make connections between authors, publishers, agents and whoever, then so much the better for others – and so much the better for you. Those you've helped will be that little bit more ready to help you in return.

➤ *Buy a bulldog*
Not all professional authors have agents, but, if you don't have one, you should almost certainly get one. Agents aren't all as good as they ought to be, but they do know more about the market than you do or ever can. They know more about publishing. They know more about contracts and what can be negotiated. You need that knowledge, so don't think you don't.

➤ *Compromise your artistic integrity*
There are things you want to write. There are things that the market wants you to write. The dead centre of the first circle is most unlikely to coincide with the dead centre of the second. You need to compromise. You're not sacrificing your immortal soul by doing so; you are shaping a product for a market. That's what you're paid to do. It's true that some of those compromises are painful. It's true that in some respects you may produce a less interesting book than the one you'd originally envisaged. At least half the time, however, the book that emerges from the compromise is a better one – cleaner, sharper, less self-indulgent. You won't feel that to start with, but you don't have to. You just have to go where the market leads you, and write the most wonderful thing you can within the parameters that you're given.

➤ *Cultivate indolence*
I know far too many professional novelists who, on completing a two-book deal, simply started off on book No. 3 or book No. 5, writing the whole darn thing 'on spec', just as they did with their very first manuscript. Sometimes this approach is unavoidable and you simply need to grit your teeth and get on with it – always bearing in mind the dreadful, but perfectly real, possibility that, as you're writing, the market will turn against you and the novel into which you've plunged so much work will be either unsaleable or saleable only for peanuts. At other times, however, it's perfectly possible to secure a contract before you've invested too much. Given how bad the market

situation has become, it's vital for writers to do as much as possible to protect themselves against excessive wasted investment of time.

This book, for example, was sold off the basis of a proposal that took me about a day to write. A previous, more ambitious and more remunerative non-fiction project was sold off the back of a 10,000-word proposal. I'm currently in the process of developing a novel that I'm hoping (perhaps foolishly) to sell off the back of a lengthy proposal, that will certainly need to include a good 25,000 or 30,000 words of actual text, and perhaps a good bit more. Selling novels in this way is certainly challenging, but you have to balance that challenge against the possible cost of spending a year or two creating something that no one wants to buy. So, whenever you can, minimise risk before investing effort.

➤ *Write with joy or don't write at all*
Lastly, if ever writing stops being a pleasure, if ever it starts feeling like *work*, then don't do it. Do something else. If you think of writing as a job, then it has to be one of the worst jobs ever invented: lonely, ill-paid, insecure, unpensioned, unpredictable, unthanked. Writing only makes sense if, like me, you think it's an amazing way to get paid for something that you want to do anyway. Just think about it! Getting *paid* to *write*! I can't even think of a suitable comparison for that, because there isn't one. I often find myself writing at weekends, bank holidays, and even at Christmas. I don't do this because I feel I ought to, but because my weekends, bank holidays and Christmases are usually pleasanter if I do. I never thought that about my past career (investment banking), nor can I think of any alternative career where the same might be true.

These feelings are common to most genuine writers. I know one fine young chap, for example, who wanted to take his laptop on honeymoon in order to work on his book proposal . . . until a wiser, older head told him that, if he wrote on his honeymoon, he'd be writing off his honeymoon. So keep the passion. If you lose it, move on.

CONCLUSION

Our revels now are ended. It seems a long time ago that your fingers withdrew astonished from that final full stop and a lot of ground has been covered since then. Yet, in dealing endlessly with the *business* of writing, we have thereby, deliberately, chosen to ignore its soul. But the soul needs the final word. Gustave Flaubert put it like this:

> It is a delicious thing to write, to be no longer yourself but to move in an entire universe of your own creation. Today, for example, as man and woman, both lover and mistress, I rode in a forest on an autumn afternoon under the yellow leaves, and I was also the horses, the leaves, the wind, the words my people uttered, even the red sun that made them almost close their love-drowned eyes. When I brood over these marvellous pleasures I have enjoyed, I would be tempted to offer God a prayer of thanks if I knew he could hear me. Praised may he be for not creating me a cotton merchant, a vaudevillian or a wit.

He's right, of course, and yet he doesn't quite press the point home to its close. Writing is a strange game, because to do it right you have to put yourself to one side almost completely. It can't be you, or Flaubert, who sets those words down on the page. If it is, then you haven't yet reached the right creative depth. Perhaps you dissolve into the book, or the book dissolves into you. Either way, it's not like making an apple pie or a set of shelves.

At the same time, though, and just as you're pulling off your disappearing act, you are also highly alert. Your brain hasn't switched off. It's still thinking hard about craft, and sentences and word choice and the rest. Yet that brain of yours is both active and subservient. Subservient to *what* I can't tell you, but it's no longer quite the boss. If your book doesn't somewhat surprise you when you're done, then you haven't done it quite right.

The process changes you. Not hugely. Not so that your friends look at you strangely and ask you if you've found God or given up booze or started some new-fangled power diet. But it's a good sort of change, nevertheless.

An enlargement. A widening out. And that's why this job, this writer's life, is worth chasing, no matter how hard the going may be. This book gives you a road map for the path ahead. Actually following it is down to you. Your enterprise, your endeavour, your luck, your talent.

From one writer to another: good luck.

FACTS AND FIGURES

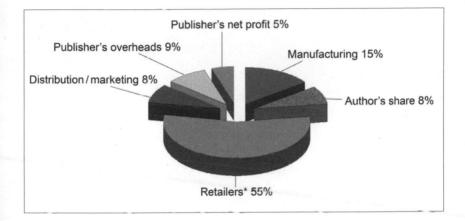

Publisher's net profit 5%

Publisher's overheads 9%

Distribution / marketing 8%

Manufacturing 15%

Author's share 8%

Retailers* 55%

If a book has a notional cover price of £10.00, the spoils are approximately divided as per the pie chart above, with the author's share equating to about 8%, or 80p on a £10 cover price.

Note that the retailers' share of the pie includes amounts paid to wholesalers, discounts offered to overseas publishers for export copies, and will also include discounts offered to customers by way of promotions. (So a £10 notional price might translate, for example, to an average selling price of just £8.) The net profits made by retailers might easily be as little as 2–5% of sales – and, indeed, a couple of high-profile names have recently found it hard to make any money from their sales at all.

Source: Tim Hely Hutchinson, The Author, 1998

PARLEZ-VOUS FRANÇAIS?

A 2005 study of international best-seller lists conducted by the Swedish book trade magazine *Svensk Bokhandel* found that the Anglo-Saxon countries are shockingly closed to authors who write in other tongues. In Britain and America, no author outside those two countries made it on to their best-seller lists. In Germany, by contrast, nearly 40% of all best-selling books were written by authors who were neither German, American nor British.   *Source: Svensk Bokhandel, Bowker*

Country	Domestic authors	American authors	British authors	Other authors
America	91%	–	9%	0%
Britain	61%	39%	–	0%
France	60%	29%	2%	0%
Germany	24%	29%	8%	39%

WHO BUYS WHAT?

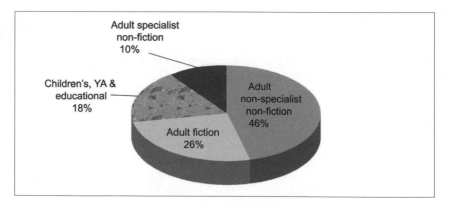

For all its prominence in the national literary culture, adult fiction takes a much smaller share of the overall books market than general adult non-fiction. The percentages above relate to the domestic UK market for 2008, which totalled about £1.8 billion. The US book market (including academic, religious and professional titles) was about $24 billion in the same year.

Sources: Nielsen, the Publishers' Association, Bowker

NON–FICTION PUBLISHING 2009

This was supposedly the year in which celebrity autobiography, having dominated the best-seller charts in recent years, crashed. In fact, reports of its demise were greatly exaggerated: celebrity chefs and personalities of other kinds still occupied nine out of the top ten places of non-fiction hits at the end of the year. There is, however, impressionistic evidence that television is having less of an impact on sales of non-fiction books of all kinds than it has recently: sales of history, science and travel books don't seem to be benefiting so much from the association, which, if they are selling, is as much for their innate qualities as for the television connection.

The 'serious' end of the market held up well and, remarkably, three books each over 1,000 pages long appeared in the best-seller lists: Diarmaid MacCulloch's A History of Christianity, *William Shawcross's* Queen Elizabeth the Queen Mother: The Official Biography *and Christopher Andrew's* The Defence of the Realm: The Authorised History of MI5. *The fad for books of quirky scientific questions begun by* Does Anything Eat Wasps? *diminished, but no successor trend clearly emerged, and there was no runaway popular best-seller of the* Eats, Shoots & Leaves *kind. Reference publishing continued its now substantial migration to the internet. Trade non-fiction still constitutes the largest share of the book market (42% value) but in 2009 declined in value by -6% in contrast to a growth in adult fiction (+1%) and in children's (+4%).*

It is difficult to say in any given year why some books sell and some books don't. With regard to 'serious' non-fiction at least there is a very great deal to be said for a book which tells us things we don't know already. Books which retell, however fluently or entertainingly, stories we know already face the difficulty that time is short, potential readers are busy, and they must seem unnecessary. New insights and new perspectives must change our view of a familiar subject significantly. When conceiving a book I think it's worth asking not what will produce a plausible, coherent or even enjoyable read (though each of those is extremely important), but what can be done that really hasn't been done before — what will make a book necessary.

STUART PROFITT
Publishing Director, Allen Lane, Penguin

A FLOOD OF WORDS

New printing technologies have made it far easier for people to self-publish their work. No solid numbers exist on what proportion of titles published today are self-published (because in many cases it's simply hard to tell), but a huge increase in the number of print-on-demand titles suggests that self-published work now accounts for a significant proportion of all new titles published. The data below relate to the US, but the same pattern would be broadly true of all English-speaking markets. Do also note that the huge increase in the number of titles being published should not be taken to indicate that it's become easier for a mainstream author of fiction or non-fiction to get commercially published, because it most certainly has not. Indeed, most large publishers have spent the last few years reducing their lists, not expanding them.   *Source: Bowker*

	2002	2008	Increase
New titles and new editions of existing titles	215,000	275,000	+28%
Print on demand	33,000	285,000	+774%
Total	248,000	560,000	+126%

YO HO HO!

Illegal piracy may be something you associate mostly with the Somali coast and music-loving teenagers, but it's increasingly becoming an issue for the publishing industry too. According to a 2009 study carried out by Attributor, a Californian technology company, the thousand or so most popularly downloaded titles were each downloaded an average of some 10,000 times each. The implied loss to publishers' revenues is equal to more than one-tenth of the total US books market.

This way of phrasing the issue does, however, rather overstate the problem, as it's not likely that each illegal download represents a lost sale. And you can draw whatever conclusion you like from the fact that the piracy problem seems most rife in books in the business and investing categories. It's also true that the pace of change in the e-book market is so swift at the moment that these issues are likely to undergo rapid changes from year to year.   *Source: Attributor*

THE BOOKED AND THE UNBOOKED

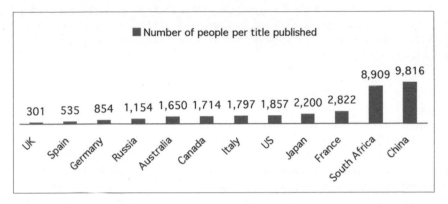

In the United Kingdom, there is around one title published for every 300 people in the population. In the United States, the figure is closer to one title published for every 1,800 people (a figure rather closer to the average for developed nations). China and South Africa are more typical of emerging markets.

Sources: UN for population data, various sources and dates for publication data

THE MARKET FOR LEMONS

In 2001, George Akerlof, Michael Spence and Joseph Stiglitz won the Nobel Prize in Economics 'for their analyses of markets with asymmetric information'. This revolution in economic thought was Akerlof's famous (to economists) paper 'The Market for Lemons'. In that work, Akerlof looked at the market for second-hand cars, where the seller was presumed to know whether his car was in good condition or whether it was, to use Akerlof's term, a lemon. Since the buyer lacked this knowledge, Akerlof was able to demonstrate mathematically that the conventional rules of supply and demand, as they had always previously been understood, would simply collapse.

The market for books is also a market in which informational asymmetries are rife. Publishers may know whether the books they are offering for sale are excellent or poor, but the buyer has almost no way to find out, other than purchasing the book and spending an hour or two finding out. Debut authors (especially of fiction) face this problem most severely, because they have no pre-existing readers to support them and will, in most cases, have limited or no review coverage either.

Other media markets either don't face this problem or don't face it to anything like the same extent. So the music market allows for radio and internet sampling, while the market for films enjoys much more extensive media and word-of-mouth coverage than does the market for books.

So how does the books world survive and thrive despite the information asymmetry that faces readers? Answer: word-of-mouth recommendations, press coverage, retail prominence . . . and, of course, that old favourite: readers who judge a book by its cover. As Akerlof would probably comment, they may have nothing else to go on.

INFLUENCES ON BOOK PURCHASING

Assessing what makes readers buy the books they do is much harder than it sounds. You can, of course, simply ask them (as the *Bookseller* did in its June 2009 'Reading the Future' survey: see data below), but what readers say and what they do may be two quite different things. Few publishers, for example, would rate newspaper reviews as being almost as important as retail prominence. Nevertheless, the *Bookseller* survey does at least tell you what readers think they think.

Source: Bookseller

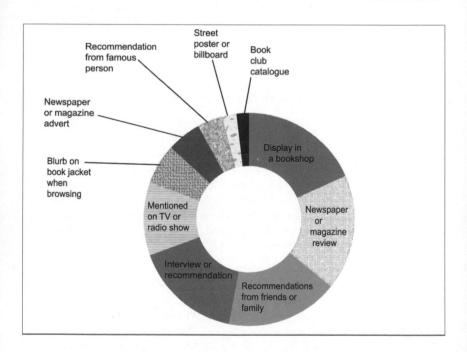

INDEX

GUIDING WRITERS AND ARTISTS
FOR OVER 100 YEARS

'... much, much better than luck'
TERRY PRATCHETT

'Essential reading ... how to survive in publishing'
KATE MOSSE

'Full of useful stuff. It answered my every question'
J.K. ROWLING

'... the book which magically contains all other books ...
an entrance ticket to the world you long for'
FAY WELDON

'... set right to it, with the Yearbook your shining armour,
your sword!'
ALEXANDER MCCALL SMITH

'Think of the Writers' & Artists' Yearbook as your sherpa'
IAN RANKIN

'...like a magic carpet that would carry the writer anywhere'
MAEVE BINCHY

'Every possible scrap of information needed
by the upcoming or established writer'
EOIN COLFER

SERIOUS ABOUT GETTING PUBLISHED?
For top tips, advice and feedback from industry specialists,
book a place on one of our writing conferences or masterclasses.
Visit www.writersandartists.co.uk for further details.